JUST
PERMANENT
INTERESTS

JUST PERMANENT INTERESTS

BLACK AMERICANS IN CONGRESS, 1870–1992

William L. Clay

U.S. CONGRESSMAN

with a Foreword by
Governor L. Douglas Wilder

Amistad

NEW YORK, NEW YORK

Direct all inquiries to: Distributed by:
  Amistad Press, Inc.   Penguin USA
  1271 Avenue of the Americas   375 Hudson Street
  New York, NY 10020   New York, NY 10014

Library of Congress Cataloging-in-Publication Data
Clay, William L.
  Just permanent interests : Black Americans in Congress, 1870–
1992 / by William L. Clay.
    p. cm.
  Includes bibliographical references and index.
  ISBN 1-56743-000-7 : $10.95
  1. Afro-American legislators—History. 2. United States
—Politics and government. 3. United States. Congress—History.
4. Afro-Americans—Politics and government. I. Title.
E185.96.C58   1992
328.73′0089′96073—dc20   92-25191
                                      CIP

Book design by Stanley S. Drate/Folio Graphics Company, Inc.

Packaged by March Tenth, Inc.

1 2 3 4 5 6 7 8 9 10

*To Gwen Giles
and Pearlie I. Evans,
two beautiful women
who played a major role
in my political success.*

Contents

Foreword

The roles played by Americans of African descent in American political history, and American history in general, have long been depicted inaccurately and downplayed. William L. Clay, Sr., has taken the time to studiously correct these historical misstatements and to provide a correct and incisive review of the proper role played by those who were not welcome to the "melting pot," where others assimilated the American Dream.

Though some of us may know the first senator or congressman of African descent—although all too few know even these bare facts—we have not been made aware of the travails, setbacks, failures, and accomplishments of these true statesmen.

For example, the mere inviting of Illinois Congressman Oscar De-Priest's wife to a social gathering by President Hoover, along with the wives of white congressmen, prompted legislative action in several states condemning the president's invitation—and threatening sanctions.

Even with the passage of the Thirteenth, Fourteenth, and Fifteenth Amendments, Congress still debated whether to seat elected members of the House when said members included African Americans. Needless to say, the sole argument made against their inclusion was the color of their skin or their being designated people of African descent. Some of them were forced to spend more time gaining admittance to elected assemblies than they did actually serving in those bodies. (Today, there is still documentation of—and reasons for concern about—double standards, excessive scrutiny, vilification, and even acts of violence against the successors to these officeholders.)

The efforts over the years to discredit officeholders, office seekers, and voters of African descent were structured, sanctioned, and condoned by the governments of majority. Overt "black codes" were

FOREWORD

enacted throughout the South, but northern states also practiced their own forms of double standard classifications and denial of voting rights.

The stereotypical premise that disfranchisement or other denial of civil rights was practiced only in the South is discredited in this work. For example, Congressman Clay points out that the state of New York did not elect its first American of African descent to the state assembly until 1916, California not until two years later in 1918, and Massachusetts did not come on board until 1946. While there were African Americans from Boston's Beacon Hill who served in municipal offices during Reconstruction, New York City did not elect its first councilman of African descent until 1941.

Most important, the author weaves a linking thematic thread, reporting a kaleidoscopic pattern of political progress, though painstakingly slow, by and on behalf of Americans of African descent. Future generations will have a rich reference source and genealogy to chart their further course in pursuit of the dream of all people to be free.

The Congressional Black Caucus—through the contributions of the men and women who comprise its membership—was founded in conscious deliberation and dedicated to eliminating the lingering barriers to equal justice and equal opportunity. The CBC serves as the continuing catalyst for prompting the Congress to adhere to the precept of "government of the people, by the people, and for the people."

—GOVERNOR L. DOUGLAS WILDER
Commonwealth of Virginia

Preface

When I first came to Congress, I was a young, angry man. Well, now I'm an old, angry man, and this book is about my anger. In reality, it is about the anger of black America and why books like this should be written. Representative Louis Stokes has often spoken about the horrendous distortion of American history brought about by omission and by downright lying. The film *Birth of a Nation*, for example, was really the shame of a nation. The way that film interprets the history of black elected officials is utterly disgraceful. It portrays black American elected officials as illiterate barefoot buffoons who eat chicken in the legislative chambers and throw the bones on the floor. Nothing could be further from the truth.

To the contrary, the twenty black Americans who served in the U.S. House of Representatives and the two who served in the Senate in the nineteenth century were the most honorable, the most educated, and the most politically experienced individuals in the Congress. They went to the finest universities in the world—in Canada, England, France. Seven were lawyers, three were ministers, one was a banker, one a publisher, two teachers, and three college presidents. None of them threw chicken bones on the floor. None of them walked around barefoot. Among them were wealthy farmers and businessmen. Most had served in the military during the Civil War and some of them spoke two and three languages. One, incidentally, spoke German, French, and Spanish and read Latin. So I say shame on the D. W.

This preface is based on a speech given by Representative Clay at the reception marking the publication of the hardcover edition of this book held at the National Building Museum in Washingtom, D.C. on September 24, 1992.

Griffiths for their immoral portrayal of those outstanding early black American elected officials who risked everything they had in the cause of justice and equality.

There are a few things you'll find in this book which you might not know. In 1875, somebody stole the Presidency of the United States. We had a President who was elected by one vote. That election affected black folk tremendously. At that time, the Hayes–Tilden election was thrown into the House of Representatives, where it was decided that a committee of fifteen persons would determine the winner. Five from the House were selected (three Democrats and two Republicans), along with five from the Senate (three Republicans and two Democrats) and five from the Supreme Court (two Democrats, two Republicans, and one Independent). The Independent on the Court—who was truly an Independent—resigned and was appointed to the Senate from the State of Illinois. A justice who was Republican took his place. And in a vote along party lines, 8–7, Republicans to Democrats, Rutherford B. Hayes was named President of the United States.

What did that mean for black folk? Hayes made a deal to get the majority vote by promising to withdraw Federal troops from the South. The day he started withdrawing those troops, organizations like the Ku Klux Klan rose up and conducted a campaign of terror and intimidation unequaled in the history of this nation. Dating from the three-year period after the withdrawal of Federal troops, not an additional black Representative was elected for forty-odd years. In 1874 there were over 100,000 black registered voters in the state of Louisiana and Mississippi each. In 1901 there were fewer than 5,000 in Louisiana and fewer than 1,000 in Mississippi. So, when George White left Congress on January 2, 1901, another black person wasn't elected to the Congress until 1928. But more lamentable than that is the fact that at the time White left, we didn't have a single black elected official anywhere in the country—North, South, East, or West.

It wasn't until 1916 that there was any kind of movement toward the election of black officials—the first being elected to the New York State Legislature. The New York City Council didn't include a black member until 1941. In 1918 the first black person was elected to the Legislature of California. But the first black member elected to the City Council of Los Angeles was not elected until 1963. The first black mayor of Cleveland was elected in 1967. The lack of black representatives wasn't the South's problem, it was the country's.

Don't fall for the propaganda that says, "If immigrants could make it, why can't blacks?" Immigrants were welcomed to this country with open arms, comparatively speaking. They were given jobs by the cities, the states, and the private sector. The cities hired them as inspectors, as clerks, as police officers, and as fire fighters. The private sector hired them as trolley car drivers, railroad conductors, bank tellers, bread and beer truck drivers, and elevator operators. None of that happened for black people.

Black leaders fought like hell politically—in both parties—trying to get some of the political gravy. In 1928, when Oscar DePriest became the first black American elected to Congress in the twentieth century, the man running for President on the Democratic ticket was the son of a mother born in Germany and a father born in Ireland, and he had served two terms as Governor of New York. He was a son of immigrants—and black people were trying to get their first elected official!

When Herbert Hoover was elected president in 1928, he invited Oscar DePriest to the White House, and Mrs. Hoover invited Mrs. DePriest to a tea. In response, the State Senate in Texas passed a resolution that said "intercourse between the White and Black races is contrary to decency, and subversive to the best interest of both parties." The Legislature of Florida passed a resolution saying that "entertaining a Negro woman on the parity with White ladies was both shameful and disgraceful, and if persisted in, will destroy the prestige of the Anglo-Saxon race, and . . . the social fabric of the country, that has for ages guarded and kept sacred the purity of our Anglo-Saxon blood." It was another seventeen years, 1945, before the second black member of Congress in the twentieth century, Adam Clayton Powell, Jr., was elected.

We talk about the beginning of the Congressional Black Caucus (CBC), when Louis Stokes and Shirley Chisholm and I first came to Congress. That was an historic day when we raised our hands and recited the oath of office behind Speaker McCormick. Joining with the six other black members, we now became nine, and that was the most blacks who had ever sat at one time in the U.S. Congress. Shirley Chisholm also made history, as she was the first black woman ever to sit in Congress, although one hundred white women had preceded her.

The CBC has grown from twenty-six members in the 102nd Congress to forty members in the 103rd Congress in 1993. Eighteen new members were elected, including Carol Moseley Braun, of Illinois, to the United States Senate. Three of them replaced incumbent CBC members: Bobby Rush, of Chicago, replaced Charles Hayes; Melvin J. Reynolds, also of Chicago, replaced Gus Savage; and Bennie Thompson, of Mississippi, replaced Mike Espy.

As Kweisi Mfume, chairman of the CBC, said when he welcomed guests to the ceremonial swearing-in for the 103rd Congress on January 5, 1993:

Much—and little—has changed since the establishment of the CBC in 1971. That first Caucus boasted only one woman; we now have ten. That first Caucus claimed no members from the South; we now have sixteen. Indeed, the founding members of the Caucus had been tested and tempered by the weight of our struggle in ways that only history can accurately describe.

The eighteen newly elected blacks to Congress are Democrats—all highly educated and all but one with prior experience in elective or appointed government office. Nine are lawyers and five served in both houses of state legislatures, while five others served in one state body. Two were on city councils; two were mayors; one was a county commissioner, and one was a federal judge. All eighteen new members hold undergraudate degrees; eight have master's degrees; two have Ph.D's. One is a Rhodes Scholar, and another graduated Phi Beta Kappa.

The CBC's composition of thirty-nine black members of the House and a lone woman in the Senate is a far cry from the original CBC in 1970. Then, twelve men and one woman in the House and one man in the Senate constituted the entire Congressional membership representing twenty-five million black Americans. Today nine women and thirty-one men are situated on key committees in both the Senate and the House, which allows them to really influence the shaping of legislation.

The eighteen black freshmen members were very successful in winning assignments on many key committees, thereby increasing dramatically the individual and collective political clout of the Congressional Black Caucus. New black members were assigned to each of the following committees: Agriculture, Post Office and Civil Service, Public Works and Transportation, Small Business, and Banking. Three were assigned to the Foreign Affairs, Merchant Marine and Fisheries, and Veterans Affairs committees. One went to Education and Labor, and two were placed on the Government Operations, Judiciary, and Science, Space and Technology committees. Two members, Carrie Meek and Mel Reynolds, were placed on one of the powerful "exclusive committees." Because these committees have a heavy workload and deal with very important legislation, a member is prohibited from serving on any other committee. Carrie Meek joined Louis Stokes and Julian Dixon on the Appropriations Committee. Mel Reynolds joined Charles Rangel, William Jefferson, and Harold Ford on the Ways and Means Committee.

The large number of new black Democratic members of Congress can make a real difference in the type and quality of legislation passing the House and in the ability of the CBC to block bills that are not in the "permanent interests" of our constituents. In the past fifteen or twenty years, key legislation affecting welfare, food stamps, educational programs, student aid, student loans, job corps, job training, and low- and moderate-income housing has passed or failed by fewer than twenty votes. Usually those votes were decided by white members of Congress who represented—not too well, however—districts with sizable numbers of black voters. At least eight of the Congressmen with anti-black, anti-poor voting records were either replaced by black members or had their districts eliminated through reapportionment.

Replacing eight negative votes with eight positive votes for civil rights, civil liberties, and civil decency is equivalent to sixteen additional votes, which should be sufficient to reverse many of the past voting outrages. This is, of course, conditioned on the thirty-eight black Democratic members voting in unison on the major issues facing the black community. I emphasize Democratic votes because the lone Republican member of the CBC, Gary Franks, of Connecticut, has consistently supported his conservative colleagues in opposing legislation critical to the welfare of blacks, including the vote against the Civil Rights Act of 1991. Franks contends that his opposition to programs so obviously beneficial to the overall welfare of black citizens reflects the sentiments of his district, which is 95 percent white. Yet white members representing 95-percent white districts courageously vote to extend the resources of government to black residents of inner-city ghettoes. What makes white voters in Franks's district different?

At any rate, the legacy of voters sending able and effective black representatives to Congress continues, as do the challenges that face them as representatives of a people long denied basic rights and freedoms. One must not expect these representatives to work miracles overnight or correct the myriad problems resulting from years of discrimination and segregation. The road ahead is still rocky and uncertain, but the path is made clearer by the arrival of reinforcements in the Congress to engage the forces of racism and poverty. The challenges and obstacles at times seem almost insurmountable. Yet one's hopes for the future remain unflagging. As the poet Maya Angelou reminds us, "History, despite its wrenching pain, cannot be unlived, and if faced with courage, need not be lived again."

Acknowledgments

Whenever you make any kind of significant accomplishment, it's always because there are other people with you, around you, behind you, ahead of you, pulling and pushing you. My chief pushers have been my wife, Carol, and my children—Vicki, my eldest daughter; my son, Missouri State Senator Bill Clay, Jr.; and Michelle, my youngest daughter. These are the people who have endured with me through my thirty-six years as an elected official. Most especially, it has been the patience, tolerance, and understanding of my wife—who suffered with me during the last four and a half to five years while I was researching and writing—who made this book possible. I wrote it at night and on weekends, and during that time she saw very little of me. Along with my family, the others who made this book possible were Time Warner and Charles Harris, of Amistad Press. I also extend thanks to Congressman Louis Stokes, of Ohio, one of the first persons I permitted to read the book when it was in manuscript form.

Several years ago, while vacationing at Martha's Vineyard, Massachusetts, I had the good fortune to meet a ninety-eight-year-old educator and former president of North Carolina AT&T University, Dr. Warmoth Gibbs. He was very helpful to me. For two hours he both impressed and overwhelmed me with information about the history of black representatives during the Reconstruction period. When Dr. Gibbs returned to his home in North Carolina, he sent me a note and included a tract that he had written forty years earlier about Hiram Revels, the first black U.S. senator from Mississippi. From this tract I learned so much about the nature and background of the black congressmembers of the period. Several months ago Dr. Gibbs, at the age of 101, died in his native state of North Carolina.

I shall always remain indebted to those individuals who have been a source of inspiration and support in this as well as other efforts which I have undertaken.

Prologue
Blacks and the Real World
of Politics

This book was written in the hope of familiarizing newly elected black officials with the occupational hazards associated with full-time careers in the field of professional politics and with the expectation of educating, not entertaining, those political science majors who are preparing themselves in the academic disciplines to pursue a professional life in government. Hopefully, the sharing of my experiences will alert newly elected black brethren to the trials and tribulations they will face, primarily because of their blackness, in the world of a white-dominated political system. And, perhaps, it will enable them to understand more clearly the motto of the Congressional Black Caucus: "Black people have no permanent friends, no permanent enemies . . . just permanent interests."

Through this medium, I am afforded an opportunity not only to expound on the outstanding qualities of black elected officials, but also to dispel the gross misimpressions and perversely vulgar attitudes about blacks that too many whites hold as truisms.

What I have written contravenes the idealistic, ideological pipe dreams that typically characterize political activities. Thirty-six years as an elected officeholder have allowed me to become reasonably acquainted with the intricacies of politics as practiced by whites and intimately knowledgeable about the nuances of politics as conducted by blacks. My opinions, based on personal experience, are far more verifiable than they are speculative.

PROLOGUE

My mission is not to inflame, to placate, or to entertain, but to educate black people who are entering public life for the first time, as well as those who may profit from a clearer insight into how this serious business is conducted. If I am able to make them aware of the many pitfalls awaiting those so engaged, I will have accomplished my primary purpose.

I can best dramatize the nature of the plight of black people, for those who are not old enough to have experienced the years of legally mandated separation of the races, by reciting an incident that occurred prior to the great civil rights movement of the sixties.

In a small, backwoods town of Mississippi where one-half of the population was black, the first time a $100,000 bond issue was floated for major financing of the three public schools, it lost by fifty votes. Four hundred black registered voters had boycotted the election. The white superintendent of schools called upon the NAACP, black educators, and black ministers, seeking support for resubmission of the ballot initiative and promising fairness in allocation of the funds. They graciously gave their approval and in the second election delivered all 400 black voters in favor of the proposition, which carried by a margin of 350 votes.

When the school board met to disburse the funds for badly needed books, teacher salaries, and building repairs, the superintendent recommended $50,000 be allocated to each of the two all-white schools. The board agreed and promptly voted the same. When the principal of the all-black school was told that nothing was left for his students, he calmly rose and said in a very distinctive voice that the decision was satisfactory to black people in his community because, if there was anything white people needed, it was more education.

That was the sixties. Today, if there is anything black people need, it is more education. If we are to break out of the doldrums of political stagnation, we must educate our people to the necessity of dealing with a white mentality that totally disregards our entitlement to certain basic considerations. We must educate our constituents to deal with the racist behavior of past, present, and possibly future generations of whites who have been and are intent on manipulating the black vote for their own personal aggrandizement. We must pound into the psyche of our people that American politics is polarized along racial lines and divided along economic groupings.

Those who advance the concept of "white politics," by their very nature, must attack blacks who promote self-expression, self-determination, and self-pride. They must automatically brand them as dangerous and radical. Those vying to use political strength to enhance the economic stability of black communities are destined to be targeted for media harassment and grand jury investigation.

The prolonged attacks on black leadership are destined to continue until the black community effectually harnesses its latent potential power and effectively develops a mechanism for disciplining those blacks who willfully betray the cause of black liberation. The exercise of raw power, sometimes offensive to accepted standards of decency, always lacking in delicacy and refinement, may be the only means for blacks to achieve a fair and equal standing in society.

There are several different kinds of power, including media power, moral power, military power, the power of monopoly. But real power in our system boils down to two basic, meaningful kinds. One is economic. The other is political. If you have one, you are respected. If you have both, you are feared. If you have neither, you are oppressed.

We are an oppressed people because we do not understand how to use power effectively. I hesitate even to mention the term "power" and certainly do not refer to it with reckless abandon. If it were possible to alert newly elected black officials without uttering the blasphemous word, I would. For history teaches us that the possessors of real power seldom allude to their power and will readily destroy anyone who advocates a modest degree of power-sharing with the underprivileged and disadvantaged.

At the peak of the civil rights movement, in the sixties, those who screamed and chanted about black power usually had no conception of power (black or otherwise). Many of the militants, those vocalizing the slogan "black power," attacked and ridiculed other proponents of black empowerment, black pride, and black politics without fully understanding the ingredients for black power, which were an effective mixture of pride and black politics.

To some of them, black power was a convenient cliche recited to evade responding to legitimate questions concerning their activities and purposes. But to others, it was a means of advancing the cause of freedom through manipulation of the media. But the mere fact that both groups talked about power indicated a lack of knowledge about the nature of the subject.

Real power has been that awesome, often destructive, imposing force that those possessing it seldom discuss. The Rockefellers, Danforths, Kennedys, Mellons, DuPonts seldom broach the subject. For to admit having it, in some way, diminishes or destroys some element of the power itself.

PROLOGUE

If there is any validity to the term "black power," it does not exist in a slogan coined by free-wheeling, inexperienced black youths. Real black power is the result of serious and long-term investment in years of suffering and sacrifice. It is the result of vibrations that come out of the entire black populace. Black pride is not the exclusive property of any unique faction of the black public. It belongs to all of us as surely as our birthright.

Carl Stokes, former mayor of Cleveland, wrote in his book *Promises of Power:* "Politics is no box of crackerjacks, it is not candy and popcorn and free prizes." I agree strongly with this realistic summary of what the state of American politics is not. If anyone is eminently qualified to address this subject, based on actual experience garnered in the trenches of American political life, it's Carl Burton Stokes. He is one of the few public servants to have distinguished himself in all three branches of government—having been twice elected mayor of Cleveland, Ohio; twice elected to Ohio's state legislature; and twice elected to Cleveland's municipal courts. He is a consummate, professional practitioner in the fine art of elective politics.

The business of effective government is neither fun nor games. It is not easy work, short hours, and unending cocktail parties. For those who grasp the fundamental values, principles, and meanings of elective politics, it is hard work. It is not fairytale fantasies, candy, spice, and everything nice. Too often, part-time adventurists scurrying on the periphery of this endeavor believe otherwise. Exaggerated opinions and misconceptions promoted by the media, detailing glamour associated with public life, ofttimes create misleading and unfortunate perceptions about politicians and their lives.

Politics is not, was not, and will never be the descriptive romanticism embodied in refined gestures and gentlemanly virtues verbalized by idealistic dreamers in academia. Educators engaged in speculative political doctrine for the purpose of mesmerizing "do-gooders" at monthly tea sips would profit immeasurably by discarding this theatrical and pristine hypothesis about professionals engaged in politics. All concerned would be better off if they described a good political campaign as trench warfare, where the troops are armed for battle and poised for attack, where the candidate serves as field marshall or general, ever ready to sacrifice a percentage of the troops in order to capture a strategic position.

If editorial writers and professors of political science actively participated in politics at the precinct level, the experience would open up for them new vistas of intense realism. The evident hollowness of their

PROLOGUE

ideological pursuits and untested hypotheses in confrontation with sharp everyday truths would send shock waves to shatter their myopic highbrowed theories. Hundreds of Carl B. Stokeses learned years ago that there is no possible way to fashion a textbook for classroom discussion that adequately spares students the pain, frustration, and conflicts inherent in the process of politics.

Partisan political activism is rough, tough business; pursued by the roughest, toughest individuals; playing for the highest stakes; under a set of established rules. Politics is a deadly serious exercise, and the rules are structured to ensure that only the strongest survive. Neophytes, weaklings, and the unprepared entering this domain are quickly entangled in a maze of confusion, baffled by contradictions, and bewildered by numerous confrontations. Those who survive belong to a special breed of people, well equipped to compete with others in this extremely laborious but rewarding enterprise. They excel because they are strong-willed, egotistical, and fanatically determined. Idealistic persons don't fit the mold for success in this deadly business. Characteristics of modesty and timidity are fatal flaws in the makeup of those pursuing political careers.

This descriptive formula for a successful operation is not intended to demean or debase those who have built careers in politics. My characterizations are not applicable to all politicians in all situations. There are a few exceptions to every rule and some few, I confess, exist in my chosen field. But the vast majority do not participate in a game plan any more sinister or reckless than that of other professionals. By no means are we unique in our natural, animalistic tendencies. Our automatic protective reflexes do not differ appreciably from common defense mechanisms inherent in most animal species. Each group tends to devour its opponents no matter how young or old they may be.

The same set of ignoble rules, somewhat unfettered by the self-serving invocation of trivial platitudes that exist in other professions—i.e., ministry, education, medicine, law, business—also guide our behavior. In each category, the motto (written or unwritten) is the same: "To the victor belong the spoils."

For centuries, each profession has attempted to develop, expand, and standardize its operational procedures and codes of ethics. Politics is no different. Basically its ethos varies no more, no less than that of other professions. For each specific criticism hurled at politicians as a whole, there is a comparable one that can be leveled against those in other fields. Elected officials do not have a monopoly on hypocrisy and callousness, or on corruption and criminality.

Percentage-wise, the rate of involvement in sordid activity is generally the same as that for other groups. The difference lies merely in the public's perception that politicians are more corrupt. Negative press coverage of criminal activities engaged in by doctors, lawyers, judges, educators, and businessmen does not receive the same degree of excessive attention and notoriety.

To grasp a full understanding of successful politicking, it is necessary to distinguish between the process of election and the subsequent role of public service. The latter reflects the behavior of those elected or appointed to office, and the former is the course of action required to attain such a position. The two are measurably different and yet uncommonly inseparable. What happens after arriving at the top of the heap does not begin to explain or to excuse what occurs while scrambling for leverage at the bottom of the heap. Persons possessing high standards of morality, once in office, tend to exercise those qualities without distasteful memories of the carnage employed to get there. Those political degenerates who ignore all ethics and principles in getting elected continue to disgrace their trust of office once elected.

Our politics must state simply and succinctly that we believe that every person must be afforded fair and impartial justice, every business must be guaranteed a fair share of the public funds, and every community must have full participation in determining how tax dollars are to be spent.

If blacks are to unshackle the chains of bondage that bind us to a status of economic and political slavery, we must learn the basic rules of the political game. Rule number one is, take what you can, give up what you must. Rule number two is, take it whenever, however, and from whomever. Rule number three is, if you are not ready to abide by the first two rules, you are not qualified for a career in politics.

So it is up to your generation to add to and improve upon the advancements of the generation preceding you. Your opportunities for success are unlimited, as long as you don't become confused about your mission in life. Always remember that your destiny is inextricably tied to the destiny of 32 million other black brothers and sisters in this country. Your struggle, our struggle, their struggle are tied irrevocably one to the other.

Pervasive black unemployment, excessive numbers of black women heading households, deplorable black-on-black crime, escalating rates

PROLOGUE

of teenage pregancies, phenomenal rates of high school dropouts and drug addiction, and all the other tragic and sordid conditions that form a panorama of the black experience should be the number one priority of black leaders.

The best advice I can give to newly elected black officeholders and to those black students majoring in political science hoping to make a career in this field is to exercise a caution based on personal integrity. If you really want credentials as a qualified leader, never profiteer from or prostitute your blackness. It's not worth it. Don't deliberately confuse the issues in public debate, and refuse to sow the seeds of community dissent in order to ingratiate yourself to the white financial power structure. In the end, it's not worth the agony.

Always remember, when tempted by offers of personal enrichment, that those who are responsible for destabilizing their own communities are usually resented by their own and not trusted by the exploiters. Don't allow yourself to become a super gladiator, paid to maim and kill the aspirations of other blacks for the gratification and entertainment of white spectators. It simply is not worth it.

At all costs, preserve your personal integrity, for in the end it is probably the most effective force you have as a leader of a people sorely in need of leadership.

JUST
PERMANENT
INTERESTS

1

The Slow March to Freedom

Black Americans have experienced all facets of the political spectrum. We have cloistered with conservatives, consorted with liberals, coalesced with independents, and coexisted with socialists. We have, to one degree or another, embraced Republicans, Democrats, Communists, Progressives, Whigs, Tories, and Bull Mooses. We have sometimes, without regard to wisdom, even involved ourselves in debates concerning internationalism versus isolationism. Black people fought the tyranny of the British Crown, were strong advocates of Cuban independence from Spain, and were outspoken critics of American military intervention in Vietnam.

Black Americans have always been a discernible force in this country's political history. The plight of our race, so often at the core of political issues, has been the catalyst and the focus for political campaign after campaign. The attitudes of whites toward the black body politic are frequently a mystery to those blacks who don't understand the dynamics of race-hating and race-baiting politics. It is difficult for blacks to comprehend why whites so often and so callously disregard our needs and disrespect our aspirations. To grasp the totality of disdain many blacks hold for white politicians and, more importantly, to fully appreciate the forthrightness of our people in publicly expressing disenchantment for so-called white politics, it is necessary to revisit every biased paragraph of every distorted chapter in every sordid account that masquerades as authentic American history. If reviewed in the context of separating fiction from fact and assessing the racist motivation of dishonest authors who pervert the truth by denigrating, disregarding, or denying black contributions to the development of this nation, the travesty becomes all too apparent. Such a reappraisal will reveal the calculated inaccuracies and gross omissions by white historians, educators, and theologians in their conspiratorial revision of American history.

To give balance and credibility to this shameful spectacle, it is important that a review of America's history be made from a black perspective. Do whites really believe in the liberty, the justice, the equality they so proudly proclaim? The inscription on Crispus Attucks' monument in Boston Common reads, ". . . on that night the foundation of American independence was laid." Attucks, one of five Bostonians who died in what is now referred to as the "Boston Massacre," was a member of a race whose right to vote and access to educational facilities were denied in most of the original thirteen colonies.

Despite their mistreatment, blacks were always willing to fight for America in each of her wars, even when their efforts were not welcomed or accepted. Until the governor of Virginia invited indentured servants to join the British army in 1775, General George Washington opposed the enlistment of black soldiers, claiming their efforts were not necessary. President Abraham Lincoln, the "Great Emancipator," issued an order calling for 75,000 brave volunteers—white men only—to protect the Union. His rejection of Jacob Dodson's offer to raise an army of 350 black volunteers to guard the nation's capital is indefensible. The "Great Emancipator's" refusal to allow 100 black students from Wilberforce University to join the Union army is inexcusable.

Once the Union forces began to suffer humiliating and embarrassing defeats at the hands of Confederate troops, black volunteers for military service were accepted grudgingly by President Lincoln. He reversed his position after top advisers persuaded him that total defeat of the Union army was a real possibility because of massive casualties.

Frederick Douglass, a friend and close adviser of President Lincoln, had agitated from the beginning of the Civil War for the acceptance of black troops in the Union army. When blacks were finally permitted to enroll, Douglass personally enlisted a large percentage of all-black units of the Fifty-fourth and Fifty-fifth Massachusetts regiments. Later, he complained to President Lincoln that black soldiers were not receiving the same pay as whites and that it was shameful that no blacks were commissioned as officers. Lincoln acknowledged the disparity but told Douglass that the country was not quite ready for racial equality.

Blacks understandably have had a hard time accepting the premise held by white America that they are not quite ready for racial equality.

President Franklin D. Roosevelt harbored views similar to those of presidents Washington and Lincoln about allowing blacks to fight for this country. On October 9, 1940, Roosevelt instructed Assistant Secretary of War Robert Patterson to draft a memorandum, which the president initialed, declaring segregation of Negro troops to be official policy. "[That policy] has been proven satisfactory over a long period of years and to make changes would produce situations destructive to the morale and detrimental to the preparations for national defense."[1]

Historians have neglected to record the racist attitudes of American presidents, and they remain particularly generous in ignoring the shortcomings of President Lincoln concerning human slavery. In 1861, Lincoln countermanded a battlefield order issued by General John C. Fremont freeing all slaves in the state of Missouri. A much publicized letter written by Lincoln to Horace Greeley sheds light on the sentiments underlying Lincoln's decision to reverse General Fremont. Lincoln wrote:

> My paramount object in this struggle is to save the Union, and is not either to save or destroy slavery. If I could save the Union without freeing any slave, I would do it; and if I could save it by freeing all the slaves, I would do it; and if I could do it by freeing some and leaving others alone, I would also do that. What I do about slavery and the Colored race, I do because I believe it helps save this Union.[2]

Consistent with his feelings as displayed in this assertion, and very much aware that Great Britain would never intervene on behalf of the South if it appeared the war were a crusade to free the slaves, Mr. Lincoln issued a preliminary proclamation in which he wrote:

> That on the 1st day of January A.D. 1863, all persons held as slaves within any State or designated part of a State the people whereof shall then be in rebellion against the United States shall be then, thenceforward, and forever free...[3]

When President Lincoln ultimately issued his Emancipation Proclamation, the slaves that General Fremont attempted to liberate were left in bondage because Missouri had not seceded from the Union. Those slaves were not freed until 1865, when a state constitutional convention convened in Saint Louis to legally abolish slavery in Missouri. The significance of the Emancipation Proclamation was to free legally 4 million men and women who resided in the Confederate

States. But 800,000 slaves in states that had not seceded from the Union remained in bondage.

Some blacks who were later elected to Congress fought in the Civil War on the side of the Union. Some raised armies or joined with other blacks who fought. Some were forced to fight with the Confederate army, but many of them escaped as soon as the chance occurrred. No black who later achieved any degree of prominence after the Civil War fought with the Old Confederacy. According to the *New York Times*: "By end of the war 178,895 blacks had served in the Union army, 10 percent of the total Union forces and approximately one-third of the Union navy's 3,222 casualties were black men."[4]

Official records reveal that blacks were enlisted in 120 infantry regiments, twelve heavy artillery regiments, ten light artillery batteries, and ten cavalry regiments. Over 200,000 black troops (including 25 percent of the total Union army) fought in the Civil War. They engaged in more than 200 battles. Of the total number of black troops, 134,111 Negroes came from slaveholding states. Louisiana led the list with 24,952.

President Lincoln's attitude about the ultimate destiny of former slaves was as laissez-faire after the Civil War as before. The issue of penalties for those who rebelled against the Union was alive and well by the time of his last public address. His sentiment for unconditionally readmitting the rebellious states and their mutinous leaders was revealed in his last public speech on April 11, 1865, when he said: ". . .finding themselves [secessionist states] safely at home, it would be utterly immaterial whether they have ever been abroad."[5]

As part of the moderate Republican wing, Lincoln did not exert any appreciable pressure to advance the rights of citizenship for blacks. He summoned a group of black leaders to the White House on July 14, 1862, and informed them that a sum of money had been appropriated by Congress and placed at his disposal for the purpose of establishing a colony in another country for persons of African descent. Therefore, he said, it became the president's "duty, as it had been for a long time his inclination, to favor that cause." He continued: "You and we are different races. We have between us a broader difference than exists between almost any other two races. Whether it is right or wrong I need not discuss, but this physical difference is a great disadvantage to us both, as I think your race suffers very greatly, many of them by living among us, while ours suffers from your presence."[6]

President Lincoln went on to urge "intelligent Colored men" to prepare themselves for colonization of some place in Central America.

Apparently he was speaking of the same colored men of quality referred to in his 1864 letter to the interim governor of Louisiana when proposing that some Coloreds be allowed to vote, especially the "very intelligent."[7]

The observation persuades many that Abraham Lincoln's interest in the question of slavery was one-dimensional—namely, how slavery affected the Union.

There is very little doubt about Lincoln's views on the question of race. By all objective measures, he has to be evaluated as believing in white supremacy. His decision to free the slaves was nothing more than a strategic military ploy designed to weaken the Confederacy by eliminating its labor force and inciting slaves to insurrection. The "Great Emancipator" actually blamed blacks and slavery for the disunity of the nation.

Senators Charles Sumner, Thaddeus Stevens, and other stalwart Republicans represented a different perspective. Their opposition to slavery was based on moral principle. They were convinced, contrary to the beliefs of our founding fathers, that every man was entitled by birth to live free. Without much help from Lincoln, the senators successfully led the fight to ratify the Thirteenth Amendment abolishing slavery. Had Lincoln not been assassinated before ratification of the Fourteenth Amendment (conferring citizenship and providing for due process) and the Fifteenth Amendment (guaranteeing the right to vote), based on prior actions, it is reasonable to speculate that he would have opposed both measures.

Indicative of the great belief white southerners had that Lincoln would lead the campaign to restore them to their previous positions of leadership and respectability is a scene from D. W. Griffith's *Birth of a Nation*. When it is announced at Cameron Hall that Lincoln is dead, Colonel Cameron sadly states: "The South has lost its best friend!"[8]

Evidence suggests that President Lincoln was predisposed to compensate former slave owners for the loss of their property. Indemnifying them for financial loss of human chattel would have been no kind and gentle gesture designed to encourage harmony and to reunite a divided country. It would have been a blatantly overt act of intolerance toward black people and their white supporters. There is no real basis for believing that President Lincoln considered the institution of slavery as immoral and repulsive.

In this regard, he was no different from most other presidents in their feelings regarding issues of race and the plight of black people.

If President Lincoln's actions involving blacks may be considered immoral by some, those of his successor, Vice President Andrew Johnson, were obscene. His vehement opposition to suffrage for newly free slaves was indicative of the deep hatred he and other leaders harbored. Johnson pardoned former slave owners and evicted blacks from land allocated to them after the war in Mississippi, South Carolina, and Georgia. Returning the "forty acres" to former slave masters left former slaves without property, without education, and without employment. In a sense, their status was now worse than before emancipation, because they were at the mercy of white over-lords who were not even motivated by the need to protect their slave property. The whites had no reason to care if their workers were adequately fed and housed, as they were simply workers for hire who could be replaced without any initial investment.

Adding insult to injury, a series of laws known as "black codes" were enacted by legislatures across the South. Their purpose was to legalize the notorious antebellum practices of unrestrained racial violence and exploitation. The intent was to establish for blacks a status barely higher than that of involuntary servitude and far short of full citizenship. President Johnson wholeheartedly sanctioned these restrictive measures. In his first annual message to the nation, he stated: "The change in their [freedmen's] condition is the substitution of labor by contract for the status of slavery."[9]

The change in their economic status, as authorized by the "black codes," meant blacks were now subjected to harsh penalties for such minor charges as vagrancy or insulting gestures or curfew violations. The South Carolina legislature, purportedly to ensure good behavior, went so far as to require the posting of a $1,000 bond by any black entering the state. It also passed a law permitting employers to inflict corporal punishment on their black workers.

The former rulers of the South were now firmly back in political control and the "carpetbaggers," "scalawags," and ex-slaves in deep trouble. Their complaints to the president and to Congress were to no avail. Surprisingly, the voters came to their rescue. In the elections of 1866, the Republicans won an overwhelming majority in Congress with a mandate to repeal the "black codes."

To nullify the oppressive effects of the "black codes," Congress passed the Civil Rights Act of 1866 and reauthorized funding of the Freedmen's Bureau, which had been created to protect the rights of newly freed slaves. President Johnson vetoed the two bills, but the Congress voted to override him in both instances. Then Congress passed the Reconstruction Act, which dissolved all governments in the rebellious states except for Tennessee, divided the South into five military districts, and stationed army troops in each district to ensure that former slaves and white Union loyalists could register to vote without fear of bodily harm. The act also mandated that each state call a convention and ratify a constitution conferring rights of citizenship on former slaves. Those states not complying would forfeit their representation in the United States Congress. For a brief moment in history, it appeared the rights of black Americans to participate in the political process were secure.

The black race has found itself at the vortex of every major thrust for improving the quality of government. Despite numerous and seemingly unending rejection, many citizens of color continue to cling to the belief that equality of opportunity can be achieved through the exercise of political action, especially where federal legislation is concerned. But only behavior, not attitudes, can be legislated, and enforcement of law cannot be taken for granted. In spite of being shortchanged in most political relationships dealing with whites, some blacks remain wide-eyed optimists, hoping for the millennium when white politicians will share the spoils of victory with their black supporters.

Others, despairing of this dream decades ago, have come to realize that the so-called "collective conscience" of this nation is a fantasy. They have been awakened rudely to the fact that white Americans will only accede to black Americans those rights which we can negotiate through pressure or take by force.

The same rules for politically indemnifying other ethnic groups in America have never been applicable to blacks. From the time of the Colored race's unyielding trust of Republican President Abraham Lincoln and his Free-the-Slave movement, until converting reluctantly to support the Democratic party by way of President Franklin D. Roosevelt and the New Dealers, frustrations have increased, disappointments multiplied, and cynicism has permeated the black community. Unswerving loyalty to either political party has not resulted in significant economic and political gains for blacks.

Chuck Stone, political analyst, author, and former special assistant to Congressman Adam Clayton Powell, Jr., discussing this state of affairs in an article in *The Black Scholar* magazine, attributed our political impotence to ignorance and blind loyalty. He ascribed powerlessness to a lack of group sophistication.

The reason the "negro vote" has rarely decided the outcome of an election is because of its political ignorance and blind, single-party loyalty. For example, in 1932 and 1936, when Americans voted overwhelmingly for a Democratic president, black people in opposite numbers voted for the Republican candidate because a Republican president had freed their ancestors seventy years ago. They were still paying political booty. Then, in 1952 and 1956, America shifted its political sentiment and voted in equally overpowering numbers for a Republican president, but black people voted Democratic 74 percent and 77 percent respectively in those two elections. This time, they were paying political booty to a Democratic president who had put food in their stomachs.[10]

Mr. Stone's assertions, while enlightening and educational, would be plausible if all things in American life were equal. But the reality is that all things are not equal for black people. White ethnics who abandon politicians and political parties that have assisted them financially, economically, and educationally do so because they are offered much more "booty" by other politicians and political parties than their present spokespersons. No such incentives or rewards are ever proffered to black constituencies. Our people are encouraged to change parties and dissolve alliances in response to such cheap, insulting, meaningless cliches as "Blacks should participate in both parties so as to have leverage with the eventual winner," or the insulting juvenile slogan "It is time for a change." Some well-educated blacks fall prey to these trite phrases and support candidates who make decisions based on the reactionary philosophies of Ronald Reagan, Jesse Helms, George Bush, and Pat Buchanan.

Black professionals who criticize blacks for not making greater political advances fail to assess the devastating impact of slavery on the psyche of black Americans: Despite tireless efforts to achieve acceptance, we have not been able to overcome the stigma of our previous status of involuntary servitude. Nor do they take fully into account the continuing strength of the cultural bias against blacks: Descendants of former slave owners cannot or will not honestly and honorably bargain with the descendants of slaves in a manner to remove the obstacles to our full citizenship. From their perspective, I suspect this seems a perfectly tenable position. Why should a society that places an inordinate value on the right to own property seriously respect the rights of men and women once legally owned as property?

Many envision the extension of rights to minorities as a diminution of their own rights. Consequently, most of their leaders oppose measures that might result in economic gains, social advancement, and political progress for nonwhites.

Congressman Jim Wright of Texas, former Speaker of the U.S. House of Representatives, wrote:

> Those who would throw roadblocks in the way of free expression are builders of intellectual walls. The builders of walls usually operate from fear. All of the legal and economic tricks which for years kept blacks and other minorities from voting and getting an education and sharing fully in the opportunities and privileges of a free society were walls. They were built, for the most part, by people who honestly feared that—unless the minorities were walled off and kept "in their place"—there would be fewer privileges left for themselves.[11]

Most blacks would take exception to the contention that whites "honestly fear" them. "Hate" is the more appropriate term for the kind of behavior whites display. An exceptional black politician, Congressman Robert Brown Elliott of South Carolina, eloquently addressed the issue in a speech on the floor of the House in 1874:

> We trust the time is not far distant when all our fellow citizens—whether they be native born or whether they first drew the breath of life on the banks of the Rhine; whether they sprang from the Orient or the Occident—no longer controlled by the teachings of false political faith, shall be touched with the inspiration of a holier sentiment and shall recognize the universal fatherhood of God and the brotherhood of man . . . [To] hasten that period we shall contribute whatever of energy, brain, and muscle we may possess, and asking only what is just and fair, we shall ever cherish the genius of our American institutions.[12]

The politics of blacks, however, have for the most part been dictated, shaped, and molded by the prejudicial attitudes and spiteful actions of white people. Throughout the development of this country, white society has failed to take into account the mental and physical pain racism has inflicted whether or not manifested in a violent way.

Callous disregard for the rights of blacks as citizens was strikingly apparent immediately following conclusion of the Revolutionary War. Whites who resisted the tryanny of British domination were just as determined to impose the same, if not a far greater, degree of oppression on their fellow black colonialists. They concurred in the notion that social and economic class segregation were perfectly legitimate, acceptable tenets of democracy.

Our founding fathers were vehemently opposed to universal suffrage, regardless of the race question. They debated the issue at the 1789 session where the language subsequently adopted in the Constitution was framed. The prevailing opinion denied the right of the vote to women, free blacks, and slaves, and even attempted to deny it to white workingmen.

Gouverneur Morris of Pennsylvania said, "Give the votes to the people who have no property, and they will sell them to the rich, who will be able to buy them." He further stated, "The ignorant and the dependent can be as little trusted with the public interest."[13]

John Dickinson of Delaware said he considered property owners as "the best guardians of liberty, and the restriction of the right to them as a necessary defense against the dangerous influence of those multitudes without property and without principle with which our country like all others will in time abound."[14]

John Rutledge of South Carolina said "the gentleman last up had spoken some of his sentiments precisely. Property was certainly the principal object of Society."[15]

The notion of reserving the right to vote to a certain privileged class was only partially rejected. What remained was applied to black people and accepted across the nation.

At the time, the total population was 3 million, but only 120,000 persons, or 3 percent, had the right to vote. Workingmen did not get full suffrage until 1825. Women, black or white, did not get it until August 26, 1920, with the adoption of the Twentieth Amendment to the Constitution.

Theoretically, black citizens had the right of suffrage in ten of the thirteen original states. Georgia, South Carolina, and Virginia were the only states to prohibit free or freed black men from voting. Between 1792 and 1838, nine of the original thirteen states revised their constitutions and again denied black citizens the right to freely exercise the ballot. They were joined in this by every new state admitted into the Union between 1800 and 1861, except Maine. By law, blacks, right up to the time of the Civil War, were denied the right to participate in the electoral process in 85 percent of the states.

North and south, east and west, black citizenship did not have the same meaning as white citizenship. Similarly today, the predominant criterion for determining an American's quality of life is race.

NOTES

1. *The Negro Almanac*, New York: The Bellwether Company, 1976, page 635.

2. Letter to Horace Greeley from Abraham Lincoln, August 22, 1862.

3. Abraham Lincoln, preliminary Emancipation Proclamation, September 22, 1862.

4. *New York Times*, December 14, 1989, page. 21.

5. Abraham Lincoln, April 11, 1865, *The World Book*, Chicago: Field Enterprises Educational Corporation, 1966, page 286.

6. *New York Times*, August 15, 1862, page 1.

7. Lincoln, quoted in *Congressional Quarterly*, June 24, 1972, Vol. XXX, no. 26, page 1524.

8. *Birth of a Nation*, 1915.

9. President Andrew Johnson, first Annual Address, December 4, 1865, *Congressional Record*, 39th Congress, first session, Appendix, page 3.

10. Chuck Stone, *The Black Scholar*, December 1969, page 9.

11. Jim Wright, *Reflections of a Public Man*, Fort Worth, Texas: Madison Publishing Co., 1984, page 116.

12. Robert Elliott, Republican from South Carolina, *Congressional Record*, 43rd Congress, second session, page 946.

13. Max Farrand II, editor, *The Records of the Federal Convention*, New Haven, Ct.: Yale Press, 1937, pages 202–203 (August 7, 1787).

14. *Ibid.*, page 202 (August 7, 1787).

15. *Ibid.*, page 534 (July 5, 1787).

2

From Emancipation to the Halls of Congress

Politicians have long had a love/hate relationship with the media, though black politicians might say the scale is heavier with hate when they are the subject of the story. Historically, the rule more than the exception has been for the media to broadcast and publish images of black elected officials—and blacks in general—that are harmful, inaccurate, and negative. There is no greater example of this bashing-by-image than the landmark D. W. Griffith film *Birth of a Nation*.

Griffith, regarded as an artistic genius of filmmaking, is credited with the first use of flashbacks, close-ups, and fade-outs. He can also be credited with using his genius to make a vile and disgusting assault on black leaders. He depicted black elected officials during the period of Reconstruction as lawless, corrupt, ignorant, ill-mannered, and uneducated. He showed blacks drinking whiskey and eating fried chicken, throwing the bones on the floor, while the legislature was in session. His distorted version of history included a scene falsely depicting a special rule requiring all members to wear shoes, while Ku Klux Klansmen were depicted as glamorous knights in shining armor who upheld the noble virtues of chivalry. A majority of white Americans at the time—and maybe even today—wanted to believe that the first black members of Congress were buffoons. But in reality, most early black elected officials were well-educated, properly trained gentlemen in every respect.

If D. W. Griffith had carefully researched the history of whites in the Congress, he would have found ample material to support a movie revealing the shenanigans of rascals and rogues on Capitol Hill. Davy Crockett, whose image so represents the western American frontier, was an uncouth, tobacco-spitting, vulgar ruffian dressed in coonskins and toting a musket—not the heroic, adventurous, larger-than-life hombre shown in movies and film. Many members of Congress in those days were pistol-packing hooligans. During one contentious debate in the House, thirty congressmen pulled their guns and threatened to do bodily harm. Henry Clay and John Randolph fought with pistols in 1839, and Congressman Jonathan Cilley killed Congressman William Graves with a rifle. (The incident precipitated a law in the District of Columbia to outlaw dueling.) Senator Charles Sumner was brutally beaten with a cane on the Senate floor in 1856 by Representative Preston S. Brooks of South Carolina. The attack took place while a civil rights bill was pending and Sumner was speaking against the evils of slavery. His injuries were so severe he walked with a limp for the rest of his life.

When a gentleman raised a point of order, declaring, "Mr. Speaker, the House is not in order," he often meant it literally during this period of congressional history. James H. Hutson, chief of the Library of Congress Manuscript Division, wrote in his book *To Make All Law, The Congress of the United States, 1789–1989,* "Two New Englanders, Matt Lyon, Republican of Vermont, and Roger Griswold, Federalist of Connecticut, were the principals [in one fracas]. At issue was Griswold's charge in a House debate in 1798 that during the Revolutionary War, Lyon had been forced to wear a wooden sword because of cowardice. Retaliating against his accuser, Lyon spit tobacco juice into Griswold's face on January 30, 1798. Fifteen days later, Griswold, armed with a 'stout hickory stick,' assaulted Lyon as he sat at his House desk."[1]

In stark contrast to this rowdiness, thirteen of the twenty-two blacks who served in Congress during Reconstruction were ex-slaves, but all twenty-two were well educated—either self-taught or formally trained. There were seven lawyers, three ministers, one banker, one publisher, two school teachers, and three college presidents among the ranks. Half of them had previous experience in state assemblies and senates. But they were seldom appointed to important committee chairmanships, and only on rare occasions were they able to see legislation of meaningful import to their black constituents or to the nation passed into law.

One congressman, Robert Smalls of South Carolina, was a war hero. His daring exploit of commanding the steamer *Planter* past Confederate guns and turning the vessel over to the Union fleet prompted President Lincoln to name him a pilot in the Union navy and promote him to the rank of captain. He was the only black to hold such a rank during the Civil War. Smalls was also awarded a very large sum of money for the delivery of such prized war booty. But his national prestige did not give him any more favorable standing in the Congress than that of other black members.

Five states—Alabama, Florida, Louisiana, Mississippi, and South Carolina—had majority black populations when the Supreme Court declared the Reconstruction Acts passed by Congress to be constitutional. These measures opened the floodgates for blacks to be elected to public office. This ruling, bolstered by the Fourteenth and Fifteenth Amendments to the Constitution, added 703,000 blacks and 627,000 whites to the voting rolls in southern states. These newly enfranchised citizens voted in large numbers, electing many of their own to local and state as well as national offices.

Brief notes on early blacks elected to Congress follow:

THE REVEREND HIRAM RHOADES REVELS, THE FIRST BLACK U.S. SENATOR

Hiram Rhoades Revels' performance as an elected official should have dispelled any negative stereotyping of black legislators. He was a person of enormous character and wit, well respected by whites and blacks alike. He was known for his big booming voice, which resounded in the chamber of the Senate as he defended the rights of black people—a voice that also resounded from the pulpit, as he was a preacher. He became pastor at the St. Paul AME church in St. Louis in 1852 and in doing so became an outlaw, practising God's law in defiance of man's law. His first act of civil disobedience was to allow slaves—as opposed to only free blacks—to worship in his church; his second illegal act was founding a school to teach black children to read and write.

In 1847, the Missouri legislature had made it a crime to educate blacks—be they free or slave. This was a part of a series of laws called "black codes," which prohibited "any white person, free Negro or mulatto" from association with slaves "at any meeting hall or place of entertainment." Those found to be in violation were liable for a fine of $300 or "twenty lashes on the back," or both.

Born in Fayetteville, North Carolina, in 1827, Hiram Revels grew into a national figure whose religious and political work took him around the country at a time when simply staying alive was an accomplishment for a black person. He did missionary work in Indiana, Illinois, Kansas, Kentucky, and Tennessee. Besides his stint as pastor of the church in St. Louis, he also served as pastor of a church in Baltimore, Maryland, in 1860. After the Civil War broke out, he organized two all-black regiments that fought for the North. He was chaplain to the units and established a school to educate the troops. The regiment to which he was assigned was sent to Mississippi. After the war he first settled in Vicksburg, then later moved to Natchez, where he became active in politics. In 1870, Revels was elected to fill the thirteen-month unexpired senatorial term of Jefferson Davis, who had resigned to become president of the Confederate States.

While the population of Mississippi was 60 percent black at the time, the body of representatives that picked Revels was not predominantly black. It was composed of one hundred whites and only forty blacks.

There were fourteen candidates seeking the Senate seat. The first order of business for the newly sworn Reconstruction state legislature was to fill three vacancies to the United States Senate. Two seats had been left open when the state seceded from the Union. The other was for a regular scheduled full term. James Lynch, a highly qualified and very likeable black politician, was the odds-on favorite to be named to one of the positions. But he had already been appointed secretary of state for Mississippi and declined to enter the contest.

In the jockeying to fill the two unexpired Senate terms and the one full six-year term, former Confederate general James L. Alcorn was elected on January 18, 1870, to fill the full term beginning on March 4, 1871, and going to March 4, 1877. He would not be sworn into office until the term of the seat vacated by Jefferson Davis had expired. Also on the same day, former Union general Adelbert Ames was elected to fill the remainder of the longer term that terminated on March 4, 1875. But it took three days and seven ballots to fill the thirteen-month unexpired term of Jefferson Davis. Hiram Revels, who was not aggressively seeking the position, won out as a compromise candidate. He received eighty-one votes, twenty-one more than required by state statute.

On January 25, 1870, the provisional governor of Mississippi, General Adelbert Ames, as authorized by the Reconstruction Act, signed the certification of election attesting that Revels had been duly elected to serve in the United States Senate. One month later, President Grant signed into law a bill entitling the state to congressional representation.

After arriving in the capital, Revels waited three weeks before the Senate scheduled a date for his swearing-in ceremony. From the very moment that he presented his credentials to the secretary of the Senate, a battle to deny him a seat was joined. The authority of a provisional military governor to certify his election was challenged by Democrats, who opposed Revel's seating. Provisional military governors had previously certified white senators from Virginia, and in those cases none of those contesting Revels' accreditation had objected. Although the credentials of some senators had been lost before they arrived in the capital, including those of at least one of the senators now opposing Revels, they had still been sworn in. But some senators were hell-bent on preserving the "racial purity" of the world's most deliberative legislative body, and consistency of procedure be damned.

Senator Garrett Davis of Kentucky, a leading opponent to the seating of Revels, railed in abusive oratory. During floor debate, he declared:

> Mr. President, this is certainly a morbid state of affairs. Never before in the history of this government has a colored been elected to the Senate of the United States. Today for the first time one presents himself here and asks admission to a seat in it. How does he get here? Did he come by the free voices, by the spontaneous choice of the free people of Mississippi? No, sir, no. The sword of a military dictator has opened the way for his easy march to the Senate of the United States, and but for that sword and that dictator, he never would have been presented here for a seat.[2]

But the acid-tongued remarks of Mr. Davis from Kentucky were not left to sully the *Congressional Record* without contest. Senator James Nye of Nevada was quick to rise in support of Mr. Revels. He spared no barbs and minced no words. He described Davis as a "mountain of prejudice—fearful of competition from blacks." Observed Nye scornfully,

> This is his [Davis's] last battlefield. It is the last opportunity he will have to make this fight . . . It seems to me this is the day long looked for, when we put into practical effect the theory that has existed as old as man. We say that men are brothers; whatever their color, all are subject to the same law, and all are eligible to fill any place within the gift of the people . . . I had

hoped that prejudice was over. Color never made a man; color never unmade a man.[3]

Boasting, bragging, further slamming the senator from Kentucky, Nye said,

> In 1861 from this hall departed two senators who were representing here the state of Mississippi; one of them who went defiantly was Jefferson Davis. He went out to establish a government whose cornerstone should be oppression and the perpetual enslavement of a race because their skin differed in color from his. Sir, what a magnificent spectacle of retributive justice is witnessed here today! In the place of that proud, defiant man, who marched out to trample under foot the Constitution and the laws of the country he had sworn to support, comes back one of that humble race whom he would have enslaved forever to take and occupy his seat upon this floor.[4]

After the question of Revels' credentials had been resolved in his favor, the next dilatory tactic employed by opponents was to contest his citizenship. Since there had been no statute defining the "legal status" of blacks until the 1866 Civil Rights Act and no judicial opinion had ever been rendered on this subject, this argument presented a thorny problem in 1870. But it did not prove to be an insurmountable obstacle, because those opposed to seating Revels simplified the issue by arrogantly acknowledging that their opposition was actually based solely on the color of Revels' skin.

They insisted that a Negro, notwithstanding his free birth (Revels had never been a slave), was unqualified for citizenship, and they argued that the *Dred Scott* decision had never been reversed or nullified by any later Supreme Court decision. Shamefully reciting rationalizations used in the *Dred Scott* decision but rejected by subsequent courts, they disdainfully echoed the discredited opinion issued in the case by Chief Justice Taney. They argued as if the question of slavery had not been decided in the bloodiest armed conflict in the nation's history—134,000 Confederate soldiers and 364,000 Union troops killed—and they totally ignored the ratification of the Thirteenth and Fourteenth amendments.

Nye was not Revels' only defender. There were others who supported his seating and spoke in his behalf. Senators Jacob Merritt Howard of Michigan, Henry Wilson and Charles Sumner of Massachusetts, Simon Cameron of Pennsylvania, and others rose to defend the right of Mississippians to decide their own representation.

Senator Wilson befriended Revels on the first day. During floor debate before the vote to seat Revels, Senator Wilson said,

> I am glad this senator is here from the state of Mississippi; that he comes as a representative of the black race—their eyes are fixed on him. They will remember these three days of debate. They will remember its significance, and so will their true and trusted friends. I welcome him here. When he takes his seat with us . . . [we will have] closed this great struggle of forty years. He will be an illustration of the power of the Constitution and the laws. This oath will soon be administered and caste and privilege disavowed forever.[5]

After three tumultuous days of debate and three dilatory procedural roll calls, Hiram Rhoades Revels was seated by a vote of 48 ayes, 8 nays, and 12 not voting. Senator Wilson accompanied him to the desk of the vice-president, where the oath of office was administered to the first black in the United States Senate. (Wilson was later elected vice-president of the United States.)

He served only one year and one month in the Senate, but in those thirteen months he established a record exceeding the expectations of many who thought the first and only black member of the body would be of no consequence. He spoke out against legislation designed to deny citizenship to Chinese; fought to protect the rights of Indians; and championed the racial integration of public education. Afterward, he returned to Mississippi to become the first president of all-black Alcorn A & M College.*

Senator Revels' return to Mississippi from the Senate was greeted with a degree of hostility in some Republican quarters. He was appointed to serve as interim secretary of state for Mississippi in 1873 while still the president of Alcorn. But the following year, Republican Governor Adelbert Ames forced his resignation as president of Alcorn, and he became pastor of a church in Holly Springs. An embittered Revels then campaigned for several Democrats in the 1875 elections.

The following year, he was interrogated by the U.S. Senate's Select Committee to Inquire into Alleged Frauds in Recent Elections in

---

*The Mississippi legislature authorized funding for the all-black college almost 100 years before James Meredith was admitted as the first black student at the University of Mississippi in 1962. Their action was motivated by the desire to keep blacks from agitating for enrollment at the all-white student body of tax-supported Ole Miss—the University of Mississippi at Oxford.

Mississippi, which was chaired by George S. Boutwell of Massachusetts. Revels, attempting to protect the Democratic governor whom he supported, lied to the committee, testifying that the elections at issue had been conducted in a peaceful, nonviolent manner. As a result of his obviously false testimony, the parishioners at Holly Springs dismissed him as pastor. The Democratic governor, John M. Stone, who had won office with Revels' assistance, reappointed him to preside over Alcorn.

BLANCHE BRUCE, FIRST FULL-TERM BLACK SENATOR

A former slave, this Oberlin College–educated man was a Mississippi state senator as well as tax assessor and sheriff in Bolivar County before becoming the first black man to serve a full six-year term in the United States Senate.

Blanche Bruce was seated four years after the departure of Senator Revels. While in office, he was appointed chairman of a committee to investigate the failure of the Freedmen's Saving and Trust Company. This was a federal bank chartered by the Congress to safeguard the earnings of ex-slaves. His investigation was thorough and extensive, uncovering massive fraud and gross incompetence. The circumstances were very similar to today's crisis in the savings and loan industry. Those assigned as watchdogs to protect the deposits of black freedmen had become lapdogs conspiring with those pilfering the deposits. Bruce's six-member congressional committee released an official report specifically naming bank officials who had absconded with money or were guilty of gross negligence. The result was that more than 61,000 depositors who had been victimized by these fraudulent schemers were returned all or at least a portion of their savings.

Senator Bruce also served on three other committees: Education and Labor; Manufactures; and Pensions. During debate on a bill that would have excluded Chinese from entering the country, Bruce chaired the session, the first black to be so honored. He also served two terms as U.S. register of treasury.

When Democrats won control of the Mississippi state legislature in 1880, Bruce was replaced by a Democrat, James Z. George. After his departure from office, he remained active in party politics. He received eleven votes for vice-president at the 1888 convention that nominated Benjamin Harrison. In 1889, President Harrison named him to a position previously held by other prominent black citizens, recorder of deeds for the District of Columbia.

AMNESTY FOR SOUTHERN INSURRECTIONISTS: A FIRST STEP TO LOSS OF BLACK POLITICAL REPRESENTATION

Every politician has his contradictions, and neither Revels nor Bruce were exceptions to the rule. While they made political decisions that promoted the interests of black people, they also made some decisions that undermined those interests. A case in point was their advocacy of legislation to lift sanctions against white Confederate insurrectionists. Both were guilty of the same flaws in judgment that some modern-day black leaders insist on repeating: They were too eager to concede to their political enemies, and often too generous to people who did not return their generosity.

Both Revels and Bruce practiced the philosophy that blacks could successfully compete on equal footing with whites, regardless of the advantages that whites had in society. Ignoring the vast social and economic disparities between the races, they argued for abstract equality before the law, demanding neither special favors for their people nor practical requirements to reduce the gap between the races. This philosophy of "fairness" was applied, come what may, to blacks or whites.

When the question of amnesty for Confederate leaders and rebel soldiers was debated on the Senate floor, Revels said,

> I am in favor of removing the disabilities of those upon whom they are imposed in the South just as fast as they can give evidence that he is a loyal man, and give that evidence in the fact that he has ceased to denounce the laws of Congress as unconstitutional, has ceased to oppose them, and respects them and favors the carrying out of them, I am in favor of removing his disabilities; and if you can find a whole State that is true of, I am in favor of removing the disabilities of all its people.[6]

Revels' position on amnesty was somewhat ambiguous. While he opposed conferring voting rights on rebel leaders who could not demonstrate their loyalty to the Union and had not reformed their rebellious ways, he did not set or demand a standard for measuring the degree of their repentance. He often brought up the number of whites who opposed secession and emphasized what he knew of individual eagerness to accept the outcome of the war and the liberation of black people—but without citing credible evidence.

Revels and Bruce thought publicly taking an oath to uphold the laws of the land was sufficient to restore all rights of citizenship to the rebels, and shortly thereafter, the nation did find "whole state(s)" willing to denounce prior behavior in order to regain political rights. And indeed, an amnesty was granted.

The actions of Senators Revels and Bruce and like-minded black representatives jeopardized the interests of the so-called scalawags—southern whites who had remained loyal to the Union; carpetbaggers—northerners who had come south to aid the blacks in the transition period; and blacks—the recently freed slaves who were grappling with serious problems of economic and political insecurity.

Both Revels and Bruce should have known better—especially Revels, whose seating in Congress was so actively opposed by white members on trumped up charges of voting fraud and incompetence. But they and others like E. D. Tinchant, a black delegate to the 1868 Louisiana Constitutional Convention, persisted in their over-optimistic view of relations between former slaves and masters. This is why Tinchant announced his opposition to a "rebel political disabilities" article, which proposed to extend penalties against rebel leaders who had not repented:

1. Because I think that all men who voluntarily aided or assisted the rebellion against the United States in any shape or manner are equally guilty and ought to be treated alike.

2. Because I have been taught to look upon the men of my race as fully equal to the white man, and able to fight their way through without the help of any partial proscriptive measure directed against their opponents.

3. Because I think this article embodies such principles as are in direct conflict with those which are the most sacred to the heart of any wise and honest Republican.[7]

Tinchant, a wise and learned black man, holding a utopian vision of a colorblind society, was himself blind to the reality that powerful interests were determined to impose a color-conscious society, as is still true today.

In Washington, Mr. Tinchant's thoughts were echoed by Jeremiah Haralson, a black representative from Alabama who served in Congress from 1875 to 1877. Haralson was obnoxious in his criticism of the use of federal troops to stop the violence aimed at black voters in the South during the 1876 elections. A close friend of Jefferson Davis, former president of the Confederacy, he boisterously protested efforts to ensure orderly voting and the protection of black voters. Apparently, the safety of voters and the sanctity of the ballot were not his major priorities. Instead, he devoted considerable time agitating for a general amnesty for former Confederates. (Some of the positions taken by black leaders during Reconstruction are very similar to positions taken today by some black people. They believe it personally advantageous to echo the duplicitous rhetoric of white politicians and business leaders, who are more often than not indifferent to the real needs of the black population.)

Another black member of the House of Representatives supporting the insane notion of amnesty without contrition was Benjamin S. Turner of Alabama. In the first session of his one and only term, Mr. Turner introduced a bill to remove all legal and political disabilities imposed on former Confederates by Section Three of the Fourteenth Amendment to the Constitution. His bill was referred to committee, where it died.

Once Congress passed the Amnesty Act, restoring full rights to Confederate leaders, including the right to vote, blacks were once again harassed and intimidated beyond all reason. Shortly after their return to power, those same white leaders for whom Senators Revels and Bruce had so passionately pleaded succeeded in enacting new state constitutions requiring literacy tests as a prerequisite for voting. These tests became the primary means of disfranchising 99 percent of all black voters in the secessionist states.

Representative Robert Brown Elliott of South Carolina was much more realistic about this subject than either Revels or Bruce. He was not unmindful of the many unrepentant ex-Confederate officials and rebel leaders. In his first speech on the House floor, debating a measure dealing with civil rights, he emphasized,

History teaches us that adequate policy is the best. In one section of the Union, crime is stronger than law. Murder, unabashed, stalks abroad in many of the southern states. If you cannot now protect the loyal men of the South, then have the loyal people of this republic done and suffered much in vain, and our free Constitution is a mockery and a snare . . . Such sir, will be the bitter reflection of all loyal men in this nation, if the Democratic party shall triumph in the states of the South through armed violence.[8]

F. L. Cardozo, a black delegate to the 1868 South Carolina Constitutional Convention, was more blunt about the subject than Elliott. He stated flatly,

> In the first place, there is an element that is opposed to us no matter what we do, which will never be reconciled. It is not that they are opposed so much to the constitution we may frame, but they are opposed to us sitting in the convention. Their objection is of such a fundamental and radical nature, that any attempt to frame a constitution to please them would be utterly abortive.[9]

THE DENIAL OF ELECTED BLACK REPRESENTATION

Black politicians should realize that the campaign waged against Revels in his efforts to be seated served as a prototype for subsequent efforts by enemies of black political power in their efforts to block blacks from obtaining representation. For the next hundred years, the discourtesies and indecencies shown Revels because of race became the standard operating procedure in abusing other black elected officials.

Five of the first twenty blacks elected to the House were denied their seats, and ten others had their terms interrupted or delayed. The charges against these individuals were frivolous and frequently fabricated, often having to do with alleged voting irregularities. James Lewis, John Willis Menard, and Pinchney B. S. Pinchback, all from Louisiana, were charged with vote fraud by individuals who themselves were the perpetrators of ballot box tampering. These elected Louisiana representatives' credentials were challenged and they were never seated in the House.

However, Menard did become the first black to speak in the U.S. House of Representatives. On February 27, 1869, he pleaded with the Congress to accept his credentials and seat him along with his white Republican running mate, Lionel Allen Sheldon. Each had received the exact same number of votes and far outdistanced their opponents. But life being what it is, Sheldon was seated and Menard was rejected. In his remarks to the body, Menard stated, "I do not expect nor do I ask that there shall be any favor shown me on account of my race or the former condition of that race."[10]

Denying a seat to Pinchney B. S. Pinchback was perhaps the most tragic because his character was so impeccable. His popularity in the state of Louisiana was second to none. Born free, the eighth of ten children, he was a leading figure in the founding of Louisiana's Republican party and had played a key role in building it into a powerful force in national politics. During the war he'd raised a company of black cavalrymen and fought on the side of the Union.

Pinchback was unique in being the only person in the history of the country ever elected to serve in both houses of Congress at the same time. In 1867, the voters of the state elected him to the House of Representatives as an at-large candidate. Simultaneously, the state legislature elected him to represent the state in the U.S. Senate. Blanche K. Bruce waged a mighty and prolonged effort on Pinchback's behalf. But despite this and the fact that no serious allegation of vote tampering had been raised in Louisiana, the influence of his enemies had grown to such an extent that they were able to prevent his being seated in either chamber of Congress.

The House moved on to seat Pinchback's Democratic opponent with little discussion and without even a serious investigation of the charges of voting irregularity against Pinchback. In the Senate, the issue was handled differently. There the debate dragged on intermittently for over three years. Finally, in a close vote, Pinchback was rejected. He was paid the salary of a senator and reimbursed for mileage while traveling back and forth from Louisiana to Washington, D.C., over the three years of the lengthy debate.

After he returned to Louisiana, he was elected to the state senate and four years later was elected president pro tempore of that legislative body. He succeeded to the position of lieutenant governor upon the death of incumbent Oscar J. Dunn, another black, and for five weeks—from December 9, 1872, to January 13, 1873—served as acting governor when the white governor, Henry Clay Warmoth, was suspended because of impeachment proceedings.

Warmoth's one term as governor was marred by scandals involving kickbacks in state aid to the railroads. He was controversial among black citizens because his commitment to racial equality, particularly his stance on the right to vote, was questionable. Because black voters represented such a large percentage of the electorate in Louisiana, the issue was critical, particularly inasmuch as blacks' rights to register and vote were not protected by the state. While some praised Warmoth for signing a bill to open all restaurants, schools, and railroad cars to people of all races, others pointed to the governor's veto of a much stronger civil rights bill. White Republicans accused him of catering to the whims and fancies of black leaders—kowtowing to "burr heads" and "tar babies"—while black Republicans attacked him for foot-dragging on civil rights. He was unable to win the Republican nomination for re-election in the closing months of his term, so chose not to run again. Angry with members of his own party, he endorsed a Democratic candidate for governor. And it was in this highly charged atmosphere that Warmoth was impeached by the legislature. Lt. Governor Pinchney B. S. Pinchback served out the remainder of the term—five weeks—as acting governor. (Warmoth was not convicted because the trial extended past the expiration of his term.)

In 1877, Pinchback followed in the footsteps of Warmoth. He, too, left the Republican party and supported a Democrat for governor. The Democrat won and for several years afterward, Pinchback held a minor post appointed by the governor. He later moved to Washington, D.C., to practice law.

Representative James Lewis, another of the three blacks from Louisiana whom Congress refused to seat, was compensated by a presidential appointment as U.S. Inspector of Customs for the Port of New Orleans. He also continued to be active in local politics. Five years after his rejection by Congress, Lewis was named chairman of the Louisiana delegation to the Republican National Convention.

THE FIRST BLACKS SEATED IN THE HOUSE OF REPRESENTATIVES

In 1870, Joseph H. Rainey of South Carolina became the first black man actually to be seated in the House. He had been elected to a four-year term in the state senate, just two months prior to winning the congressional seat, which was being vacated because of the resignation of the incumbent, who had been accused of selling appointments to military academies. Rainey was slated as the Republican nominee and defeated his Democratic opponent in a special election. After serving the partial term in the Forty-first Congress, he won re-election without opposition in 1872.

But Rainey's election was challenged in 1874 and again in 1876. The first challenge came after a narrow victory over an independent Democrat. The House took several months to reject the challenge and finally seat Rainey. In the second instance, his defeated Democratic opponent contended that federal soldiers and gun-toting members of black political clubs had intimidated his supporters in the election. Rainey was seated while the House investigated the merits of the challenge. One and a half years later, the investigating committee recommended that the seat be declared vacant, but the full House refused to vote on the matter, referring it back to committee.

Rainey was very active and vocal during his tenure of office. He spoke on behalf of the civil rights bill sponsored by Senator Charles Sumner that made racial discrimination in schools, transportation, and public accommodations illegal. He argued that unless certain protections for blacks were firmly established by federal law, there should be no amnesty for former Confederate officials.

He also fought to expand educational opportunities. Insisting that federal aid to education was not a sectional or racial issue, but one of great national import, he produced data showing that 126,946 school-age children in Illinois did not attend school; 308,312 in Indiana were not attending; 666,394 in Louisiana were not enrolled; and in Arkansas, of the 180,000 total school-age population only 40,000 were in daily attendance. In the congressional debate, Rainey said,

> I would have it known that this ignorance is widespread; it is not confined to any one State. This mental midnight, we might justly say, is a national calamity, and not necessarily sectional. We should, therefore, avail power to avert its direful effects. The great remedy, in my judgment, is free schools, established and aided by the government throughout the land.[11]

Rainey was defeated in 1878 by the candidate who had challenged him in the previous election. The Democrats by this time had taken control of politics in most of the South. Following Rutherford B. Hayes' ascendancy to the presidency and the withdrawal of federal troops from the South, the question of protecting the right of blacks to participate in the electoral process became moot. The violence and intimidation of black voters in the southern states where they were still somewhat politically active was intensified. It was impossible for blacks to exercise the right to vote without fear of death or serious bodily harm.

Jefferson Franklin Long, a black representative from Georgia who had been elected to fill an abbreviated term in 1871, was among those actively opposing a bill to restore political rights to former Confederate officials. The measure passed, though, by a vote of 118 to 90. President Grant permitted it to become law without his signature.

By this time, violence against black candidates and black voters was escalating at a tremendous pace across the South, and Long was subjected to an attack that was typical of the times. Bruce A. Ragsdale and Joel D. Treese, in their book on blacks in Congress, wrote:

> Returning to Georgia, [Long] continued to campaign for Republicans and on election day, 1872, addressed a large gathering of Macon blacks who then marched to the polls and were met by angry armed whites. A brief riot broke out, instigated by Democrats wanting to "redeem" Macon and Bibb County from the Reconstruction government. Long was unharmed, but four people were killed. Most black voters left the polls without casting their ballots.[12]

South Carolina's Robert C. DeLarge also fell victim to trumped-up charges of violations of voting laws after defeating a fellow Republican, Christopher C. Bowen, a white man, by 986 out of more than 32,000 votes cast in the 1870 election. His opponent challenged the results in the face of evidence that Bowen's supporters were guilty of most of the voting irregularities that had occurred. DeLarge was sworn into office in 1871 with this cloud of allegations hanging over his head. After he'd served twenty-two months of the twenty-four-month term of office, his seat was declared vacant.

During the time he served in the Forty-second Congress, DeLarge successfully offered amendments to several bills. He fought to keep political restrictions on former Confederate officials and soldiers, advocating instead to protect southern whites who had been loyal to the Union and were now subject to a reign of terror by former Confederates. Denying the need for an amnesty, he pointed out that thousands of "rehabilitated" white southerners were already holding high elected office. He opined that those still denied the right to vote and to hold public office were the diehards, the recalcitrants, the ones who refused to recognize the Union victory in the recent war. According to DeLarge, continued disfranchisement was appropriate punishment for those hell-bent on returning blacks to the status of noncitizen.

DeLarge, citing poor health, declined to seek re-election in 1872. The seat was then won by another black, Lt. Governor Alonzo J. Ransier. Ransier, a former member of the state house of representatives, was sworn in on March 3, 1873, and appointed to the Committee on Manufactures.

John Mercer Langston, the only black ever elected to Congress from the state of Virginia, was another man denied a seat in the House—in his case for almost two years. The Republican party had refused to nominate him for Congress in the 1888 campaign, so he filed for the seat as an independent. In the three-way race, Langston ran ahead of the Republican but behind the Democratic candidate by some 641 votes. Then it was discovered that the Democrat had received several thousand fraudulent votes. Langston challenged the election returns, but Republicans controlling the House were angry because he had siphoned off enough black votes to deny the white Republican candidate the victory, and they delayed consideration of his petition. Not until September 1890, just three months before the next election, was he seated. And all of the Democrats in the House boycotted the swearing-in ceremony.

In the next election, Langston was defeated by a white Democrat, James Epes, by almost 3,000 votes. Again Langston filed an appeal with the House of Representatives, alleging voting fraud and other irregularities. In the national elections that year, the Democrats had captured control of the House, and his appeal was quickly denied.

Langston, an attorney, educator, author, orator, and rich landowner, had already distinguished himself as an important personality well before his election to public office. He'd earned both a bachelor of arts and master of arts degree from Oberlin College in Ohio. Denied admission to two law schools because of his race, Langston, determined to become a barrister, read law under Judge Philemon Bliss in Elyria, Ohio, and was subsequently admitted to the Ohio bar. In 1871, President Grant appointed him resident minister to Haiti and chargé d'affaires in Santo Domingo. He later served as vice-president of Howard University, and, in 1884 and 1885, was acting president of that institution. Later in 1885, he was named president of Virginia Normal and Collegiate Institute in Petersburg, Virginia.

Josiah Thomas Walls was the only black member of Congress unseated twice by opponents contesting his election. He was elected in 1870 to Congress from Florida, presented his credentials, and was seated in 1871 and assigned to several committees. But his white Democratic opponent, Silas L. Niblack, disputed the vote count, and in January 1873 the House Committee on Elections unseated Walls by declaring Niblack the winner.

Walls, born a slave in Winchester, Virginia, had been forced to fight with the Confederate army. However, Yankee troops captured him in the siege of Yorktown, Virginia, and within months he had enlisted in the Union army with the Third Infantry Regiment, United Colored

Troops, at Philadelphia. After the war, he taught school for a short time in Alachua County, Florida.

In 1872, Walls won re-election by the narrow margin of 371 votes over his white Democratic opponent, Jesse J. Finley. The outcome was contested and referred to the House Committee on Elections, which was controlled by the Democrats. The six Democrats supported the claim that the votes in one precinct of Columbia County had been tampered with by a Republican state senate candidate who later had been murdered under mysterious circumstances. The three Republicans on the committee contended that the disputed ballots that had been burned in the county courthouse by a fire believed to be arson-related had not been cast illegally. The Democrat-controlled House supported the majority report of the committee and Walls was not seated. In the next campaign, Walls lost his bid for re-election in the primary, but the following year he was elected to the Florida State Senate.

It was difficult enough for black politicians to get elected and be seated in the Congress between 1870 and 1899. Once they got there, they were often confronted and denigrated by hostile white members. They were continually subjected to discourteous verbal attacks, and it was routine for white members to disparage and vilify black people in the presence of black representatives. Typical of such barbarous behavior are the remarks of Representative David A. DeArmond of Missouri, who, in one session of Congress, described black citizens as "almost too ignorant to eat, scarcely wise enough to breathe, mere existing human machines."[13]

During debate of the Civil Rights Bill of 1874, Congressman James B. Beck of Kentucky assaulted the reasoning processes of intelligent people and displayed his own profound ignorance and abysmal bigotry, in asserting:

> I suppose there are gentlemen on this floor who would arrest, imprison, and fine a young [white] woman in any state of the South if she were to refuse to marry a Negro man on account of color, race, or previous condition of servitude, in the event of his making her a proposal of marriage, and her refusing on that ground. That would be depriving him of a right he had under the amendment, and Congress would be asked to take it up and say, 'This insolent white woman must be taught to know that it is a misdemeanor to deny a man marriage because of race, color, or previous condition of servitude'; and Congress will be urged to say after a while that sort

of thing must be put to a stop to, and your conventions of colored men will come here asking you to enforce that right.[14]

Representative Robert Brown Elliott, a black Republican from South Carolina, during the same debate took to task a white member from Virginia, Mr. John T. Harris, for stating that remarks he (Harris) had made were addressed to white men alone. Mr. Elliott said:

> I shall have no word of reply. Let him feel that a Negro was not only too magnanimous to smite him in his weakness, but was even charitable enough to grant him the mercy of his silence. (Laughter and applause on the floor and in the galleries.) I shall, sir, leave to others less charitable the unenviable and fatiguing task of sifting out of that mass of chaff the few grains of sense that may, perchance, deserve notice.[15]

Republican Thomes E. Miller, a lawyer from Beaufort, South Carolina, served in that state's senate before being elected to Congress in 1889.

Miller, a respected orator in the House chamber, addressed the House in 1891 in rebuttal to a polemic delivered in the Senate by Senator Alfred H. Colquitt of Georgia. Mr. Colquitt had attacked blacks as "backwards and uncouth" and blamed them for retarding the economic development of the South. Miller called the speech insulting to all decent people, describing it as an "offensive mixture of theology and political economy that contained groundless slanders against black Americans." White southerners, he said, were the real culprits in the South's economic failures because of their policies, which were "motivated by bigotry and vengefulness in denying blacks the full rights of citizenship." After his term in Congress, Miller was named president of the State Colored College at Orangeburg, South Carolina.

Robert Brown Elliott, a lawyer from South Carolina, served two terms in the House of Representatives (1871–1875). He'd graduated with high honors from Eton University in England and was indeed a talented politician. There is some controversy surrounding Elliott's background and early childhood. He claimed to have been born in Boston and to have served in the Union army. It was claimed by others that he was born in Liverpool, England, and had learned the typesetter's trade. Whether he served in the Union army or in the British navy—as some contend—it is agreed that Elliott excelled in various disciplines. He was well versed in several languages, able to read German, Spanish, French, and Latin. His was a respected voice at the 1868 South Carolina State Constitutional Convention, and he emerged as the one person most responsible for defeating a proposition to impose a poll tax and literacy test as requirements for voting in South Carolina.

In Congress, he served on the Education and Labor Committee and the Committee on the Militia. Elliott was a great orator and an uncompromising defender of the civil rights of minority citizens. He gained national acclaim for his championing of black rights during the 1874 congressional debate of an omnibus civil rights bill.

James T. Rapier, who served in the House from 1873 to 1875, studied at Montreal College in Canada, at the University of Glasgow in Scotland, and at Franklin College in Nashville, Tennessee. He was born in Florence, Alabama, the son of a man set free from slavery in 1829.

A successful cotton planter who provided low-interest loans for sharecroppers, Rapier entered politics to organize recently enfranchised blacks into an effective political machine. He won the 1872 election for Congress from the Second Congressional District of Alabama, becoming the state's second black elected to the Congress, where he was appointed to the Education and Labor Committee.

Representative Rapier's most prized legislative feat, though, was the passage of a bill designating the state capital, Montgomery, Alabama, a port of delivery to be managed by a federally appointed collector of customs. He also successfully steered through Congress legislation appropriating funds for maintaining common schools to fight illiteracy and educate blacks in southern districts.

In 1875, Congressman Rapier was defeated by a former Confederate army major, Jeremiah Williams. This election offers a classic example of the tactics used by whites in regaining control of the political machinery in southern states. Ballot boxes were stolen and destroyed, replaced with others containing stuffed or illegally cast ballots. There were numerous incidents of bribery, fradulent counts, and armed intimidation. Many blacks on their way to vote were forced by white marauders, at gunpoint, to return home. Several blacks attempting to cast votes were murdered at polling places.

The following year, Rapier moved his political operation to Lowndes County, near Montgomery. He filed for Congress from the only remaining district in the state predominantly populated by blacks and won the Republican nomination by defeating the incumbent, black Congressman Jeremiah Haralson. Haralson then chose to run as an independent candidate. His presence on the ticket in the general election had the effect of splitting the black vote and enabled a white Democrat, Charles Shelley, to win the election. In this instance, there was no suspicion of collusion between Haralson and white Democrats.

Haralson's opposition to Rapier was more likely prompted by bitterness on his part—an embarrassed politician seeking revenge against what he considered an ungrateful constituency. The nomination of Rapier in his place in the district he had represented in Congress was a hard pill for Haralson to swallow.

The political career of Congressman Benjamin S. Turner of Alabama ended in a similar manner. After serving a first term in the House of Representatives and winning the party nomination for re-election, he saw another black, Phillip Joseph, file as an independent candidate. Joseph siphoned off enough black votes to allow a white Democrat, Frederick G. Bromberg, to win the election. There is no evidence here either that Mr. Joseph was enticed by white Democrats to enter the race, but his decision to run effectively made him a tool of white political interests. Any reasonably intelligent individual should have anticipated the adverse effect another black in the race would have on either's chance for election. If Joseph had truly been concerned for the welfare of the black community, he would not have set out to split the black vote.

Eight of the blacks who served in the House of Representatives during Reconstruction were elected from the state of South Carolina. North Carolina sent four blacks to the House, and Alabama elected three. Five other states—Georgia, Florida, Mississippi, Louisiana, and Virginia—were each served in the House by one black.

Mississippi elected two blacks to the United States Senate. Louisiana was the only other state to send a black to the Senate, but as we have seen, he was denied his seat by that body.

South Carolina was the lone state to have more than one black serving simultaneously in the same Congress. From 1871 to 1873, three black South Carolinians—Joseph H. Rainey, Robert C. DeLarge, and Robert B. Elliott—were in the House. The state of Louisiana would also have had three blacks serving simultaneously, had the House not refused to seat them.

FROM EMANCIPATION TO THE HALLS OF CONGRESS

John Roy Lynch is a fine example of the quality of black persons who served in government in the years immediately following emancipation. Born a slave in Concordia Parish, Louisiana, he was reared in Natchez, Mississippi. After obtaining his freedom, he worked days and went to school at night. He started a business as a photographer that grew into such a prosperous enterprise that he was able to invest substantial sums in real estate.

Mr. Lynch, the only black representative from the state of Mississippi for more than a hundred years, had himself a hectic but interesting political career. First elected in 1873 at age twenty-five, he was very young for a member of Congress. He had been elected to the Mississippi State House of Representatives at the age of twenty-one, and three years later his colleagues there named him Speaker of the House.

As Speaker, Lynch engaged in a little old-fashioned politicking as he drew the boundaries of the six congressional districts for the state. Of the six congressional districts, five were drawn to ensure the safe election of Republicans. Gerrymander accurately describes the boundaries of the five seats.

In the very next election, Lynch entered the Republican primary and defeated the white incumbent. He went on to handily beat the Democratic candidate in the general election. In the House he was appointed to the Committee on Mines and Mining and the Committee on Expenditures in the Interior Department.

Lynch took an active role in the debates on the Civil Rights Act of 1875. Many of the southern states had already enacted laws similar to the one being argued in the Congress. Black southerners such as Lynch had seen these laws enacted to protect the rights of blacks without seeing any material change in whites' attitudes toward blacks. Basically, the federal law would extend legal protection black people were supposed to have won in the South to states in the North. It was in this vein that Lynch delivered the following remarks:

The opposition to civil rights in the South is not so general or intense as a great many would have the country believe. It is a mistaken idea that all the white people in the South outside of the Republican party are bitterly opposed to this bill . . . It is true they would not vote for it, but they reason from this standpoint: The civil rights bill does not confer upon the colored people of Mississippi any rights that they are not entitled to already under the constitution and laws of the state. We certainly have no objection, then, to allowing the colored people in the other states to enjoy the same rights they are entitled to in our own state.[16]

It is hard to know if Representative Lynch really meant some of the things he said or if he mentioned them only to allay unfounded fears of northern Republicans. What followed in his speech suggested that passage of the bill would not cause any appreciable socializing between the races:

> But let the bill be passed and become a law, and you will find that in a few months reasonable men, liberal men, moderate men, sensible men, who now question the propriety of passing this bill, will arrive at the conclusion that it is not such a bad thing as they supposed it was . . . They will find that there is no more social equality than before. That the whites and blacks do not intermarry any more than they did before the passage of this bill. In short, they will find that there is nothing in the bill but the recognition by law of equal rights of citizens before the law.[17]

In 1874, an organization known as the White League embarked on a widespread campaign of violence and intimidation to keep Mississippi blacks from participating in the electoral process and to replace Lynch in Congress. Despite their efforts, he narrowly defeated his Democratic opponent and was sworn in as a duly elected member of Congress.

Lynch was a renowned orator and constitutional scholar and demonstrated keen political skills when debating a bill in the Forty-third Congress to provide funding for public education. Lynch opposed an amendment to finance separate schools for black and white students—in fact, opposed all forms of discrimination that separated groups by either religion or race.

> The colored people in asking the passage of this bill just as it passed the Senate do not thereby admit that their children can be better educated in white than in colored schools, nor that white teachers, because they are white, are better qualified to teach than colored ones. But they recognize the fact [that] the distinction when made and tolerated by law is an unjust and odious proscription; that you make their color a ground of objection, and consequently a crime.[18]

Democrats eventually gained control of the Mississippi state political machinery, and in the next election a Democrat, James R. Chalmers, a former general and cavalry commander in the Confederate army, unseated Lynch.

Lynch ran and lost a second time to Representative Chalmers in 1880. He ran again two years later and lost, but successfully challenged the election results and was seated on April 29, 1882. During this session, he was appointed to the Committee on Education and Labor and the Committee on the Militia. He also introduced legislation to divide Mississippi into two federal judicial districts and to reimburse the Protestant Orphan Asylum in Natchez $10,000 for damage caused by Union forces during the war.

Lynch was defeated for re-election in 1886 by less than 1,000 votes. Returning to Mississippi, he was admitted to the bar. The following year, he opened an office in the District of Columbia, where he practiced until 1898, when he joined the army. During the Spanish-American War, he was appointed a major in the army by President McKinley and served as a paymaster.

In 1911, he resigned his military commission and settled in Chicago to practice law.

Lynch wrote two books dealing with his life as a politician and the times in which he lived. The first was entitled *The Facts of Reconstruction* and documented the years of Reconstruction, with an emphasis on his involvement in the state of Mississippi. The second was his autobiography, *Reminiscences of an Active Life*, which highlighted the struggle he waged with others to preserve the civil rights of freed slaves.

Upon his death, the *New York Times* eulogized Lynch as "one of the most fluent and forceful speakers in the politics of the 1870s and 80s."[19]

THE DRIVE TO EXCLUDE BLACKS FROM CONGRESS

The presidential election of 1876 marked the beginning of events that would greatly weaken black political power and lead to the subsequent inability to elect blacks to Congress.

On election night 1876, virtually every major newspaper in the country announced that Samuel Tilden, the Democratic candidate, had won the presidency. He had clearly won the popular vote and at least 184 electoral votes, just one shy of the requirement for election. But twenty contested electoral votes—nineteen from southern states and one from Oregon—threw the disputed election into Congress for resolution. Citizen committees were established in several southern states to challenge the validity of electors and different sets of returns were submitted by electors of each political party.

There is no provision in the United States Constitution for resolving disputed elections. The only reference to the subject is Article II, Section 1, which states that the president of the Senate "shall open all the certificates, and the votes shall then be counted."

The Congress was equally divided between the two parties. Democrats held a majority in the House; Republicans controlled the Senate. In this atmosphere and under these circumstances, Congress enacted a law establishing a fifteen-member commission to decide the validity of the challenges. The commission was composed of five members of the Senate (three Republicans and two Democrats); five members of the House (three Democrats and two Republicans); and five members of the Supreme Court (two Republicans, two Democrats, and one independent). Theoretically, Democrats and Republicans were evenly balanced on the committee (seven each) and a truly independent person held the balance of power.

Justice David Davis, the independent jurist, had been appointed to the Supreme Court by his old friend from Bloomington, Illinois, President Abraham Lincoln. But in a strange turn of events, Davis resigned from both the Supreme Court and the congressional commission, and the same day the Illinois state legislature elected him to fill a vacancy in the United States Senate.

Davis's replacement on the commission was Supreme Court Justice Joseph P. Bradley. Though he was tagged an independent, Bradley clearly had Republican affiliations and sympathies. He cast the decisive vote that determined who would be the next president of the United States. By a one-vote margin—seven Republicans and the one Republican-inclined independent to seven Democrats—all challenges to Samuel Tilden's electors were upheld. The declared final count was 185 electoral votes for Republican Rutherford B. Hayes to 184 for Democrat Samuel Tilden.

The basis of the sordid compromise that allowed the Republican candidate to win the presidency was an agreement concurred in by Republicans and Democrats alike. In return for Hayes' recognition as president, all federal troops were to be removed from the South. That pernicious promise was honored in April 1877, when the Democrat-controlled House of Representatives and the Republican-controlled

Senate voted to deny appropriations for army troops stationed in the southern states.

This conspiratorial act between the Congress and the president effectively repealed the Reconstruction Act and gave unfettered license to any hate group wishing to intimidate black voters. A reign of terror was inflicted upon blacks throughout the South by secret organizations such as the Ku Klux Klan, the Jayhawkers, and the Black Horse Cavalry. Many other hate groups also sprang up. These groups created a "de facto" criminal justice system throughout the South. They became judge, jury, and executioner in the dispensation of punishment to blacks seeking to exercise their legal rights.

E. Dorian Gadsden, a graduate of the Howard University School of Law and later a federal administrative law judge, summed up the situation in his book *Progress Against the Tide*:

Between 1867 and 1877, other such terrorist organizations as the Knights of the White Camellia, the Pale Faces, the White Brotherhood, the 76 Association, and the Knights of the Ku Klux Klan all fought to acquire absolute control over freed blacks, to drive them and their white allies from power, to end radical reconstruction, and establish what became known as "white supremacy." Armed with weapons (guns and swords), their members disguised themselves and their actions and patrolled parts of the South, eluding the Union troops. They utilized force, intimidation, bribery at the polls, ostracism of businesses, arson, and even murder to achieve their mission. The community condoned and supported their activities.[20]

Terrorism was widespread throughout the South. *The Charleston News* of November 7, 1870, referring to the outcome of one election, ranted,

We understand, therefore, and accept the solid black vote cast against the nominees of the Reform party as a declaration of war by the Negro race against the white race, by ignorance against intelligence, by poverty against actual or potential wealth. This issue we have striven to avoid, but the Negroes will have nothing else. They will not allow us to work with them. We must, if necessary, work against them. Conciliation, argument, persuasion, all have been worse than useless. The white people stand alone. And they must organize themselves, and arm themselves, not as "a white man's party," but because the past and present prove that decency, purity, and political freedom, as well as the preservation of society, are identical with the interests of the white people of the state.[21]

This venomous sort of journalism was generally indulged in by a majority of southern newspapers. In comparison to other public statements, however, the *Charleston News* diatribe was mild. The same paper on January 31, 1871, reported an official order of the Ku Klux Klan posted in the office of the York County, South Carolina, auditor:

Headquarters K.K.K., January 22, 1871.

Resolved, That in all cases of incendiarism ten of the leading colored people and two white sympathizers shall be executed in that vicinity. That if any armed bands of colored people are found hereafter picketing the roads, the officers of the company to which the pickets belong shall be executed. That all persons reported as using incendiary language shall be tried by the high court of this order and be punished at their discretion. The different officers are charged with the execution of these resolutions.

By order of K.K.K.

In conducting its reign of terror, the posting of orders from the Klan became common practice and there was uncommon adherence to the edicts. The *Spartanburg Republican* newspaper of South Carolina reported on March 22, 1871:

The Ku Klux last week posted a notice on the bulletin-board at the courthouse in Union to the effect that the county commissioners, the school commissioner, and the members of the legislature must resign their positions by the 27th instant.

We understand that the sheriff, the school commissioner, and the clerk of the county commissioners have, in obedience to this order, tendered their resignations, and it is thought that other officers will follow their example.

The following is a copy of the document found posted in Union:

Ignorance is the curse of God. For this reason we are determined that members of the legislature, the school commissioner, and the county commissioners of Union shall no longer officiate. Fifteen days' notice from this date is therefore given, and if they, one and all, do not at once and forever resign their present inhuman, disgraceful, and outrageous rule, then retributive justice will as surely be used as night follows day.

Also, "An honest man is the noblest work of God." For this reason, if the clerk of the said board of county commissioners and school commissioners does not immediately renounce and relinquish his present position, then harsher measures than this will most assuredly and certainly be used. For confirmation, reference to the orders heretofore published in the *Union Weekly Times* and *Yorkville Enquirer* will more fully and completely show our intention.

By order Grand Chief: A.O., Grand Secretary.[24]

The Columbia, South Carolina, *Daily Union* newspaper expressed its irritation with the reporting of the numerous threats made by the Klan. In a story dated March 10, 1871, the paper cited this testimony of an army officer:

A dispatch-bearer, Major Whitehead, United States Army, from the post of United States troops at Yorkville, brought yesterday the following important intelligence from that locality. The dispatches explain themselves, and we submit them with the voucher of bare and naked truth, having tired long ago of the monotony of chronicling these daily outrages. The Governor has telegraphed to Washington the facts, and also to General Terry, commanding the department, stating that fighting is going on in that county:

HEADQUARTERS CAMP SHERIDAN
Yorkville, South Carolina, March 8, 1870

GOVERNOR: I respectfully state that, on Monday morning last, the company of militia known as the "Carmel Hill Company" was attacked by a portion of the organization styled "Ku Klux Klan," and after a running fight, lasting nearly three days, arrived in close proximity to this place. . .[25]

The Ku Klux Klan and other similar groups had succeeded beyond their wildest expectations. Their campaigns of terror, harassment, intimidation, and brutality against blacks became the standard procedure for disfranchising black voters. In addition to threats of bodily harm, a campaign was launched to frustrate blacks attempting to cast votes. Unpublicized polling places in black precincts were stationed in the backwoods, swamps, and other places equally inaccessible. When blacks learned of the locations and appeared ready to vote nevertheless, they were told that the polls had closed. Those who protested were beaten, jailed, and in some cases never seen again.

More scandalous than this unprovoked violence was the fact that these hate groups were permitted to operate with impunity by both state and federal agents of governments. Their efforts were so successful that by 1912 enactment of laws imposing stringent and discriminatory conditions for blacks to qualify as voters had totally disfranchised blacks nationwide. The poll tax was adopted in most southern states to keep blacks and poor whites off the rolls. But in many areas, white employers paid the taxes for their poor white workers and later cast votes in their behalf.

Then there was the imposition of the infamous literacy tests. In some communities where prominent black educators and other professionals resided, not one black ever passed the test. Blacks with Ph.D's seeking to register were asked such obnoxious questions as "How many bubbles in a bar of soap?" by white registrars who had not finished elementary school. Illiterate white election judges asked black professionals to recite verbatim the Bill of Rights or the Declaration of Independence. Another favorite gimmick was a cute innocent-sounding ploy called a "grandfather clause." Under its provisions, any black who could not prove that he was registered to vote before 1867 was automatically disqualified.

Then we witnessed the ingenuity of white America in a scheme established to disfranchise black voters and yet give the impression of allowing them to participate in the electoral process. Blacks in some areas were permitted to register but could only vote in the general election. At that phase of the electoral process in a one-party state, voting is a meaningless gesture. And that is precisely what happened in the South, where Democrats controlled the legislatures. "All-white" Democratic primaries were established by state law. The legislation provided that all voters in a primary must be a member of the political party fielding candidates for public office, and then allowed political parties to deny membership based on the race of the applicant.

This inimically perverted law allowing political parties to function as private social clubs remained on the statute books in most southern states for more than thirty-five years. Finally, a suit was filed in 1927 challenging the constitutionality of the Texas law, and the federal courts, after many years of litigation, struck it down as an unconstitutional denial of citizenship rights. In ruling on the case, Supreme Court Justice Louis D. Brandeis said:

> States may do a good deal of classifying that it is difficult to believe rational, but there are limits, and it is too clear for extended argument that color cannot be made the basis of a statutory classification affecting the right set-up in this case. . . . The duty of the law maker is to know no race, no color, no religion, no nationality, except to prevent distinctions on these grounds, so far as the law is concerned.[26]

During that thirty-five-year period, black voters were reduced to noncitizens by the denial of their right to participate fully and freely in the political process. They were almost totally purged from voter lists in the eleven southern states of Alabama, Arkansas, Florida, Kentucky, Louisiana, Mississippi, North Carolina, South Carolina, Tennessee, Texas, and Virginia.

The diminution of black political power eventually resulted in the virtual disfranchisement of 90 percent of the black populace. This process started in earnest after the election of Rutherford B. Hayes to the presidency. Within twenty years, eight states had imposed the devastating literacy tests as requirements for blacks to register and vote. In the South, this was accomplished by changing state constitutions to effectively evade the constraints of the Fifteenth Amendment. First it was Mississippi in 1890, then South Carolina in 1895, and Louisiana in 1898—each changing its constitution to exclude from voting those who did not pay the poll tax; those who had been convicted of burglary, theft, bribery, arson, murder, perjury, or bigamy; and "persons who could not read, understand, or give a reasonable interpretation of any section of the state constitution."[27]

Mississippi's restrictions reduced the number of qualified black voters from over 135,000 to almost nil. Louisiana went one step further in imposing a "grandfather clause" stipulating that in order to register, both the person's father and grandfather had to be qualified to vote on January 1, 1867. The number of black voters almost instantly decreased from 100,000 to less than 5,000.

When Rutherford B. Hayes was elected to office, eight blacks were members of the U.S. Congress. From the fateful day that Mr. Hayes took office in 1876 until 1928, fifty-two years later, only six blacks were elected to Congress.

THE LAST BLACKS TO SERVE IN CONGRESS IN THE NINETEENTH CENTURY

Henry Plummer Cheatham was the next to last black member to serve in the U.S. Congress in the nineteenth century. Before being elected to Congress, he had received a bachelor of arts degree from Shaw University in Raleigh, North Carolina. He was an experienced educator and researcher. Much of his time was spent writing about the contributions and achievements of black citizens.

After winning his first election to Congress in 1888 by 653 votes out of a total of 32,000 cast, Mr. Cheatham was assigned to the Education Committee and the Committee on Expenditures. Like so many other black legislators during this period, he introduced numerous bills and resolutions, only to see them die in committee or defeated on the floor. He supported efforts to reimburse those who lost their money in the Freedmen's Savings and Loan scandal and backed funding for public schools.

In 1890, he was re-elected. Two other blacks in the House seeking re-election that year, John M. Langston and Thomas E. Miller, were both defeated. That left Cheatham as the only black serving in the Fifty-second Congress.

He was defeated by a white Democrat in the 1892 general election. Two years later, he attempted a comeback. He edged out George H. White, his brother-in-law, in the Republican primary. Cheatham, however, was defeated in the general election by Democrat Frederick A. Woodard, the white incumbent. In 1896, Cheatham and White again went head-to-head in the Republican primary. This time White won the nomination and also defeated the incumbent.

George H. White, of North Carolina, who took his seat in 1897, was the last black to serve in Congress in the nineteenth century. He said in his final address to Congress on January 29, 1901:

This, Mr. Chairman, is perhaps the Negroes' temporary farewell to the American Congress. But let me say, phoenix-like, he will rise up someday and come again. These parting words are in behalf of an outraged, heartbroken, bruised and bleeding people, but God fearing people, faithful, industrious, loyal people . . . rising people, full of potential.[28]

NOTES

1. James H. Huston, *To Make All Laws, The Congress of the United States, 1789–1989,* Library of Congress: Washington, D.C., 1989, page 41.
2. *Congressional Globe,* February 23, 1870, 41st Congress, second session, page 1508.
3. Maurice Christopher, *Black Americans in Congress,* New York: Thomas Y. Crowell, 1976, page 3.
4. *Ibid.,* pages 3–4.
5. *Congressional Globe,* February 23, 1870, 41st Congress, second session, page 1542.
6. *Afro-American History: Reconstruction,* 1865–77, page 10.
7. *Journal of Louisiana Constitutional Convention 1868,* page 259, cited by

Warmoth T. Gibbs, "Hiram Revels and His Times," *Quarterly Review of Higher Education Among Negroes*, 1940.

8. *The Congressional Globe*, April 1, 1871, page 392.

9. F. L. Cardozo, March 4, 1868, South Carolina Convention, reported by J. Woodruff, printed by Denny and Perry, page 705.

10. Carter G. Woodson, *Negro Orators and Their Orations*, Washington, D.C.: The Associated Press, Inc., 1925, page 268.

11. *Congressional Globe*, 42nd Congress, second session, February 3, 1872, Appendix, page 16.

12. Bruce A. Ragsdale and Joel D. Treese, *Black Americans in Congress, 1870–1968*, U.S. Government Printing Office: Washington, D.C., 1990, page 82.

13. *Congressional Record*, April 25, 1898, 55th Congress, second session, Appendix, page 362.

14. *Congressional Record*, January 6, 1874, page 409.

15. *Congressional Record*, January 6, 1874, page 410.

16. *Congressional Record*, February 3, 1875, 43rd Congress, second session, pages 946–947.

17. *Ibid.*, page 947.

18. *Congressional Record*, February 3, 1875, 43rd Congress, second session, page 945.

19. *New York Times*, November 3, 1939, obituary, page 21.

20. E. Dorian Gadsden, *Progress Against the Tide*, New York: Vantage Press, 1989, page 47.

21. *Charleston News*, November 7, 1870.

22. *Ibid.*

23. *The Spartanburg Republican*, March 22, 1871.

24. *Ibid.*

25. Columbia, South Carolina, *Daily Union*, March 10, 1870.

26. Justice Louis D. Brandeis, *Nixon* v. *Herndon*, 273 U.S. 536, 1927.

27. Mississippi state constitution, Article 12, Section 244, adopted 1890.

28. *Congressional Record*, 46th Congress, second session, January 29, 1901, page 1638.

3

The Barren Years: Taxation Without Representation

The living conditions "enjoyed" by free black people before the Civil War did not improve to any great measure after the war. For most, it was equally harsh and dismal during both periods. The situation for those who were not slaves was almost as intolerable as it was for slaves. Free black men, both those never held in bondage and those who had won their freedom, generally lived a miserable existence.

The Republic of Liberia in Africa was established by blacks who mostly had been free men in the United States. The 1849 Declaration of Independence written by them for Liberia neatly describes the circumstances faced by black Americans during this period of time.

> In some parts of that country [the United States of America], we were debarred by law from all rights and privileges of men—in other parts, public sentiment, more powerful than law, frowned us down.
>
> We were everywhere shut out from all civil office. We were excluded from all participation in the government. We were taxed without our consent. We were compelled to contribute to the resources of a country which gave us no protection.[1]

Following the defeat of Representative George White by a white candidate in the 1900 election, black people were without a single spokesman in the United States Congress. For the next twenty-seven years, millions of black citizens watched helplessly, as their legal and constitutional rights were systematically erased, while no voice at any level of government was effectively raised on their behalf.

Indeed, that dreadful reality of unrepresentative government imposed on the American colonists by the British—which James Otis had spoken out against so eloquently—was now ruthlessly revisited upon the land. This time, it was 10 million black citizens who were being taxed without a scintilla of representation.

Shortly after the 1896 Supreme Court decision in *Plessy* v. *Ferguson* sanctioned "separate but equal" facilities for the races, a widespread campaign was launched to deny blacks any appreciable amount of government services. Public education for black students was separate but certainly not equal. In most southern states, efforts were waged with considerable community support to spend only the amount of tax dollars on black public schools that was collected from black property owners.

But this vengeful, racist act soon lost all its support when the recorder of deeds in county after county found out that blacks were paying *more* taxes than they were receiving in return. For example, in Mississippi, which was fairly typical of the southern states, blacks were paying 30 percent more than the actual state tax funding for black services. In other words, taxes of black people were being used to subsidize the public education of white children.

The revelation is not surprising in view of the fact that black people in America, mostly in the South, numbered almost 10 million and owned 25 million acres of land.

Our race has encountered every obstacle and every barrier possible. Indignities upon indignities, similar to those imposed on early immigrants also seeking their niche in society, have been heaped upon us. The difference, of course, is that most European immigrants within a reasonable length of time eventually achieved their political and economic aspirations. To this day, blacks are still awaiting the coming of the political Messiah.

During the 1920s, our grandparents were fighting for positions as precinct co-captains and block chairmen in ward organizations supposedly representing all-black neighborhoods, hoping to be rewarded with menial jobs at city hall. But white hostility toward blacks was so intense throughout the nation that it was impossible to make social, economic, or political gains through active participation in politics. A case in point: Attorney E. E. Brown was appointed assistant health commissioner for the city of Boston in 1907. Mayor Fitzgerald, a Democrat, took a courageous step in making the appointment, which played a role in a Republican's winning the mayoralty in the next election. According to one newspaper report, Brown's appointment was the "best position any colored man ever had in Boston." The newspaper went on to say, "The appointment of a colored man to such a high-salaried position [$2,500 a year] displeased all color-prejudiced white politicians." Incoming Mayor Hubbard, a Republican, removed Brown from the job by abolishing the position, saying it was not needed.[2]

European ethnic groups meanwhile had already achieved an awesome amount of political influence. They had been selected for the highest party positions and hired to top-level patronage jobs. They had elected their own as councilmen, mayors, and governors. They were insiders in both political parties, making decisions regarding candidate slates in all areas of the country where they outnumbered native-born white Americans.

During the 1910s European immigrants became generally accepted by established political forces in both parties. Some had become so influential that they were organizing their own political machines. In contrast, native-born blacks were still grappling to win meager concessions from recalcitrant white leaders. Political bosses in northern urban centers and plantation bosses in sleepy southern rural towns had no intention of allowing black people the right to freely participate or to wield meaningful political power in the affairs of local, state, or national government. The federal government had no intention of protecting the rights of black people who sought to participate freely in the electoral process. Resistance by white leaders and by the press to granting blacks the right to vote and the right to hold public office was total, universal, unequivocal—in many instances, criminal.

At the 1928 Republican National Convention, held in Houston, Texas, the same year that the Republican party was electing Oscar DePriest, the first black congressman in the twentieth century, only 100 black spectators were admitted to the convention site, and they were segregated in the rear of the balcony—cordoned off by chicken wire.

To illustrate the depth of hatred harnessed against black people, it is only necessary to cite an anecdote of sordid proportion that took place in Florida during this period.

Shortly after Herbert Hoover assumed the presidency in 1929, the Florida state legislature, after considerable and inflammatory debate, passed a resolution condemning the president for inviting the wife of the only black member of Congress to the White House for a social event. The mere presence of one black woman, the wife of a congressman, caused the pot of racial intolerance in the Florida legislative body to boil over. Unfortunately, these elected officials accurately represented the sentiments of most whites.

The full text of Resolution No. 15, which was introduced by Mr. Way, a Democrat from Pinellas County, follows:

WHEREAS, it has become common knowledge that at a social function held in the city of Washington at the White House, the official residence of the president of the United States, presided over by the wife of the president, a Negro woman by the name of DePriest was entertained and received on terms of equality with the white ladies present;

AND WHEREAS, we believe that social intercourse between the white and black races is contrary to decency and subversive of the best interests of all parties concerned;

AND WHEREAS, there has always existed in the southern states, and always shall exist, a line of demarkation between the social status of the white and Negro races;

AND WHEREAS, during the presidential campaign in the year 1928 the charge was made that Herbert Hoover, then a candidate for president of the United States, and now president, had by order as secretary of commerce directed that no distinction, so far as segregation was concerned, should be made between the white and Negro employees of said department, which charge was denied by the allies and supporters of the said Herbert Hoover;

AND WHEREAS, the electorate of the state of Florida, believing that the said Herbert Hoover would discourage social equality and deny to the Negro that which has always been denied, did give to the said Herbert Hoover a majority of the votes cast in the national election held on the 6th day of November 1928, and the electoral vote of said state of Florida;

NOW THEREFORE, be it resolved by the House of Representatives of the state of Florida that the act of Mrs. Hoover in thus entertaining a Negro woman on a parity with white ladies was both shameful and disgraceful and if persisted in will destroy the prestige of the Anglo-Saxon race and set at naught the social fabric of the country that has for ages guarded and kept sacred the purity of our Anglo-Saxon blood which stands for the highest type of Americanism.[3]

The vote approving of a resolution that ended with a further resolve that "it [the resolution] may stand for all time as a protest against any effort to accord to the Negro race social equality with the white race,"[4] passed the body by a vote of 71 yeas to 14 nays.

Claude Pepper, later elected to the U.S. Senate and U.S. House of Representatives, was one of the fourteen who voted against the resolution. He stated in the record immediately following the vote, "I am a southerner and a Democrat like my ancestors before me and have always voted for the Democratic nominees, but I consider such a resolution as this out of place as an act of this body."[5]

Another who voted against the resolution, Representative J. M. Lee of Highlands County, gave a reason very unlike that of Mr. Pepper. He said immediately following the vote and for the record,

> If white supremacy has been imperiled by this act, it was by reason of the sacrifice made by the white ladies who accepted entertainment at the hands of their host on a social parity with a Negro woman and they should be the recipients of the condemnation of a white Democratic deliberative body and not the first lady of the land. I believe in applying the chastising lash to the sinful child without respect of person or position.[6]

Democrats who controlled the Florida state legislature were angry because they had looked for vindication of their rebellion against the national party leadership. During the presidential election campaign, they had established across the state Democratic committees for Republican candidate Herbert Hoover—to openly demonstrate another of their chief biases, protesting their party's nomination of Roman Catholic Al Smith.

Needling his colleagues, Representative S. P. Robineau stated,

> I voted NO to the House resolution [because] . . . the whole nation, and the Republican party knows through the grim experiences of bloodiest combat, and therefore does not need to learn by formal reiteration through House resolution the deep-seated convictions of southern Democrats concerning the social segregation of the white and Negro races.
>
> These racial convictions do or do not constitute paramount principles in the sociological and political policies of the Democratic party of the South. And no Democrat, who truly considered these convictions as paramount principles of his political faith, could have left the ranks of his party during the recent campaign.
>
> It is therefore only those Democrats who were persuaded or self-deluded into the notion that the Republican party would protect them against such shocks to their sincerest and keenest sensibilities, that have any right or cause to protest against the recent social feature in the White House. The regular Southern Democrats did not expect anything else and said so throughout the campaign.
>
> Therefore, I see no occasion for a Democratic assembly doing anything to

make the lot of the unsteadfast Florida Democrats any more comfortable than it is. I find peculiar relish in watching the Hoover Democrats of Florida stewing in the juices of their recent political errors. I cannot resist the impulse to say to them: "I told you so!"[7]

Florida was not alone in its condemnation of the president for inviting a black to the White House. The state senate of Texas had previously passed a similar resolution just as racist. They condemned Mr. Hoover for promoting "social equality" and resolved that "the only way that this beloved South land of ours can expect to maintain its dignity and Anglo-Saxon supremacy is to stand as a whole for the eternal principles of democracy and Anglo-Saxon superiority."[8]

While the nation was festering in hostile reaction to Mrs. DePriest's appearance at the White House, two of her husband's fellow House members refused to occupy office space next door to his.

A CONTINUING PATTERN OF PREJUDICE

European immigrants—foreign-born whites and their progeny—had much different experiences. In the preceding year, 1928, first generation children of European immigrants had risen so fast and so high in the world of politics that one of them was carrying the banner of the national Democratic party as its candidate for president of the United States. Alfred Emanuel Smith, four-term governor of New York, a reformer in the progressive mode, and the first Roman Catholic nominated by a major political party for the highest office in the land, exemplified this group's rapid rise to political power.

Smith's father was an immigrant of German and Italian descent. His immigrant mother was the daughter of Irish parents. Al Smith's family lineage was typical of many early immigrants. Extensive intermarriage among immigrants of different ethnic and cultural backgrounds served to contradict the rantings of those who promoted the virulent virtues of "racial purity." Racial or ethnic intermingling and intermarrying were common practice. Blacks and whites, however, were prohibited by law to mingle and intermarry in most states or, where no formal legal restraints existed, precluded from doing so by social customs. There was little chance for blacks to slide unobtrusively into that big, imaginary American "melting pot," because of these laws and customs.

It is often asked why, if penniless immigrants, uneducated and unable to speak the language, made it in our society despite the odds, blacks are still floundering at the bottom of the social, economic, and political ladder.

The answer is complex, yet simple and, most assuredly, not blowing in the wind. There are many theories but only one reason.

The failure of our people to advance and progress at a pace commensurate with our contributions is best explained by citing society's hostility toward us. August Wilson, author of the critically acclaimed Broadway stage plays *Fences*, *Joe Turner's Come and Gone*, and *Ma Rainey's Black Bottom*, delves into the heart and soul of the problem. He explains the most obvious reason for immigrant successes and black failures, when he writes:

> Near the turn of the century, the destitute of Europe sprang on the city with tenacious claws and an honest and solid dream. The city devoured them. They swelled its belly until it burst into a thousand furnaces and sewing machines, a thousand butcher shops and bakers' ovens, a thousand churches and hospitals and funeral parlors and money-lenders . . . the descendants of African slaves were offered no such welcome or participation.[9]

Wilson touches on the elementary difference between white and black politics and the reasons European immigrants have outdistanced us in personal and group accomplishment. The dissimilarity is found in that attitude of nonwelcome and nonparticipation afforded dark-skinned people.

Economically disadvantaged white Europeans gained political influence and economic power in tandem. Democrats and Republicans vied for their support, bartered for their votes, and traded political favors for their attention. They were hired by municipal and state governments as policemen, firemen, city inspectors, and municipal clerks. The private sector employed them as trolley car drivers, railroad conductors, bank tellers, bakers, milk and beer deliverymen, elevator operators, and retail salesmen. Banks extended loans to them for first-time business ventures; educational communities integrated them at all levels of employment in both public and private school systems. None of these opportunities was available anywhere in the United States of America to black people, who also "sprang on the city with tenacious claws and an honest and solid dream."

We were shamefully rebuffed in our efforts to reap economic stability through political involvement, and unjustly rejected in attempts to enhance our political status through loyal support of party organizations. Almost every accomplishment and every advance has been the result of hard-fought battles. The turf we possess is the turf we took. We invited candidates from both parties into our homes, entertained them lavishly, uncorked the finest champagne, and still they spit in our faces.

August Wilson's assessment of the advantages accorded new arrivals to our shores is neither original nor singularly held. American blacks who resettled in Liberia prior to the Civil War were agitated by the same difference in treatment and wrote a similar appraisal:

> We were made a separate and distinct class, and against us every avenue to improvement was effectively closed. Strangers from all lands, of a color different from ours, were preferred before us.[10]

Assimilation of the immigrant population into what was commonly called "the great American melting pot" was a great American fantasy. This slick public relations euphemism was conceived to cover up a devious plot designed to exploit human labor. It was a myth propagated by enterprising industrialists to lead a work force blindly into labor-intensive sweatshops to increase productivity and maximize profits. There never was any demonstrative attempt to "melt" into society the newcomers' languages, religions, customs, or cultures. Those who succeeded learned a new language, changed their names, abandoned the religious practices of many generations, and altered centuries-old customs and cultures while "melting down" into the pot. In the final analysis, it was an exercise in group capitulation by the new arrivals to Ellis Island. They were expected to, and did, conform to the prevailing mores of a Calvinist Protestant majority.

Dr. Robert L. Green, former president of the University of the District of Columbia, in analyzing the situation, stated perceptively:

> . . . American society actually required conformity to a narrow range of characteristics evolved from the original English colonists. The "Anglos" had established themselves in America solidly prior to independence, and they established the rules regulating the participation of subsequent immigrants. Newcomers willing and able to conform to the life-style deemed appropriate by "old stock" Americans were allowed to compete fully in American life. Groups too unlike the elite—too distant in race, language, and culture, for example—were consigned to inferior positions in the social order. The elite established laws, including first slavery and later segregation, that mandated routines of interaction based upon differential status.[11]

Blacks striving to emulate European immigrants in their upward mobility were hard pressed in the endeavor. Not only were they impaired by poverty and crippled by the impediment of skin color, but they were also disadvantaged by the teachings of an amoral religious power. White theologians cast black people as only one generation removed from monkeys and apes.

Undoubtedly, the greatest tragedy of slavery in the United States consisted of brainwashing millions of the black victims. Psychologically conditioning them to accept as infallible truth the brutalizing concept of self-worthlessness was a vile stroke of genius for those who devised the legal and moral basis for imposing a system of involuntary servitude on their fellow humans.

From infancy the average black person has been handicapped—constantly informed of his nonhuman qualities, consistently regarded as incompatible with other humans, and conspicuously designated as an outcast among genteel people. This forced indoctrination has produced a sense of freakishness, causing blacks to believe themselves hybrids of nature rather than purposefully designed creatures of God.

A strong sense of group identification and an awareness of black contributions to the culture go a long way toward arming us in the face of campaigns waged against us by the protagonists of white supremacy. The building of national pride requires all of a nation's citizens to be aware of their distinctive achievements as a group as well as of any achievements of the dominant class. That is why the plea of the Reverend Jesse Jackson for blacks to recite "I am somebody" is so very important in the process of restoring confidence and self-worth. It also is why celebration of Black History Month is so critical to the establishment of a meaningful value system for black folk. And it explains why many of us do not cherish the Stars and Stripes with the same patriotic fervor as others. The campaign to demean, ignore, or ridicule our accomplishments has too often succeeded, invariably led by people who have wrapped themselves in the flag.

The need to reinforce group identity and a positive self-image among blacks became increasingly significant when, at the end of the First World War, many black soldiers opted to remain in the large cities instead of returning to rural areas in the South. This decision, plus extensive southern migration northward, produced large blocs of blacks in many cities.

THE POVERTY OF BLACK POLITICAL REPRESENTATION

From the turn of the century until the election of Oscar DePriest to Congress in 1928, being black in America meant "taxation without representation." At the time of DePriest's election, only a handful of blacks held elected office in any American legislative body.

Black representation, at all levels of government, was sparse. The state of New York elected its first black, E. A. Johnson, to the state assembly in 1916. California elected its first black, Fred Roberts, to the state assembly in 1918, and Missouri followed suit in 1920 by electing Walthal Moore to the state legislature. The great Commonwealth of Massachusetts did not elect its first black in the twentieth century to the state legislature until Lawrence Banks of Boston won office in 1946. His solitary holding of office must be contrasted with the twenty blacks from the Beacon Hill section of Boston who held public office during the period of Reconstruction. Ten years after Banks went to the Massachusetts legislature, Illinois sent its first black, Cecil Partee, to the state capital in Springfield.

At the time of DePriest's election in 1928, major industrial cities with large concentrations of black residents like Memphis, Atlanta, Pittsburgh, Baltimore, Little Rock, Charleston, Charlotte, Richmond, New Orleans, Cleveland, Cincinnati, Louisville, Washington, D.C., Philadelphia, Boston, Buffalo, Savannah, Birmingham, and Detroit had no elected black officials. It is sad but true that the prospects of electing blacks at that time to any office in any of these cities was very remote. The cities of New York and St. Louis elected their first blacks to the city councils in 1941 and 1943, respectively. Los Angeles did not elect its first black city councilman until 1963.

After Oscar Stanton DePriest became the first black man of the twentieth century to be elected to the United States House of Representatives, it would be another seventeen years before as many as two blacks served simultaneously in the Congress. This legislative color barrier was hurdled in 1945 when Adam Clayton Powell, Jr., was elected from a district in New York's upper Manhattan Borough. Powell's presence theoretically provided the occasion for someone at least to second a motion in committee or to speak on behalf of an amendment offered on the floor by the only other black member at that time, William Dawson of Chicago. (It was 1966 before a black, Edward Brooke of Massachusetts, would sit in the United States Senate.)

A TALE OF THREE CITIES

Fortunately, there was some progress in the exercise of black political power, albeit slow, painstaking progress. The first breakthroughs were seen in the cities of St. Louis, Cincinnati, and Chicago.

St. Louis was more politically advanced where blacks were concerned, compared to other cities in the South, yet much in its politics was typical, in that a general disrespect for blacks dominated political attitudes. The concerns and plight of blacks in St. Louis were the same as those of people of color in every major city. Lacking political and economic power, they were relegated to the lowest status of citizenship, required to take the most menial of jobs, and denied equal protection of the law.

But there was a germ of black restlessness in St. Louis that crystallized in a meeting at the Pythian Hall on December 17, 1919. There, a group of disheartened young black men including Crittenden Clark, George L. Vaughn, J. E. Mitchell, Aaron W. Lloyd, Captain Walter Lowe, and Charles Udell Turpin formed the Citizens' Liberty League. Each man in his own sphere was a source of considerable influence. Each in his own right commanded respect as a leader and spokesperson for his people.

Mitchell, publisher of the *St. Louis Argus* newspaper; Lloyd, the Grand Chancellor of the Knights of Pythias; Turpin, owner of the Booker T. Washington Theater; Vaughn and Clark, prominent attorneys; and the others were individuals of unquestionable ability with undisputed credentials. They constituted a legitimate core of leadership in the community. Their followers numbered about 85 percent of the 40,000 registered Negro voters in the city.

These men decided the time had come to reap some benefit from political involvement. Blacks in St. Louis held no public offices, sparingly received the most menial type of political patronage and, of course, made no major decisions affecting their own community. At that meeting at Pythian Hall, a list of thirteen proposals was approved and published. Today that would not be earth-shaking news, but in the climate of the early 1900s, it was revolutionary. The mere putting in writing and public announcement of specific conditions for continued support of the party was viewed as an act of high political treason by white Republicans.

In serving notice on the Republican party, whose winning of 80 percent of the black vote enabled the party totally to dominate city politics, the Pythian rebels defied a cardinal principle of white politics:

Blacks should not get uppity. However, these black leaders insisted on their conditions being met or their community would discontinue its overwhelming support of Republican candidates.

The following demands were made:

1. A Negro to be elected from the state of Missouri to serve as a congressman in Washington, D.C.
2. A Negro to be elected as a judge (justice of the peace, similar to the presiding officer in small claims court).
3. A Negro to be elected as constable (the executive officer assisting a justice of the peace).
4. A Negro to be elected as the committeeman of a ward.
5. A Negro woman to be elected as committeewoman, if women obtained the right to vote and hold office in time for the next election, or as soon as possible after women received the right.
6. A Negro to be appointed superintendent of garbage collection.
7. Negroes to serve on the grand juries, which consisted of twenty-four persons (generally made up of intellectuals, persons in business, or other professionals).
8. Negroes to be selected to serve on the petit juries.
9. A Negro city undertaker (to bury paupers).
10. Negro uniformed policemen. (There were several Negro detectives in plain clothes.)
11. A Negro on the board of education.
12. A Negro fire department (really a fire station).
13. A city hospital staffed entirely by Negro doctors, nurses, and orderlies.

From that day forth, relations between the white establishment of St. Louis and the black community were dramatically redefined and permanently altered. Unnoticed by both groups was a realignment of power. Passive indifference on the part of a once condescending group gave way overnight to an aggressive political activism in a coalition held together by racial considerations. This activism was destined to continue—to grow and to flourish for the next several generations. It was destined to alter the way white officials dealt with the minority community.

The Pythian declaration emphatically denounced the system of begging for political crumbs and discarded the idea that those who provided the most in terms of political muscle had to suffer the most in terms of personal humiliation and disgrace. This determined group no longer was seeking political philanthropy from benevolent white leaders, but insisting on measures of equity.

Prior to this time, whites made all decisions affecting the lives and lifestyles of Negro people in St. Louis. Those decisions were rarely questioned, and almost never opposed by a group believing itself powerless to protest. As meager as the demands of the Citizens' Liberty League appear today, their bold act set in motion a confrontation of radical import. No longer would Negroes be content to let outsiders decide for them what was good or bad, what was or was not in their best interests.

The bottom line had been reached and the Republican party in St. Louis was confronted with a fish-or-cut-bait predicament. The pleasant platitudes and paternalistic phrases usually employed to soothe the restless "beast" in ghetto supporters no longer sufficed. Republicans of color were outraged by the absence of "meat and bread" rewards for their noble efforts. Coal in the bin, vittles on the table, and jobs for the faithful dictated the issues on their agenda. A spirited defiance permeated the newly organized group and carried over into the general populace.

The Pythian document outlined a litany of priorities that for the next forty years consumed much of the community's attention. The group's action detonated a chain of events aimed at achieving those goals. Miraculously, some of the objectives were attained within a matter of months. Others were not accomplished until the early 1950s and late 1960s. Less than twelve months after issuance of the manifesto, Charles Udell Turpin, a Republican and member of the original organizing group, was elected the first Negro constable. His election, however, was not without vehement opposition from powerful quarters within the ruling Republican party.

The morning after the election the daily press, in banner headlines, announced that Turpin had been defeated by an overwhelming margin. History blurs at this point in its record of what happened next. What is certain is that for six months the count was contested in the courts. Some contend that blacks seized ballot boxes at gunpoint. The other story is more plausible: Twelve police officers were assigned to protect the ballots around the clock. Six months later, the court finally declared Turpin the winner by a margin of two to one. "And so a black man," stated St. Louis historian Nathan B. Young, "who was born in Georgia, lived in Mississippi, was a gold prospector and one-time jewelry salesman in Mexico became the first black man to be elected to public office in the city of St. Louis and the state of Missouri."[12]

The next year, 1920, another Republican, Walthal M. Moore, became the first Negro elected to the Missouri House of Representatives. He represented the Third District until his defeat in 1922. In 1925, he returned to the state house from the Sixth District for three more terms (1925–1930).

Richard Kent, a taxicab owner, was elected the first Negro committeeman of the Sixth Ward in 1920. Within three years after the Pythian meeting, Negroes had been trained to serve as uniformed police, to operate two fire stations, to bury the bodies of unclaimed Negro paupers for the city, to serve on both petit juries and grand juries, and to supervise garbage and trash collection. After passage of the Nineteenth Amendment to the U.S. Constitution ratifying suffrage for women in 1920, a Negro woman, Rosa Madison, was elected committeewoman for the Sixth Ward.

What began as a list of overly optimistic requests, perceived by whites as a publicity stunt, materialized into an impressive fait accompli. The success of the campaign so inspired the black community that they did not relax until the remaining five conditions were met: a Negro in Congress, a black justice of the peace, a black member of the board of education, a black member of the board of aldermen, and a city hospital staffed by Negroes. Attainment of these goals became the cause celebre to Negroes for the next five decades. The flame of hope sparked by the effectiveness of the Pythian group never dimmed in the political circles of St. Louis's minority community.

Blacks in Cincinnati, Ohio, were forced to resort to tactics similar to those of the Pythian group in St. Louis. They, too, had routinely voted in disproportionate numbers for Republican candidates. In the 1921 city-wide elections for city council, the Republicans received 68,000 votes to the Democrats' 61,000. (All officeholders were elected citywide instead of by districts.) Republicans won thirty-one of the thirty-two seats on the city council because black folk cast 98 percent of their votes for white Republicans, and this provided the margin of victory. However, not a single Negro was elected to the council or to any other office. The two black Republicans who ran on the 1921 ticket were soundly defeated in all white wards, including those that white Republicans won by a landslide.

In 1925, the system of electing the city council was changed and the total number of seats was reduced. Under something referred to as a reform movement, the strong mayor type of government was replaced with a city-manager type, and the council was reduced to nine members elected by proportional representation. Presumably, voters, re-gardless of where they lived in the city, could cast their ballots for nine candidates in a weighted fashion. The total number of ballots divided by the number of contested seats (nine) would establish the quota for election. Each voter was permitted to vote for one first choice, one second choice, and so on, and the election was decided by attainment of the quota.

In 1927, the very next election, blacks, who comprised about 11 percent of Cincinnati's population, believed they were entitled to a seat on the council. But when a group of black leaders conferred with white Republican leaders about the party's supporting a black, they were rejected outright, this despite the fact that for years it had been the black vote that provided the margin of victory for white Republicans and accounted for their uninterrupted control of city politics. Despite the refusal of Republican party leaders, two blacks, Frank A. B. Hall, a retired city detective, and Abraham Lincoln Dalton, ran as independents. Both lost. Of the twenty-five candidates, Hall was eleventh in first-choice votes recorded, and under the proportional representation system used, was eliminated, as his total second-place votes distributed by other candidates were insufficient to make him one of the top nine vote getters overall.

In 1929, Hall filed again for office and this time was joined by a well-respected, active black Republican, George W. B. Conrad, an attorney with the Pennsylvania Railroad. Both sought the endorsement of the Republican party but were rebuffed. The party leaders again refused to put a black on their ballot, publicly announcing that to do so would hurt their ticket in white areas.

But this time blacks were more organized and more determined to elect one of their own. The issue had become one of national interest in black America. Republican Congressman Oscar DePriest of Chicago, ignoring threats against his life, appeared at rallies in Cincinnati to support Hall and Conrad, who ran as independent candidates. At one of the meetings where DePriest spoke, a local black leader, A. Lee Beaty, aroused the crowd of over 2,000 to loud indignation when he complained, ". . . both local parties [have] granted recognition to every group—Catholic, Protestant, Jew, Irish, German, Labor—but not the Negro."[13]

Both Hall and Conrad lost, but they made a better showing than expected. Of twenty-five candidates, Hall came in eighth with 6,781 first-place votes; Conrad finished twentieth with 1,179 votes on the first count. After the election, leaders of the black community, livid over the Republicans' refusal to support black candidates, issued a terse statement:

> We are serving notice upon the Republican organization that "the old order" in Hamilton County is gone and that the Negro district never again will be a transitory playground for unwholesome ambition and alien leadership.
>
> In the future the Republicans must look upon the Negro's secession from the ranks as a new order of things and a demand for real leadership which has been sucking the very vitals out of Negroes for the sole purpose of vote getting. The defection is permanent.[14]

In the next election, that of 1931, the Republican party finally placed Mr. Hall on the ticket. He ran second on the first count with 11,690 votes and was the fourth candidate to reach the quota, thus becoming the first black to be elected to the Cincinnati City Council. In the following election, A. Lee Beaty became the first black ward committeeman in the history of the city.

In 1920, more than 49,000, or 50 percent of Chicago's black population, lived in the First Congressional District. They represented 44.7 percent of the district's total population and constituted 40 percent of the voters in the district. More importantly, blacks cast 60 percent of the district's Republican vote in the primary and general elections.

The First District of Illinois had elected Martin B. Madden, a white Republican, to represent them in Congress since 1908. His political career was similar to that of other whites in major northern cities, whose districts were drawn so as to prevent blacks from becoming a majority. Their careers, however, were rather unusual, because in some areas blacks comprised more than 40 percent of the district population.

Undoubtedly, if this had been true of any other ethnic or religious group, one of their own would long since have been sent to represent them in Congress. White Anglo-Saxon, American-born Protestant party leaders would have understood the ethnic pride, the human desire, and the political necessity for electing indigenous leadership. In a district so composed, all party leaders would have been representatives from the indigenous group. Anglo-Saxon, American-born Protestants would have had nothing to say about the outcome.

But blacks are never given these opportunities. When other ethnic groups agitate for self-representation, their actions are described as the American way. When blacks do so, they are labeled racists, branded troublemakers, and assaulted by those in the power structure.

In 1924, Congressman Madden was opposed in the Republican primary by Nathan S. Taylor, a black lawyer. To the chagrin of party bigwigs and to the shock of the incumbent, this little-known black man, unaffiliated with any political machine and conducting a pitifully underfinanced campaign, received 40 percent, or approximately 8,500, of the 21,000 votes cast.

Four years later, something far more strange and far more difficult to explain took place. In the Republican primary, William L. Dawson, a graduate of Fisk University and Northwestern University School of Law who was reasonably known in the area and very active in politics, filed against Madden. Dawson was much more aggressive in his campaign and more articulate than either incumbent or challenger had been four years earlier. He chose to make "race" the principal issue against his white opponent. In his quest for election, Dawson carried the message of race pride to every part of the district. Again and again, he told large crowds of blacks, "By birth, training, and experience I am better fitted to represent the district at Washington than any of the candidates now in the field . . . Mr. Madden, the present congressman, does not even live in the district. He is a white man. Therefore, for those two reasons, if no others, he can hardly voice the hopes, ideals, and sentiment of the majority of the district."[15]

Indeed, by education, temperament, training, and ethnicity, Dawson was clearly better qualified to represent the First District of Illinois. But the black electorate either ignored his plea based on consideration of race and sided with the white incumbent, or their votes were not accurately tallied. Dawson received only 29 percent of the total after waging a more spirited and better organized campaign than a black candidate who four years prior had received 40 percent of the vote. By the time of this election, a majority of those living in the congressional district were black. The 1930 census showed 233,903 blacks living in Chicago, and 54,606 of those resided in the First Congressional District, constituting 58 percent of the district's total population.

Several days following the primary in which Attorney Dawson was defeated, Congressman Madden suffered a fatal heart attack in the nation's capital. At the time of Madden's death, Oscar Stanton De-Priest, then a local black leader who had supported Madden, was vacationing in Westbaden, Indiana, with black political cronies and other Chicago black leaders, among whom were Charlie Jackson, Alderman Louis B. Anderson, and Bishop Archibald Carey. They had joined DePriest to recuperate from the hard-fought primary. All of them had supported the now deceased white incumbent.

When word came of Madden's death, DePriest immediately took steps to secure support for replacing Mr. Madden in Congress. Without informing his vacationing friends, he dispatched telegrams to each of the elected Republican committeemen in the congressional district and to Mayor William ("Big Bill") Thompson, indicating his interest in becoming the nominee for the vacant seat.

The next morning, cutting his vacation short, DePriest appeared in the office of Mayor Thompson to seek his endorsement. "Big Bill" Thompson agreed and so did the other elected committeemen in the district. The vote was unanimous. Members of the committee included Dan Jackson, a black gambling kingpin; Daniel Serritella, a close associate of mobster Al Capone; W. S. Finucane, a white ward heeler; John ("Dingbat") Oberta, a racketeer who was later assassinated in gangland style; and DePriest himself.

The unsavory backgrounds of DePriest's white political bedfellows raised doubts among some blacks about his ability to act in an independent fashion. Consequently, some who were not identified with the regular Republican ward organizations expressed outrage at the selection procedure for the party's candidate for Congress and encouraged William H. Harrison, a black, to challenge DePriest. There is evidence that a double standard was being applied to DePriest, though, as the same unsavory characters who supported him had for eighteen years provided major support for the white incumbent. Nobody had ever protested the white politician's support from them.

But Harrison's entry into the race as an independent placed DePriest's chances of election in jeopardy. There was no certainty that white Republicans would support a black nominee of the party, even one so trusted and faithful, to the same extent blacks had traditionally supported whites. In fact, it was suspected that most white Republicans would vote for Harry Baker, a perennial white candidate chosen by the Democratic party to head their ticket. Baker became the odds-on favorite to receive the lion's share of defecting Republicans and win the election.

For years the First District was a Republican party stronghold because a majority of both races voted the same straight party ticket. Madden usually won by as much as a 15,000-vote plurality. In the special election to fill this seat, DePriest campaigned hard in all sectors of the district, reminding white voters of his loyalty to Madden and to other white leaders. The final tabulation showed DePriest receiving 24,479, Baker 20,664, and Harrison 5,861 of the votes cast. DePriest's slim margin of victory, only 3,800 votes, was the result of Harrison's siphoning off several thousand black votes and substantial voter defection by white Republicans who threw their support to the white Democratic candidate. Obviously race, not party, was the decisive factor for their switching allegiances.

Oscar Stanton DePriest thus became the first black elected to Congress in the twentieth century. He stood six feet four inches tall, handsome to the bone, with blue eyes, sandy hair, and a very light complexion. His reputation in politics and in business was varied and somewhat controversial.

Before the city of Chicago changed its method of nominating candidates for public office to balloting in primary elections instead of selection by party convention, it was possible for minorities to get elected county-wide. This was possible because voters rarely knew the racial identity of candidates. Once the party convention nominated candidates, their names went on a slate with others for all offices in the entire county. The slate was then promoted as a package, and most voters in one area of town were unaware of the backgrounds of the several hundred candidates from other wards among those vying for hundreds of positions. Even whites from different areas of town were unknown to other whites on the slate.

Prior to 1910 and under the old system, several blacks had been elected on a county-wide basis in Cook County, which was then 90 percent white. In 1904 and 1906, Oscar DePriest was nominated by the Republican County Convention and elected by the voters to the county board of commissioners. In 1908, after a squabble with party bigwigs, including Congressman Madden, he was dropped from the slate and defeated for re-election. It's likely 99 percent of the people who voted to put him in office did not know he was black—and that 99 percent of those who voted to take him out of office did not know it either.

DePriest remained in political limbo for seven years. Ostracized by the Madden faction and ignored by black politicians aligned with the machine organization, he devoted much of his time to speculating in real estate and the stockmarket and became a very wealthy man. Several sources accused him of engaging in the unethical practice of neighborhood "blockbusting." They alleged that he leased apartment buildings fully occupied by whites, panicked the tenants by leaking word that blacks were moving in, and in turn relet the buildings to blacks who were charged twice the rent of former white occupants.

An account of the situtation is given in a book written by Harold F. Gosnell:

> . . . when the migration began he would lease whole buildings in sections where white people had lived and were paying twenty dollars a unit rent and rent them to colored for forty dollars, while his obligation for the same unit ran about ten dollars, thus leaving a thirty dollar profit. Negroes weren't aware of being overcharged anyway. Times were good and they didn't mind. And if DePriest hadn't gotten it, someone else would have.[16]

In 1915, after seven years of forced political hiatus, DePriest made peace with the Madden group by rallying grassroots black voter support for several white incumbents whose election outcome was in peril because of aggressive campaigns launched by black contenders. Because the opposition was not of the usual token nature, Congressman Madden needed a person of DePriest's skills and connections to keep a portion of the black vote in the regular organization's column. In return, Madden showed his gratitude by supporting DePriest for the board of aldermen.

Congressman Madden's endorsement was helpful but by no means the only reason for DePriest's successful campaign to become the first black on the city council. During the seven-year period when DePriest was in political exile he had developed an organization outside the reach of the regulars. Putting together a formidable group consisting of black ministers, small businessmen, and personal friends, he was in a position to offer unwanted and unneeded competition to the Madden organization. He won election to the board of aldermen by a plurality of 10,599 in a race where the total vote was divided among four candidates.

His term on the board of aldermen lasted for two years and earned him a reputation of providing exceptionally efficient and prompt municipal services to his constituents. In addition to securing the usual street cleaning and garbage collection services expected of an elected official, he was particularly adept at using his vote and influence to put many on the payroll at city hall. Since black constituents in Chicago had never been hired for municipal jobs in any large numbers—or in any small numbers for that matter—DePriest became very popular in the community for his judicious use of power.

It was DePriest's alliance with Mayor "Big Bill" Thompson that made these accomplishments possible. The mayor befriended many black politicians and rewarded the black community for its support much more demonstratively than had any of his predecessors. He appointed so many blacks to white collar jobs in the water department and to clerical positions in the health department that the daily newspapers began referring to city hall derisively and cynically as "Uncle Tom's Cabin."

But DePriest's climb up the political ladder did not insulate him from the same kind of harassment reserved for black leaders today. One month before the 1917 aldermanic primary, a grand jury indicted him—along with the chief of police, three police lieutenants, a black nightclub owner, and a few underworld characters—on a charge of conspiring to allow gambling operations and permitting houses of prostitution. The black club owner entered into a plea bargaining arrangement, admitted guilt, and testified for the state. He said during the trial that he had paid DePriest the sum of $2,500 over a four-month period to give protection to illegal activities in his business establishment.

It is highly probable that DePriest's indictment was politically motivated. Without question, the state attorney was very selective in singling him out for this precedent-setting accusation. Scores of other Chicago politicians could justifiably have been cited for the same criminal violation—and probably prosecuted successfully. Why then was the only black elected official in the entire city selected? This question poses a twister for those who claim no racial overtones were involved in the indictment. At any rate, under the circumstances, DePriest decided not to seek re-election.

The Democratic state attorney who charged DePriest with "accepting bribes from gamblers in exchange for protection" had been elected five years earlier in 1912, chiefly because of support provided by DePriest. However, two years later, after DePriest and Madden smoked the peace pipe and renewed their friendly alliance, DePriest threw his support in the 1916 election to a Republican candidate for state attorney backed by Congressman Madden. It's reasonable, as well as understandable, to believe that the incumbent state attorney, after winning re-election, was in a mood to seek a pint of blood and a pound of flesh. Indicting a black who had opposed him was the pint of blood. Taking out his revenge on both Congressman Madden, the white who master-minded the attempted coup, and the white candidate who opposed him would have satisfied his lust for a "pound of flesh." The state attorney's failure to do so beclouds the argument that the charges were lodged purely as political retribution. Racism was a clear contributing factor.

At his trial, DePriest was defended by Clarence Darrow, the world-renowned criminal lawyer. In his deliberate, methodical manner, Darrow succeeded in ridiculing the prosecutor and poking gaping holes in the case presented by the state. Charging racial bias, arguing selective prosecution, and describing cash payments made as no more than ordinary campaign contributions, Darrow persuaded the jury to acquit DePriest on all counts.

OSCAR STANTON DePRIEST TAKES HIS SEAT IN CONGRESS

History is strange, sometimes cruel, and often repeats itself. Twelve years later, shortly after DePriest's nomination to fill the vacancy created by Congressman Madden's death, an odd and unexpected event occurred: He was again indicted on almost identical charges as those handed down by the 1917 grand jury. This time, he was accused of "aiding, abetting, and inducing" gangsters who operated "gambling houses and disorderly places." How nebulous a charge to level against DePriest, a black politician in the most corrupt political system in the country. But this latest assault on his honesty and integrity prompted speculation and cast doubt on his chances of being seated in Congress even should he be elected. His black opponent, Bill Harrison, raised on every possible occasion the ugly specter of a convicted felon presenting his credentials to Congress and being rejected.

After the election, that possibility loomed larger than daybreak at Cape Cod. Many in Congress, especially those from southern and border states, were predisposed to challenge the right of any black man to be seated in *their* august assembly. They relished the thought of opposing a black who had been convicted of a felony and was seeking admission to their private club. Fortunately for DePriest and the black community, shortly after the election, the state dropped all charges, and he was sworn into office in an aura of suspense but with no real drama.

A key player in the plan to assure the seating of DePriest was Ruth Hannah McCormick. She was the widow of former U.S. Senator Medill McCormick of Illinois and very friendly with politicians aligned with former Congressman Madden. Mrs. McCormick also had a close personal relationship with Alice Roosevelt Longworth, wife of the Republican Speaker of the House of Representatives and the daughter of President Theodore Roosevelt. It is generally acknowledged that Mrs.

McCormick persuaded Mrs. Longworth to intervene with her husband on behalf of Oscar DePriest.

Speaker Nicholas Longworth devised a strategy for outmaneuvering the southern Democrats who were preparing a floor fight to oppose the seating of DePriest. The customary procedure for swearing members into the House was by state delegations in alphabetical order. Southern congressmen from Alabama, Arkansas, Florida, and Georgia normally would have been seated prior to those from Illinois. Under the rules, anyone already sworn in could offer a motion challenging the seating of any member whose name was presented later. But Speaker Longworth caught DePriest's enemies off-guard when he announced that all members would stand and be administered the oath of office at the same time. The ploy worked. Simultaneously alongside 434 others, DePriest took his seat as a member of the most prestigious legislative body in the world.

When he finished reciting the oath of office after Speaker Longworth and his hand dropped back to his side, Oscar Stanton DePriest had become the most powerful and most influential black in America. Black people across the land—in every city, town, and hamlet—identified with him. He became a widely sought after speaker at rallies and banquets. His election was the culmination of a dream long deferred, a hope long cherished, an act of justice long delayed.

Not only was DePriest the lone black member of Congress, but he also was the first black congressman elected in twenty-seven years, the first black congressman elected in the twentieth century, and the first black congressman from a northern city. He had reason to be proud, and blacks from one end of the country to the other had reason to take pride in the man who had accomplished so notable a feat: overcoming racism and racists to achieve one of the federal government's highest elective offices.

THE EFFORT TO ELECT A BLACK CONGRESSMAN FROM ST. LOUIS

At the same time DePriest was winning in Chicago, blacks in St. Louis were making a major thrust to elect one of their own to the U.S. House of Representatives. The effort, however, differed in several ways. St. Louisans concentrated on winning a seat through the Democratic party. The major emphasis was placed on blacks' voting in favor of their basic racial interests by switching their loyalty from the Republican party and deserting the ghost of Abraham Lincoln.

Joseph L. McLemore, a black attorney, filed for Congress. He conducted a hard-hitting, educationally enlightening campaign, winning the Democratic primary in the Twelfth District. While a student at Howard University, he had been sponsored by the white incumbent Congressman and appointed by the House sergeant-at-arms as an elevator operator in the Capitol. Now he was opposing his patronage benefactor for the seat in Congress.

In this race, the Democratic party officially endorsed a black congressional candidate for the first time. In the general election, McLemore was pitted against the white Republican incumbent, Congressman L. C. Dyer, who had represented the heavily black populated district since 1910 and had never been seriously challenged during his nine terms in office.

In 1928, most blacks were still aligned with the party of Abraham Lincoln and saw nothing admirable or worthwhile in supporting a Democrat, even a highly qualified black Democrat. Lincoln had been credited with freeing the slaves, and that was sufficient reason for their loyalty to the inheritors of his party.

In St. Louis, many refused to recognize the advantages that a black congressman, Democrat or Republican, could bring to the legislative arena. Despite a spirited, issue-oriented campaign waged by McLemore in his effort to corral black support, he lost by 7,000 votes, receiving 17,609 to Congressman Dyer's 24,701. Substantial support for Dyer in black precincts was the difference between victory and defeat for black candidate Joseph L. McLemore.

Black St. Louis Republicans, like blacks in other cities, to a great extent were persuaded by party propaganda accusing McLemore and other black Democrats of running merely to garner electoral votes for Al Smith, the Democratic candidate for president. At the time, the black vote played a key role in determining which candidates would win four states: Ohio, Kentucky, Maryland, and Missouri. Blacks feared that a Democratic victory would mean the rebirth of the policies of Woodrow Wilson and once again the appointment of bigoted southern white Democrats to key government positions. Since a majority of blacks were Republicans and Baptists, Al Smith, a Democrat and Catholic, had two strikes against him from the start. Political loyalty and religious bigotry prevailed as both McLemore and Smith were defeated in Missouri's Twelfth District.

McLemore's chances would have been better if Congressman L. C.

Dyer had not been so popular a national figure among black voters. His image was exalted when James Weldon Johnson, the secretary of the National Association for the Advancement of Colored People (NAACP) persuaded him in 1921 to introduce an anti-lynching bill that would "assure to persons within the jurisdiction of every state the equal protection of the laws, and to punish the crime of lynching."

Dyer's bill, similar to the first anti-lynching bill, which was introduced on January 20, 1900, by the last black congressman of the Reconstruction era, George H. White, was debated in the House and stringently opposed by southern congressmen who openly advocated mob rule as the only remedy for maintaining "civilized" conditions in their areas. Despite their acrimonious rantings, the anti-lynching bill passed the House by a vote of 230–119, and Representative Dyer earned the respect and loyalty of many Negro citizens. The bill was stalled in the Senate by a filibuster led by senators from Mississippi and Alabama.

Lynching was a very emotional issue in black communities and Dyer's introduction of the bill to take government action against it was a meaningful political gesture as far as blacks were concerned. Between 1889 and 1922, 3,436 blacks had been officially designated lynch victims. Between 1918 and 1921, twenty-eight black people were publicly burned in the streets by white mobs. Thousands more had died at the hands of terrorists but were not recorded as having been lynched, because the circumstances did not precisely meet the definition of a lynching: an act of mob violence resulting in the death or maiming of a person taken from the custody of a law enforcement official.

DEPRIEST'S PERFORMANCE IN CONGRESS

While Oscar Stanton DePriest was viewed by many to be the most influential black in America, his fellow white colleagues in the House treated him the same as they did any ordinary "nigger."

The separation of the races was such an established fact of life in America that even the Congress of the United States indulged in its rancorous practices. When DePriest's son and personal secretary sought service in a public restaurant on the grounds of the United States Capitol, they were refused. The chairman of the House Committee on Accounts, Democratic Representative Lindsay C. Warren of North Carolina, who had jurisdiction over the restaurants, personally ordered the two blacks to leave the premises. He snidely informed them that a special eating facility had been provided for people of their race in the basement of the House of Representatives.

DePriest secured 145 signatures asking the House of Representatives to sit *en banc* as an investigative committee. The move was an attempt to bypass the Democrat-controlled Committee on Accounts. But instead, the Democratic Speaker of the House appointed a special committee composed of three Democrats and two Republicans. The committee, voting along party lines, refused to change the policy of segregated eating facilities in the Capitol building.

This was not the first time DePriest expressed his outrage at racism and displayed his courage in challenging it. Describing the actions of DePriest during the bloody Chicago race riot of 1919, William L. Dawson, who had recently just returned from the battlefields of Europe, remarked:

What great admiration I had for Oscar DePriest as a man who really had "guts." I remember seeing him put on a policeman's cap and uniform and drive a patrol wagon into the stockyards to bring out the Negroes who were trapped inside during the riot of 1919. He was respected as a former alderman, and he did what not a single policeman had the courage to do. Again and again he went into the stockyards, bringing Negroes out with him in the patrol wagon until finally he had rescued all of them from the white mob.[17]

It was not mentioned in Dawson's letter, but the fact that DePriest's complexion was virtually white helped him considerably in his heroic deed. The white mob guarding the perimeter of the stockyards in all probability believed him to be a white police officer in the act of arresting black rioters.

In Congress, DePriest, like his black predecessors during Reconstruction, was assigned to three insignificant committees: Enrolled Bills, Indian Affairs, and Invalid Pensions. Legislative initiatives he offered to improve the lot of black citizens were invariably rejected.

In March 1931, DePriest introduced a bill providing for a $75 monthly pension to ex-slaves above the age of seventy-five. It died in committee. Later, he introduced bills to make Abraham Lincoln's birthday a legal public holiday and to hold states and counties legally responsible for the prevention of lynching. Both bills died in committee. On one occasion DePriest was successful in attaching an antidiscrimination amendment to a $300-million unemployment relief and reforestation measure. It was deleted by the Senate when they met in conference with the House to reconcile their differences in the bills.

ANOTHER BLACK DEFEATS DEPRIEST

In 1934, Arthur W. Mitchell defeated Oscar DePriest in his bid for re-election to a fourth term. Several factors played an important role in Mitchell's surprise upset of the incumbent. As late as the day before election, political pundits and ward insiders were predicting that DePriest would win in a landslide. What was not taken into account was the special appeal that President Roosevelt's social programs had for many black constituents. Neither was it recognized that DePriest's opposition to such programs as the Works Project Administration (WPA), Civilian Conservation Corps (CCC), and the National Industrial Revitalization Administration (NIRA) had caused serious erosion in his political base in the black community.

In addition, the Communist party had launched an extensive attack on DePriest for his insensitivity toward poor black people. Their publicity campaign castigated him for evicting unemployed black families from his apartments without showing any compassion or any understanding of their plight.

Another important factor in Mitchell's victorious campaign was the 1933 slaying of Chicago Mayor Anton J. Cermak and the attempted assassination of President Franklin D. Roosevelt. Cermak was replaced as mayor of Chicago by Edward J. Kelly, his long-time friend. Kelly, as mayor, approached the black community in a manner similar to that of his predecessor. He, too, aggressively reached out to black voters. He made a series of public statements attacking racism and expanded on Mayor Cermak's policies for increasing the number of black Democrats by sharing with them the spoils of office.

Kelly's liberal credentials were so much in order that Bill Dawson and Robert W. Jackson, the two black Republicans on the board of aldermen, joined forty-five Democratic councilmen in voting for him to fill the unexpired term of Cermak. Shortly after assuming office, he made two significant appointments of black leaders. One was named assistant corporation counsel and the other was placed on the Chicago Library Board.*

---

*The corporation counsel appointment was important, but not a first for a black. Ten years earlier in 1923, Earl B. Dickerson had been appointed to the same position by Mayor William E. Dever.

When Arthur Mitchell filed for Congress against Oscar DePriest, Mayor Kelly not only endorsed him but vigorously supported his campaign efforts. This was the first time that Democrats in Chicago had endorsed a black person for Congress.

Mitchell's political rise followed a path similar to that of his predecessor, DePriest. Harry Baker, the winner of the Democratic primary, died before election day and Mitchell was selected by the Democratic committee as the substitute Democratic candidate.

With almost solid support from the white political organization, Mitchell narrowly defeated DePriest. He won by 3,130 votes out of a total 52,810 cast. The returns showed Mitchell with 27,970 to DePriest's 24,840. Mitchell won handily in the two all-white wards while losing in every all-black ward. But his large majority in the white community was sufficient to offset DePriest's slim margins in the black wards. Both Mitchell and Roosevelt lost heavily in the black precincts. Black voters in Chicago knew very little about President Roosevelt's previous accomplishments as governor of New York; recognized FDR's health problems; and feared the possibility of Roosevelt's Texan vice-president, John Nance Garner, becoming president.

Arthur W. Mitchell was an individual obsessed by politics and fascinated by political life. He was educated at Tuskegee Institute, Columbia University, and Harvard University's School of Law. He was the founder of Armstrong Agriculture School in West Butler, Alabama. He'd earned a fortune in land speculation while practicing law in Washington, D.C., and then moved to Chicago specifically to oppose Oscar DePriest for Congress in the 1934 election.

Mitchell's victory was a personal triumph for him. But it was a disaster for the black community. He totally ignored the fact that he, as a black man, was expected both by his constituents and blacks elsewhere to champion the cause of black liberation. He ignored their wishes and deserted their cause. Mitchell made it unmistakably clear that as the only black member of Congress, he felt no obligation nor intended to become the spokesman for 12 million blacks nationwide. On one occasion he openly declared: "I do not represent Negro people in any way, but the First District of Illinois."[18]

And Mitchell meant exactly what he said. Not once during his tenure in Congress did he identify with any universal cause of black people. He spent most of his time and efforts catering to the interests of white businesses located in the Chicago Loop, which was a part of his district.

Like his predecessor, Oscar DePriest, Mitchell was unable to pass any legislation, meaningful or otherwise. According to *The Negro Almanac*, a reference work on the African-American:

> Mitchell's most significant victory on behalf of civil rights came, not in the legislative chamber, but in the courts. In 1937, Mitchell brought suit against the Chicago and Rock Island Railroad after having been forced to leave his first-class accommodations en route to Hot Springs, Arkansas, and sit in a "Jim Crow" car. He argued his own case before the Supreme Court in 1941, and won a decision which declared "Jim Crow" practices illegal.[19]

Mitchell, in defeating Oscar DePriest, was the first black Democrat to qualify for a seat in the United States Congress. At the 1936 Democratic Convention, he and eleven other blacks were elected delegates. That was a far cry from 1924, when the first black delegate in history was allowed to participate at a Democratic Convention. That year A. P. Collins of New York City, a black alternate delegate, replaced a white delegate who was unable to attend the convention because of illness.

Congressman Mitchell's presence on the podium to address the 1936 assembly was used as an excuse for a U.S. senator from South Carolina and eight other delegates to stage a walkout in protest. But even that demonstration was mild compared to what had happened in previous conventions of both the Democratic and Republican parties when blacks sought to participate.

In 1877, racist elements of the Democratic party attacked the Republican white–black coalition as being the "Nigger Party." In response, the Republicans established what was officially known as "the Black and Tan Republican Party" within the party. White Republicans from the South established all-white Republican clubs, which came to be known as "Lily-white Republicans." When white Republicans tried to wrest control from blacks at the 1888 state convention in Texas, a race riot broke out.

The next year, President Benjamin Harrison recognized "Lily-white Republicans" as the only bona fide Republican party members. Four years later, however, President McKinley garnered enough support from Black and Tan Republicans to defeat the "Lily-whites" and to clinch the nomination. In 1908 and again in 1912, President William Taft received enough "Black and Tan" votes to win the Republican nomination against Teddy Roosevelt. In 1928, even though it was the votes of black delegates that gave Herbert Hoover the nomination, he sided with the "Lily-whites" after being elected and in effect changed the party rules to end any significant influence blacks might wield at future Republican conventions.

This was the classic treatment accorded blacks throughout their long association with the party of Abraham Lincoln. This was the situation black Americans involved in politics faced when Democrat Arthur Mitchell defeated Republican Oscar DePriest for Congress.

Congressman Mitchell's election marked the beginning of a new dynamic in black politics. For the next fifty or so years, blacks would be in alliance with a new political party. Forty-three of the next forty-six blacks elected to Congress came from the ranks of the Democratic party. The three exceptions were Senator Edward Brooke of Massachusetts, Representative Gary Franks of Connecticut, and Melvin Evans, a nonvoting delegate from the Virgin Islands, each of whom was a Republican.

NOTES

1. Declaration of Independence, the Republic of Liberia, 1849, from Frederick Starr's "Liberia," cited in "Hiram Revels and His Times" by Warmoth T. Gibbs, *Quarterly Review of Higher Education Among Negroes*, Vol. 8., 1940, page 8.

2. See *African-Americans in Boston*, by Robert C. Hayden, Boston: Trustees of the Public Library of the City of Boston, 1991, page 95.

3. *Journal of the Florida House of Representatives*, in Extraordinary Session, Monday, June 17, 1929, page 1145.

4. *Ibid.*

5. *Ibid.*,page 1146.

6. *Ibid.*, pages 1145–1146.

7. *Ibid.*

8. *Texas House Journal and Senate Proceedings*, 41st Legislature, second session, June 18, 1929, pages 326–327.

9. August Wilson, in the 1987 Broadway play *Fences*, New York City, New York, and Scarborough, Ontario: a Plume Book, New American Library, page xvii.

10. Declaration of Independence of the Republic of Liberia, 1849, cited in "Hiram Revels and His Times," Warmoth T. Gibbs, *Quarterly Review of Higher Education Among Negroes*, Vol. 8, 1940, page 25.

11. Robert L. Green, *CBC Foundation Souvenir Program Book*, Fourteenth Annual Legislative Weekend, September 1984, page 71.

12. Nathan B. Young, editor, *Your St. Louis and Mine*, St Louis: N. B. Young, 1938, page 39.

13. Ralph A. Straetz, *PR Politics in Cincinnati: Thirty-Two Years of City Government Through Proportional Representation*, New York: N.Y. University Press, 1958, page 109.

14. *Ibid.*, page 117.

15. Harold F. Gosnell, *Negro Politicians: The Rise of Negro Politics in Chicago*, Chicago: University of Chicago Press, 1935 (reissued 1969), page 79.

16. *Ibid.*, page 169.

17. Dempsey J. Travis, *An Autobiography of Black Politics*, Chicago: Urban Research, 1987, page 71.

18. *Ibid.*, page 127.

19. *The Negro Almanac*, New York: The Bellwether Company, 1976, page 325.

4

The Lonely Years: Few Blacks in Congress

The first three blacks elected to Congress in the twentieth century—Oscar DePriest, Arthur Mitchell, and William Dawson—each lived in the First Congressional District on the South Side of Chicago, Illinois. And at times while serving each was the only member of his race to sit in Congress. Their terms of office can best be described as "the loneliest years" of service ever spent in the Congress by anyone, before or since.

In the magnificent halls of the "most deliberative legislative body in the world," each black member was considered persona non grata. Black members were not invited to share in the festivities nor to join the inner circles of this prestigious cabal. Institutional perks, a given for members of Congress, were denied to them. Haircuts, manicures, pedicures, restaurants—the extra fringe benefits, subsidized by the taxpayers and exclusively reserved for members of Congress—were explicitly designated off-limits to all black members of Congress.

Life outside Capitol Hill in the city of Washington, D.C., was equally uncivil and uncharitable. Establishments licensed to serve the public would not provide food or lodging to persons of color, be they members of Congress or not. Not a single restaurant, hotel, or movie house in the downtown area would admit DePriest, Mitchell, or Dawson as patrons.

Each during his time in office slept at the colored YMCA or at the homes of friends and admirers. They had a choice of driving five miles from work to enjoy a restaurant in a black neighborhood, brown bagging it, or eating in the place reserved for all black employees of Congress at that time, the basement of the Capitol.

WILLIAM L. DAWSON, THE PREMIER POLITICIAN

William Dawson grew up in a well-to-do middle class family that had produced an array of doctors, attorneys, school teachers, and businessmen. A native of Albany, Georgia, born in 1886, he graduated *magna cum laude* from Fisk University. He attended Kent College before being commissioned an officer in the U.S. Expeditionary Forces in 1917 and distinguished himself as a combat soldier in Europe during World War I. He was hospitalized twice, first as a victim of poison gas and then from wounds that shattered his leg and left him with a permanent limp. His brother, Dr. Julian Dawson, was one of very few blacks commissioned as a general in the United States Army during the 1950s.

Following World War I, Bill Dawson finished Northwestern University School of Law. After practicing in Chicago for almost nine years, he challenged the incumbent white congressman from the First District in the 1928 Republican primary. Garnering 29 percent of the vote in a predominantly black district, Dawson made white party leaders aware that race was a viable issue. His vigorous campaigning in the primary and his exhortations inciting blacks to vote for blacks in the district indirectly led to the nomination and election of Oscar De-Priest.

When the incumbent white congressman died after defeating Dawson in the primary but before the general election, GOP committeemen in the district named DePriest as his successor on the ticket. In all probability, a black man would not have been selected for this position had Dawson not so energetically raised the issue of race-conscious voting.

Seven years later, in 1935, Bill Dawson, running on the Republican ticket, was elected to the board of aldermen. In 1938, he ran against Mitchell for Congress on the Republican ticket and was defeated, losing by 4,000 votes. While a member of the city council, he sometimes acted more like a Roosevelt Democrat than a Hoover Republican. Crossing party lines on several occasions, including declaring support for Franklin D. Roosevelt for president in 1936, he established a firm base among Democrats while maintaining the loyalty of most of his Republican admirers. In 1940, he officially left the Republican party by filing in the Democratic primary and was elected committee-man of the Second Ward.

In 1942, Congressman Mitchell announced that he would not seek re-election. William Dawson, by this time a Democratic officeholder, filed for Congress and was elected in a closely contested campaign. His Republican opponent, William E. King, received 23,537 votes to Dawson's 26,280 votes.

During twenty-seven years in Congress, Dawson was never accused of losing touch with his constituency. He was a consummate politician who lived each day to advance the interests of his district and political machine. This is how Congressman Dawson is described in a book recently published by the Library of Congress:

In many respects Dawson was an atypical politician and machine leader. He disliked personal publicity, regarded the media with wariness and lived in an unpretentious manner. When in his district Dawson spent part of each day at his headquarters listening to complaints, requests, and opinions from a parade of constituents. He kept a tight grip on his share of power in Chicago, dispensing patronage and favors through his political machine and its ancillary organizations.[1]

Dawson was a strong advocate of equal rights for blacks. In the late 1940s, he assumed the chairmanship of the House Committee on Expenditures in Executive Departments. Later it was renamed the Committee on Government Operations. This was the first time in history that a black had been elevated to chairmanship of a full committee. Dawson retained that position (except for a two-year period when Republicans controlled the House) until his retirement from Congress in 1970 at the age of eighty-four.

In 1944, he was appointed assistant chairman of the Democratic National Committee and soon became the first black to be elected vice-chairman. In his later years, Dawson toned down his rhetoric considerably, but without ever abandoning his mission of seeking equality of citizenship. During his tenure in Congress, he fought for appointment of blacks to key positions in the federal civil service and to the federal bench.

In 1951, Dawson was primarily responsible for the defeat of the Winstead Amendment in the House. That provision would have per-mitted military personnel the option of choosing between all-white units and racially integrated ones. In an impassioned floor speech,

Congressman Dawson successfully implored his colleagues to defeat the measure.

You see this mark on my forehead. It is the result of German mustard gas and this left shoulder is today a slip joint. I served in a segregated outfit as a citizen trying to save this country. I would give up this life of mine to preserve this country and every American in it, white or black.

Deny to me if you will all that American citizenship stands for, and I will still fight for you, hoping that under the Constitution of the United States all these restrictions will be removed, and that we will move forward as one people, American people, joined in a democracy toward all the world.

I say to you, who claim to love America in this hour of its stress, that the greatest argument the Soviet Union is using among the black people of the world to turn them against us is your treatment of me, an American citizen.[2]

When Dawson spoke of giving his life for America, he was referring to the fact that he had been too old to be drafted but volunteered to fight for his country in the First World War. Commissioned a lieutenant in the infantry, he led troops in battle against the Germans.

Congressman Dawson's role in the House was described in the weekly *Washington North Star* in an article by Eddie T. Arnold and Dr. Bobby Williams:

Dawson presented a sharp contrast to his soon-to-be ally Adam Clayton Powell, Jr., who loudly blasted discrimination wherever he found it. . . . Mr. Inside (Dawson) and Mr. Outside (Powell) worked together for more than ten years setting the agenda and dialogue around desegregation of American life and the establishment of civil rights for black Americans.[3]

Dawson retired in 1971 and died a year later in his beloved city of Chicago.

ADAM CLAYTON POWELL, THE PEOPLE'S VOICE

The most productive legislator and the most flamboyant personality in the 200-year history of the U.S. Congress, black or white, was Adam Clayton Powell, Jr. He was elected to Congress in 1944 to represent the predominantly black district of Harlem in New York City. Like his father, Adam, Sr., he was pastor of the 15,000-member Abyssinian Baptist Church on 138th Street in Harlem. The young Reverend Powell encouraged members of his congregation to fight racial discrimination in public facilities and to advance the political interests of black people. He also was in the forefront of the struggle to elevate the economic and political status of blacks. After five black doctors were arbitrarily dismissed from the staff at Harlem Hospital, Powell led the campaign to initiate reforms in the hiring and promotion of blacks at that institution. He also organized rent strikes against absentee slumlords and forced them to put some of the rental money into escrow accounts for repairing housing units.

The young Reverend Powell set up soup kitchens during the depression years of the 1930s that fed hundreds of people on a daily basis. He organized picket lines and led boycotts in an effort to end discrimination against and segregation of black Harlemites. He organized picket lines at restaurants that refused to serve black customers and boycotts of retail merchants who refused to hire black employees. Through his efforts, the merchants in Harlem were forced to enter into agreements to hire blacks as one-third of their total workforce. He was the chief organizer of campaigns that forced bus companies, gas and light utilities, the telephone company, and Harlem Hospital to hire thousands of blacks in jobs ranging from menial to top administrative and professional positions.

In 1941, Adam Powell, Jr., the most popular person in all of Harlem, ran as an independent and was elected to the New York City Council. He was so well known and so well liked that he won the seat with the third highest number of votes ever cast in a New York City municipal election.

Three years later, Powell ran for Congress unopposed in the general election and won with 83,140 votes. Within months, he had developed a national following and established himself as the undisputed leader of black America. He challenged the evils of segregation and discrimination at every opportunity. Immediately he clashed with one of the House's most influential members, John E. Rankin of Mississippi. Mr. Rankin was an arch-segregationist who recoiled in anger at Mr. Powell's audacity in sponsoring legislation to outlaw lynching and the poll tax, and at Powell's support of a ban on discrimination in the armed forces, housing, employment, and transportation.

J. Wyatt Mondesire, in his book *High Priest of Harlem*, describes Adam C. Powell, Jr., almost poetically:

He was prophetically named. At the genesis of black political power—before Jesse, before Andy, before Martin, before Malcolm, there was Adam. This man called Adam, more accurately Adam Clayton Powell, Jr.—parson of black America's most prestigious house of prayer, populist, author, twelve-term congressman and committee chairman and flagrant knave—was the seed from which contemporary black power evolved.[4]

For more than twenty years, Adam's voice rang out in clarion tones, trumpeting the frustrations of black Americans and censuring white America for not fulfilling its promises of liberty and justice for all. His voice was one of the most forceful and most respected in all the land. Whenever politics or civil rights or economic injustices were discussed, his opinion was always sought. He was a silver-tongued orator with a penchant for high living and a cavalier attitude about white folks' disdain for his lifestyle. Adam C. Powell, Jr., was the premier spokesman for black America. His basic political philosophy was summed up in one statement that he incorporated into a "Black Position Paper" he issued in 1965. In Point 4 of his seventeen-point document, he stated:

> The black masses must demand and refuse to accept nothing less than that proportionate share of political jobs and appointments which are equal to their proportion in the electorate. Where we are 20 percent of the voters, we should command 20 percent of the top jobs, 20 percent of the judgeships, 20 percent of the commissionerships, and 20 percent of all political appointments.[5]

Congressman Powell was an effective and outspoken critic of racial discrimination in the U.S. military and worked feverishly to end "Jim Crow" practices at federal and congressional facilities. The famous "Powell Amendment" denying federal funds to any project where racial discrimination existed was first attached to the Flanagan School Lunch Bill in 1946. When it finally passed both houses of Congress and was signed by the president, Powell became the first black member of Congress to sponsor and see enacted a civil rights law of major national import. For the next several years, this amendment was attached to all appropriations bills passing the House.

On one occasion, an attempt to attach the Powell Amendment to a school-aid bill caused a fist fight in the committee room. According to several committee members present, Adam Powell was floored by a right-handed punch thrown by Representative Cleveland M. Bailey, a Democrat from West Virginia. In a disagreement over the amendment, Bailey allegedly accused Powell of "trying to wreck the public school system through his anti-segregation amendment to a school construction bill."[6]

The bill under consideration by the House Education and Labor Committee authorized $1.6 billion in federal aid to states over a four-year period for the construction of public schools. The amendment was actually offered by Representative Stuyvesant Wainwright, a Republican from Long Island, New York. Powell was of the opinion that the amendment should be offered on the floor of Congress instead of in committee, contending that the Rules Committee, under the chairmanship of a die-hard segregationist, Howard W. Smith of Virginia, would strip the amendment from the bill and set the rules for debate in such a manner that any effort to restore it on the House floor would not succeed.

At any rate, the disturbance took place in a closed meeting of Democratic committee members. When Mr. Powell stated that it was a lie to describe his intentions to amend the bill as an effort to kill it, Bailey allegedly threw a punch that caught Powell off-guard. Powell lost his balance and fell over a chair. Despite the provocation, Powell, twenty-three years younger than the sixty-nine-year-old Bailey and twenty pounds heavier, did not return the blow. Later both men shook hands and denied the incident took place.

Seniority had prevailed in the Congress for many decades. But when Powell was the No. 2 member in seniority on the Education and Labor Committee, Chairman Graham Barden of North Carolina nevertheless bypassed him for a subcommittee chairmanship.

The sixty pieces of major legislation Adam Clayton Powell, Jr., steered through the Congress remain a record of individual accomplishment in the House of Representatives. Under his later leadership as chairman of the House Education and Labor Committee such landmark legislation as the Title 1 Educational Act, Headstart, the Manpower Development and Training Act, the Vocational Education Act, and the National Defense Education Act all became law. Moreover, in the seven-year period he served as chairman of the committee, only two bills reported from his committee to the House floor were defeated.

Powell constantly promoted the impression that he was the personification of black politics—the role model to be emulated by blacks seeking to become the perfect representative of their community. But Powell was much more. His political agenda was based on the realization that basic black hopes and aspirations could not be achieved without addressing basic social and legal problems also facing the average white citizen. Therefore, he advocated increased low-income housing, school lunch programs for the poor, college grants for economically needy students, and government-guaranteed loans for middle class students. All of these programs affected a high percentage of blacks but many more whites. His support of civil rights measures was intelligently calculated and intermingled with demands to increase the minimum wage, provide for adequate health care, and develop programs to assist senior citizens.

Adam Clayton Powell, Jr., led at least three public lives: Adam the dynamic preacher; Adam the legislator par excellence; and Adam the fast, high-living womanizer. His attacks on institutional racism, his controversial legislative initiatives, and his personal lifestyle guaranteed that he would be a prime target for media intimidation and government harassment. He was dramatic in gesture and militant and confrontational in speech, especially when exposing racism. From the time of his elevation to committee chairman in 1961 until 1967, when he was denied his seat in the House, the media paid him mostly unwanted and hurtful attention. It was as if he satisfied a need for a kind of villain generally unreported in their coverage of American politics.

The press overdramatized the smallest events in his daily life and pictured his every action as sinister, corrupt, and uppity. The incessant scrutiny of his personal life and the excessive coverage of insignificant events gave the false impression that Adam Clayton Powell, Jr., was the most incorrigible member of Congress. In fact, the accusations against him could have been leveled against every chairman of every full committee in the House of Representatives. He did no more, and no less, than any other in terms of exercising traditional legal privileges that accompanied the powerful position of committee chairman. His private life, including intimate relations with numerous and glamorous women, was routine activity for many members of Congress, committee chairmen or not.

The two most damaging incidents in Powell's career were his indictment for criminal evasion of federal income taxes in 1958 and his conviction for contempt of court in a New York civil suit. He was indicted on three counts in the income tax case, but never convicted. Two of the charges eventually were dropped and the other count ended in a hung jury. The government refused to ask for a new trial. But it was the civil contempt case that caused Powell the most trouble and eventually led to his being dethroned from his lofty perch of power in the Congress.

In 1960, Powell was struggling to extricate himself from the charge of income tax evasion and, as he often did in difficult situations, attempted to divert attention away from the matter. In this instance, he engaged in a high-profile publicity campaign attacking the Mafia and the New York Police Department. He accused the Mafia of controlling gambling in Harlem. He attacked the police for providing protection for the gamblers and their "numbers" business.

As long as he confined his remarks to the House floor and the *Congressional Record*, Powell was protected from libel suits under the Speech and Debate Clause of the Constitution. But when he appeared on a radio station in New York City and referred to Mrs. Esther James, a black woman with close ties to underworld figures, as a "bag lady," he no longer had immunity. Although very few doubted her association with mobsters, she was encouraged by some of Powell's enemies to sue the radio station, the program sponsor, and the congressman for defamation of character. The radio station and the sponsor were given the option of apologizing and paying a small fee as retribution. They agreed and arranged an out-of-court settlement for $1,500 each.

Powell refused to negotiate with attorneys representing Mrs. James. He sneered at the offer, mocked the suit, and ignored numerous pleas from his own attorney to appear in court. In April 1963, a jury returned a verdict in favor of Mrs. James, awarding her $200,000 for punitive damages and $11,500 for compensatory damages. Failing to make good on the judgment, Powell was cited for civil contempt of court.

Under New York state law, court arrest warrants in civil contempt cases could not be processed on Sunday. This legal quirk was a loophole made in heaven for the Right Reverend Powell. For more than two years, the congressman and pastor of the largest congregation in the city sashayed into town each Sunday after sunrise and scampered out again before sundown.

Excessive and derogatory media coverage alleging that Powell was guilty of misappropriating congressional funds and abusing his authority as chairman led some elected officials and taxpayers to demand his ouster from Congress. *The New York Times* was leader of the parade. The racism involved in the massive campaign to legislatively castrate Mr. Powell was quite apparent. National hysteria surrounded the activities of the powerful black congressman from Harlem.

On January 9, 1967, in an emotionally laden atmosphere—very similar to that of a lynch mob—the House Democratic Caucus voted 122 to 80 to strip Powell of his committee chairmanship. This stern, unprecedented action was taken even before any formal investigation had been conducted by the House of Representatives. The judgment was based entirely on newspaper accounts of Powell's behavior.

The next day, Representative Lionel Van Deerlin of California objected to seating Powell as a member of the House. According to longstanding procedures, Powell was then asked by the Speaker to stand aside. At this point Congressman Morris Udall of Arizona offered a resolution to seat Powell and to establish a committee of seven persons to examine witnesses, documents, and accusations relating to his conduct. The recommendation called for the select committee to report its findings back to the House within sixty days. Udall's resolution was rejected by a vote of 126 yeas to 305 nays.

At this point, Representative Gerald Ford of Michigan offered a motion to establish a committee of nine members to decide the question of Powell's right to be seated and to investigate the allegations. He also called for a delay in seating Powell until the committee reported back within five weeks. After much debate, that measure carried by a vote of 363 yeas to 65 nays, with three not voting.

The select committee appointed was chaired by Congressman Emanuel Celler of New York. The other eight members consisted of five democrats and four Republicans: James Corman (D–California), Claude Pepper (D–Florida), John Conyers (D–Michigan), Andy Jacobs (D–Indiana), Arch A. Moore (R–West Virginia), Charles M. Teague (R–California), Clark MacGregor (R–Minnesota), Vernon W. Thomson (R–Wisconsin). The committee conducted its investigation during the five-week period called for in the Ford motion and concluded:

> . . . Mr. Powell has repeatedly asserted a privilege and immunity from the processes of the courts of the state of New York not authorized by the Constitution.
>
> . . . As a member of Congress, Mr. Powell wrongfully and willfully appropriated $28,505.34 of public funds for his own use from July 31, 1965, to January 1, 1967, by allowing salary to be drawn on behalf of Y. Marjorie Flores as a clerk-hire employee when, in fact, she was his wife and not an employee in that she performed no official duties. . . .
>
> . . . Mr. Powell wrongfully and willfully appropriated $15,683.27 of public funds to his own use . . . by allowing clerk-hire to be drawn on behalf of Y. Marjorie Flores . . . when any duties performed by her were not performed by her in the state of New York or Washington, D.C., in violation of House Resolution 294. . . .
>
> . . . wrongfully and willfully appropriated $214.79 to his own use by

allowing Sylvia Givens to be placed on the staff . . . in order that she do domestic work in Bimini, the Bahama Islands. . . .

. . . wrongfully and willfully appropriated $72 by ordering committee air travel card to be used to purchase transportation for his son. . . .

. . . As chairman of the Committee on Education and Labor, Mr. Powell made false reports on expenditures of foreign exchange currency to the Committee on House Administration.[7]

In making its findings, the committee recommended that Powell be permitted to take the oath of office, be censured and condemned by the House, forfeit $40,000 in salary, be stripped of all seniority, and terminate the salary of Corrine Huff.

On March 1, 1967, the day the committee reported back to the full House, Gerald Ford, then the minority leader of the House (and later president of the United States), opposed the recommendations of the Celler Committee and the full House voted 222 to 202 to reject the report. That prepared the House for a vote not to seat the gentleman from New York.

A hurriedly drafted, handwritten amendment prepared by Arch Moore of the committee was offered by Congressman Thomas Curtis of Missouri as a substitute to the committee resolution. It read:

Resolved, that said Adam Clayton Powell, member-elect from the Eighteenth District of the state of New York, be and the same hereby is excluded from membership in the Ninetieth Congress and the Speaker shall notify the governor of the state of New York of the existing vacancy.[8]

The resolution passed by a vote of 307 to 116 with the support of many Democrats from both northern and southern districts. The next month, in a special election, the constituents of the Harlem district re-elected Powell by a margin of seven to one. But the House once again refused to seat him and the people of Harlem were without congressional representation for the next two years. In the interim, Powell remained in Bimini, his island retreat in the Bahamas.

After the federal district court and the federal court of appeals refused to hear Powell's case, he appealed to the Supreme Court of the United States. The Court ruled that Powell did meet all constitutional requirements for holding office, and in January 1969, on the same day that Shirley Chisholm, Louis Stokes, and I were sworn into office for the first time, Adam Clayton Powell, Jr., took the oath of office for the last time.

The Supreme Court did not have the power, however, to restore Powell to his former status as committee chairman. That prerogative was exclusively in the hands of the Democratic majority in the House of Representatives.

Powell, a once proud and powerful black man, now humiliated, depressed, and angry, literally gave up on the political system. Two years after the Court's decision in 1970, Charles Rangel defeated him for re-election by a margin of 150 votes. In 1972, Powell died of cancer at the age of sixty-three. His body was cremated and the ashes strewn over the waters near his beloved Bimini home.

CHARLES C. DIGGS, THE FATHER OF AFRICAN-AMERICAN FOREIGN RELATIONS

Charles C. Diggs, Jr., who hailed from Detroit, Michigan, was the next to join Dawson and Powell in the House of Representatives, swelling the ranks of blacks there to the impressive number of three. Black people, who constituted 12 percent of the population, now had the grand sum of less than 0.5 percent of the congressional representation.

Diggs was educated at the University of Michigan, Fisk University, and Wayne State University. While a law student in 1951, he became the youngest member ever elected to the Michigan State Senate. His father, Charles Sr., had been the first black member of the state senate.

In 1953, Diggs ran unsuccessfully for a seat on the Detroit Common Council. The following year, at the age of thirty-two, he was elected to the United States Congress and sworn in as one of its youngest members. The majority of his colleagues were well into their fifties and sixties. Many were in their eighties. In those days, because retirement benefits were so dismal, very few congressmen retired.

Diggs received nationwide publicity as a result of his eagerness to speak out against violence afflicted upon black people that was sanctioned by the larger white community. He was immediately inundated with requests to investigate specific incidents of racial injustice. I myself was prompted to call upon him for assistance even before he was sworn into the Congress.

In late 1954, I was a member of the Army Chemical Corps stationed at Fort McClellan, Alabama. In direct contravention of President Harry S. Truman's 1948 Executive Order 9981 banning racial segregation on military facilities, the post was thoroughly and officially segregated by race. Despite the sincere efforts of President Dwight D. Eisenhower to wipe away the last vestiges of racial separation in the military, in 1954, Fort McClellan still resisted with all the insobriety of the last Confederate general and the insolence of the last Confederate infantryman. I was forced to soldier at a military facility that prohibited blacks from getting a haircut except on Saturday, when a black barber was brought in from a nearby town; that closed the NCO club to blacks on Thursdays, when white girls were imported from Anniston, Alabama, for dances; that had a "whites only" PX restaurant; and that kept blacks out of the swimming pool by claiming it was reserved for National Guardsmen in training.

Under the circumstances, I became incensed and organized a campaign among the black soldiers to protest these illegal activities. We picketed the post restaurant, blocked the doors at the NCO club, boycotted the barbershop for several months (many refused to get haircuts), and I, along with my wife and several kids from the housing project where we lived off post, swept past the guard at the swimming pool and integrated it.

At that point, the commanding officer of the post threatened to court-martial me. I immediately appealed to Congressman-elect Diggs to investigate the situation and also to inquire into the allegations of racial discrimination at the newly constructed Women's Army Corps (WAC) unit. The story made national news, and shortly thereafter I was transferred back to an army base in Missouri. Later Diggs did initiate a full-scale investigation.

Diggs was involved in many similar matters. He was a prominent figure in attempting to bring to justice the gang of white Mississippi hooligans who lynched Emmett Till, a fourteen-year-old black child from Chicago.

During the period of outright war against blacks in the South, Diggs was there on many occasions when it was extremely dangerous. On one such occasion he was in Mississippi encouraging blacks to register and demanding that the Department of Justice give them protection in exercising their right to vote. While he was a guest in the home of Aaron Henry, president of the state NAACP, a bomb completely destroyed Henry's home. Miraculously, Diggs, Henry, and Henry's wife and daughter emerged from the rubble unharmed.

In 1970, at the age of forty-eight, upon the retirement of Bill Dawson and the death of Adam Powell, Diggs became the senior black member of Congress.

His leadership in espousing the causes of black Africans and exposing the racist policies of this country in dealing with them significantly raised the level of black consciousness about the importance of strengthening ties with the African continent. As chairman of the Subcommittee on Africa for more than a decade, he succeeded in obtaining financial assistance programs for newly independent African states. He was considered by his colleagues as the principal authority on and spokesman for U.S.–Africa relations.

The people of Africa became very attached to Charlie Diggs and held him in high esteem because of his efforts in promoting programs beneficial to their interests. In 1959, Diggs was appointed to the Committee on Foreign Affairs, a slot he had coveted since coming to Congress four years earlier. His interest in Africa peaked in 1957, when he accompanied Vice President Richard Nixon on a tour of Africa, and then in 1958, when he attended the All-African Peoples Conference in Accra, Ghana.

After becoming chairman of the Subcommittee on African Affairs, Diggs intensified his efforts to assist the grossly neglected countries of sub-Sahara Africa. In 1973, he was made chairman of an eighteen-group coalition that lobbied the government to provide $30 million in famine relief to the drought-stricken Sahel region.

On one occasion, Representatives Louis Stokes, Walter Fauntroy, and I accompanied him to five African countries. The welcome Diggs received in each was befitting a head of state. In Sierra Leone, our plane did not arrive until after one o'clock in the morning. But when it did land, more than 10,000 people who had waited almost four hours to greet Congressman Diggs honored him in song and dance as if he were a Messiah, not a black congressman from Detroit.

During his twenty-six years in the House, Diggs led black Americans to a more caring, more sensitive, more enlightened foreign policy toward Africa and the Caribbean. He had such strong convictions that he walked out of the Twenty-sixth Session of the United Nations General Assembly in protest of American policy toward Africa, thereby bringing public attention to the issue. He stormed out of the General Assembly because the White House had instructed him to vote against several key resolutions condemning South Africa's system of apartheid.

Another significant contribution by Diggs was the establishment of TransAfrica as the major Washington, D.C., lobbying group for African nations. Diggs was not the founder of the organization; however, Randall Robinson, its executive director and founder, cut his wisdom teeth on black African issues while serving as a staff assistant to Diggs.

Diggs consistently allowed Robinson the flexibility and provided him with the opportunity to meet key players in most of the independent black countries.

The long and glorious career of Congressman Diggs ended sadly with his resignation in 1980, shortly after he was convicted of federal income tax evasion and misuse of public funds. It is unfortunate that his sterling record of accomplishment was blemished in this fashion. But even more tragic is that after Diggs suffered his personal humiliation and served his time in prison, not one African nation offered him a contract to represent their interests here in the United States.*

*These same African nations hire hundreds of consultants and other agents, some of whom also run afoul of the law. Most African countries are represented by large white law firms that employ many ex-members of Congress. Seldom, if ever, do they check to ascertain if any professional staff include former white officeholders who have been forced to resign from Congress or from the presidential staff.

There is nothing novel or unusual about friends in foreign countries affording preferential treatment to former government officials who get in trouble with the law. The case of Vice President Spiro T. Agnew is typical of the way in which some politicians are rewarded for past services. He was forced to resign from office in 1973 after pleading "no contest" (guilty) to income tax evasion. In return, the government agreed not to prosecute him for extortion and bribery. He was sentenced to three years unsupervised probation and fined $10,000.

During his period of probation, Agnew became wealthy as an agent of many firms controlled by the same Arab interests that he protected while vice-president.

Richard Nixon left the presidency in shame and disgrace, but friends who profited financially from his recognition of Communist China provided handsomely for his luxurious living.

Consideration should have been given to Diggs, a stalwart defender and promoter of black Africa's interests. But black African nations persist in hiring only white firms to represent them. These nations spend millions of dollars annually in this country with white-owned firms. Not a single African nation has entered into a meaningful contract with a black-owned American company.

In 1990, a white public relations firm, ProService, handled Nelson Mandela's tour of the United States. Niger, Zaire, and Liberia are represented in the United States by a white-owned public relations firm whose president is a convicted felon. Edward J. van Kloberg III, the head of van Kloberg and Associates, in Washington, D.C., was sentenced in U.S. federal court to five years probation and 100 hours community service in 1984 for fraud.

Liberia's President Samuel K. Doe signed an $800,000, nineteen-month public relations contract with van Kloberg even though Liberia at the time was $800 million in debt and rice and gasoline were running short in the country.

Paul Manafort admitted during criminal investigations of scandals at the Department of Housing and Urban Development that he had engaged in "influence-peddling" while pursuing HUD contracts for clients. Manafort is a

It is too bad that the "prophet" of the continent could not himself "profit" from the tens of millions of dollars he was responsible for delivering to African governments and to firms doing business in African nations.

ROBERT NIX, AN ORGANIZATION MAN

In 1958, Robert N. C. Nix of Philadelphia joined Dawson, Powell, and Diggs as the fourth black sitting in Congress. His election represented a personal reward for many years of dedicated, tireless battles in the political trenches of Philadelphia. He was an organization man who earned his way to the top by working the precincts in South Philly. He was first elected committeeman of the Forty-fourth Ward back in 1932 and held that position for more than thirty years. A graduate of the University of Pennsylvania Law School, he later served as special state deputy attorney and then as special assistant deputy attorney for the Commonwealth of Pennsylvania.

Bob Nix, unlike Ralph Metcalfe, a black congressman associated with the political machine of Chicago's Mayor Daley, was never able to divorce himself from the white-run political machine that hand-picked him to represent the black inner-city congressional district in Philadelphia. For his entire tenure, he continued to function as a ward politician. Promoting the national black agenda was definitely not on his list of priorities. He often insisted that he was a "congressman first, a Democrat second, and a black third."

When named chairman of the House Post Office and Civil Service Committee, Nix became only the third member of his race to chair a full committee of the United States House of Representatives. His elevation to the chairmanship was made possible by the decision of Representative David Henderson of North Carolina not to seek re-election. This left a vacancy that everyone expected to be filled by Morris Udall of Arizona, who was next in seniority. But the election of Jim Wright (D–Texas) to House majority leader altered the situation by opening up two other committee chairmanships—Public Works and Interior. Udall opted for the Interior Committee because of its relatively greater value to his state.

Some younger white members of the Post Office and Civil Service

senior partner in the firm of Black, Manafort, Stone and Kelly, which represents Jonas Savimbi and the UNITA faction in Angola and also President Daniel Arap Moi of Kenya.

Committee and even a few committee staffers organized a campaign to oppose Nix's rise to chairman. They contended that his age, sixty-eight years old, and his "record of inactivity" made him unfit for the position. They supported James Hanley, a New York congressman, but their scheme faltered and died when I intervened on behalf of the Congressional Black Caucus.

"Clay worked it very cleverly," one committee member said. "He took it on almost by himself. He called a meeting of the [Democratic] committee members, including Nix, and said that the committee would fare well under Nix because he would give the members wide latitude. He also threatened that he and other members of the [Black] Caucus would make a big fuss if Nix didn't get the chairmanship," the committee member said.[9]

The committee member was extremely kind in describing my remarks as threatening to "make a big fuss." Actually, I threatened to "kick some ass." I did say that members would have "wide latitude." Those code words were a state-of-the-art phrase meant to allay any fears on the part of several members that Nix would prove domineering and also indicating my conviction that Nix would be cooperative with other committee members. I never dreamed, however, that he would totally abdicate his authority and surrender the power vested in a chairman.

His election as chairman accrued no particular benefits to those of us struggling to increase the power of blacks in the House. Under his leadership, white staffers continued to hold all of the high-paying committee positions, and white congressmen continued to make all of the major decisions.

After many arguments and a few loud confrontations between the two of us, Nix finally agreed to hire a black attorney. But when the white staff director refused to assign the newly hired attorney any meaningful committee tasks, Nix sided with the staff director. For three years, this black professional was never included in staff meetings and was permitted to drift aimlessly until finally he resigned in disgust.

Chairman Nix also allowed himself to be manipulated by President Carter, who attempted to undermine the basic interests of federal employees by changing the law to drastically reduce employee job security. Carter proclaimed civil service reform the centerpiece of his domestic policy. The 1978 Civil Service Reform Act debate was a classic case of the executive branch and the Congress disagreeing, sometimes strenuously, on the means to achieve that goal.

In transmitting his proposed legislation to Congress, President Carter said it was "intended to increase the government's efficiency by placing new emphasis on the quality of performance by federal workers . . . [and] to reduce the red tape and costly delay in the present personnel system."[10]

A cursory reading of the bill quickly revealed that what the president wanted was to reduce employee rights and protection. The media barrage accompanying the announcement stressed how difficult it was to "fire" employees and how few had been removed during the preceding year. According to Carter, "The sad fact is that it is easier to promote and transfer incompetent employees than to get rid of them."[11]

Two stated purposes of the bill were, first, to improve labor–management relations and, second, to appoint a special counsel to investigate and prosecute political abuses and merit system violations. The problem was the bill did not contain any labor–management relations provisions and the proposed special counsel was a "paper tiger."

The proposal met with little enthusiasm in the Post Office and Civil Service Committee. The president sensed the determination of members on the subcommittee, which I chaired, to protect basic, long-standing employee rights. Congressman Bill Ford of Michigan, Congresswoman Pat Schroeder of Colorado, and I insisted on providing "due process" for federal employees. To get around our position, Carter entered into an underhanded deal with Nix and Udall to ignore time-honored committee procedure, and Chairman Nix refused to refer the bill to my subcommittee. Instead, he agreed to handle the bill at the full committee level and appointed Udall to chair special hearings.

The Carter-Nix-Udall combine proceeded to "develop" its own labor–management relations proposal without consulting those of us who were most familiar with the subject. They chose instead to "negotiate" with the largest federal employee union, the American Federation of Government Employees (AFGE). Particularly disturbing to us were elements of the proposals that would reduce long-standing statutory protection enjoyed by civil servants. Due process rights would be diluted significantly, the degree of proof necessary to fire a worker for cause would be lessened considerably, and the measures protecting so-called whistle-blowers were all empty vessels. The proposals brought to the committee included no improvements in such key areas as the scope of bargaining, union security, and processes for resolution of disputes. All federal employee unions other than the AFGE soundly criticized the plan and joined forces with those of us on the committee who opposed it.

While the Carter administration was negotiating with AFGE, Ford, Schroeder, and I developed our own bill (H.R. 9094), which eventually became the labor–management relations vehicle in the House. We were able to push through so many amendments to the bill that Title VII, the labor–management relations section, emerged virtually as our bill. At one point I succeeded in attaching the Hatch Act Reform legislation as an amendment. During subsequent consideration by the full House, this provision was stripped from the bill through a parliamentary maneuver. However, the House on September 13, 1978, voted 381 to 0 to adopt a substitute amendment offered by Mr. Udall that embodied the agreements reached between the Carter administration and us.

In 1978, Nix faced stiff opposition for re-election. A young black minister, William Gray, challenged him for a second time. Two years earlier, Nix had defeated the Reverend Gray by less than 300 votes. I remember as if it were yesterday a high-ranking officer of the American Postal Workers Union and a top White House staffer visiting me on Capitol Hill and pleading with me to visit Philadelphia to campaign for Nix. I also remember what a pleasure it was to inform them that black citizens would be better represented by the young pastor of Bright Hope Baptist Church.

After being elected ten consecutive times and serving twenty years in office, Congressman Robert N. C. Nix was defeated in 1978 by the Reverend William H. Gray III.

AUGUSTUS F. HAWKINS, THE FATHER OF FULL EMPLOYMENT

Augustus F. Hawkins, affectionately called by his friends the half-century man of elective politics, came to the House of Representatives from the city of Los Angeles in 1963. He was first elected to public office in 1934 as a member of the California State Assembly and served there continuously for the next twenty-eight years. Often, during that period, he was the only black in the assembly. He would probably still be in the state assembly if he had remained the only black member through 1962.

That same year, as the Democrat with the most seniority in the assembly, Hawkins ran for the position of Speaker. He lost that race to Jesse Unrah by one vote. The one-vote difference was cast by none other than the only other black member of the legislative body, Byron Rumford, a druggist from Berkeley. Ironically, Hawkins had played an instrumental role in raising money to elect Rumford to the assembly.

At the time of the race for Speaker, Hawkins was actively supporting a proposal by Governor Earl Warren to institute prepaid health insurance. The California medical community, doctors in particular, were vehemently opposed to the plan. Apparently, Rumford felt a closer allegiance to the medical community than to the black community, which would have benefited significantly from passage of the measure. Another vote that could have made the difference for Hawkins was cast instead for Jesse Unrah by the most prominent white liberal in the assembly, Phillip Burton.

At any rate, disappointed by losing the race for Speaker, Hawkins ran for and was elected to Congress the following year. Many years later, Jim Wright defeated the same Phil Burton by one vote for the position of majority leader of the United States House of Representatives. Capitol Hill insiders claim that Hawkins engaged in a little payback activity and cast that one decisive vote.

Hawkins' fifty-eight years as an elected official marked him as one of the nation's most experienced legislators. He was dubbed the "Silent Warrior" by fellow Black Caucus members because of his quiet, patient demeanor. He was described by friend and foe alike as one who pursued legislative goals untiringly and approached the resolution of problems in a methodical way.

The Hawkins-Humphrey Full Employment Bill

Hawkins' greatest accomplishment was undoubtedly H.R. 50, the Full Employment and Balanced Growth Act, better known as the Hawkins-Humphrey Full Employment Act. (He was coauthor of the bill with Senator Hubert H. Humphrey.) Hawkins was architect and chief engineer in promoting passage of the bill in the House. He was responsible for drafting the nuts and bolts part of the bill and presided over 200 hours of hearings at which noted economists, fiscal officers, labor leaders, and corporate executives testified. (Hawkins was chairman of the Education and Labor Committee, which followed a stint as chairman of the Committee on House Administration.)

Thanks to the efforts of Leon Keyserling, who had been chairman of the Council of Economic Advisers during the Truman administration, the original bill was a tough, no-nonsense piece of legislation calling for effective remedies to redress the woes of unemployment in the American economic system. It envisioned the federal government as the employer of "last resort," mandating full employment even if the government had to create public service jobs through programs such as those created during the Great Depression.

H.R. 50 was cosponsored by sixty-nine members of the House, including the entire membership of the Congressional Black Caucus. Hawkins, in rallying support for the full employment bill, made many public appearances. Speaking before the first National Full Employment Conference, held on June 24, 1975, at the Statler-Hilton Hotel in Washington, D.C., he said:

> To be in the business of merely transferring jobs from males to females, or from white to blacks . . . makes no sense at all . . . unless we, of course, reject full employment as a dream which must be postponed for better days. . . . Let us not be fooled or divided by misuse of the phrase "full employment" as indicating a tolerable level of unemployment. H.R. 50 rejects this meaning. . . . Impertinent are the claims of our friends who endorse full employment as a concept but reject it as politically unfeasible.[12]

Perhaps the biggest enemy of the original bill's concept was President Jimmy Carter. He insisted on the inclusion of crippling provisions in exchange for his support. Some original cosponsors of the bill found his actions so obnoxious and so disgusting that they literally held their noses when voting for its passage. Carter's insistence on an amendment calling for the rate of inflation to drop to 3 percent by 1988 before the provisions of the bill would be triggered rendered the final version totally impotent. That bail-out amendment gutted the legislation to the point that even though the bill was signed into law by President Carter on October 27, 1978, no one was ever required to obey it.

The Carter administration in its 1979 Economic Report projected unemployment rates of 6.2 percent, 5.4 percent, 4.6 percent, and 4 percent, respectively, for the next four years. Projections for 1979 and 1980 were obviously too high, and Representative Hawkins argued that the administration's economic plan was a violation of the intent of the Hawkins-Humphrey Act. He said the plan would make it all but impossible to reach the mid-1983 goals of 4 percent unemployment overall and 3 percent for those aged twenty and older. Keyserling accused the Carter administration of being "in flagrant violation of the Humphrey-Hawkins Full Employment and Balanced Growth Act of 1978."[13]

Hawkins termed the president's actions a violation of "the letter and spirit of the law" and called for policy alternatives to those proposed by the president. Senator Jacob Javits of New York joined him in his demand for a review of the Carter timetable. Carter ignored the criticism and lost the 1980 presidential election to Ronald Reagan, an election in which many blacks refused to actively support an incumbent Democrat whose domestic economic policies did less for workers and the poor than those of his Republican predecessors, Nixon and Ford.

Congressman Hawkins, during his tenure of office, was also instrumental in the creation of the Action Volunteer Agency, which administers such programs as the Peace Corps, VISTA, and Foster Grandparents.

He announced in January 1990 that he would not seek re-election after serving twenty-eight years in the House of Representatives. Following in the footsteps of former chairmen of the Education and Labor Committee Adam C. Powell and Carl Perkins, Hawkins frequently found himself in the "eye of the legislative storm." (The committee is still the breeding ground for initiatives on controversial issues such as child care, pension rights, labor policy, and educational entitlements, not to mention a score of other hotly contested legislative proposals.)

JOHN CONYERS, JR., MR. CIVIL LIBERTY

John Conyers, Jr., was elected from the First District of Michigan to represent the city of Detroit in 1964. The creation of a new predominantly black-populated congressional district enticed many candidates to seek the position. But only two emerged as serious contenders, John Conyers, Jr., and Richard Austin. Austin, Michigan's first black certified public accountant, was owner of an accounting firm and active in community affairs. Conyers, a referee in the Michigan Workmen's Compensation Department and senior partner in the law firm of Conyers, Bell and Townsend, had substantial support among members of the United Auto Workers Union, where his father was a union organizer.

There was a remarkable difference in the style of the campaigns conducted by Austin and Conyers and between the views expressed by the two. Conyers took the initiative in promoting a bold program calling for jobs, justice, and peace. He also attacked the local police for brutalizing black citizens. Charges of police brutality were widespread not only in the usual confines of the poorer neighborhoods, but also in upper middle-class areas. Black professionals driving Cadillacs in tree-lined affluent residential neighborhoods did not feel any safer in the presence of white law enforcement officers than blacks loitering on street corners in the ghettoes.

Although Austin differed very little with Conyers on the question of jobs, justice, and police brutality, he was less aggressive in pursuing these matters as bedrock campaign issues. In addition, because of his nonconfrontational behavior, he was seen by some as a typical establishment candidate.

The major and perhaps decisive issue, however, was the war in Southeast Asia. Austin supported the efforts of President Johnson in waging the Vietnam "police action." Conyers, on the other hand, was an outspoken critic of the war. He denied there was a legitimate American interest to be fought for in Vietnam, and attacked the president, the military/industrial complex, and his opponent for supporting a costly, senseless endeavor that was disrupting communities and wreaking havoc on families.

Many political analysts credit his position on this issue for Conyers' narrow victory over Austin. Out of the 60,000 votes cast in the Democratic primary for the numerous candidates, Conyers received 16,249 votes to beat Richard Austin by a slim margin of 108 votes. In a recount, the margin was reduced to 45 votes.*

In the 1964 general election, the path for Conyers was much smoother. He faced a black candidate, Robert B. Blackwell, and defeated him with 84 percent of the vote (138,589 to 25,735).

Dapper, articulate, and smart, John Conyers, Jr., was welcomed to the Washington scene with an unusual but complimentary display of fanfare. Labeled a visionary and a revolutionary by the press, he was regarded as a man of uncharacteristic courage and tenacity. The civil rights and civil liberties community recognized his militant voice would bolster and complement the efforts of veteran black legislators such as Powell, Dawson, and Hawkins.

It was not necessary for Conyers to spend countless months familiar-

---

*Austin ran for mayor of Detroit in 1969 and lost by only 6,000 votes. In 1970, he ran statewide for the office of Michigan secretary of state and was elected. Both times John Conyers supported his efforts. Austin is still the secretary of state.

izing himself with Capitol Hill procedures, because he'd spent three years as a legislative assistant to Democratic Congressman John Dingell of Michigan.

Within days of taking the oath of office, Conyers was deeply immersed in promoting the Medicare legislation recommended by President Johnson, and also in leading the fight for passage of the 1965 Voting Rights Act.

Over the years John Conyers has used the prestige of his office to fight the crippling ravages of racism and sexism. During his many years in Congress, Conyers has won particular acclaim for legislative initiatives in the areas of social justice and economic opportunity. Perhaps his greatest legislative feat was the passage of the Martin Luther King, Jr., Holiday Bill.

The Fight for a Federal Dr. Martin Luther King, Jr., Holiday

It took fifteen arduous years to realize the dream of establishing a national holiday celebrating Dr. Martin Luther King, Jr.'s, birthday. Only three individuals in the history of this country had previously been honored by having a federal holiday declared in their names: George Washington, our first president, Abraham Lincoln, and Christopher Columbus, generally acknowledged as discoverer of the New World.

During those fifteen years the legislative battle was spearheaded by Representative Conyers and the Congressional Black Caucus (CBC). Conyers' efforts were stymied in four successive presidential administrations: those of Nixon, Ford, Carter, and Reagan. Three of the presidents openly opposed the bill. The other, Jimmy Carter, was much more subtle but equally effective in blocking its passage. His hidden agenda was more detrimental than the others because it was less known but, in effect, just as callous.

The bill was initially introduced by Conyers in 1968, only four days after Dr. King's assassination. But it failed to reach the House floor for a vote. At the time, support for the bill was sparse and many thought its introduction merely a political gesture on the part of Conyers. Few realized his dogged determination and persistence in building a groundswell of support for the bill.

Conyers enlisted the aid of the King family and the Southern Christian Leadership Conference (SCLC) in this endeavor. The Reverend Ralph Abernathy, who succeeded Dr. King as president of the

SCLC, started a petition drive that resulted in 800,000 signatures. He traveled to Washington and personally presented the petition to President Nixon, but to no avail.

Conyers reintroduced his bill again in 1971, and Senator Edward Brooke did the same in the Senate. This time the Reverend Abernathy launched a petition drive that secured more than 3 million signatures and personally brought them by train to the White House. At one point, the corridors of the Cannon House Office Building were lined with U.S. Postal Service bags containing more than a million pieces of mail from supporters of the bill.

Later, Conyers and twenty-four other House members met with sixty-five mayors, urging them to make their own proclamations and to engage in their own January 15 celebrations. Shortly thereafter, Nelson Rockefeller, governor of New York, and John Lindsay, mayor of New York City, organized celebrations for state and city employees. The mayor of St. Louis and the governor of Maine also proclaimed the date a holiday and arranged for appropriate tributes to Dr. King.

By the time of final passage of the bill, ten states and the District of Columbia had legally established January 15 as the Dr. King holiday. These were: California, Connecticut, Illinois, Kentucky, Maine, Massachusetts, New Jersey, Rhode Island, South Carolina and Wisconsin. Four others—New York, Michigan, Ohio, and West Virginia—designated a different date to honor Dr. King's contributions to his country. However, for nine consecutive years, the Georgia legislature refused to enact a bill declaring a holiday in honor of its native son, the most celebrated crusader for freedom and justice. (Today, all but two states—New Hampshire and Montana—celebrate Dr. King's birthday as a holiday.)

House Speaker Thomas P. ("Tip") O'Neill, Jr., appointed Congressmen Stokes and Fauntroy to conduct official investigations into the assassinations of John F. Kennedy and Dr. Martin Luther King, Jr. When their committee concluded the inquiries and issued final reports, pressure to pass the Dr. King Holiday Bill increased dramatically.

In 1980, the bill fell a mere five votes short of passage. Conyers said, "We were short a few votes. But I think the momentum that builds up every year around King is sincere and genuine across America. And I think that we're finally coming to the period where we're going to do it."[14]

President Carter Opposes the Bill

The greatest disappointment to proponents of the King holiday legislation was the lack of support from President James Earl Carter. "Jimmy" would not have have been elected president without the efforts of the Reverend Martin L. King, Sr., Coretta King, and Andrew Young. It was their activity among black voters on his behalf in the early Democratic primaries that put him so far ahead of the other candidates that they were never able to catch up.

After the election and throughout Carter's four years in office, the attitude coming from the White House toward the bill was so negative that Coretta King openly voiced dissatisfaction with the manner in which Carter was acting. The Reverend Joseph Lowery, president of the SCLC, and Bill Lucy, secretary-treasurer of the American Federation of State, County and Municipal Workers Union, publicly attacked the president for his neutral stance on the bill.

While the president publicly conveyed the impression of neither supporting nor opposing the bill, his political operatives were actively working behind the scenes for its defeat. On December 5, 1979, during the final days of the Ninety-fifth Congress, a substitute to the Conyers' bill was offered by Representative Beard of Tennessee, calling for the celebration of Dr. King's birthday on the third Sunday in January. Conyers argued,

> [It] is patently clear that if we are to follow the precepts of this legislation that has been in the House for eleven years, we can in no way assume that we will be passing a legal holiday for Martin Luther King with an amendment that specifically says this will not be a legal holiday.[15]

Despite vigorous opposition by Conyers and other members of the Black Caucus, this crippling amendment passed by a vote of 207 to 191.

No White House lobbyists were in evidence during the debate, but Hamilton Jordan, a chief aide to President Carter, was reported to have called legislators from Georgia, Alabama, and Mississippi to encourage their opposition to the Conyers bill. Apparently, Jordan worked his list quite effectively. On the key motion offered by Beard, nine of eleven congressmen from the president's home state of Georgia voted to cripple the legislation. Only Wyche Fowler and Billy Evans supported the Congressional Black Caucus position.

THE LONELY YEARS: FEW BLACKS IN CONGRESS

Popular songwriter, singer, composer, and activist Steveland "Stevie" Wonder provided the movement with a tremendous rallying instrument in 1981 when he wrote a song in honor of Dr. King's birthday entitled "Happy Birthday." That emotional uplift, plus the march to the Capitol that Wonder organized for King's birthday, dramatized the urgency of the issue and enlisted millions of grassroots supporters to press for passage of the bill.

In 1983, Congressman William Ford, chairman of the House Post Office and Civil Service Committee and like Conyers a Democrat from Michigan, supported Katie Hall, a freshman House member from Indiana, for chairman of the subcommittee that had primary jurisdiction over the Conyers holiday bill. Hall introduced her own bill designating the third Monday in January as the day to commemorate Dr. King. Her committee held hearings and on July 3, 1983, passed the bill out of subcommittee. Chairman Ford, a key supporter of the bill, called for a full committee mark-up and reported the bill to the House floor for a vote in August.

Once again Conyers went about organizing grassroots groups to pressure their representatives to vote for the Dr. King Holiday Bill. He argued once again that it was imperative that a day be set aside to review our history in order to portray the ideas for which Dr. King lived, preached, taught, and died. This time the vote was more favorable than the last, as the House passed the bill by an overwhelming majority, 338 to 90.

Senate Majority Leader Howard Baker, also a supporter of the legislation, permitted the House version of the bill to bypass time-consuming committee review procedures by sending it directly to the floor of the Senate for a vote. In spite of the objections of senators such as North Carolina's Jesse Helms, the measure passed the Senate by a vote of 78 to 22.

Conyers, who had led the struggle to enact the holiday bill, and other supporters were fully aware of the Carter administration's hostility toward the bill.

Enactment of the Dr. King Holiday Bill represented a strange twist of fate. Jimmy Carter, who owed his election to the King family and to black voters, was president when both houses of Congress were controlled by members of his party, yet claimed to be unable to persuade Congress to enact the Dr. King Holiday Bill. On the other hand, Ronald Reagan, an avowed opponent of both Dr. King and the holiday bill, serving with the Republicans in control of the Senate, had the distinction of signing into law the bill designating a national holiday for Dr. Martin Luther King, Jr.*

As of 1992, John Conyers, Jr., following in the footsteps of Bill Dawson, is chairman of the House Committee on Government Operations and also a senior member of the Judiciary Committee.

THE STAYING POWER OF BLACK CONGRESSPERSONS

Those lonely years experienced by DePriest, Dawson, Powell, and others in the beginning were not to become a permanent condition for black members of Congress. In the early seventies, a dramatic increase occurred in the number of black elected officials at local, state, and national levels. In the House of Representatives the number of blacks increased from six in 1968 to sixteen in 1973.

Three events were primarily responsible for this significant increase in black officials: First, passage of the 1965 Voting Rights Act by Congress enabled blacks to register and vote in large numbers throughout the southern states. Second, the 1964 Supreme Court ruling affirming "one man, one vote" required redrawing legislative districts at all levels of elective government, with equal weight given to each vote cast. Third, the federal court decision declaring unconstitutional the "gerrymandering" of districts to diminish the influence of minority voters played an important role in the increase of black elected officials in every sector of the country.

Prior to these legislative and judicial fiats, most state laws failed to give adequate protection to the rights of the minority voting public. Government tacitly approved the monopoly of power in the hands of politicoes who flagrantly disregarded the rights of American citizens.

In Illinois, which was by no means an exception to the rule, 914,053 persons constituted one congressional district, while in rural Michigan there was a district with only 177,431 residents. The disproportionate ratio meant that voters in the Michigan district were five times more

---

*Just two weeks prior to signing the bill on November 22, 1983, President Reagan had restated his opposition to the legislation, taking sides with Senator Helms. In response to a question from the press asking if the senator was justified in demanding that the FBI release files allegedly showing Dr. King as a communist, President Reagan glibly remarked, "Well, we'll know in thirty-five years, won't we?" Later he apologized to Mrs. Coretta King, widow of the slain civil rights crusader.

represented than those in the Illinois district. Put another way, it meant that one vote in the Michigan district was equal to five votes in the Illinois district.

In both the North and the South, most districts where large numbers of blacks resided were so drawn as to dilute the importance of the black vote.

After the "one man, one vote" decision, state legislatures were forced to create districts that made it possible for blacks and other minorities to be elected. As a result, as of early 1992 twenty-five blacks sit in the House of Representatives as compared to only six in the mid-sixties. A majority have been elected from districts much like those held by southern Democrats prior to the Voting Rights Act and the court decision outlawing districts designed to dilute the voting strength of minority citizens.

Blacks elected to Congress in the twentieth century, as a group, rate in the top percentile on all criteria used for measuring effective legislative performance. We are rated above the national average in educational attainment, intelligence, oratorical skills, and ability to work amiably with colleagues. Most importantly, we come from districts respectful enough and appreciative enough to send us back time and again, so that we accumulate that most precious asset, seniority.

The defeat of Arthur Mitchell of Chicago by William H. Dawson in 1942 signaled the beginning of a new era for blacks in national politics. It inaugurated a procession of black members to Congress who gained tenure through longevity. Dawson became the first of a long line of blacks elected to Congress who were consistently re-elected and amassed sufficient seniority to wield significant influence on legislation.

Dawson was the first, but certainly not the last, to be re-elected time and time again. The four blacks following him each served more than twenty years. Since power in the House of Representatives is decided on the basis of seniority, political pundits sanction this kind of constituent behavior (re-electing the incumbent) and hail it as the most practical and intelligent use of the right to vote.

Government positions, including seats in the United States Congress, are not as attractive to a large segment of upper middle-class whites as they are to the elite of black America. Whites with an above average education, intelligence, communication skills, and ability to get along with others fare much better in the private sector than in government. Opportunities providing far greater financial and social remuneration await them in companies listed in the *Fortune* 500.

On the other hand, blacks who succeed in getting elected to public office are viewed by their constituents as having reached the top of the ladder. Because opportunities in business, academia, law, medicine, and other professions are so limited, a career in politics becomes attractive to some of the best talent in the black community.

When I came to Congress in 1969, white Democrats from southern and border states who represented less than 20 percent of House members chaired 71 percent of the standing House committees. They held absolute authority over fifteen of the twenty-one House committees. The state of Texas alone had four persons serving as full committee chairmen: W. R. Poage, Agriculture; George H. Mahon, Appropriations; Wright Patman, Banking and Currency; and Olin E. Teague, Veterans Affairs.

Wilbur Mills of Arkansas chaired the powerful Ways and Means Committee. South Carolina had two chairpersons: L. Mendel Rivers, Armed Services; and John L. McMillan, District of Columbia. William Colmer of Mississippi chaired the Rules Committee, and Carl D. Perkins of Kentucky presided over Education and Labor. Representatives from border states chaired another four committees: Samuel N. Friedel, Edward Garmatz, and George H. Fallon of Maryland chaired House Administration, Merchant Marines, and Public Works, respectively. Richard Ichord of Missouri was chairman of the Internal Security Committee. All these assignments were based solely on seniority.

Today, black members of Congress have compiled a record of seniority comparable to that of their southern colleagues in past Congresses. By virtue of our longevity, we are now moving into positions of influence on important committees. In 1988, blacks chaired five full committees and two special committees: Augustus Hawkins, Education and Labor; Ron Dellums, District of Columbia; Louis Stokes, Permanent Select Committee on Intelligence; Julian Dixon, Standards of Official Conduct; and William Gray, Budget. Charles Rangel chaired the Select Committee on Narcotics Abuse and Control. Mickey Leland chaired the Select Committee on Hunger. Eighteen black members chaired key subcommittees. When most of us first entered the Congress, we opposed the system of seniority as archaic and unfair. But the longer we stay, the more modern and progressive it appears.

Of the fifteen blacks elected to the House from the time of Dawson in 1942 until Parren Mitchell of Baltimore in 1970, eleven served more than twenty years. Two of the four who did not, Ralph Metcalfe and George Collins, both of Chicago, died while in office. Collins was killed in an airplane crash. His wife replaced him and has been re-elected for nine two-year terms. Shirley Chisholm of New York and Parren Mitchell of Maryland voluntarily stepped down after serving fourteen years each.

Election to Congress is a great honor and a unique distinction. During the more than 200-year history of the country, only 2,683 persons have served in the United States Senate and only 9,421 in the House of Representatives.

Election to ten terms or more is an even more singular honor. Through the One Hundredth Congress, which ended December 1988, only 434 had achieved the status of serving twenty years or more. Twelve black members are in that special group: Dawson, Powell, Nix, Diggs, Hawkins, Conyers, Stokes, Dellums, Rangel, Fauntroy, Collins, and I.

In his book *Black Political Power in America*, author Chuck Stone predicts, "In a nation that owes its viability to politics, black politicians will continue to grow in prestige and numbers, and their stars will not fall before the world has 'rightly gauged their brightness.' "[16]

True! The real history of blacks in politics has always been written by courageous men and women hitching their bright stars to the ballot box, men and women who have not hesitated to wage a constant battle against prejudice and the threat of political annihilation.

NOTES

1. Bruce A. Ragsdale and Joel D. Treese, *Black Americans in Congress 1870–1989*, Washington, D.C.: Library of Congress, 1989, page 30.

2. Congressman William L. Dawson, speech on the floor of the House, *Congressional Record*, April 12, 1951, page 3765.

3. Eddie T. Arnold and Dr. Bobby Williams, *The Washington North Star*, September 22, 1983, page S-2.

4. J. Wyatt Mondesire, *High Priest of Harlem*, cited in *Point of View*, CBC Foundation publication, Winter 1987, page 26.

5. Adam Clayton Powell, Jr., Black Position Paper, cited in the *Black Scholar*, December 1969, page 10.

6. *New York Times*, July 21, 1955, page 14, column 4.

7. Excerpts from Report of the House Select Committee to Investigate Adam Clayton Powell, *Congressional Record*, March 1, 1967, page 4997.

8. *Ibid.*, page 5020.

9. Warren Brown, in the *Washington Post*, January 1, 1977.

10. Message from the president of the United States, James Carter, transmitting a draft of Proposed Legislation to Reform the Civil Service Laws, House Concurrent Resolution 95-299, 95th Congress, second session.

11. *Ibid.*, page 3.

12. Copy of speech delivered by Congressman Hawkins, Statler-Hilton Hotel, Washington, D.C., June 24, 1975.

13. Leon Keyserling, February 22, 1979, in hearings before the Joint Economic Committee, Congress of the United States, 96th Congress, first session, Washington, D.C.: Government Printing Office, page 53.

14. Congressman John Conyers

15. *Congressional Record*, December 5, 1979, page 34760.

16. Chuck Stone, *Black Political Power in America*, Indianapolis: Bobbs-Merrill, 1984, page 10.

5

Birth of the Congressional
Black Caucus

For almost a century, the open and bloody warfare waged by white terrorist groups against innocent black citizens went virtually unchallenged by local, state, or national governments. The lynching of fourteen-year-old Emmett Till by a white Mississippi mob in 1955 was just one such typically gruesome event. The following year, white rioters blocked the doors at the University of Alabama to keep a black woman, Autherine Lucy, from entering. The year after that, local NAACP president Daisy Bates and the nine black students she represented were traumatized by their attempt to enroll at Little Rock's Central High School. In the decade of the sixties, white mobs invaded the campus of the University of Mississippi in defiance of a court order to admit James Meredith; civil rights leader Medgar Evers was assassinated in Jackson, Mississippi; and four black children were killed in the bombing of a Birmingham, Alabama, church. In 1964, Michael Schwerner, James Chaney, and Andrew Goodman, three young civil rights workers, were murdered in Philadelphia, Mississippi. The next year, Viola Gregg Liuzzo was killed on a lonely road near Selma, Alabama, because she had helped blacks register to vote.

Then came the riots. Watts burned for six days in 1965, leaving thirty-four persons dead, 1,000 wounded, and more than 4,000 arrested. The Newark, New Jersey, riot saw twenty-three killed and 1,500 wounded. In Detroit, forty-three were killed—thirty-three of them black—with 2,000 wounded. Following the assassination of Dr. Martin Luther King, Jr., the most effective leader of the black struggle for equal rights and a proponent of nonviolent social activism, sixty-five cities were ignited by enraged blacks, and more than fifty college campuses saw students pitted against the National Guard and the United States Army. Black insurrection was the order of the day.

However, not all the political action took place in the streets. History was made in mainstream politics on January 2, 1969, when House Speaker John McCormick asked Shirley Chisholm of New York, Louis Stokes of Ohio, and me, Bill Clay of Missouri, to swear the oath of office given to members of the United States Congress. Nine blacks serving simultaneously in the House of Representatives represented a new milestone in the advancement of our political agenda. The other black congressmen, already sitting, were William L. Dawson, Chicago (1943–1970); Adam Clayton Powell, Jr., New York (1945–1970); Charles C. Diggs, Detroit (1955–1980); Robert N. C. Nix, Philadelphia (1957–1978); August F. Hawkins, Los Angeles (1963–1990), and John Conyers, Jr., Detroit (1965 to the present).

While 100 white women had served in Congress since Jeannette Rankin of Montana became the first in 1917, it was fifty-two years later before Shirley Chisholm became the first black woman so honored. The greatest number of black members sitting at any one time in any prior Congress were in office in 1875, when seven House members—all from southern states, all Republicans—served: Joseph Rainey of South Carolina; Josiah T. Walls of Florida; John R. Lynch of Mississippi; Jeremiah Haralson of Alabama; John A. Hyman of North Carolina; Charles E. Nash of Louisiana; and Robert Smalls of South Carolina. Blanche K. Bruce was then serving in the Senate.

In 1901, Representative George Henry White predicted that blacks one day would be "rising phoenix-like, full of potential." And in 1970, they did. George W. Collins of Illinois; Ronald V. Dellums of California; Ralph H. Metcalfe, who replaced the recently deceased William Dawson of Illinois; Parren J . Mitchell of Maryland; Charlie Rangel, who had defeated Congressman Adam Clayton Powell of New York; and Walter E. Fauntroy of the District of Columbia, in the newly created position of nonvoting delegate for the District—increased the representative ranks of blacks by four.

THE GROWTH OF BLACK MILITANCE

The watershed of increased black representation grew out of the civil rights movement and the efforts of black activists of prior years.

But something more was to emerge in these changing times. While white liberals and black moderates were patting each other on the back for improvements in race relations achieved during the forties and the fifties, visions of a new reality were being seen and acted upon by black activists whose strategies would shake the nation and the world in the sixties and the seventies. The differences between the younger generation and the old guard were deep enough to occasion bedlam in the ranks of the civil rights movement.

Militant, proud young blacks questioned the relevance of Roy Wilkins of the NAACP and Whitney Young, Jr., of the Urban League, well-respected, venerable black leaders, to the issues of the day. Highly vocal proponents of nonviolent, passive resistance like Dr. Martin Luther King, Jr., of the Southern Christian Leadership Conference (SCLC) and James Farmer, executive director of the Congress of Racial Equality (C.O.R.E.), considered extremist by the white establishment, were merely tolerated by many radical voices of the struggle who went beyond nonviolent strategies of social protest. Malcolm X, Stokely Carmichael, Amiri Baraka, and H. Rap Brown, advocating self-defense as a tactical weapon, offered an attractive option to those who had despaired of strategies promoting racial gradualism and passive resistance.

The younger generation was not about to be content with the meager accomplishments in racial progress up to that point, or to genuflect to liberal whites promoting policies of racial gradualism. They were disrespectful of "for whites only" signs in theaters, bathrooms, restaurants, and hotels because they refused to acquiesce to a life of exclusion. They were impatient with the hypocrisy of the legislative process and contemptuous of time-consuming legal battles. They took their anger to the streets, confronting racist institutions with acts of civil disobedience. There were the Montgomery bus boycott of 1955; the student sit-ins at Greensboro, North Carolina, in 1960; the Freedom Bus rides in 1961. Sympathetic whites were disturbed and moderate blacks embarrassed, but civil disobedience worked; it played a major role in the enactment of the 1964 Civil Rights Act, which outlawed segregation in places of public accommodation, and the passage of the 1965 Voting Rights Act.

The nation was presented with a challenge it was unprepared to address. White America found its status of privilege and advantage crumbling under the weight of massive and disruptive protests on the one hand, and legislated away by enactment of new laws that abolished preferential treatment on the other.

Frederick Douglass had forewarned the nation of this possibility in 1886 when he said at the twenty-fourth anniversary of the Emancipation Proclamation, "Where justice is denied, where poverty is enforced, where ignorance prevails and where one class is made to feel that society is an organized conspiracy to oppress, rob and degrade them, neither persons nor property will be safe."[1]

White America reacted with anger and frustration as their methods for pacifying restless black Americans failed. In the past, in order to quell black discontent they had only to call a conference at the White House, invite a few carefully selected black leaders, propose some nebulous fair employment program, and then publicize it highly in the black media. The glare of lights from camera flashbulbs alone was often sufficient to overwhelm the agenda of the black leadership. The pomp and glory of the Oval Office served to distract everyone from the original purpose for the meeting, and the black leadership would end up forgiving—or worse, praising—the culprits they had come to chastise. But it was no longer easy for the old-style black leaders to get away with this. Their magic had worn off with their own constituencies. When they settled for political gimmickry and preached assimilation now, the reaction from the black community was outright disgust.

Leadership in the ghettoes had become diversified, localized, and independent, so no three or four individuals could operate as national spokesmen for 25 million disgruntled citizens. Indigenous neighborhood leadership had become a reality.

Hosting a presidential dinner for a small cadre of celebrated leaders who had never seen the inside of a Mississippi jail or never felt the end of a billy club wielded by a Georgia sheriff just didn't impress those who had suffered such gross injustices. These battle-scarred, denim-clad warriors were not ready to be silenced by the same old promise of a special, underfunded jobs program geared to help some unspecified minority residing somewhere who might have been miserably trapped in the claws of systemic unemployment. Clearly, the new mood of black people inclined them to blame the totality of white America for the legacy of historic wrongs heaped upon the entire black community. It was a mood not susceptible to compromise and compassion.

Civil rights organizations that continued to propagate the impractical wisdom of "appealing to conscience" were ridiculed and ignored by a substantial number of blacks, who had concluded that 200 years of experience had encouraged whites to see our patience as cowardice, our acquiescence as apathy, and our tolerance as satisfaction.

The uncompromising, militant slogans calling for "freedom now" with cultlike chants of "black power" and "burn, baby, burn," became more common as the protest struggle intensified. Soon they replaced such moderate phrases as "cooling-off time" and "give decent white people a chance." This attitude on the part of young blacks was the result of their generation's being exposed to and conditioned by a series of the most gruesome acts ever inflicted against a defenseless people.

Congressional elections of 1968 reflected the changing fortune of blacks in American politics. Shirley Chisholm, Louis Stokes, and I considered ourselves, along with other black representatives, to have a mandate to speak forcefully and loudly in behalf of equitable treatment of minorities by government.

THE ELECTION OF SHIRLEY CHISHOLM

Shirley Chisholm was elected in 1968 to represent the Twelfth District of New York (Brooklyn). The forty-four-year-old Brooklyn-born political activist had built a significant rapport with blacks and Puerto Ricans in the newly drawn district. Her mother, a seamstress, hailed from Barbados. Her father came from British Guiana (now Guyana). At the age of three, Chisholm went to Barbados to live with relatives and remained there for eight years. Returning to Brooklyn, she finished elementary and high school before going on to earn a bachelor's degree at Brooklyn College and a master's degree in elementary education from Columbia University.

As a nursery school teacher, director of a day care center, and educational consultant, she engaged in many one-on-one experiences with voters in the area. Capitalizing on those relationships, Mrs. Chisholm ran for and was elected to the state assembly. She served four years in that body before entering the campaign for Congress. While in the state legislature, she sponsored measures to improve education and assist the poor. During her tenure in the assembly, she successfully sponsored a bill titled SEEK (Search for Elevation, Education and Knowledge), which was designed to help black and Puerto Rican students who had not finished high school but had the potential to go to college. She also sponsored bills establishing publicly supported day care centers and providing unemployment insurance for domestic workers.

In the Democratic primary, Mrs. Chisholm defeated William C. Thompson, a candidate supported by the Brooklyn political organization who was favored to win. Her upset victory added momentum to her hard-fought campaign in the general election. In that election, she and former national chairman of C.O.R.E., James Farmer engaged in a heated battle that involved both candidates citing their liberal credentials as justification for their election.

Farmer, a pioneer in the civil rights movement, was the candidate on the Republican-Liberal ticket. Mrs. Chisholm successfully labeled her opponent as an intruder sent by the white liberal bosses to impose their will on the black community. She said, "Mr. Farmer and I agreed on practically everything. But the main issue was that the people considered him a carpetbagger. Since he lived in Manhattan, it would have made more sense for him to run in Harlem."[2]

Both were opposed to the war in Vietnam. Both believed that the anti-poverty programs created during the Johnson administration should be continued. Both believed that presidential candidate Richard Nixon's call for "law and order" was merely a code signaling a government crackdown on protesters against racial discrimination and demonstrators against the war. The major factor determining the outcome was the political preference of the voters. The district was overwhelmingly Democratic.

The campaign was the subject of considerable national media coverage, and the two candidates uttered many quotable statements. The outcome on election night was in line with early predictions: Shirley Chisholm beat James Farmer by a margin of two and a half to one (34,885 votes to 13,777).

THE ELECTION OF LOUIS STOKES

Louis Stokes was elected in 1968 to the Twenty-first Congressional District in Cleveland, Ohio, which had been drawn by the federal courts. The suit to redraw the district was originally filed on behalf of Charles P. Lucas, a black Republican political leader, and tried in federal court by his attorney—Stokes, a Democrat. Both Lucas and Stokes, the front runners of their respective parties, were well respected in the civil rights community. Stokes, however, was better known politically because his brother was the dynamic, charismatic

Carl Stokes, who had been elected mayor of Cleveland the previous year. In addition, Louis was aligned with many civil rights activists whom he'd represented, pro bono, following their arrests for demonstrating. It also helped that the district was overwhelmingly Democratic.

It is ironic that in the general election to determine who would represent the district, Stokes and Lucas faced off against each other.

Seeking that congressional seat were ten black candidates—seven Democrats and three Republicans. Seven whites also filed in the district, which was 65 percent black. But the likelihood of a white winning in a divided black community was improbable. In fact, the white incumbent in the district for many years, Charles A. Vanik, had moved into the Twenty-second District to challenge veteran Congresswoman Frances P. Bolton. In defeating Mrs. Bolton, he ended her twenty-eight years in Congress and forty years of Bolton influence—her husband had preceded her in the House.

Among the whites aspiring to the office was an avowed racist, Robert W. Annabel, who preached "segregation now and segregation forever." His message failed to convince many of the 70,000 voters in the Democratic primary—he received only 361 votes. Other whites waging more credible campaigns were fourth-term city councilman Edward F. Katalinas and thirteenth-term city councilman Jack P. Russell. They, too, were unsuccessful in their bids, receiving 9,724 and 3,567 votes respectively.

Of the three black Republicans, Charles P. Lucas, a real estate agent, defeated Frank C. Lyons and Clarence E. McLeod, one an attorney and the other a former member of the Ohio Parole and Pardon Commission. In the Democratic contest, three black city councilmen, George Forbes, Leo A. Jackson, and George W. White, all had solid political bases in the black wards. Louis Stokes, however, entered the primary with the most impressive community group endorsements. He was the choice of the Joint Citizens Committee, which was composed of leading ministers and a coalition of community organizations.

In the primary, Stokes beat his nearest challenger, Leo A. Jackson, by a vote of 28,680 to 15,110. Lucas won the Republican primary over his two opponents with 4,020 votes. In the general election, Stokes and Lucas engaged in several debates. The big issue was "law and order." Both expressed respect for and demanded enforcement of all laws. But the difference was readily apparent. Lucas confined himself to dealing with the slogans surrounding the controversy, while Stokes tied Lucas to Republicans Richard Nixon and Strom Thurmond, who had repeatedly demonstrated their disrespect for laws that protected blacks. Stokes also described the two presidential candidates, Republican Richard Nixon and independent George Wallace, as one and the same in terms of policies and prejudices, asserting that Lucas would be forced to support Nixon's policies if elected. In one speech Stokes called Wallace's candidacy a victory for disunity and accused Nixon of not being a man of principle but a man in need of principle. In the election, Stokes defeated Lucas by a three-to-one margin (86,000 to 31,000).

THE ELECTION OF WILLIAM ("BILL") CLAY

I was elected in 1968 to represent the First District of Missouri (St. Louis) when the incumbent of twenty-two years, Frank Karsten, announced he would not seek re-election. Eleven persons filed for the Democratic nomination (seven whites and four blacks) in a district that was 55 percent black. Five of the seven whites were major candidates with considerable political experience—Walter Meyers, committeeman of St. Ferdinand Township and state representative; Edward Roche, ward committeeman and constable; Milton Carpenter, former Saint Louis comptroller, state auditor, state treasurer, and businessman; Patrick Boyle and Francis Stokes held no elective office but were well known in political circles. The other two were of little consequence. All four blacks were major players in the political field— Joseph W. B. Clark, civil rights activist and city alderman; James P. Troupe, ward committeeman and state representative; Ernest Calloway, president of the St. Louis NAACP and director of research for Teamsters Union Local 688; and myself, a ward committeeman, former city alderman, and civil rights activist.

Four of the major white candidates withdrew on the same day after meeting with white leaders of the Democratic party. Each formally endorsed the candidacy of Milton Carpenter, virtually assuring his victory if all four blacks remained in the race. This action gave Carpenter full support of the white community. Ministers, publishers, and businessmen in the black area made a serious effort to rally the community around my candidacy because I had the most political and grassroots support. But the effort to achieve black political unity was not as successful as that in the white community. Alderman Clark quietly withdrew, took a verbal swipe at me, and refused to endorse my candidacy. State Representative Troupe eventually withdrew and endorsed me, but too late to get his name off the ballot. Union leader Calloway remained in the race and spent considerable funds in a deliberate attempt to split the black vote.

Calloway's efforts were for naught. He received only 6,405 votes, mostly in the white precincts. Troupe, who actively and enthusiastically campaigned for me, received 3,186, mostly in the black wards. Carpenter was the recipient of 16,927 votes, and I outpolled him with 23,758 votes. The two minor white candidates Harry S. Leahey and John J. Relles received 1,571 and 1,258 votes respectively.

Calloway's decision to stay in the race was influenced by his boss, Harold Gibbons. Gibbons and I had repeatedly done battle over the failure of dairy, soda, and beer warehousing companies under Teamsters Union contract to hire blacks in any meaningful capacity. Despite the large number of black Teamsters Union members residing in the congressional district, the union's endorsement had little effect in the black community because Milton Carpenter, the candidate Calloway intended to help, was a symbol of white resistance to black equality. In 1959, when I was already an elected member of the St. Louis Board of Aldermen, I was arrested at a Howard Johnson restaurant while seeking to be served there, in a public place. Carpenter and his family owned that restaurant and went into circuit court seeking an injunction to stop the demonstrations conducted by the Congress of Racial Equality (C.O.R.E.) that followed.

Curtis Crawford, a black attorney, won the Republican nomination. I defeated him in the general election, 79,295 to 44,316. Most of his votes came from the heavily Democratic white precincts in St. Ferdinand and Washington townships, where my civil rights involvement was deemed anathema to local interests. Crawford received 21,011 votes to my 13,198 in the area, but I rolled up a 63,876–22,098 margin in the black precincts.

In both elections, I took the law and order issue away from conservative candidates Carpenter and Crawford. My position was consistent with my views on civil rights: attacking police brutality and calling for more federal assistance to law enforcement agencies. Other issues that I stressed were job opportunities for blacks and increased government-sponsored educational programs.

The emphasis and intensity of my campaign can best be summarized by quoting from a letter leading into my platform, which was entitled "Platform for First Power." I am sure that Chisholm and Stokes had similar messages for their constituents. My commitments were in the area of employment, federal housing, private sector housing, education, mass media, health, welfare, and equal justice before the law.

The needs and hopes and dreams of many people, like the people of our First Congressional District, are the subjects of many political talks, unending academic studies, best selling books, radio and television documentaries, religious statements, and revolving government programs from Urban Renewal to Model Cities.

In studying statements from these sources and listening to the people in the community, one conclusion always stands out: That is, an effective fight to solve the problems of the First District can only be waged at the federal level. The battle is on a national level. Anything less will fall short of solution.

The magnitude of the problems demands a national campaign. The urgency of these problems demands not money for programs alone, but democratic participation in the decisions by the people whose lives are affected.

The conditions of poverty found in the First District and other areas of this country must be immediately addressed by our federal government to bring faith and hope to our people, before we can talk of quelling unrest and civil disorder.

It is at the federal level where we must fight that all men and women may respect their neighborhoods and see in them a decent way of life for themselves and their families. Only when people feel they are a part of their government will they respond with respect for the "law of the land" and work together in dignity and equality.[3]

INCREASED BLACK REPRESENTATION AND THE FIRST MOVES TOWARD A CONGRESSIONAL BLACK CAUCUS

The three of us—Stokes, Chisholm, and I—came to Washington determined to seize the moment, to fight for justice, to raise issues too long ignored and too little debated. We were described by the media as militant, aggressive new leaders determined to make changes in the way black members of Congress had been viewed in the past. And we wasted no time seeking to establish a forum for articulating our concerns.

Stokes and I decided that nine of us representing such a collage of talent and experience and coming mostly from politically safe districts constituted a power bloc deserving respect within the institution. We discussed the merits of organizing a group with rules, regulations, and bylaws and made our feelings known to the other seven. It was our opinion that a more formal, more structured organization based on solidarity of purpose and program would enable the nine of us to wield a significant amount of influence in the House.

On New Year's Eve 1970, I drafted a memo and circulated it to all members of the Democratic Select Committee, warning, "Without adequate programming and planning, we [the Democratic Select Committee, a loose-knit group under the leadership of Charles Diggs that met periodically with the Speaker of the House] might well degenerate into a Kongressional Koffee Klatch Klub."[4]

The memo called for (1) formal election of a chairman, vice-chairman, secretary, and treasurer; (2) establishment of an executive committee as the major policy-making instrumentality, with authority to act on behalf of the group in cases of emergency; and (3) subcommittees to be formed in specific areas of concern to black Americans.

Two days later, the number of black House members increased to twelve with the swearing-in of George W. Collins (D–Illinois); Ronald V. Dellums (D–California); Ralph H. Metcalfe (D–Illinois); Parren J. Mitchell (D–Maryland); and Charles B. Rangel (D–New York). Rangel replaced Adam Clayton Powell, Jr., and Metcalfe replaced Bill Dawson. The other three replaced white incumbents. Collins was elected to fill the vacancy of an incumbent who won the primary but died before the general election.

The new members, especially Dellums and Mitchell, brought additional pressure to bear on the black members of Congress for militancy, if not outright radicalism. Rangel, of course, was under pressure to continue the high-profile militant stance of his legendary predecessor. Metcalfe and Collins were more conservative than the rest, except for Bob Nix. The three of them were all products of old-line, patronage-laden political machines run by reactionary white political bosses.

Ronald Dellums

Ronald Dellums was elected to Congress from the Seventh District of California, which, according to the media, was comprised of the most radical constituents in America. Its black population (only 22 percent of the district's population) was based in the ghetto of Oakland, home of Bobby Seale and Huey Newton, founders of the Black Panthers party. The majority of the district's constituents were white radicals from the University of California Berkeley campus and its environs, the place where the Free Speech movement was born. The district was also the center of the youth rebellion that sparked massive demonstrations in opposition to the war in Vietnam and promoted a cultural revolution to establish new values and new views about women's rights, gay rights, and civil rights.

The question of war and peace was by far the most important issue affecting the voters of the Seventh District, and Dellums was by far the most outspoken opponent of U.S. intervention in the Indochina war. His position enabled him to forge a coalition with the most militant and most radical groups in a victorious campaign to defeat the liberal incumbent of twelve years, Jeffrey Cohelan. Despite Cohelan's almost total support from the AFL-CIO and the huge amount of funds available in his campaign coffers, Dellums received 42,778 votes (55 percent) to 35,223 for the incumbent in the Democratic primary. In the November general election, Dellums defeated Republican challenger John E. Healy by a vote of 89,784 to 64,691.

Parren J. Mitchell

Parren J. Mitchell was elected to represent the Seventh Congressional District in and around Baltimore. At the time, there were a substantial number of Jews residing in the district, and the incumbent of some twenty years, Samuel Friedel, was the representative in what was considered Maryland's safe Jewish district. Mitchell's victory was made possible when a bitter fight developed between two factions in the Jewish community. Incumbent Friedel and another Jewish candidate with a similar name, Friedler, engaged in a hard-hitting, no-holds-barred campaign that sufficiently split the Jewish vote to allow Parren Mitchell to eke out a win by the unbelievably slim margin of 46 votes. He received 24,265; Friedel 24,227; Carl L. Friedler 16,909; and Walter T. Dixon 3,504.

In the general election, Mitchell defeated his Republican opponent, Peter Parker, 60,390 to 42,566. By the next election in 1972, the district had been redrawn as required after every ten-year census and contained a majority of black voters.

Charles Rangel

In a five-way race, Charles B. Rangel defeated Adam Clayton Powell, Jr., for Congress in the Twelfth District of New York by 150 votes. The three others challenging the legendary incumbent were Jesse Gray, a community activist who had led several successful rent strikes in Harlem slums; Ramon Martinez, an attorney of Puerto Rican descent with a sizeable political following in East Harlem (Spanish Harlem); and John Young, who had run against Powell in 1968 and made an impressive showing.

Initially, Powell considered the other candidates the same kind of perfunctory opposition he had faced in past elections. He was of the impression that the voters in the district were too awed by his past accomplishments and too indebted to him for his leadership in passing major civil rights and anti-poverty legislation in the Congress to unseat him. That was par for the course, as the incomparable Mr. Powell considered the office his personal possession and assumed that voters would back his candidacy in each election without his having to participate in the mundane practice of asking for their votes.

But this time he misread tea leaves from the wrong cup. After twenty-six years, the voters had grown tired of his seeming neglect and refusal to earnestly involve himself in the affairs of Harlem. There was growing discontent in the district, centering around his lackadaisical, cavalier attitude toward important issues in the Congress.

Powell had not waged a campaign for re-election in twelve years. No serious candidate had challenged him since he'd beaten Assemblyman Hulan Jack and the Tammany Hall machine in 1958. The overwhelming majorities Powell amassed in previous elections without even opening a headquarters or mailing out literature were the result of black constituents' letting the *New York Times*, the Congress, and America in general know that only black people would decide who would represent them in the House of Representatives. Thus, the Powell mystique had gone untested for an extended period of time.

But this time Charlie Rangel, with the aid of seasoned black politicians from Harlem, conducted a hard-hitting campaign. There could be no valid accusations of an "outside" factor or "white carpetbaggers" intrusion. Rangel was able to garner the support of such well-known personalities as Jackie Robinson, Roy Campanella, and Lionel Hampton. He was supported by the Reverend Wyatt T. Walker, a former top aide to Dr. Martin Luther King, Jr., and pastor of a very large congregation in Harlem. His political endorsements came from a variety of influential officials, including David Dinkins, Paul O'Dwyer, and Percy Sutton. The closest thing to white interlopers into the campaign was support from Jimmy Breslin and editorial endorsements by the *New York Times* and the *New York Post*.

While Rangel was conducting an effective door-to-door campaign, hitting hard on Powell's absenteeism from Congress and from the district, attacking him for taking Harlem residents for granted, Powell was barnstorming the country making speeches and collecting honoraria. He returned to the district only each Sunday to preach at his church, Abyssinian Baptist. In one handbill distributed by the Rangel campaign committee, Powell was accused of missing fourteen votes during 1969 on key legislation, including extension of the Elementary and Secondary Education Act Program; extension and expansion of permanent special milk programs for children; extension and improvements in the federal-state unemployment compensation system; extension of the Voting Rights Act; and appropriation of $6 billion for the anti-poverty program.

In the end, Rangel was victorious. He received 7,804 votes, Powell 7,599. A recount reduced the difference to 150 votes. Martinez received 4,327, Gray 2,562, and Young 1,627.

The general election was no contest. Rangel beat his opponent on the Liberal ticket, Charles Taylor, 52,851 to 6,385.

Ralph Metcalfe

Ralph Metcalfe was elected from the First District of Illinois located on the South Side of Chicago, which constituted the most heavily black populated district in the nation. Blacks had represented the district since Oscar DePriest was elected in 1928 as the first black congressman of the twentieth century. Metcalfe was an important cog in Mayor Daley's political machine and in the primary defeated by a margin of two to one an insurgent black alderman allied with an anti-Daley, racially integrated reform movement. In the general election, Metcalfe received 43,272 votes and his Republican challenger, Janet R. Jennings, received 9,267.

George Collins

George Collins was elected from the Sixth District of Illinois to fill the vacancy caused by the death of Daniel J. Ronan. He defeated his primary opponent, Brenetta M. Howell, 36,350 to 5,940. In the general election, he defeated Alex J. Zabrosky by a vote of 68,182 to 14,942. Collins, a trusted member of the Daley machine, had no problem getting organizational support in the white areas that were traditionally delivered by the machine politicians. Collins, a former member of the Democratic City Central Committee and a former member of the board of aldermen, had moved up the ladder in the organization through hard work and patience and earned the respect of other Daley allies.

With the increased number of black House members, Diggs called a meeting to consider the recommendations mentioned in my 1970 New Year's Eve memorandum. In addition to authorizing formal elections of officers, naming an executive committee, and establishing subcommittees, also under consideration was an appropriate name for the group. Proposed designations ranged from Congressional Committee on Minority Rights to Congressional Committee for the Protection of Minority Rights. Some wanted a kind of all-inclusive nomenclature so that at a future time Chicano, Puerto Rican, and Jewish members could join. But the name "Black" won out because we recognized that protecting black interests was the primary reason most of us were elected, and the term also adequately described our mission.

The February 2, 1971, minutes of the Democratic Select Committee reflect that ". . . at this point it was unanimously agreed that the Caucus be composed of only black members and that the word 'black' remain in the name." Mr. Rangel reiterated his suggestion for using the name "Congressional Black Caucus," and it was agreed that would be the name used.

After formally organizing, it was necessary to raise funds and hire professional staff to implement the ambitious program envisioned by members of the Congressional Black Caucus. Congressman Hawkins proposed that we hire a staff and purchase a building that would enable us to pool resources and address problems jointly. "We represent not only our own districts but every black person in America," he said. "It is very hard to reject the many letters we get from other areas where persons feel they are not getting sympathetic treatment from their congressman. By combining expertise, we can serve this function."[5]

Hawkins recalled that while on a congressional trip to the Far East, he and I had met with and were impressed by Howard Robinson, an experienced administrator who was working for the American embassy in Tokyo as labor attaché with the State Department. We recommended him for the position of executive director.

Robinson was elated to be considered for the position. In responding to Chairman Diggs' letter, he wrote:

[I accept] the job with the full recognition that the Caucus may not, at this time, be in a position to match my current salary. But, because I believe that the purposes and objectives outlined by the Caucus are basic to the future of all black Americans, I am willing to abandon my position as a senior Foreign Service officer, in order to dedicate the next years of my life to the objectives that you in the Caucus have set out to achieve.[6]

Robinson arranged a two-year leave of absence from the Department of State and assumed the task of organizing the technical staff of the original Congressional Black Caucus.

The road of the black race's struggle for justice and equality is littered with disheartened groups and individuals coining slogans and proclaiming mandates for birth of new movements. While some efforts to combat racism were authentic and sincere, others were fraudulent schemes promoted by charlatans, unrealistic adventurers, and self-righteous posturing neophytes.

This time, however, the chemistry was different. Blacks in legislative bodies, including those in the United States Congress, were rising "phoenix-like" and had captured the respect and support of the vast majority of America's black citizens. The thirteen black members of Congress were uniquely situated and sharply primed to lead an all-out assault on the institution of racism. In addition, they were in positions of power because black people put them there. That, too, made a difference in the chemistry. Their success or failure did not depend on the fickle whims of a white electorate.

THE BLACK MANIFESTO

Black America was in an angry mood in 1969, and in the midst of this climate a group of grassroots organizations under the leadership of James Forman drafted a "Black Manifesto." They demanded that white Christian churches and Jewish synagogues reimburse the black community to the tune of $500 million in reparations for past racial injustices. The Manifesto was delivered at a meeting of the National Black Economic Development Conference in Detroit, Michigan. The Manifesto in part stated:

We have been forced to come together because racist white America has exploited our resources, our minds, our bodies, our labor. For centuries we have been forced to live as colonized people inside the United States, victimized by the most vicious, racist system in the world. We have helped to build the most industrial country in the world.

We are not unaware that the exploitation of colored peoples around the world is aided and abetted by the white Christian churches and synagogues. . . . Fifteen dollars for every black brother and sister is only a beginning of reparations due us as a people who have been exploited and degraded, brutalized, killed and persecuted.[7]

On July 6, 1969, the Washington Square United Methodist Church in New York City donated $15,000 to James Forman toward the reparations demanded. Two months later, the Episcopal Church's House of Deputies awarded $200,000 to the National Black Economic Development Conference.

It might seem ironic that religious organizations would be asked to pay reparations for racial injustice, but racism's most reliable tool has always been religion, in particular the religious values propagated by overzealous Christian missionaries. Great numbers of white Americans hold that race determines human traits and capabilities, and doggedly believe that whites are inherently superior to blacks—even spiritually so.

History vividly documents the seriousness of racism in America but trivializes the subject by artfully and meticulously failing to identify any specific Americans as racists. Politics and politicians are by no means immune to the fallacious supposition of white superiority. In politics, as in all other disciplines, bigotry against blacks is as "American as apple pie." Members of our race have endured more discrimination and more rejection at the hands of political leaders than any other minority group. No other segment of society has been more dedicated to the democratic process than blacks, more faithful to political parties than blacks, and more loyal to individual office-seekers than blacks. Yet no group has been so abused, so misused, so mistreated as black Americans seeking reciprocity for their contributions. The political legacy bequeathed us is one of unkept promises and unmet needs. Two hundred years of unfulfilled pledges by white politicians who eagerly sought and readily received maximum support from black voters have left our leaders embarrassed and our people embittered.

Many black people felt the demand for indemnification was proper. The prevailing sentiment was that the profits from American slavery, spawned by the immoral interpretation of Christian theology, had provided financial security to the grandchildren of those who traded in human flesh. Although modern-day Christians were not deemed individually guilty, it was not beyond the pale of reason to hypothesize that they were personally enriched by the investments their progenitors had made in the sordid business of human bondage.

In order to justify more than 300 years of dehumanizing "de jure" slavery and at least 100 additional years of "de facto" racial serfdom, it was necessary for these forces of evil to construct a moral thesis relieving Christian zealots of any individual feelings of guilt. In very simple terms, the so-called disciples of Jesus Christ accomplished this apostolic mission by rejecting the most basic tenet of Christianity— that all men have souls and therefore are redeemable.

Intellectually dishonest men rationalized that some men, black men in particular, were soul-less creatures, thus unacceptable candidates for conversion to Christianity. The Church willingly prostituted itself to the economic greed of those "uncircumcised Philistines" who invested in slavery for profit, consenting to drastic changes in all previously acceptable practices of slave–master relationships.

To accommodate the financial interests of greedy slave owners, this country permitted a radical redefinition of the bounds of humane treatment previously accorded those in bondage. America allowed for a vastly different interpretation of the rules normally imposed in situations of "involuntary servitude." The difference was precisely that highlighted by the contrasting terms: "slavery," as distinguished from "servitude." Human beings were considered nothing more than chattel or property. This simple variation changed the historic relationship between the conquered and the conquistadors. Once blacks held in bondage were defined as chattel the same as hogs, chickens, and farm land, the next step in this nefarious scheme of mental masturbation was predictable.

Apparently, the gross profitability associated with buying and selling human cargo overshadowed the gross profanity involved in the institution of slavery itself. The Reverend William A. Jones, Jr., described the religious and moral decadence associated with slavery:

Such a massive program of peddling and killing humans could not have developed without the approval of churches on both sides of the Atlantic. "From the beginning," states Pierre Berton, "it was the Church that put its blessing on slavery and sanctioned a caste system that continues to this day." Being pious religionists, churchmen had to tailor their theology to fit their sociology.[8]

When the Black Manifesto was issued, it seemed as if 250 million American citizens were in an angry mood. Blacks seeking redress for 200 years of forced subjugation and restitution for involuntary servitude were also angry and justifiably bitter. Whites in the "establishment" were confused, contemptuous, and angry. White liberals were perplexed and petulant and publicly expressed their anger that blacks no longer solicited their counsel nor cherished their companionship. White conservatives were angry because they felt blacks were biting the gracious hand of "Mother Liberty" who had fed them (grits and fatback) for so many years. The vast majority of white Americans, the "know-nothings, do-nothings," always in the middle on all issues of epic proportion, as usual had no educated opinion whatsoever. They were just angry.

What the white majority viewed as the destructive behavior of civil rights protesters was perceived by the black minority as the only constructive option available to them for removing the shackles of racial oppression.

The term "black power" coined by black militants and promoted by the white media was offensive to those who had always possessed and defended the concept of white power—and had always prospered by it. They now felt aggrieved because blacks demanded first class treatment as a right of citizenship, not as a privilege conferred by a benevolent majority.

It boggles the mind to think that the descendants of those who defiantly threw bales of tea into Boston Harbor and took up arms to oppose repression now felt outraged because some blacks advocated the use of force to gain their rights.

By massively resisting Supreme Court edicts that outlawed racial segregation, whites flaunted their contempt and scorn for the concept of racial equality. In the process, they made a mockery of their oft-stated commitment to the principle of "law and order." Foot by foot, street by street, city by city, blacks were compelled to do battle in order to dislodge white persons from entrenched political and community positions they held simply because they were white.

A NEW FOCUS FOR BLACK POLITICAL POWER

At the end of the sixties, Richard Nixon, who was often seen waving two fingers for victory, was elected the thirty-seventh president of the United States in a very close election. When he and his conservative cadre marched into Washington, D.C., they carried what they insisted was a mandate from the voters to repeal all of the Johnson Great Society programs. Low-income housing, school lunches, child nutrition programs, CETA, the Job Corps, and college loans and grants were all slated for revision or elimination. The Republicans were determined to use their newly gained power to reverse more than ten years of steady progress in the area of minority accomplishments. Their attacks on Great Society programs were not couched in anti-black rhetoric, but the end result was the same. Blacks had benefited tremendously from these government programs, and what the new administration offered as replacement was more ideological than substantive.

Such massive attacks from the political right necessitated a new, bold direction to be taken by blacks. The most easily recognized and readily equipped force capable of organizing a black national constituency, galvanizing effective opposition to the purveyors of regressive change, and launching a counterattack were black members of Congress. The thirteen congresspersons were best situated to assume that role because of their prestigious positions, institutional resources, national appeal, and well-publicized previous successes in fighting racism. The thirteen members were: Charles D. Diggs, Jr. (D–Michigan); John Conyers (D–Michigan); Robert N. C. Nix (D–Pennsylvania); Augustus Hawkins (D–California); Shirley Chisholm (D–New York); Louis Stokes (D–Ohio); George Collins (D–Illinois); Ronald Dellums (D–California); Walter Fauntroy (D–District of Columbia); Ralph Metcalfe (D–Illinois); Parren J. Mitchell (D–Maryland); Charles Rangel (D–New York); and yours truly, Bill Clay (D–Missouri).

THE JOINT CENTER FOR POLITICAL STUDIES

Prior to the founding of the Congressional Black Caucus, Congressman Diggs had pulled together the black members to form the Democratic Select Committee. It was a loosely organized confederation established for the purpose of communicating the concerns of black members and their constituents to the House Democratic leadership. Diggs had taken the lead in initiating activities and serving as spokesperson for the group.

Perhaps the most noteworthy accomplishment of the Democratic Select Committee, the one that made a lasting and important difference, was the role it played in bringing into existence the Joint Center for Political Studies.

Just prior to formally organizing the CBC, Representative Hawkins discussed the need to establish a vehicle with the research capability to furnish reliable information for legislative purposes. He deemed it critical that a data bank be established for compiling and distributing information to black candidates for public office and to incumbents in legislative bodies. So a proposal justifying such a need and outlining a structure was drawn up.

Contacts were made by Hawkins and Diggs with various nonprofit foundations that funded similar activities for white groups. The Ford Foundation agreed to put up seed money for the newly constituted Congressional Black Caucus to begin developing a plan to meet the legislative needs of the black members of Congress and those in state legislatures. Congressmen Hawkins and Diggs initiated a series of meetings with black educators and researchers to discuss staffing requirements and budgetary needs.

Frank Reeves, a faculty member at Howard University Law School in Washington, D.C., agreed to serve as executive director of the newly created organization, heading a staff of six professionals and five clerical personnel. Initially, a plan establishing joint responsibility between Howard University, Metropolitan Applied Research Corporation (MARC) of New York City, and the Congressional Black Caucus was reached. MARC was headed by Dr. Kenneth Clark, a Ph.D. in psychology. The tripartite arrangement constituted the reason for the name "Joint Center for Political Studies."

The Ford Foundation authorized a two-year grant of $410,000 per annum but then reconsidered the political implications and balked at the CBC's direct participation. Fearing that the Caucus was too political in nature and might jeopardize the tax-exempt status of the charitable foundation, it was agreed that the fund recipients would be only Howard University and MARC.

The Joint Center would become a clearinghouse to receive and disseminate information in cooperation with other agencies like the Urban Coalition, the National Council of Negro Women, and the Urban League. The Caucus would have a special relationship with the newly created organization.

The Joint Center was also to be a service agency, not a policy-making unit. This arrangement satisfied legal provisions of the new tax reform act covering foundations.

The Caucus had a tacit understanding with Frank Reeves, the executive director, and Louis Martin, the first chairman of the board, that the Center would hire consultants for certain projects and make them available to us. Additionally, the Caucus would receive interns sponsored by the Joint Center, and our respective staffs would work closely to complement mutual efforts of the two organizations.

THE BLACK PANTHER MURDER HEARINGS

Before being replaced by the Congressional Black Caucus, the Select Democratic Committee also conducted several public hearings and inquired into discrimination against blacks in the military. Its first nationally publicized investigation took place when black elected officials in Chicago asked for assistance in a review of police actions in the killing of two Black Panther leaders.

Under the leadership of Fred Hampton, a gang of thirty-three black youths on Chicago's West Side was transformed into a well-organized, anti-establishment, reform-minded grassroots organization. Hampton was regional coordinator in Chicago for the San Francisco–based parent group of Black Panthers and in less than sixteen months increased active membership to more than 1,000. He put into place a free daily breakfast program that fed thousands of ghetto children and instituted a system for dispensing free quality medical care.

Implementation of these relief-type public programs embarrassed the political machine of Mayor Richard Daley and damaged the image of Chicago as a city that provided for its needy, revealing government efforts to be nothing more than propaganda stunts.

Retaliation against the Hampton-led group was swift and decisive. Agents of the Justice Department tapped the telephones of the Black Panther headquarters and the homes of its leaders. Law enforcement agencies, including the FBI, constantly harassed members of the group. FBI Director J. Edgar Hoover, by any definition a cunning fascist of the highest order, publicly called for the extermination of all Black Panthers. He labeled the Panther movement as "the single most dangerous threat to the internal security of the United States." That same terminology had been used by Mr. Hoover six years earlier in seeking permission to wiretap the telephones of Dr. Martin L. King, Jr.—Hoover had described the civil rights leader in those precise words to Attorney General Robert Kennedy. The conniving, devious-minded J. Edgar Hoover lacked a talent for creative expression. He had used identical phraseology forty years prior to the Dr. King episode to discredit another black leader in his very first assignment as a young FBI agent. In that instance, it was the charismatic crusader for black separatism Marcus Garvey whom he hounded, eventually framed, and sent to jail.

Police and the local media in Chicago played a major role in the campaign against the Panthers. They conspired over a period of twelve months to paint an image of Black Panther leaders as lawless hooligans seeking the violent overthrow of the government. The Chicago Police Department engaged in a campaign of disinformation against the organization, and the daily press printed word-for-word all statements issued by the department as if they were gospel truth.

At 4:00 A.M. on the morning of December 4, 1969, one of the most reprehensible acts of racial brutality in the history of official government lawlessness took place. Fifteen Chicago policemen, under instructions from Cook County's state attorney, Edward V. Hanrahan, arrived in unmarked cars at the West Side dwelling of Black Panther members. Armed with .38-caliber revolvers, .30-caliber carbines, .357 magnums, and .45 Thompson submachine guns, Chicago's finest, within a matter of minutes, destroyed the wood-framed residence and assassinated Panther leaders Mark Clark and Fred Hampton.

Hundreds of bullets were discharged by police into the flimsy dwelling that housed Hampton, Clark, and seven others. The police had been supplied a detailed map of the house by federal agents. It accurately pinpointed the sleeping quarters of each resident. Twenty-five bullet holes were found in the wall of the bedroom where Chairman Hampton was asleep. Forty-two bullet holes entered the living room area where Clark slept.

State's Attorney Edward Hanrahan bragged the following day that police officers had performed a public service of "heroic" proportions. The press printed the official police account verbatim and raised no questions suggesting any official impropriety.

But all was not that simple. Black Chicagoans were outraged by the carnage and shocked by photographs appearing in the newspapers that showed the extent to which the house had been riddled with bullets. Civil rights leader the Reverend C. T. Vivian, speaking for a black community-based organization, called for a dust-to-dawn curfew of whites in black neighborhoods.

Black persons from all walks of life and from all sections of the country came to pay last respects to Fred Hampton. Thousands waited outdoors for hours in below-zero weather to parade past his coffin in the First Baptist Church in Melrose, Illinois. Among those in attendance were Dr. Benjamin Spock, the politically active baby doctor, and the Reverend Ralph D. Abernathy, president of the Southern

Christian Leadership Conference. A Catholic priest, Father George Clements, spoke to the throng of mourners. In his eulogy he proclaimed, "You can kill a revolutionary, but you can't kill the revolution." Per press reports, the mourners showed their agreement by chanting in response, "Right on."[9]

Many agreed with the statement of the national chief of staff of the Black Panther party, David Hillard: "We see the vicious murder of Hampton and Clark as a checkered flag which signals a systematic plot of genocide against the Black Panther party."[10]

Some elected officials in the Windy City called for a full inquiry. Black aldermen William Cousins, Jr., and A. A. ("Sammy") Rainer, joined by Alderman Leon Despres (white), issued blistering attacks on the police for their inept handling of the affair and called for a federal investigation.

Nine members of Congress wrote to Milton S. Eisenhower, chairman of the Commission on the Causes and Prevention of Violence, stating the raid had caused "great controversy" and noting that "a commission investigation would be far more credible than a report made by local authorities. . . . The incident threatens to add to the suspicion and distrust which already characterizes the relations of blacks and whites in many communities."[11]

The letter was signed by Congresspersons Abner J. Mikva of Illinois, Shirley Chisholm and William R. Ryan of New York, John Conyers of Michigan, Don Edwards and Augustus Hawkins of California, Robert W. Kastenmeier of Wisconsin, Louis Stokes of Ohio, and me.

Joseph L. Rauh, a white attorney and vice-chairman of Americans for Democratic Action, requested that Representative Emanuel Celler, chairman of the House Judiciary Committee, convene hearings to investigate police conduct in the shootings.

A group representing 110 organizations in the Chicago area also met and decided to take the case for the safety and well-being of black Americans before the United Nations. They charged the United States with pursuing a plan of genocide toward militant blacks.

Reuters reported that the NAACP, in calling on Attorney General John Mitchell, Governor Ogilvie of Illinois, and Mayor Daley of Chicago to conduct inquiries, branded the Panther killings "murder and modern-day lynching."[12]

A citizens' inquiry group consisting of twenty-eight prominent church officials, legal scholars, and civil rights leaders was impaneled to investigate official violence against the Black Panthers. Among the panelists were former Attorney General Ramsey Clark; former Supreme Court Justice Arthur J. Goldberg; NAACP Executive Director Roy Wilkins; Jack Greenberg, counsel for the NAACP Legal Defense Fund; Clifford Alexander, former chairman of the United States Equal Employment Opportunity Commission; Richard G. Hatcher, mayor of Gary, Indiana; Louis Pollak, dean of law at Yale University; Whitney Young, Jr., executive director of the Urban League; Julian Bond, state representative of Georgia; and Phillip Hoffman, president of the American Jewish Committee. The commission had no legal status and no authority to issue subpoenas, and its operating expenses were financed by civil rights groups. Many prominent legal scholars donated time and talent to further the inquiry.

Black Illinois state senators Charles Chew and Richard Newhouse, joining with then State Representative Harold Washington, invited the Congressional Democratic Select Committee to Chicago for a public hearing. On December 20, 1969, Charles Diggs, chairman of the committee, joined by eight other members—Chisholm, Conyers, Diggs, Hawkins, Nix, Powell, Stokes, and I—convened a hearing at A. R. Leaks Colonial House at 914 East Seventy-ninth Street. It lasted from ten in the morning until eight in the evening, with a short break to survey the scene of the crime. Testimony was transcribed by a court stenographer. Witnesses included locally elected and appointed officials, representatives of concerned organizations, private citizens, and members of the Black Panther party. Also testifying before the committee were three persons who later would be elected to Congress and become members of the Congressional Black Caucus: Alderman Ralph Metcalfe, State Representative Harold Washington, and publisher Gus Savage.

Our ad hoc committee released a special report on January 26, 1970, titled "Investigation of Panther Slayings." In the introduction, it stated:

The events of December 4, 1969, which resulted in the death of the Chairman of the Illinois Black Panther Party and a leader of a downstate chapter have been labeled by citizens all over the country as brutal and unwarranted—a label reinforced by motion pictures of the scene of the shootings and a look at the grim pictures of Panther–police clashes over the past two years. The incident calls into question police conduct on that day and necessarily leads to questions about other events. What is particularly clear is that the several "official" police versions are inconsistent with each other, and further are inconsistent with certain independent facts.[13]

Among facts cited in the report, were these:

A police firearms expert testified at the Coroner's inquest that among the
expended ammunition recovered from the apartment were the shell casings
of five .32 caliber bullets. He said that these did not match any of the alleged
Panther weapons the police say they found and that the list of police
weapons carried on the raid did not include any of .32 caliber. The same
police expert, John M. Sadunas, testified that none of the 130-odd expended
shell casings and slugs recovered from the apartment matched seventeen of
the nineteen weapons police say they seized. He said three shotgun cartridge
casings matched the remaining two shotguns but no slugs or shotgun pellets
were recovered from the areas where the shotguns were supposed to have
been fired.

Dr. Levine, a pathologist, examined Mr. Hampton's body and said he found
heavy traces of the barbiturate seconal in the blood—three times the
amount necessary to put a man Mr. Hampton's size and weight to sleep.
The implication being that Mr. Hampton was either unconscious or too
drowsy with drugs to have been firing at the police at the time of death.[14]

As a result of the Select Democratic Committee's hearing, which
found sufficient evidence to raise serious questions about the administration of justice in this matter, and the widespread publicity accorded the investigation by the Citizens Inquiry Commission, the
United States Department of Justice launched its own investigation of
the incident. A federal grand jury was impaneled to consider criminal
charges against those involved in the obvious massacre of the two
Black Panthers.

State Attorney Edward V. Hanrahan and thirteen codefendants were
indicted. The judge presiding at the trial was a product of the local
political organization and had been recommended for appointment to
the bench by Mayor Daley. He revealed his personal bias for federal
prosecutors at every stage of the proceedings. Mr. Hanrahan was
acquitted on the charge of conspiracy. Charges of murder, a state
offense, were never filed against him by Mayor Daley's prosecutors.
But Hanrahan was not destined to get off scot free.

The black community was furious and vengeful. In the November
1972 general elections, black voters extracted their "pound of flesh."
Mayor Daley suffered one of the most humiliating political defeats of
his long and illustrious career. Black voters, angered by this travesty
of justice, cast over 60 percent of their ballots for the Republican

candidate challenging Hanrahan. This kind of black support to a Republican was unprecedented and caused a major political upset. Bernard Carey, the Republican, defeated Hanrahan for the office of Cook County prosecutor by 129,000 votes.

THE JACKSON STATE COLLEGE KILLINGS

The members of the Select Democratic Committee, as we were then called, next became involved in the Jackson, Mississippi, police killing and injuring of students on the campus of Jackson State College. In May 1970, several days after the U.S. invasion of Cambodia, and shortly after the killing of four antiwar students protesting at Kent State College in Ohio, students at the all-black Jackson State College engaged in a protest on their campus.

The temperature on the day of the confrontation was in excess of 100 degrees. Classrooms and dormitories were overcrowded and not air conditioned. The conditions were ripe for short tempers to flare. For years, students and faculty at the school had complained that city traffic through their campus—whites who lived in the suburbs driving to work in town—was both a nuisance and a danger. Their request that this street leading through the center of the campus be converted to a cul-de-sac and closed to through traffic was to no avail. On this particular day, some students began to throw rocks at cars driven through the campus by local white citizens. Although no injuries were reported after the rock throwing incident, local police felt compelled to teach the black students a lesson about proper respect for the safety of white folk.

At midnight, the campus of Jackson State College became a war zone. In a well-lighted area that housed students, police from the city of Jackson and the Mississippi State Highway Patrol converged on the campus and opened fire on unarmed students who were casually walking around the grounds. The twenty-eight-second barrage of gunfire resulted in the death of two students and the wounding of twelve others. The all-black student body of 4,500 was left in a state of shock.

The women's dormitory, housing 1,050 female students, was strafed with 400 bullets and shotgun pellets. Police claimed they had spotted a sniper somewhere on one of the upper floors. No evidence of such a person was ever produced, nor did any eyewitnesses ever come forward to attest to the same.

There was the usual request for a federal investigation and the usual response from the FBI that evidence was insufficient to warrant federal intervention. But the unexpected happened when Russell Davis, the white mayor of Jackson, contravened all standard operating procedures for southern politicians. At the behest of the local NAACP, he appointed a biracial committee to look into the affair. He further broke with the customs of mint julep–drinking southern gentlemen by appointing two black civil rights activists to the five-member panel.

Governor John Bell Williams, appearing on television, was visibly shaken by the mayor's action. He immediately ordered the highway patrol not to cooperate with the investigation. City Commissioner Ed Gates, an aspirant for state attorney general, also encouraged city police not to cooperate and insisted that the mayor's commission had no legal standing. Later some police officers did testify and denied firing any shots. Mayor Davis, on the basis of this testimony, exonerated his own police force of wrongful use of force, laying any blame at the door of the highway patrol. Ballistic tests conducted by the FBI later disproved the city police testimony.

Governor Williams issued a statement completely exonerating the city police and highway patrol of any wrongdoing. In justifying the actions of those participating in the apparent massacre, the governor cited a report issued by his appointed group. Although no one from his investigating team visited the campus, inspected any photographs of the debacle, or interviewed any students, they concluded that the police acted in a proper manner.

The mayor's commission, on the other hand, conducted a full-scale inquiry. It subpoenaed evidence and interviewed eyewitnesses. All the witnesses, with the exception of the head of the highway patrol, admitted that the students were running away from the scene when the police started shooting. They also testified that no tear gas canisters were tossed to disperse students, no verbal warning issued, no warning shots fired, and no order to fire ever given.

Inspector Lloyd Jones, commander of the Mississippi State Highway Patrol, on the night of the fiasco, radioed his headquarters the following message, which was taped:

> I think there are about three more nigger males over there, one of 'em shot in the arm, one of 'em shot in the leg and one of 'em somewhere else. They ain't hurt all that bad. Them gals, it was two nigger gals . . . shot in the arm, I believe . . . There are two nigger females and three males we just discovered; that's a total of ten . . . Here's another one; let me see what this is . . . We got two students 10-7 here.[15]

In radio code, 10-7 means "out of service." Gibbs and Green were dead.

The mayor's commission interviewed numerous eyewitnesses, subpoenaed evidence, and concluded among other things, "The patrol has proven itself undisciplined in riot situations."[16]

No official action was ever taken against the police, and no one was ever charged with killing two unarmed students.

A few days following the disruption and killings, members of the Select Democratic Committee, led by Chairman Charles Diggs, chartered a plane and visited the campus. In addition to the black members of the House, several white colleagues joined the panel. Three members of the Senate, Birch Bayh of Indiana, Walter Mondale of Minnesota, and Edward Kennedy of Massachusetts, also accompanied the group. The inquiry was held in the school auditorium. Testimony was given by many eyewitnesses.

The Nixon administration sought to muffle public outcry for a federal investigation of the killings. Nixon wanted to stop the investigation because it posed a threat to his "Southern Strategy" and its potential for attracting white Democrats to the Republican party. It is alleged that he used Senator Edward Brooke to achieve this goal.

Senator Brooke was invited to travel on the plane chartered by the black members of the House. But, for reasons best known to him, he chose to arrive in town twenty-four hours earlier. He met with segregationist Governor John Bell Williams, called a press conference, and implied that the disturbance was merely one big misunderstanding. His statement was carried by all three national television networks and appeared the next day on the front pages of all major daily newspapers.

At the press conference, Governor Williams stated, "In the interest of self-preservation . . . the officers did not instigate the problem; they did not encourage it. The responsibility must rest with the protestors."[17] The governor implied that the community should return to business as usual. Senator Brooke, by not contradicting the absurdity of the misstatements, gave tacit agreement. Members of the Select Committee were livid.

Senator Brooke's solo excursion into the bowels of local racist politics, meeting with obnoxious proponents of racism, caught us by surprise. It also took the newsworthy edge off the Select Democratic Committee's investigation. One black member of Congress remarked, "Brooke's skin is nearly black, but his mind isn't black."[18]

That attack on the students was without justification and there was no reason for Senator Brooke to participate in such an act of sabotage. After all, he had never previously functioned as a rubber stamp for the Nixon administration or its policies. On numerous occasions he had taken issue with the president for neglecting the concerns of blacks and for failing to enforce antidiscrimination laws. Later, he voted against three of President Nixon's nominees to the Supreme Court: Clement F. Haynesworth, Jr.; G. Harold Carswell; and William H. Rehnquist. In addition, the senator was an outspoken critic of the president's continued support of the war in Southeast Asia. During the Watergate revelation of Mr. Nixon's involvement in criminal matters, Senator Edward Brooke was the first member of the United States Senate to call publicly for Mr. Nixon's resignation from office. He said that the president did not possess the public confidence to govern effectively. But just as in the case of Senators Revels and Bruce in the days of Reconstruction, we politicians often have our contradictions.

If members of the Democratic Select Committee were bitter because few, if any positive results came out of the Jackson, Mississippi, inquiry, we should have looked back in history and expected no more. During Reconstruction, a white mob stormed a courthouse in Carrollton, Mississippi—just a few miles from the Jackson campus—where seven whites were on trial for assaulting two blacks. The mob of crazed individuals stormed into the courtroom and opened fire on all blacks in sight. They killed eleven blacks and wounded nine others.

Congressman James Edward O'Hara, a black from North Carolina, one of two blacks then sitting in the Congress, introduced a resolution calling for a five-member committee to investigate the incident. Speaker John G. Carlisle casually referred the matter to the Rules Committee, where it died.

History is replete with accounts of individuals, organizations, and institutions, each or all waiting for the optimum time to emerge as leaders of a national movement. In this instance, it happened to be thirteen black legislators in the United States Congress. We were strategically positioned to challenge the system, which doomed black citizens to an abysmal life of hopelessness and despair. We were prepared and willing to raise pertinent issues, review them under a microscope, transcend timid excuses for lack of progress, and mount an effective campaign for social freedom and economic justice. We were in a position to speak out freely and forcefully on such issues as contract set-asides, job creation, and economic enhancements for black folk when others were reluctant or unable to do so. We were committed to representing all black Americans, whether they lived in our respective districts or not. As Congressman Augustus Hawkins put it:

> The leadership belongs not to the loudest, not to those who beat on the drums or blow the trumpet, but to those who day in and day out, in all seasons, work for the practical realization of a better world—those who have the stamina to persist and to remain honest and dedicated. To these belong the leadership.[19]

Congressman Charles Diggs put it another way:

> It was not the numbers. But it seemed we had the chemistry at that point. The timing was right. People were raising serious questions about using confrontation techniques. We had the strength and the know-how to use them.[20]

Hawkins prophetically foretold the "manifest destiny" of the Congressional Black Caucus. As a postscript, Diggs precisely and correctly analyzed the situation.

The strength of the CBC was found in our ability to align with certain dynamics in black communities around the country. We could call a meeting, invite the heads of important black institutions, and receive their affirmative reply within a matter of days. The black church, the black media, black professionals, black activists all looked to us as the catalyst for organizing and unifying efforts in the struggle to attain equal opportunity and impartial justice. The masses of the black populace depended on us to discern black interests and to articulate the black perspective. Indeed, the black members of Congress, as loosely organized as we were, had become the flagship in the continuing struggle for equal rights.

There was a great need for black elected officials to come together and fashion a program to combat the racist politics of both major parties. It was imperative to establish a mechanism for ensuring the survival of the black race. So we came together as a group determined to reach decisions by consensus, with one spokesperson speaking for all.

NOTES

1. Frederick Douglass, April 1886, Washington, D.C., cited in *Pioneers in Protest*, by Lerone Bennett, Jr., Baltimore, Md.: Penguin Books, 1968, page 212.

2. *Ebony* magazine, February 1969, page 59.

3. Cover letter accompanying the "Bill Clay Bulletin" outlining his campaign platform, 1968.

4. Clay, memo, December 31, 1970.

5. *St. Louis Post Dispatch*, March 1, 1970, page 3B.

6. Letter from Howard Robinson, dated February 25, 1971, American Embassy, Tokyo, Japan.

7. The Black Manifesto, National Black Economic Development Conference, Detroit, Michigan, 1969.

8. Reverend William A. Jones, Jr., *God in the Ghetto*, Elgin, Illinois: Progressive Baptist Publishing House, 1970, page 51.

9. *Washington Post*, December 10, 1969, page 3A.

10. Dempsey J. Travis, *An Autobiography of Black Politics*, Chicago: Urban Research Press, 1987, page 443.

11. *New York Times*, December 10, 1969, page 43.

12. *Washington Post*, December 6, 1969, page A3.

13. Interim Report, The Ad Hoc Committee of Black Representatives, January 26, 1970.

14. *Ibid.*

15. Stephen Lesher, "Jackson State a Year After," *The New York Times Magazine*, March 21, 1971, page 25.

16. *Ibid.*

17. *Ibid.*

18. *Newsweek*, June 7, 1971, page 33.

19. Augustus Hawkins, *Politically Black*, Washington, D.C.: Alrag Productions, Twin Image Lithographers, 1972, in the Introduction.

20. Paul R. Hathaway, "The Black Caucus," *Essence* magazine, October 1971, page 40.

6

The Nixon Administration Tries to Ignore the CBC

The consensus in the Congressional Black Caucus in 1970 was that a "deep and dangerous alienation" of the country's 25 million blacks existed and we needed to take the matter up with the president, then Richard Nixon. Primarily, we felt it was necessary to call the president to task because of his own inflammatory, race-baiting rhetoric and insensitivity toward the adverse effects his program funding cuts were having on the black and the poor.

Congressman Charles Diggs requested a meeting between the CBC and the president. Two months later, a curt note of rejection from the president arrived. To add insult to injury, it was signed by a low-level White House staffer. In response, we, the CBC, boycotted Nixon's State of the Union address. That action was unprecedented and the event became international news. The Soviet news agency TASS, the BBC, and Communist China's Radio Peking saturated Europe, Asia, and Africa with reports of Nixon's affront to black leaders. Major media outlets around the world, with the exception of the United States' Radio Free Europe and the normal USIA news outlets, reported the Black Caucus snub by their president.

This error in judgment on the part of Richard Nixon was an effective propaganda weapon for Marxist adherents so, of course, it became a source of embarrassment to the U.S. government. It caused serious problems for American diplomats stationed in Third World countries, where Russia, China, and the United States were engaged in a philosophical tug-of-war. And at home the president's disrespect of black

Americans led many to question whether the United States could truly be considered "the land of the free."

While President Nixon continued to ignore the CBC's request for a meeting, the black media, through news accounts and editorials, criticized his attempts to eliminate programs that had begun to improve the quality of life for blacks and other minorities. Black-owned newspapers, with the exception of a few—notably the *Cleveland Call & Post* and the *Atlanta Daily World*—were highly critical of Nixon's efforts to dismantle government agencies that promoted agendas advancing the causes of minorities. The *Call & Post* and *Daily World* printed the administration's press releases verbatim and editorially endorsed Nixon's initiatives to retard the civil rights advances of black people.*

The Nixon White House issued manicured, nonsensical press statements describing benefits for black people—benefits that, in our eyes, did not exist. So in a countereffort Chairman Diggs in late 1970 appointed a "shadow cabinet" consisting of black professionals highly knowledgeable about government workings. Each was given a title corresponding to a member of Nixon's cabinet. The mission of the shadow cabinet was to monitor activities of top Nixon appointees and report on them to the community. Publicity-wise it was a brilliant coup. Every time a cabinet member or head of an agency presented a new program or new policy initiative, his or her counterpart in Diggs' shadow cabinet responded with clarity to document the negative effects each proposal would have on the black community.

Meanwhile, a number of us in the House proceeded to escalate the battle of words. I addressed the House of Representatives:

> To make known at this time our outright disgust with the president's policies and his refusal to give us an audience . . . there is no doubt where Mr. Nixon has placed his priorities. . . . He has traveled more than 35,000 miles in foreign countries. He has entertained hundreds of foreign dignitaries but refuses to meet with elected representatives of the Black "nation"

---

*The *Atlanta Daily World* was a black daily owned by the Scott family. The publisher's son, Stanley Scott, the first black reporter for United Press International, was an aide to President Nixon, and showing partiality to Republican officeholders had become something of a trademark of that newspaper.

W. O. Walker, publisher of the *Call & Post* and a decent, affable, but uncompromising Abraham Lincoln–style Republican apologist, apparently had a blind side when interpreting the regressive intent and accomplishments of Republican officeholders. His conciliatory approach to President Nixon's debilitating domestic policies infuriated many of his fellow black journalists.

within this country. . . . While he has been too busy to confer with us, the chief executive has found time for meetings with eleven veteran and patriotic groups, association executives, the head nurse of a Vietnamese children's hospital—and for many cocktail parties and state dinners. . . . It is pathetic that the well-traveled president has not seen the suffering and deprivation in Watts, Hough, Harlem, Fillmore, and the other United States ghettos. His failure to give priority to such domestic concerns as poverty, housing, and unemployment testifies to his apathy not only toward black people, but toward all poor Americans, who since January 1969 have truly known what it means to be forgotten.[1]

On advice from Republican legislative leaders and John Ehrlichman, the White House chief of staff, the president steadfastly refused to discuss the plight of black citizens with members of the CBC. Ehrlichman was quoted in the March 1, 1971, issue of *Newsweek* as saying, "We try not to permit opportunities to use the presidency as a grandstand."[2]

Describing Caucus members as a bunch of publicity seekers struck a sensitive nerve among our constituents and served as a catalyst for crystallizing support among blacks from all walks of life for our demand for a meeting with the president. Ehrlichman's callous description of the highest black elected officials was an insult not only to us, but also to those who had elected us.

For over a year President Nixon refused to meet with the Black Caucus. Representative Hawkins expressed his feelings in the same March issue of *Newsweek* in which Ehrlichman had been quoted: "The time has come to tell the president respectfully that unless he faces up to the problems of black Americans, there will be chaos. . . . It's not too late, but we can't wait two more years to do it."[3]

In an effort to increase pressure for the meeting, I addressed the House again on December 15, 1970.

Mr. Speaker, Roberta Scott, thirteen, Wichita, Kansas, was selected 1970 poster child for the National Association of Retarded Children. Roberta also happens to be black. It is an interesting fact that the president has refused to have his picture taken with this youngster.

This is not the first time that President Nixon has refused to meet with blacks. When the nine black members of the House requested a meeting with the president, we received a brief note from a White House staff assistant stating, "We had hoped to be able to work this out, but the president's schedule has been such that we just have not been able to work it in."

That same presidential aide has written the National Association of Retarded Children stating that, because of the president's heavy schedule, Mr. Nixon could not meet Roberta. The question remains—when will the president find time to fit blacks into his schedule? Joe Brooke, executive director of the Wichita-Sedgwick County Association, said this was the first time within memory that a president has declined to meet the NARC poster child. The president's refusal came as a great disappointment to Roberta's parents. . . .[4]

My statement prompted freshman Senator Bob Dole of Kansas, four days later, to write me a letter.

It is regrettable that you would attack the president of the United States without at least ascertaining the facts or at least visiting with some members of the Kansas delegation. . . . I would hope we share the view that it serves no useful purpose to attempt to further divide Americans. . . .[5]

I then responded to him in a letter of my own:

Your intentions are probably sincere, but your great perceptive powers failed you in discerning the point of my attack. Your invitation for this black congressman to visit with some of the members of the Kansas delegation did not mention visiting with the real culprit of racial division and disharmony, President Richard M. Nixon.[6]

So on the day of the president's State of the Union address in January 1971, Congressman Stokes suggested more drastic action.

Congressman Clay and I were seated on the floor of the House on the day Nixon was to deliver his State of the Union address in 1971. I told Clay we just had to do something dramatic. I suggested a boycott of Nixon's address by all black House members. Diggs called a meeting of black House members to negotiate the parameters of the boycott. Clay drafted the news release announcing the boycott. We got attention and recognition overnight.[7]

When the president delivered his message to the nation later that evening, Senator Ed Brooke was the only black member of Congress in attendance. Breaking rank with the other black members, he explained his presence: "I respect the office of president and the man who holds that office, and I will give careful consideration to his proposals. It is my duty as a United States senator to be present, to listen and to consider his recommendations."[8]

Senator Brooke's political situation was somewhat different from that of the CBC members. Not only was he the only black Republican in either body, but his constituency was about 94 percent white. Congressman Hawkins explained the uniqueness in this way:

> It would be nice to have a Republican to remove any suspicion that we are a partisan group. But Senator Brooke's problems are somewhat different from ours. We represent ghettos. Our problems are the problems of the ghettos. He represents a state, and a state with a small black population. Nonetheless, he has spoken out in his own way.[9]

After the boycott, Donald Riegle, a Republican member from Michigan, said on the House floor, "This administration has . . . consciously pursued a racial policy of 'benign neglect,' pursued an overt southern strategy, tried to diffuse the Voting Rights Act, nominated G. Harrold Carswell to the Supreme Court. Refused to meet with the black members of Congress for over a year."[10]

THE PRESIDENT AGREES TO MEET WITH THE CBC

Under attack from black and white Republicans, Nixon finally capitulated to the CBC request for a meeting. The twelve-month impasse was broken when Senator Brooke, acting as a go-between, arranged for the president and the CBC to come face to face at the White House. In order to let Nixon "save face," to use Brooke's words, the president would announce the meeting to take place after Congressman Diggs returned from a scheduled trip to Africa. It was held one month later, on March 25, 1971. How the delay allowed Nixon to "save face" puzzled us in the Caucus.

In the one-month interim, Carl Holman, national chairman of the Urban Coalition; attorney Frankie Freeman, national president of the Delta Sigma Theta sorority; Ofield Dukes, a public relations specialist; and Edward Sylvester, chief staffer for Congressman Diggs, organized a task force to prepare a document worthy of presentation to the president of the United States. Academicians, economists, lawyers, and civil rights activists assembled in Washington, D.C., to document "the State of the Black Nation." By the time the final version of the document was drafted, we had sought the opinions and advice of students, educators, elected officials, and others. Whitney Young, Jr., of the Urban League; Roy Wilkins, of the NAACP; Bayard Rustin, of the A. Phillip Randolph Institute; and the Reverend Theodore Hesburgh, president of Notre Dame University and member of the United States Civil Rights Commission, were just a few who supported the effort.

In all, a total of 400 position papers were submitted to the screening committee. A team of nine persons meeting day and night in the D.C. national headquarters of the Delta Sigma Theta sorority spent several weeks culling through reports before arriving at sixty recommendations to be offered to the president. Never before had a president of the United States been presented with such a professional, thoroughly studied case for addressing the complexity of needs and concerns facing black Americans.

The meeting was scheduled for a Thursday at 5 P.M. That was the worst kind of timing for the black print media. In industry jargon, it put them in a "time box" that would allow for no more than a tag line for their readers before network television would feature the story on the late evening news. Most black weeklies published on Tuesdays and Wednesdays, so a Thursday event would not be reported until the next week. The White House meeting would be thoroughly analyzed by the white media long before the black weeklies covering the meeting hit the streets.

Jimmy Booker, a black political writer covering the Capitol Hill scene for *Jet* magazine, wrote a confidential memorandum to Caucus members asking,

1. . . . that a representative of the black press be present at the two White House briefings held by Ron Zeigler on Thursday.
2. [that the] CBC release, on an embargo basis, a limited number of copies of the document . . . to insure that [the black press] will have time to digest it to meet early deadlines. . . .
3. [that the CBC] give [the black press] copies of the documents on Wednesday in order that those in Washington can be on time with the daily press. . . .
4. . . . that the members of the Caucus state after the meeting that we "have no further comment this evening, because of the lateness of the hour and because we wish to discuss among ourselves our reactions to this meet-

ing. We will hold an in-depth briefing and have a more formal statement regarding this meeting with the president at 10 A.M. Friday morning."

The Caucus, though, decided not to accommodate Booker's request. They were appreciative and respectful of the black press and sensitive to their needs, but they were also knowledgeable about the inner workings of the Nixon administration and the national media. We felt that such a delay would render any statement from the Congressional Black Caucus anticlimactic. By Friday morning, the spin given by the administration, unrebutted by the Caucus, would be viewed as the whole truth and nothing but the truth by a majority of American citizens. So press statements were issued by both sides immediately following the meeting.

THE SIXTY CBC RECOMMENDATIONS TO THE PRESIDENT

On March 25, 1971, President Nixon received the sixty recommendations, each buttressed by research data supporting Caucus positions. It was designed to provide the president with a serviceable understanding of complex problems. He accepted the "black paper" in the Oval Office at the White House in the presence of camera crews from almost every nation in the world. The historic document was referred to in the mass media as "sixty CBC demands," but the statement was clearly nonconfrontational and throughout referred to the expectation of cooperation with the president. At one point, it read:

> We do not underestimate the power of the presidency in achieving progressive change. Every sector of our society tends to look to the White House for cues to direction that the society is taking. . . . In discussing these [recommendations] with you, we will be focusing on executive action that can be taken immediately, as well as legislative programs whose success may depend on the nature and intensity of the support they receive from the White House.[12]

Representing the administration at the summit meeting were Secretary of Housing and Urban Development (HUD) George Romney; Secretary of Labor James Hodgson; Assistant Secretary of Labor Arthur Fletcher; Assistant Secretary of HUD Samuel Jackson; Undersecretary of Health, Education and Welfare (HEW) John Veneman; Assistant Secretary of Defense Roger Kelly; Assistant Secretary of Commerce Abraham Venable. From the White House staff, there were Leonard Garment, Robert Brown, Robert Finch, Donald Rumsfeld, George Shultz, Clark MacGregor, and Ronald Zeigler. In addition to the twelve members of the Caucus and two staffers, Walter Fauntroy also attended. He was invited by special invitation of President Nixon. (Fauntroy was not officially a member of the Caucus on our meeting date. He was elected delegate of the District of Columbia just two days prior to the meeting and had not yet been sworn in as a member of Congress.)

The meeting opened with President Nixon entering the Oval Office and shaking hands with each Caucus member. His exceptional political acumen, developed over twenty-five years of public service, was immediately noticeable as he made an appropriate personal comment to each Caucus member. He knew which districts the members hailed from and little tidbits about their backgrounds.

President Nixon said he welcomed the opportunity for the meeting and indicated that he and his staff had thoroughly digested the contents of the document that had been forwarded a week in advance of the meeting. He then proceeded to introduce members of the cabinet and the White House staff.

Congressman Diggs was the first to speak. He informed the president that the sixty recommendations represented not only the views of CBC but expressed the concerns of organizations and individuals from all over the country. "Our people are no longer asking for equality as a rhetorical promise," he said. "They are demanding from the national administration and from elected officials without regard to party affiliation, the only kind of equality that ultimately has any real meaning—equality of results."[13]

The president was asked to support legislation that would create 1.1 million public service jobs, to immediately increase aid to black businesses, and to recommend a guaranteed minimum income of $6,400 for families of four. In addition, he was asked to

... abandon plans to destroy the Office of Economic Opportunity (OEO); support legislation to provide quality integrated education; discard his general revenue-sharing plan in favor of a nationalized welfare program; provide more, not less, money for educational aid-in-grants and work-study payments to needy students; declare drug abuse and addiction a major national crisis, and devote all government resources to preventing entry of drugs; create an independent, publicly funded development bank to aid minority businesses; establish a National Legal Services Corporation; support full congressional representation and home rule for the District of Columbia; and disengagement from Southeast Asia as soon as possible.[14]

Following Diggs' statement, Congressman Hawkins outlined the need for government-supported job creation programs. He cited the necessity of establishing full-time employment for 1 million in-school youth as a number one priority in dealing with the prospects of a "long hot summer."

Congresswoman Shirley Chisholm highlighted the problems of black veterans and called for a civil rights division in the Department of Defense to ensure a greater degree of justice for black soldiers. The president interrupted briefly to apologize for not having someone from the State Department or the Defense Department present and said that Chisholm's recommendations would be passed on to the appropriate officials.

Congressman Conyers implored the president to have the Justice Department investigate allegations of voting fraud in Gary, Indiana.

Congressman Rangel expressed grave concern about the minority problems of narcotics and drug addiction.

Congressman Mitchell called for the release of $150 million in low-income housing funds.

Congressman Stokes asked for release of $800 million that had been appropriated for but not spent on domestic programs.

Congressman Dellums discussed the need for a swift and prompt end to the war in Southeast Asia, and a redirection of the funds into programs affecting the lives of a substantial number of blacks.

I recommended student grants instead of student loans, noting that 65 percent of black students in college came from families earning $5,200 a year or less and could not afford to repay loans.

In responding, the president said he did not consider the document a "laundry list," but rather an expression of serious concerns requiring proper response. He further stated, "I appreciate the candor with which you have expressed your concerns."

Nixon was gracious to the CBC; the session lasted almost one hour past the allotted time that had been agreed on. His wife and a group of women patiently waited as our meeting overlapped into their appointed time to meet the president. During the two-hour session, each member of the CBC took between two and three minutes to explain the reason and rationale for the sixty proposals and asked the president to reconsider his declared intentions of repealing Great Society programs.

Near the end of the session, President Nixon turned to Undersecretary of Labor Arthur Fletcher, one of his highest-ranking black appointees, and asked if he cared to comment on what Caucus members had presented. In a most revealing statement, Fletcher said, "No, Mr. President. I have been telling you for fifteen months the same things as these congressmen, and nobody's been paying any attention to me."[16]

Clark MacGregor, counsel to the president, was assigned to work out details with Caucus members for an investigation of allegations that the Justice Department was engaging in illegal and unconstitutional activity against black people. Special consultant Leonard Garment was appointed the chief liaison officer between the CBC and the White House.

As the meeting was closing, Congressman Rangel called upon the president to set a high moral tone of racial tolerance for the nation to follow. He asked the president to set the tone in the area of equal employment opportunity. He said that his plea was neither partisan nor parochial, but in the best interest of the country. He cited an article written by Kevin Phillips, an influential conservative ideologue, remarking on the damage the article had done to race relations.

Rangel apparently impressed Nixon, who expressed shock that the article had been so disparaging of the Caucus. Nixon was flustered at the mention of the article but, as a gracious host as well as a superb politician, had the last word:

> You presented the recommendations as you should—this is one country— there are some good citizens—there are some bad citizens—I know the frustrations. If I were black, I would present my case just as you have presented your case. I know that historically blacks have not been treated fairly in this country. I also know why many in the white community think they should not do any more. I am happy for this kind of meeting. You were elected just like I was elected. You can be heard. Where we can we will help. I always consider that there is one real great sin, and the greatest is demagoguery and overpromising; particularly in this era it creates enormous frustrations. We need action. We will try to give as much as we can. I want you to be heard. We can't promise to do everything. I think this meeting has been worthwhile to me.[17]

At the close of the meeting, Chairman Diggs requested that the president respond to the recommendations by May 17, 1971. He politely but firmly let the president know the Caucus was about serious business. May 17, 1971, Diggs explained, was chosen to commemorate the landmark 1954 Supreme Court decision outlawing racial segregation in public schools.

One of the ironies of this episode was the behavior of a black White House staffer, Robert Brown. He took it upon himself to explain why President Nixon had refused for over a year to meet with the nation's highest black elected officials. "When [the CBC] came up on the list, they got in, just like anyone else. Some wait three years. The president can't see everybody."[18]

Those "some" referred to certainly were not twelve members of the United States Congress. And surely many of those invited to meet with the president did not speak for more than 25 million American citizens.

John Ehrlichman's prediction of our "grandstanding" did not come to pass either. However, several members of the Caucus did express dissatisfaction with the president's responses. One remarked that Nixon listened but did not hear. Congressman Parren Mitchell repeated what he had told the president during the meeting in the Oval Office: "The black community has not been blackjacked into silence or lulled into apathy . . . [and] he might, therefore, be sitting on a powder keg."[19]

Many in the white media were critical of the CBC's public statements following the presidential meeting. Others expressed concern for what they described as partisan political attacks, because all of the CBC members were Democrats. Still others like columnist Victor Riesel of Publishers-Hall Syndicate were brutally hostile. Riesel called Congressman Mitchell a "full-fashioned fire eater," and accused him of letting go with a "verbal mortar."[20] He described Congressman Dellums in the same column as one "who not only spits fire when he talks, but eats it for breakfast."[21]

While awaiting an official reply from the White House, Chairman Diggs dispatched another letter to the president, commenting,

Some of these issues are at critical junctures in the legislative and executive process and we are especially concerned that our comments be considered before such determinations are made . . . We think therefore it would be extremely useful if conferences can be arranged by the White House with the policy makers on these issues as soon as possible.[22]

On May 18, missing the target date by twenty-four hours, President Nixon responded in writing to the sixty recommendations. Throughout his voluminous report, he indicated agreement with the thrust and goals of the CBC. However, the conclusions he drew did not concur with those of the Caucus. Expressing dismay, one CBC member said anyone reading the Nixon report would think it's a wonderful world that we live in.

The Reverend Theodore Hesburgh was much more tolerant in assessing the president's response, but candid nonetheless. "The dinosaur has opened one eye," he said.[23]

President Nixon's reply took two months to prepare, consisted of 115 pages, and by his own admission, was compiled by more than 200 people. The man-hour costs of federal employees working sixty days on the document were staggering.

Yet the politically partisan report said little to indicate that Nixon recognized the severity of the situation. It basically reaffirmed current administration policies and programs, while avoiding efforts to honestly address questions about the fairness and the soundness of those policies and programs.

Director of the Office of Management and Budget George P. Shultz admitted at a press conference that the president had not proposed a single change to accommodate the recommendations of the CBC:

Is it fair to say of this document that it codifies everything the administration has already said and done about the issues raised? The answer to that is certainly yes, and at the same time I think that it is a summary document.[24]

The consensus of the CBC was that Nixon

1. Was defending his intention to spin off to other departments all programs under the Office of Economic Opportunity (OEO), leaving it only as an innovative branch, not an administrative one;
2. Was persisting in defending his aim to divert education funds into general revenue sharing;
3. Was justifying revision of federal aid to higher education and a reduction in grants, shifting the responsibility of educating the disadvantaged—the poor and minority groups—to the states;
4. Was maintaining that the Equal Employment Opportunity Commission (EEOC) should not have the power to issue cease-and-desist orders to prevent employers from discriminating;
5. Was challenging the need for a new development bank with an initial appropriation of $1 billion to aid minority businesses; and

6. Had nixed the suggestion of using Federal Deposit Insurance Corporation assets to provide assistance to minority firms.

CBC MEMBERS APPEAR ON "MEET THE PRESS"

When it was announced that three members of the Congressional Black Caucus would appear on the nationally televised "Meet the Press" to discuss Nixon's reply to the sixty recommendations, the president hurriedly assembled a meeting of black supporters at the White House.

The day before the Sunday broadcast, thirty-six black Republicans were hosted in the Rose Garden and encouraged to counter whatever the three Caucus members would say in opposition to the president's response.

On May 23, 1971, the Sunday immediately following the release of Nixon's official response, Diggs, Hawkins, and I appeared on "Meet the Press." The following are selected excerpts from that program:

MR. SPIVAK: Mr. Diggs, President Nixon has now responded to your recommendations. Will you give us your general appraisal of his response?

MR. DIGGS: Mr. Spivak, I think it is the consensus of our group that the report is deeply disappointing. I think it is more of a reply than a response, and when one considers the amount of manpower and brainpower that went into the creation of this document, our opinion is reinforced.

MR. SPIVAK: Mr. Hawkins, will you give us your appraisal of the response?

MR. HAWKINS: I recall that the president said he should be judged not by his words but by his deeds. I can now understand, because his words have very little meaning, and I think the enumeration of his deeds in terms of the accomplishments that he attempted to justify was certainly very faulted.

MR. SPIVAK: Mr. Clay, you have already been reported as saying that President Nixon's response is "a charade, a farce, a misconception, all kinds of trickery." Is there really anything the president could have said or done that would have satisfied you?

MR. CLAY: I think that the president could have been responsive to the sixty recommendations . . . Instead, he attempted to document his present policies. We already know those policies. We already contend those policies are having a devastating effect on poor and black Americans.

MR. ROSENTHAL: Congressman Diggs, there is a danger in so long a list of recommendations and responses that we begin to lose sight of an issue that I know is important . . . what single issue would you focus on; would it be welfare reform, would it be housing, would it be the economy?

MR. DIGGS: All of these things are overdue . . . the main thing . . . it is necessary to come up with some new approaches to these problems if we are going to get our country moving along.

MR. GRAHAM: Mr. Clay, in your response . . . you referred specifically to aid to black colleges. The president's report indicated that he was doubling that amount.

MR. CLAY: . . . but the fact is that he hasn't given an extra nickel to black colleges. The fact tends to bear out that last year for the twelve Land Grant colleges in the four states in the South, six white and six black, the federal government spent $72.4 million . . . but the six white colleges got $71.8 million of it and the six black colleges got only $497,000. The student ratio in those schools is only six to one, but the federal expenditure was $140 to every $1 given to black students.

MR. SPIVAK: Mr. Diggs . . . you said, "Our people are no longer asking for equality as a rhetorical promise. They are demanding equality of results." Can you tell us how President Nixon . . . can guarantee equality of results, really, without instituting a dictatorship?

MR. DIGGS: . . . institutional racism [which] exists in this country has to be met by institutional response. We are going to have to have all of the resources of our government and from the private sector converging on this matter. . . .

THE NIXON ADMINISTRATION TRIES TO IGNORE THE CBC

MR. SPIVAK: The president says that we are already making significant progress . . . toward those goals.

MR. DIGGS: I like the word "change" rather than "progress." . . . Obviously we have a difference of opinion. The president's letter frames progress in one way, but the reply from the bureaucrats that was designed to answer each one of our specified recommendations was in an entirely different vein and represented a gap between promise and performance.

MR. ROSENTHAL: Congressman Hawkins, there is a political problem in that, I would guess, for the three of you and for all members of the Black Caucus. The minute blacks begin to find the freedom to move out to the suburbs [a reference to our request for fair housing legislation], doesn't that mean there goes your political base?

MR. HAWKINS: Yes, I think we are not thinking of ourselves in this regard. Most of us represent ghettos that are almost [sic] black, at least from 50 to 80 percent black. I think that we are thinking of the individuals whom we represent, our constituencies. There is no reason why an individual should have to travel all day and sometimes half the night to return home in order to earn a job, and the jobs certainly are in the suburbs.

MR. KILPATRICK: The Black Caucus has been very critical of this massive response by the president. It has been termed "deeply disappointing," a "charade," a "farce," and so on. The president says that of the 115 judges he has nominated so far, eleven, or 10 percent of the total, are black. In your judgment, Mr. Clay, is that change, or is that progress?

MR. CLAY: I think that is part of the sham and charade that I spoke of earlier.

MR. KILPATRICK: The figures are incorrect?

MR. CLAY: The president has appointed 127 judges. Only ten have been black. But the question here is the kind of blacks that he has appointed . . . one in California was a replacement for a Johnson hold-over which was never confirmed by the Senate . . . one appointed to the Virgin Islands, which traditionally has been reserved for blacks, and eight black judges in the District of Columbia, which is 71 percent black. Seven of the eight have term appointments, not lifetime appointments. So in effect, this president has not appointed a black judge in the East, in the Northwest, in the Midwest, or in the South. . . .

MR. MONROE: I am sorry to interrupt. Our time is up. Thank you, gentlemen, for being with us today on "Meet the Press."[25]

THE CBC "REPORT TO THE NATION"

The day following the television appearance, the Caucus released a document entitled "Report to the Nation," which outlined our frustrations and disappointments with present and prior occupants of the White House for their disregard of "both the symbolic and real political expression of [black] aspirations and needs." The statement said in part:

. . . But in reality [Nixon's] document constitutes less a response than a reply, couched predominantly in the form of bureaucratic reports intent on justifying the status quo. The challenge we tried to catalyze—fresh thinking, the matching of implementation with need, the degree of courage and commitment national leadership has brought to other efforts in the past—appears for the most part to have been ignored.

. . . The president, in the transmittal letter which accompanied the replies from the agencies, stated that we and his administration are in agreement on "broad goals." We would very much wish that to be so. But "goals" are undergirded by basic assumptions which give words their meaning. We of the Congressional Black Caucus place the dignity of human beings above the balancing of books at their expense and the perfection of management techniques. We place constitutional guarantees for citizens above preservation of order through force. We believe that our constituencies have the right and the ability to determine their own affairs. In our view, volunteerism is no substitute for effective enforcement of the law. There is no better evidence of our differences with the administration on these basic issues than our respective views on economic development, welfare reform, and revenue sharing.[26]

In January 1972, eight months after we issued our "Report to the Nation," Caucus vice-chairman Hawkins assailed President Nixon for not responding to CBC recommendations in his State of the Union address.

> The president said that he had presented "ninety proposals" that still needed real action by Congress, but completely overlooked and refused to even mention any of more than sixty proposals presented to him by the Congressional Black Caucus.
>
> The entire message, in our view, was evangelistic meandering with nothing encouraging or helpful for the situation of black people in the United States. The issue of civil rights, for instance, was virtually omitted. . . .[27]

The same press release stated:

> We offer this paper as a political guide for those who could possibly be misled by the factual shortcomings of the president's civil rights highlights. . . . Indeed, this is the administration which developed the political concepts of a "southern strategy" and a "benign neglect."[28]

THE TRUE STATE OF THE UNION

One month after President Nixon was sworn into office for his second term, he shamefully perverted the message of John F. Kennedy in his January 20, 1973, State of the Union address. He exhorted the American people: "In our own lives, let each of us ask—not just what will government do for me, but what can I do for myself?"[29]

That question was a sinister one in an era when people's ability to help themselves was dwindling because the federal commitment to humanity was being eroded by callous, insensitive policies promoted by the Nixon administration.

CBC members were outraged by the message imparted by the president. We issued a call for a "True State of the Union" and vowed not to sit idly on the sidelines while corporate and other vested interests "take bread from the mouths of the poor."

> Over the past four years, we have learned that self-reliance is a virtue which is demanded only from minorities, the poor, and the disadvantaged; no one told Lockheed and Penn Central to pull themselves up by their bootstraps. That is the central fallacy in Mr. Nixon's exhortation. It is one which the CBC intends to expose and to combat—with legislative programs and congressional action.

We, too, would like to believe in self-reliance, but we see it as a goal. It is not, as Mr. Nixon would have us believe, a means. The means to the end of self-reliance lie in a federal commitment to the fulfillment of human and social needs.[30]

Pursuant to a House special order, Caucus members were given the opportunity to deliver a "True State of the Union" address before the House of Representatives on January 31, 1973. Members of the Caucus assumed responsibility for specific areas of concern and spoke to the body about pressing needs of minorities. We dealt with domestic needs, foreign policy, poverty, welfare reform, housing, Africa and Third World countries, employment and the economy, health, minority economic development, crime and narcotics addiction, racism in the military, education, the criminal justice system, civil rights, rural development, and revenue sharing.
Our message said in part:

We begin from the premise that, in this richest and most advanced technological nation, poverty is a shameful anachronism. The federal government has the power to eradicate poverty. In the absence of jobs, the welfare system must be revised to provide an adequate income for every American citizen. At the same time, the government must institute a program of full employment.

We do not believe that inflation should or can be fought with unemployment. The proper means of combatting inflation is an effective stabilization program. . . .

We will watch the implementation of the revenue-sharing program with close attention. . . . Special attention will be paid to civil rights compliance within the revenue-sharing program.

Recent years have witnessed a great disparity between promise and performance in education, health, and housing. It is to the everlasting discredit of this president that he has vetoed an unprecedented number of education, health, and housing bills. Where the veto has failed, impoundment has succeeded.[31]

Each member of the Caucus devoted his energies to one specific topic and addressed that issue on the floor of the House. Concluding the two-hour session, Congressman Louis Stokes, chairman of the CBC, stated:

> Mr. Speaker, we have now heard from the members of the Congressional Black Caucus. We have set forth our views as to the true state of the Union and the path we feel this nation must follow. We hope to help stimulate the revival of the Congress as an effective, innovative, co-equal branch of government. We must begin a massive new effort to meet the human needs of this country. Our foreign policy, so long corrupted by the Indochina war, must be redirected toward helping the underdeveloped nations. To accomplish our goals, we will need to work with our colleagues in the Congress. Many of our colleagues are here today to join us in discussing the true state of the Union. Let us now begin to hear their views.[32]

NOTES

1. Congressman Clay, House of Representatives, *Congressional Record*, December 15, 1970, page 41723.

2. *Newsweek*, March 1, 1971, page 23.

3. *Ibid.*, page 24.

4. Congressman William L. Clay, *Congressional Record*, December 15, 1970, page 41723.

5. Letter from Senator Robert Dole, December 19, 1970.

6. Letter from Congressman Clay, December 29, 1970.

7. Congressman Stokes, *The Washington North Star*, September 22, 1983, page S-3.

8. *St. Louis Globe-Democrat*, January 23/24, 1971, page 1A.

9. *St. Louis Post Dispatch*, March 1, 1970, page 3b.

10. Congressman Donald Riegle, *Congressional Record*, March 17, 1971, page H-1628.

11. Jimmy Booker, March 23, 1971, Washington, D.C.

12. CBC Recommendations to the President of the United States, a Position Paper on the State of Black Americans, Presented to President Nixon on March 25, 1971, inserted in *Congressional Record*, March 30, 1971, 92nd Congress, first session, page 24798.

13. *The Afro-American* newspaper, April 3, 1971, page 1.

14. Confidential report of comments made during Black Caucus meeting with President Richard N. Nixon, Thursday, March 25, 1971, the Cabinet Room of the White House, transcribed by Caucus staffer.

15. *Ibid.*, page 6.

16. *Ibid.*

17. *Ibid.*, pages 8–9.

18. Robert Brown, special assistant to President Nixon, quoted by Dom Bonafede, *National Journal*, June 24, 1972, page 1066.

19. Congressman Parren Mitchell, 1971 *Congressional Quarterly*, page 659.

20. Victor Riesel, Publishers-Hall Syndicate, March 29, 1971.

21. *Ibid.*

22. Diggs, letter to President Nixon, April 5, 1971.

23. *Washington Post*, May 20, 1971, page A3.

24. George Shultz, press conference, Washington, D.C., May 19, 1971, White House press release, page 3.

25. "Meet the Press," NBC, live television broadcast, Sunday, May 23, 1971, reprinted with permission of NBC News.

26. "Report to the Nation," issued by the Congressional Black Caucus, May 24, 1971.

27. Congressman Hawkins, CBC press release entitled "From the Administration Which Gave Us Benign Neglect," March 1972.

28. *Ibid*.

29. President Richard Nixon, State of the Union address, *Congressional Record*, 93rd Congress, first session, January 20, 1973, page 1660.

30. CBC press release, January 26, 1973.

31. CBC "True State of the Union" address before the House of Representatives, January 31, 1973, *Congressional Record*, pages 2830–38.

32. *Ibid.*, page 2838.

7

The First Annual Congressional Black Caucus Dinner

The Annual Congressional Black Caucus Dinner has become an institution unto itself. It is both symbolic and real in its significance, bringing together the movers and shakers of black America for celebration and for dialogue. It was first held in June 1971 at the swank Sheraton-Park Hotel in Washington, D.C. The $100-a-plate gala presented a unique opportunity to establish "a new direction" in black politics. The dinner was timely because the most recent events summoned us to ask again what the central purpose of politics in our society was. It had the potential to catalyze a collective voice for black Americans. If that collective voice was heard, it could change dramatically the nature of political decision-making in the black community and stand in contrast to the role traditionally played by individual charismatic black leaders, who more often than not depended on the generosity of white philanthropists rather than the financial support of their own constituency. It challenged the leadership process in general, for both the black and white community, because most leaders—even those heading civil rights organizations—were never great advocates for group decision-making or attuned to heeding the guidance of a collective voice.

A clarion voice was desperately needed to defy the blatant attempts of a sinister president and an accommodating Congress to dismantle people-oriented social programs. President Nixon had called for and the Congress was accepting willingly elimination of or drastic cuts in funds for the nation's elementary and secondary schools, for manpower training, for student loans and grants, for public service employment, for Model Cities programs and housing, for child health research and school lunches, and for a reduction in emergency health services.

The country was in crisis and turmoil because of our involvement in a war in Southeast Asia and because of the stubborn resistance to racial and economic justice here at home. The nation was clouded with internal unrest and beset by external war. There were 9 million known alcoholics, 4 million drug abusers, 25 million poverty stricken, 15 million welfare recipients, 5 million unemployed, and 30 million who went to bed nightly hungry and undernourished.

This was the situation confronting the nation when the Caucus convened black leaders in the capital to address the problems. The Caucus had the potential to fulfill the void created in national leadership by the election to office of Nixon, Agnew, and a wave of ultraconservatives. Proceeds from the dinner would enable us to hire the necessary staff to engage the enemy.

Much credit for the success of the first dinner goes to businessman A. L. Nellum, president and chief executive officer of a management consulting firm by the same name, and Ofield Dukes, a journalist and public relations specialist who had formerly handled media relations for Vice President Hubert H. Humphrey. Nellum's company absorbed most of the administrative costs associated with promoting the affair, and Dukes used his skills, resources, and expertise to acquaint the media with the importance of the event and to interpret for them the historical significance of black people convening such a gathering.

Nellum brought on board a crew of highly qualified professionals to function as dinner coordinators: Carol Payne, Lucia Jamieson, Carole Brooks, Diane Williams, Carol Pittman, and Denise Edgecombe. Each was adept in organizing affairs of this nature. Soon after, Ivanhoe Donaldson, Carole Hoover, Marianne Nils, Valerie Pinson, and John Wilson joined the team. Bill Cosby, W. Averell Harriman, and Henry G. Parks agreed to serve as national cochairmen.

Some of the most publicized names in the world of entertainment, including Nancy Wilson, Dick Gregory, Billy Eckstine, and Ossie Davis, were asked to be present on stage. Caucus members successfully enlisted the support of the most prominent civil rights leaders to assemble in the audience. People like Coretta Scott King, the Reverend Ralph Abernathy, the Reverend Jesse Jackson, James Farmer, Whitney Young, Dorothy Height, Bayard Rustin, Andrew Young, Stokely Carmichael, and John Lewis did not hesitate to accept our invitation to attend. Distinguished educators and scholars like Charles Hamilton, Amiri Baraka, Andrew Billingsley, Robert Green, James Cheek, and Lerone Bennett also accepted our invitation. Dynamic elected officials such as Julian Bond, Percy Sutton, Bruce Watkins, Carl Stokes, Maynard Jackson, Ken Gibson, Barbara Jordan, Willie Brown, Merv Dymally, George Brown, Richard Hatcher, and Yvonne Brathwaite agreed to attend and offered their services to promote the dinner.

Dukes developed a definitive, well-structured PR program, hiring professionals to handle the day-to-day activities of answering press inquiries, sending information, preparing news releases, and arranging press interviews with members of the Caucus for radio, television, and newspaper coverage. He also monitored the implementation of the overall PR plan.

CBC Chairman Diggs and I, as dinner chairman, knew that college presidents, ambassadors, doctors, cab drivers, hairdressers, barbers, and business people all felt compelled to attend in order to revalidate their credentials as bona fide in-the-know community leaders. We were aware that the ins and the outs, the haves and the have-nots, the would-be's, the could-be's, the never-will-be's would all make a pilgrimage to participate in this, the most memorable political event for black Americans since the 1963 march on Washington. In convening this meeting, the Caucus took a giant step in advancing the cause of black people by solidifying broadbased, national support for the development of a black agenda.

Some Caucus members questioned the wisdom of hosting a high-priced fund-raising event. They felt a $100-plate dinner signaled a catering to rich corporations and the abandonment of our commitment to the poor. Other members viewed the concept of "unified power," "group decisions," and a "one-for-all spokesperson" as a direct threat to their status as national black leaders. The media had tacitly conferred on several black officials the title of "premier" spokespersons for all blacks. Some wanted to believe that one or two celebrated leaders, elevated to levels approaching deification, were preferable to thirteen respected and strong voices articulating as one the concerns of black Americans. Even several Caucus members held to delusions of omnipotence, hoping to inherit the mantle of leadership formerly worn by Congressman Adam Clayton Powell, Jr. However, most Caucus members supported the idea of a $100-plate dinner and, thank God, most insisted on pursuing a course whereby minority communities would hear one united voice—reflected, articulated, and acted upon in the overall interests of the poor and disadvantaged.

In preparation for the program, Diggs discussed with other members and with Howard Robinson, CBC executive director, the roles each of us would play at the dinner. Speech-making before so distinguished an audience was an important consideration. What was said could propel the Caucus into national prominence. What was not said could resign the CBC to a minimal role in the field of national politics. The eyes and ears of the nation would be watching and listening to those who commanded the microphone at this very special occasion.

It was decided that substance, not rhetoric, would be the criterion for developing an acceptable but different kind of political treatise. A perspective capable of alerting our people to a new kind of adversary was desirable and necessary. We sensed that blacks expected a more sophisticated response to problem-solving than had so far been displayed, and they wanted to be involved somehow in the planning for the continued struggle to stop the oppressive forces in our anti-black society.

We proceeded with caution in devising solutions to the problems. In recent times, circumstances had changed dramatically. It was important that we create new methods of combatting a new, subtle kind of racism. We needed innovative initiatives. It was important that we re-evaluate the concept of black power. The times called for clear, unequivocal, authoritative exhortation. It was necessary for those delivering speeches to use the kind of language that would convince friend and foe alike that the CBC was in the best position to lead the fight for black political liberation. And what had to be said must be said regardless of the hurt some of our friends might suffer.

We served notice that what was perceived of in the late fifties as a "Negro problem" needing special assistance and expert direction from whites for proper resolution was now, in the seventies, viewed as a problem that blacks themselves would address. We knew our actions would be viewed as hostile and provocative by some. Yet we were willing to risk the loss of support from influential white groups and individuals in order to acquire control of the apparatus governing the quality of our lives.

We decided to define as well as refine the role that blacks would permit whites to play in our continuing struggle for economic and political emancipation. It was imperative they be made aware that blacks would control the politics in their own communities. We believed that no one, black or white, should leave the banquet with any doubt about who was authorized to speak for our people.

Those of us planning the program for the dinner were well aware of

Frederick Douglass' teachings and prepared to implement his radical concepts. He once said, "Neither institutions nor friends can make a race to stand unless it has strength in its own legs . . . races like individuals, must stand or fall by their own merits. . . ."[1]

On another occasion, addressing the same subject, Douglass stated:

> Common sense affirms and only folly denies, that the man who has suffered the wrong is the man to demand the redress—that the man struck is the man to cry out—and that he who has endured the cruel pain of slavery is the man to advocate liberty. It is evident that we must be our own representatives and advocates—not exclusively, but particularly—not distinct from, but in connection with our white friends. . . .[2]

Participants at the dinner shared the common memory of 300 years of resentment of official and unofficial lawlessness that had kept our people in bondage. The most difficult task ahead was to put into words the frustrations, the disappointments, the disillusionment of ten generations of black people and not totally alienate those nonblack forces that would otherwise help and support us in achieving our ends. But more important, our mandate, if there was one, was to promote a new strategy devised by black people themselves to confront racial repression and defy racist oppressors.

NO PERMANENT FRIENDS, NO PERMANENT ENEMIES, JUST PERMANENT INTERESTS

More than 2,700 people packed the ballroom of the Sheraton-Park Hotel on the evening of June 18, 1971, as Father Clements, a Catholic priest from a ghetto parish on Chicago's South Side, delivered the invocation for the first fund-raising dinner.* He paraphrased a prayer by St. Francis of Assisi, inserting the name of each CBC member.

Congressman Diggs, the first speaker of the evening, was received warmly. He said:

*Later Clements earned national acclaim by instituting an adoption program for black children that succeeded in reducing the waiting list considerably for those orphans. In public defiance of his archbishop, he took the unprecedented step of adopting the first child in the program. Later, he adopted two more children. Twenty years later, the program could claim the adoption of more than 11,000 children, almost 100 percent of them black.

I welcome you on behalf of the thirteen members of the Congressional Black Caucus. But we welcome you, too, on behalf of our colleagues from cities and states all over the nation who have done us the honor of joining us here, and of the millions not physically present tonight who have over the past several years mounted a quiet revolution through their ballots—a revolution which is changing both the direction—and the complexion—of municipal, county, and state governments north, south, east, and west.

We meet tonight in the majority-black capital of this most powerful nation in the world which somehow seems powerless to solve its most fundamental problems. We meet to assert the common bonds that unite men and women of all races, creeds, and generations who share a fierce determination to liberate the legions of the oppressed. We come together to arm and equip ourselves to fight more effectively than ever before for those who are too seldom victors, too often victims. The victims of poverty and racism, of a senseless war, of an economy which offers neither enough jobs nor the dignity of an adequate income. The victims of unequal justice, of basic benefits callously denied—victims of that contemporary plague, drug addiction, which is now visiting upon our soldiers and the citizens of the suburbs the same human destruction to which our country paid little heed when the casualties were largely confined to the black and brown youth of our urban ghettos.

The response which your generous outpouring of aid and encouragement tonight represents, reflects the range and depth of support which the Caucus has had the rare good fortune to receive since its inception.

. . . With the staff and resources we plan to assemble after tonight, we hope to be clearer, more persistent, and more effective than blacks in the national Congress have ever been in fashioning an agenda not only for 1972, but for years to come.

. . . As it happens, all of us are Democrats. But what we are hearing with increasing insistence from our constituents is that there are times when they would have us judge our interests by something more substantial than party labels. And there are likely to be times when we must challenge both major parties and candidates of every persuasion, at every level, to address forthrightly the unmet needs of our people.

. . . Even as we celebrate, even as we enjoy the wit, beauty, and soul of some of the most gifted artists in America, let us not forget that it is by no easy path that we have arrived at this night. And the journey is far from over. We are the grateful heirs of Douglass, DuBois, and Bethune—of Medgar Evers, Malcolm, Martin Luther King, and Whitney Young. We build on the labors of Thurgood Marshall, Adam Clayton Powell, Roy Wilkins, the young men and women of the civil rights movement of the sixties, and the black thrust toward long-denied power and liberation which is part of the world-wide revolution of color and the rejection of caste. . . .[3]

As chairman of the dinner, I had the privilege of following Diggs to the podium and introducing the keynote speaker, Ossie Davis. Before performing that task, the program called for me to give ten minutes of remarks. One sentence in my text, paraphrased from other historical statements, subsequently was adopted as the official motto of the Congressional Black Caucus: "Black people have no permanent friends, no permanent enemies, just permanent interests."[4]

The Caucus, in voting to make that statement its motto, felt those words adequately grasped the mood of the times in black America and properly reflected the attitude of Caucus members. It signaled what we hoped would be a higher level of determination, maturity, and sophistication among black elected officials in dealing with the white establishment.

In the introductory remarks I sounded the theme of the new politics when I said, "We shall accept nothing less than meaningful participation at the center of power. Our goals are to obtain freedom and justice. In order to do this, we must be united—to successfully achieve these objectives, we must stay united."

The following are points made in my speech:

The name of the game is not black issues, or women's issues or poverty issues, or economic issues, or peace issues—but human issues.

Coalition implies that each coalescing group will bring some clout, some muscle to the bargaining table.

Black politicians must become less radical in their statements and more radical on the issues.

Too many of our people are ill-housed and ill-fed; our children are kept by the public schools for twelve years and turned out on society with eight years of education.

For it has to be our positive assumption that the achievement of our goals [is] essential for the maintenance of an orderly American society.

Our politics at one time was based on the theory of appeasing the white majority. Today, the old politics of accommodation has been replaced by the new politics of confrontation.

There exists a new breed of blacks who demand a re-evaluation of the old concept that "what's good for the nation is good for minorities." We now couch our thinking in the fundamental concept that what's good for minorities is also good for the nation.[5]

Whatever gems of wisdom Diggs and I imparted were totally eclipsed by the brilliance and eloquence of the principal speaker of the evening, Ossie Davis. He worked the crowd with an artistic ability consistent with his many years of training as an actor, director, and producer par excellence. Davis electrified the audience with his grace, dignity, depth, and humor. His thought-provoking appeals to racial pride were in perfect harmony with the energy of the people in the room, many of whom had journeyed from the farthest of the fifty states to express their support for the Congressional Black Caucus. Sentence after sentence, the crowd was on its feet, shouting and applauding, interrupting his presentation.

Davis's address was titled "The Plan, Not the Man." Here is a portion of his keynote address:

> Ladies, gentlemen. Brothers, sisters. And friends. This is an historic occasion, a moment we have dreamed and worked and fought for longer than we ourselves have been alive. The light that kept our fathers and our mothers turned into possibilities of a better future when they were slaves. The insights they gleaned, the hopes they hoped, the prayers they prayed, have come one step closer to being answered by what you have collectively done by your presence here tonight [*applause*].
>
> I have been told that there are 2,800 of us here [*applause*] and we occupy facilities which were meant for 2,400. That's a pretty good indication of what price we place on our freedom and on the men and women who are dedicated to fighting for it [*applause*].
>
> You might have wondered why I, who am an actor and a performer, among other things, was chosen to give the keynote address tonight. And I, myself, when called upon to do so, had moments of hesitation and doubt and I wondered, why choose me for such an important task? I guess the one reason which makes sense is that I represent that aspect of black culture which began in Africa with the storytellers and came down to the great rhetorical giants who have stirred us by their words in the past.
>
> But I think the time has perhaps come when rhetoric will begin to take a back seat [*applause*]. And I was so stirred by that possibility that I decided tonight to give my few remarks a subject, a title, a text, which I want you to listen to very carefully.

In his characteristic deep, melodic voice, Ossie gave clear interpretation to the black experience.

The text is very simply: It's not the man, it's the plan [*applause*]. And, for those of us who need more explicit information, those of us still caught up in the dream that rhetoric will solve our problems, let me state it another way . . . it's not the rap, it's the map [*applause*].

We have been blessed in our past with many great leaders. Leaders whose qualifications have been proven by what they did and what they said and even by the fact that when the time came they didn't hesitate to give their lives. And their dedication and their hard work has been borne to fruition . . . bears fruition by where we are tonight. And I don't call for a moment of silence and gratitude for what the fathers have given us, but we shouldn't go forward without remembering that we are a continuous chain. We celebrate tonight, but we don't celebrate the past. We celebrate the future, and if anybody has a right to celebrate the future, I'm sure that we must be that particular people.

We have had great leaders in the past who have stirred us with their words, with their hopes, and with their dreams. I remember coming to Washington in 1963 when Dr. Martin Luther King stood at the Washington Memorial [*applause*] and he said to the world and to the Congress and to the nation, "I have a dream!" Now that dream of 1963 was not realized then, it was not realized at the time of his death, and it has not been realized now.

At the time when Dr. King died in 1968 he was in the process of organizing his forces and calling upon his people to come one more time to Washington, D.C. And I have a feeling that had he come that time he would not have said, "I have a dream," he would have said, "I have a plan" [*applause*]. And I feel that that plan that he had might have made the difference. . . .

And that's why, tonight, the burden of my appeal is to you, to the thirteen Congressional Black Caucus members, to give us a plan of action. Give us a plan of action . . . a Ten Black Commandments, simple, strong, that we can carry in our hearts and in our memories no matter where we are and reach out and touch and feel the reassurance that there is behind everything we do a simple, moral, intelligent plan that must be fulfilled in the course of time even if all of our leaders, one by one, fall in battle. Somebody will rise and say [*applause*] "Brother!" Someone will rise and say [*applause*], "Our leader died while we were on page three of the plan. Now that the funeral is over, let us proceed to page four."

. . . From our noble thirteen, we need that they think the problems out; that they investigate the possible solution; that they codify their results, and they present their program to us, the people, so that we may ratify what they have thought and organized and left to us as a program for action.

. . . And we might think tonight that we are at that particular junction, and in some degrees we are. We have become hep to the meaning of political power and that's why we are here. This is an exercise in power tonight. We've eaten a good meal, we've paid good money for it. We've had good fellowship. We've heard good music and entertainment. But, brothers and sisters, the name of the game is power, and if you ain't playing power, you're in the wrong place.

. . . The fires of rebellion are burning brightly because human beings can only be repressed and ignored and maltreated for so long. Then they must rise.

What is the response of the black people in our inner cities to this endemic unemployment? What happens to our youth who suffers from 25 percent to 50 percent unemployment? Some of them take to drugs. Some of them take to crime. Some of them apply themselves and say the solution to the problem is education; the solution is preparing ourselves to deal with an automated society, to deal with a computerized economy. There are others who say that the society has no alternative, nothing to give me but a tour of duty in Vietnam. Still others say the only recourse is revolution. . . .

What we need from you, our honored leaders—I choose the word advisedly, our honored leaders—what we need from you are your best thoughts, your sincerest dedication. We need from you a reassurance that there is a new political alignment, even in the black community. Now we no longer elect leaders by the value we find that they bring to us from the white community.

. . . Ladies and gentlemen, I think I have said enough. There's much that could be talked about tonight, but we're here and the fact that we are here is itself eloquent. This is a dinner that could have served without a single word, because we know the historical significance of just sitting, looking, talking to each other of what this moment means. And if you think that there are others that don't know what this moment means, you should be somewhere where the listening devices are turned up very high. But all I'm saying to the world, all I'm saying to that cadre of black leadership that we have—that we want a plan. We want a plan so simple, so easy to remember that we can carry it in our heads, so that if the storm of oppression should wipe us all out but one family and that family was crouching somewhere in the dark, one brother would reach out to another and say, "Hey, hey, man, what's the plan?"[6]

A PROMISING BEGINNING

The First Annual CBC Dinner was not only a success in terms of support and participation, it was a financial success as well. A. L.

Nellum and Associates donated staff and assumed all overhead expenses for space, office equipment, telephones, and clerical work. Nellum issued a final report representing an overview and summary of all activities involved in the planning and staging of the dinner. He reconstructed and explained the level of support activities necessary to carry out the affair, documented and analyzed the response to the dinner, and presented a transitional financial statement.

The total cash received was $212,524.43. The total disbursements were $67,689.99. The net profit was $144,843.44. In terms of the Consumer Price Index, the net profit of $144,843 in 1971 is equivalent to $510,000 in 1990 dollars. The primary reasons that net profit was so high on this initial venture was that all talent was 100 percent donated, except for musicians, who were paid union scale, and that most overhead expenses, including space, office equipment, telephone bills, and clerical help were donated by A. L. Nellum and Associates.

Nellum's report stated that white liberals in the United States Congress purchased only 57 tickets; civil rights and liberal organizations purchased only 110 tickets, with black groups buying half of those; labor unions purchased only 131 tickets, with more than half of those coming from black locals; and corporations bought only 169 tickets. The Great Atlantic and Pacific Tea Company, R. J. Reynolds, General Motors Corporation, and Gulf Oil Corporation purchased tables of 10 tickets. Senator Edward Kennedy (D–Massachusetts) and George McGovern (D–South Dakota), a candidate for president, each purchased $2,500 tables. Of the 2,700 people in attendance, less than 15 percent were white. So this is one instance where we know that success was achieved by blacks from all regions of the country and from all walks of life coming together to make something happen for themselves. We did not need big corporations and labor unions to bankroll our program. What we needed and got were enough black people who identified with a new hope and a new direction for the political future for blacks as a whole to do what needed to be done.

The First Annual CBC Dinner marked the beginning of an elaborate educational process aimed at sensitizing the black electorate to the paramount indices for effectively exercising real political power. Somehow, some way, black voters had to be convinced to use the ballot more judiciously than in the past. A national voter education program had to be launched to inform blacks that those whites who came into their neighborhoods every two or four years to kiss black babies and call senior citizens by their first names were not necessarily their best friends. And those who had a record of opposing measures beneficial to the community should be branded persona non grata at all times.

Those blacks masquerading as tough crusaders for the rights of their constituents while sipping champagne, nibbling caviar, and selling out the community at exclusive country clubs had to be dealt with as well.

But the single most important obstacle to a free, independent, effective black electorate was the unrealistic expectation that electorate had of its black representatives. They expected little or nothing from white officials and the impossible from blacks. They expected black leaders invariably to perform miracles but made no demands on whites to perform even ordinary tasks of representation.

The next most vexing problem for black elected officials was their relationship with the white media and the measure of disregard most reporters had (and still have) for the intelligence of black leaders. White reporters always insist on asking that stupid question never presented to white leaders: What is the single, most critical problem facing black Americans? The answer, of course, could very well be the question itself and the inherent racism in it.

Why will the media not perceive the problems of black Americans as being just as complex and multifaceted as those of other citizens? Lack of access to adequate health care is a grave problem for both black and white Americans. It's not assumed that it is the single most critical problem facing white Americans. Poor housing is a serious problem for both groups, but it is never conceived of as possibly the single most important problem of white Americans. Quality education, economic justice, and safety from the AIDS epidemic are just as illusory for some whites as they are for many blacks. But the question "What is the single most important issue facing white America?" is never asked of George Bush or Bill Clinton.

Just as white leaders dare not confine their attention to one problem, we must teach our people that black leaders cannot limit themselves to single issues either.

NOTES

1. Frederick Douglass, *Freedom's Journal*, date unknown.
2. Frederick Douglass, cited in the *Washington North Star*, September 22, 1983, page S-2.
3. Congressman Charles Diggs, Sheraton-Park Hotel, Washington, D.C.,

THE FIRST ANNUAL CONGRESSIONAL BLACK CAUCUS DINNER

June 18, 1971, manuscript department Moorland-Spingarn Center, Howard University, Washington, D.C., pages 1–2.

4. Congressman William L. Clay, Sheraton-Park Hotel, Washington, D.C., June 18, 1971, *ibid.*, page 2.

5. *Ibid.*, page 3.

6. Ossie Davis, keynote address, Sheraton-Park Hotel, Washington, D.C., June 18, 1971, *The Washington North Star*, September 22, 1983, page S-4.

8

Early Days of the Caucus

For all the enthusiastic support that the CBC received in its nascent days of development, there were individuals and groups in the civil rights and labor movements, liberal ranks, and local politics—all natural allies—who did not support us initially. There were some misunderstandings and misconceptions of the role we were to play. Leaders of civil rights groups felt the Caucus was trying to usurp their traditional role of establishing the civil rights agenda and dictating the course of action to be taken in racial confrontations. Some black local and state elected officials sensed that we wanted to become a national clearinghouse for local problems and issues confronting black Americans.

Labor leaders believed that any group of prominent blacks not financially or politically obligated to organized labor was a threat to their ability to mobilize the black community for their various political and economic purposes. Seven of the nine new members of the Caucus won election over opposition from AFL-CIO and Teamster locals.

Many in the business community were skeptical of politicians, black or white, who did not fear reprisals from the National Chamber of Commerce and the National Association of Manufacturers. The Caucus had never forged a relationship with either group and was not indebted to any particular business consortium for substantial financial support. In fact, most proposals advanced by business interests were considered by black officials to be anathema to the interests of our constituents.

Liberal whites seemed flabbergasted that a group of blacks would attempt to plan a course for their own people independent of and without prior approval from them and their institutions. In the minds of many whites, there was something injurious, something heretical, something sinister about the formation of an all-black political unit to protect and advance the interests of black people. A black-based, black-inspired, black-nourished group created to educate the black community politically somehow posed an imminent danger to friendly white folk. In reality, the Caucus was merely transferring from them and their groups the right to anoint our own spokespersons and to confer on them the mantle of legitimate, respectable leadership.

White liberals, in particular, were caught off-guard and their irritation was displayed in none too subtle ways. Obviously frustrated, they bemoaned the fact that black congressmen (less than 4 percent of the 435 members of the House of Representatives) had assumed the role of deciding how far and how fast black people would demand progress in the struggle for their rights. Even more disturbing was that the black agenda was to be developed without consulting them. Expressing dismay at our arrogance, liberals, moderates, and conservatives accused us of polarizing the Congress along racial lines and promoting racial separatism in the country.

The Saint Louis Globe-Democrat, one of the most racist publications in the United States, editorialized: "Congressman William L. Clay's 'black politics' is no more justified than would be 'white politics' promoted by a white politician. . . . Racism under any guise is racism—and detestable by any name."[1]

Most white liberals had parlayed themselves into positions of importance in various organizations by befriending large segments of the black community and using that relationship as a wedge to gain control of certain institutions. Liberal whites and labor leaders both benefitted from this one-sided, illicit arrangement. Prior to 1965, white America generally was predisposed to accept anybody except a black for any position of leadership and authority. Unless an organization was 51 percent black, the best we could hope for was a liberal-thinking and acting white person winning control of the group. Consequently, liberals assessed the situation and developed strategies to reap personal benefits. Using blacks as shock troops allowed them to amass power for themselves in labor unions and the Democratic party far beyond their numbers.

Members of the CBC did not fit into traditional molds ascribed to black leaders. We did not owe our election in any large measure to support from liberal and labor organizations. We were not beholden to them for any particular financial support. George Meany, Ralph Nader, the Sierra Club, the League of Women Voters were not decisive factors in shaping public opinion in our districts nor marginally influential in our elections. *The Washington Post*, the *New York Times*, *Time* magazine, and the *Chicago Sun-Times* had no appreciable effect on our bids for election or for re-election. We were truly uninhibited, really free to decide our own issues, formulate our own policies, and advance our own programs.

Our mission was clear. We had to parlay massive voting potential into concrete economic results. The possibility of our corraling black anger and funneling it into positive political retaliatory power frightened many whites. Why such fear abounded mystified us. We are still puzzled by the initial reaction to our forming the Black Caucus.

Chuck Stone explained why blacks had not moved to exert their power much sooner. He opined:

> . . . proportionate control of the political process has been manipulated by the Irish, the Italians, the Jews, and the Polish in virtually every major city in America. Ethnic bloc voting and ethnic political loyalty has been a feverish adjunct of every ethnic group in America except black people. We've been too busy trying to get "integrated" . . . instead of trying to build political power bases.[2]

CONGRESSIONAL AND OTHER ATTITUDES TOWARD THE CBC

Despite various perceptions, the CBC pushed onward. On April 5, 1971, Chairman Diggs forwarded letters to the leaders of the House of Representatives and the Senate:

> As you know, the Congressional Black Caucus submitted recommendations to the president on March 25, 1971. . . . Included in this statement was a reference to the role of the Congress in resolving the concerns of the black community. . . . The Caucus is prepared to confer with you and comment on the aforementioned at your convenience.[3]

Speaker Albert, Senator Byrd, and Congressmen Ford, Anderson, and Arends complied with the request, and a very fruitful session was held with them. Senator Mansfield rejected the invitation outright and publicly denounced the Congressional Black Caucus in negative terms, referring to us as a separatist group. In refusing to meet with the Caucus, the Senate leader took the same position as most pseudo-liberals, objecting to black members organizing our own lobbying apparatus. Those of us determined to make decisions affecting our own lives were perceived as uppity and ungrateful "niggers."

Mansfield denied Caucus members an opportunity to meet and discuss legislative proposals with him. His action mirrored the overall attitude of white liberals and epitomized the contempt they held for black leadership. When Senator Mansfield at a press conference called the Congressional Black Caucus a "special interest" group seeking publicity and racial preferences, it signaled his belief that blacks planning programs and executing policies were unwarranted intrusions into affairs best reserved for white people.

We were insulted by the insensitivity of the Democratic Senate majority leader. We were incensed because the record clearly shows that, as a group, black members of Congress more consistently and more aggressively represented the nation's "general interests" than any other bloc.

The Senate majority leader's refusal to meet with us and his public condemnation were not the only manifestations of open hostility toward the Caucus. Many whites in Congress and heads of civic, political, and business organizations considered us presumptuous in attempting to speak for the 25 million black citizens. We repeatedly heard ourselves described as a "separatist" and "racially exclusive" group.

But rebuffs from Senator Mansfield, Averell Harriman, and other liberals did not discourage or dissuade us in our efforts to proceed. Harriman exhibited discomfort, if not outright embarrassment, several weeks after agreeing to serve as honorary cochairman of the First Annual CBC Dinner. Apparently, he was subjected to some pressure to dissociate himself from our activity. In a telephone conversation, just before slamming down the receiver, Harriman informed me that he "would not personally contribute any money to the CBC dinner, would not raise any money and probably would not attend the affair." His negative attitude was par for the course among many liberals during the formative days of the Caucus.

Harsh criticism, however, was not forthcoming only from white leaders who feared for some real or imagined reason that our banding together would hurt them. The Reverend Joseph Jackson, president of the 6.3-million-member all-black National Baptist Convention, played his customary role of attacking black leaders who spoke out forcibly for equality of the races. For many years and in many high places, Jackson had been labeled "the Most Right Reverend Uncle Tom." He was noted for amusing the white media and white financial contributors to his ministry by lambasting and vilifying black leaders.

The reverend assailed James Forman and others who attempted to win reparations from religious groups for their previous support of slavery. He also attacked the National Council of Churches for setting up a black development corporation to advance funds to black causes. But perhaps his most embarrassing and most preposterous exhibition of hatred for a black leader was displayed when the Chicago Board of Aldermen renamed South Parkway Boulevard the Dr. Martin Luther King, Jr., Drive. In a shameful, intemperate reaction, the Reverend Jackson spent almost $20,000 to move the entrance of his church around the corner from Dr. Martin Luther King, Jr., Drive to 405 East Thirty-first Street.

In characteristic style, Jackson described the Congressional Black Caucus in very negative terms. In attacking the members, he said, "[The CBC is] a segregated pattern of life that serves the cause of the old form of discrimination and segregation more than it serves the rights of any people. . . . If segregation is wrong according to principle, it can bring deliverance to no race."[4]

The hypocrisy and the gall of this "Elmer Gantry"–type religious guru pandered to the racist inclinations of white America. Why the all-black, racially segregated National Baptist Convention, which he headed, did not merge with all-white groups such as the American Baptist Convention, the Southern Baptist Convention of America, or the National Baptist Convention, U.S.A., poses the question of the sincerity of the Reverend Jackson.

When it came to a lack of support from other legislators in the House of Representatives, Congressman Charles Rangel summed up the situation beautifully:

> None of us needed the problem. But we couldn't run away from it. First we had to allay the fears of those legislative groups that somehow thought the Caucus was competing with them. We weren't. There was a vacuum and we felt we had the resources, the expertise and the talent to fill the void.[5]

Initially, the efforts of the CBC were met with resistance from several other quarters of the Congress. Some white members reacted in disbelief that blacks would organize into a racially exclusive group. They declared indignantly that black segregation was as invidious as white segregation. Most predicted that, because of the highly volatile mix of egos and styles and personalities, the Congressional Black Caucus would not last a month. But Congressman Hawkins of California put it in perspective when he defended our right to organize around skin color. Forecasting the permanence of our togetherness and educating friend and foe, he commented, "We may not love each other, but we're all in the same bag."[6]

Rebutting attacks by the white media and white politicians, the CBC took the position that most interest groups in Congress organized caucuses to protect their interests, and blacks would be remiss if we did not also do so. In fact, there were many other caucuses in the House: peanut, potato, cotton, Republican, Democrat, liberal, conservative, state-based, and regional caucuses, to mention just a few. Black members belonged to many of them.

Specifically, there were formally organized, structured caucuses such as the conservative Democratic Research Organization; the liberal Democratic Study Group; the liberal to moderate Republicans in the Wednesday Group; a regional delegation, the New England Caucus; the 150 House and Senate members who belonged to Members of Congress for Peace Through Law; and the middle-of-the-road Democrats comprising the United Democrats. Black members belonged to several of these as well as the Congressional Black Caucus. In fact, in the early years, I was vice-chairman of the Democratic Study Group.

Congressman Stokes was perplexed by the oft-posed question Why should there be a black caucus? As chairman of the CBC he issued a statement, decrying the ignorance of white Americans in some cases and their hypocrisy in others. He scolded those who belonged to many caucuses, most of them void of any black membership.

Many people have raised the familiar questions: Why a separate caucus of black congresspersons? Why is it necessary? What is the role of the Congressional Black Caucus? What are its primary objectives?

It is common knowledge that the history of American politics began with coalitions based on common interests involving economic, social, religious, and ethnic groups. Today, on Capitol Hill, there are many caucuses, both formal and informal. Generally, these caucuses are based on partisan politics, political philosophy, geography, social issues, and special interests.

In this context, the Congressional Black Caucus is not a maverick organization. Instead, we are a coalition of U.S. congresspersons deeply concerned about the issues, needs, and aspirations of minority Americans. We are, therefore, interested in developing, introducing, and passing progressive legislation which will meet the needs of millions of neglected citizens. . . .[7]

By this time, members of the media were preoccupied with racial incidents and publicizing responses of individual Caucus members to them. The black media already showered attention on us, but now we were the focus of the white media as well. CBC members were invited to appear on national talk shows and were featured in in-depth newspaper stories.

We were newsworthy before we organized as a Caucus, but after we did so, the attention received heightened. This stood to reason, though, because many of the events of the day were quite dramatic—for example, our confrontation with Governor Lester Maddox of Georgia.

Governor Maddox, one of the most visible and notorious racists of the day, was in Washington, D.C., on February 24, 1970, to testify against the Voting Rights Act before the Senate Judiciary Committee, chaired by Senator Birch Bayh of Indiana. Maddox supported provisions that would have weakened the act. Under sharp questioning from Senator Bayh, the governor at one point stood up and threatened to walk out of the hearing room.

Later that morning, in the House dining room, Governor Maddox attempted to distribute his famous "ax handles" advertising his Pickwick Drumstick restaurant in Atlanta and his racist politics. Congressman Charles Diggs of Michigan was in the dining room.

In the presence of House members and their special guests, Diggs and Maddox engaged in a shouting match over the governor's insistence on distributing "ax handles." The ax handles were Paul Bunyanesque in size—three feet long and weighing four pounds. Souvenirs they were not. Promotional trinkets they were not. They were exact replicas of the baseball bat–size ax handles that Maddox used in chasing black people from his restaurant, and they were being passed out in the congressional dining hall with the assistance of uniformed Georgia state troopers.

Diggs informed Maddox that it was illegal to distribute campaign paraphernalia or advertisements of any type on federal property. In the heated exchange, Diggs called the ax handles an offensive racist symbol. Maddox told Diggs, ". . . you are acting more like an ass and a baboon than a member of Congress."[8]

At that point Diggs summoned Kermit Crown, the House restaurant manager and Congressman John C. Kluczynski of Illinois, who was chairman of the House Restaurant Committee. Diggs demanded that the governor be removed from the premises. He saw Maddox, as an invited guest in facilities reserved for members of Congress, imposing on his host with arrogant and insolent behavior. This was not 1946, when it was still permissible to subject black politicians to the kind of humiliation then suffered by Congressmen Dawson and Powell. Neither Diggs nor the rest of the black congressmen present would tolerate it. Diggs insisted that Capitol Hill police relieve the Georgia state highway patrolmen of their cache of ax handles or eject the governor and his entourage from federal property. Maddox and his state troopers decided to leave the premises of their own volition.

Some members of Congress enjoyed a Roman holiday of press coverage, showing disgust for the governor and his misplaced values. The famous chicken-selling, ax-wielding Georgia tyrant was assailed from the floor of the House of Representatives.

Immediately after the incident, Congressman John Conyers took the floor of the House and was recognized by the Speaker.

> Mr. Speaker, this may not have much to do with the legislative business at hand today, but it does have a great deal to do with the dignity in which this House should conduct its business. Only a few minutes ago the governor of Georgia, Mr. Lester Maddox, while enjoying the privileges of the members' dining room, engaged in the most shocking conduct. He distributed to all who would accept them full-size, full-length ax handles. . . .[9]

Following Conyers' remarks, other members rose to lambast Governor Maddox for his rude and indiscreet racist act. Included in the group of protesters were Congressmen Brock Adams of Washington State; Bill Ryan, Leonard Farbstein, Edward Koch, and Allard Lowenstein of New York; Lucien Nedzi and William D. Ford of Michigan; Jeff Cohelan, Thomas Rees, Jerome Waldie of California.

Congressman James C. Corman of California fulminated,

> Mr. Speaker, it is alleged, and I have every reason to believe, that an unconscionable act against decency and dignity was performed in the members' dining room by the governor of Georgia, Lester Maddox, as he passed out full-size full-length ax handles as souvenirs—replicas of the instrument with which he denied Negroes the right to come into his public restaurant a few years ago. . . . Perhaps we can expect no less from a man whose private and public career has been dedicated to lawlessness and to persistent attacks on both the morality and constitutional precepts which undergird this great democracy. . . .[10]

The Honorable Shirley Chisholm protested,

Mr. Speaker, today Mr. Lester Maddox, the governor of Georgia, was allowed to present one of the most flagrant anti-American displays ever performed in this nation's capital.

As a black woman, I am dismayed by the fact that within the Capitol restaurant he was allowed to pass out ax handles, his personal symbol of resistance to the orders of the highest court and the laws of this Congress. Such symbolism is basically racist.[11]

Congressman Louis Stokes then took the floor.

Mr. Speaker, I should like the House to know that I personally attended the House restaurant with the gentleman from Michigan and personally witnessed the matter.

Mr. Speaker, the act which the governor of Georgia performed in the restaurant today was despicable and the act was characteristic of the man. He is obviously the same sick man today that he was when he stood in the doorway of his restaurant with his ax handle, defying black people to come into his public restaurant. This man today represents everything that is sick about the society in which we live.

. . . I call upon all of my colleagues in this House to forthrightly and unqualifiedly denounce the actions of Governor Maddox and all that this sick human being stands for. History will record for all time that today, February 24, 1970, the doors of the House of Representatives swung open and that a fool walked in.[12]

Following Congressman Stokes, I was privileged to conclude the discussion about Governor Maddox's indiscretion.

Mr. Speaker, today, the cancer of racial bigotry unleashed itself in our Capitol dining room in the person of Lester Maddox, governor of the state of Georgia. This idiot invaded our cafeteria and proceeded to pass out "ax handles." . . . [His] ax handles are not just political souvenirs. They represent an appeal to those who believe in white supremacy, and those who would deny black people their constitutional rights. . . .

It is not only ironic, but tragic, that a lunatic from the state of Georgia, was not arrested for invading the Capitol to promote the barbaric doctrine of human slavery. . . .[13]

Despite instant celebrity, the lives of black congressmen went on as before. Attacks on the CBC by outside groups and counterattacks by the Caucus intensified. The disagreement between Nixon administration spokesmen, members of the CBC, and supporters of each continued to make front-page news. In March 1970, twenty-one civil rights leaders lambasted the Nixon administration for a "calculated . . . systemic effort" to overturn the civil rights gains of the 1950s and 1960s. In October 1970, the Civil Rights Commission complained, ". . . total civil rights policy has not been developed [by the Nixon administration], nor have overall national civil rights goals been established to govern components of the federal civil rights efforts."[14]

A year later, the Civil Rights Commission criticized what it described as "inertia on the part of the federal bureaucracy, in some cases a blind, unthinking, fidelity to the status quo, in others a calculated determination to do nothing to advance the cause of civil rights."[15]

THE VICE-PRESIDENT ATTACKS THE CBC

Vice President Spiro T. Agnew entered the fray and launched a blistering attack on American black leaders. This White House Neanderthal proceeded to castigate in caveman style those who disagreed with Richard Nixon's Stone Age policies for revising American society.

Agnew chose Africa as the setting for lashing out at American black leadership. While traveling from the Congo to Spain aboard Air Force One, Agnew observed that black leaders in America could "learn much" from three African leaders—Jomo Kenyatta of Kenya, Emperor Haile Selassie of Ethiopia, and President Joseph Mobutu of the Congo (now Zaire)—with whom he met on his safari visit. He was quoted in the *New York Times* as calling these men

> . . . dedicated, enlightened, dynamic and extremely apt for the task that faces them. . . . This quality of leadership is in distinct contrast with those black leaders in the U.S. who arrogated unto themselves the positions of leaders and spend their time in querulous complaint and constant recrimination against the rest of society instead of undertaking constructive action.[16]

He also said, ". . . many black people in the U.S. are tired of this constant complaining and carping [and] would like to see some constructive action from those people [black congressmen]."[17]

In gratuitously advising blacks to emulate these three African leaders, our vice-president conveniently ignored the fact that thousands of innocent, noncombatant black and white people were murdered by these ruthless men in their rise to political power.

The response from black leaders was immediate and cutting. The Reverend David Abernathy of the Southern Christian Leadership Conference said, "I just think Mr. Agnew has done it again. . . . [He] put his foot in his mouth to take attention from the real issues in the country."[18]

Roy Wilkins, executive director of the NAACP, said of the vice-president's statement, "I can't guess what Mr. Agnew is talking about. It has become evident that one of the impossible tasks of this country is to try to find out what Mr. Agnew means."[19]

William Raspberry, a columnist for the *Washington Post*, wrote:

Show me a black leader in the United States and I'll show you a "querulous" complainer. . . . Take the Congressional Black Caucus, those people who have "arrogated unto themselves" the position of black leaders in spite of the fact that they were mostly elected by black, not white people. They engage in "carping and complaining" . . . because they sought, and were refused for fourteen months, an audience with the president. . . .

And so it goes. About the only black leader who isn't behaving querulously, who in fact spends a lot of time praising the Nixon-Agnew administration, is Clay Claiborne, head of the Black Silent Majority Committee. Since the seed money for Claiborne's organization was put up by the National Republican Congressional Committee (which is to say, white people), it appears he has taken the traditional route to black leadership. It still isn't clear who his followers are.[20]

Members of the Congressional Black Caucus were not as reserved or as kind in their counterattacks on the vice-president.

Congressman Charles Diggs, speaking to the House of Representatives, said,

This apparently is the vice-president's way of fiddling while Rome burns, of telling the world it is marching out of step with him. His attack was new only in the fact that his harangue from Spain is the first time in memory that any head of government has gone abroad to attack citizens of the country he represents. . . .

Although his statements are very difficult to follow with any degree of logic, it is not hard to understand that times and the people have indeed passed him by. The vice-president also seems unaware that the matter of black leadership is not within his province to decide. . . .[21]

Representative John Conyers of Michigan remarked,

Mr. Agnew's ill-founded outburst represents the maneuvering of a demagogue, searching for a scapegoat. . . .

. . . Mr. Agnew's attack on black leadership would be ludicrous if it were not so tragic, if it were not so shallow and insensitive. In no other single area of American life is Mr. Agnew's lack of knowledge and understanding more clearly demonstrated than when he comments on black Americans . . . Mr. Agnew is to be pitied.[22]

Congressman Stokes followed Conyers to the microphone:

. . . and again, black Americans have been slapped in the face by the Nixon-Agnew combine. Not a single gain was cited, and his remarks, instead of being those of a statesman, were those of a backroom politician intent upon hacking up his political adversaries . . .[23]

Congressman Charles Rangel of New York said,

. . . it is particularly embarrassing to me as a member of a minority group to have a person who alleges to be my vice-president and the vice-president of all of the people of this country who goes to a foreign land and who insults those of us who are struggling to make this a better country. . . .

I think it is incumbent upon President Nixon to repudiate the odious and repugnant remarks made by Vice President Agnew during the week of his visits with African heads of state. . . .

Finally, I find it preposterous to ask black Americans who are fighting for rights guaranteed them by the Constitution to be "grateful" like black African leaders who are putting forth their finest diplomatic etiquette to get more foreign aid.[24]

Congressman George Collins of Illinois followed Rangel to the well of the House.

Mr. Speaker, I say, Mr. Agnew, take off those rose-colored glasses. When the black leadership talks about social, economic, and financial conditions of the black and the poor, it is very real. . . . One should not have to be told that there is a housing shortage and funds have been withheld and houses are not being built. It is evident that unemployment is at an all-time high It is quite clear that there has been an increase in applications for unemployment compensation, which has led to an increase in welfare rolls for lack of employment. Schools have not been built to provide much-needed education facilities, particularly in the highly congested communities. . . .

No, Mr. Agnew, do not listen to the black leaders. Take the rose-colored glasses off and see the conditions of the black and the poor for yourself.[25]

My remarks also were caustic:

Admittedly, our vice-president is a clown, but his tricks are no joking matter. . . . It is truly amazing that Vice President Agnew, who has demonstrated his complete inability to properly assess white leadership, now purports to be an expert on black leadership. . . .

In my opinion, Mr. Speaker, our vice-president is seriously ill. He has all the symptoms of an intellectual misfit. His recent tirade against black leadership is just part of a game played by him—called mental masturbation. Apparently, Mr. Agnew is an intellectual sadist who experiences intellectual orgasms by attacking, humiliating, and kicking the oppressed.[26]

House Minority Leader Gerald Ford was irate. Particularly angered by my remarks, he said,

I cannot imagine somebody in this body . . . using language of that kind on the floor of the House in reference to the second-ranking member of the U.S. Government. . . . It seems to me that the gentleman from Missouri, Mr. Clay, for having used that language, owes an apology to the vice-president.[27]

Ford demanded that I apologize both to the vice-president and to the members of the House. I curtly refused, citing the 116 days I had spent in jail during civil rights demonstrations, when I could have been released much earlier simply by apologizing to the judge for disobeying a court order. Adding a line from President Johnson's repertoire, I admonished the Republican leader, "Gerald Ford suffers from the same illness Agnew suffers. Part of his problem is that he played football in college without a helmet."[28]

Agnew was subsequently driven from public office for accepting cash kickbacks in the basement of the White House. His personification of profound ignorance and his unique talent for race baiting were never more in evidence than in his uncivil diatribe against black leadership.

THE CBC GROWS TO FIFTEEN

While we were engaging in verbal wars with our political enemies, our group increased to fifteen in 1972 with the addition of two beautiful folks, Yvonne Braithwaite Burke of California and Barbara Jordan of Texas.

Burke served in Congress for eight years before stepping down to run for attorney general of the state of California. During her tenure, she served on the powerful House Committee on Appropriations and the Select Committee on Assassinations. She was also a chairperson of the Congressional Black Caucus.

Burke successfully attached amendments to legislation that benefited black businesses immeasurably. She was the architect of an equal opportunity amendment to the Outer Continental Shelf Lands Act to ensure subcontracts for minority- and female-owned firms seeking business related to new oil leases on the outer continental shelf. She also sponsored the "Burke Amendment," which ensured that black contractors received a fair share of the work on the multi-billion-dollar Trans-Alaska pipeline. Her amendments resulted in millions of dollars being awarded in contracts with minority- and female-owned firms.

Jordan served until 1978 as representative from the Eighteenth District of Texas. During her tenure, Jordan was responsible for engineering the successful passage of several major legislative initiatives, including: amendments to the Voting Rights Act to expand coverage and provide for the printing of bilingual ballots; mandatory civil rights enforcement procedures for the Law Enforcement Assistance Administration and the Office of Revenue Sharing; and the repeal of federal authorization for state "fair trade" laws that sanctioned vertical price-fixing schemes.

Jordan served as a member of the Committee on Government Operations, the Steering and Policy Committee of the Democratic Caucus, and the House Committee on the Judiciary. As a member of the Judiciary Committee, which investigated the infamous Watergate crimes, her inquiries and interrogation of witnesses brought her to national attention. During the impeachment hearings of President Richard Nixon, she mesmerized the American public with her probing questions and profound statements.

The Caucus paid tribute to both Congresswomen Burke and Jordan at the Eighth Annual CBC Awards Dinner in 1978. Both had announced that they would not seek re-election. Barbara Jordan was retiring from public office to accept a professorship at the University of Texas School of Law, and Yvonne Burke was already campaigning for attorney general for the state of California.

I had the great privilege of paying tribute to Ms. Jordan. In my salute, I said,

Tonight the Congressional Black Caucus presents its Special Awards to two outstanding members of our organization. My privilege, indeed my honor, is to acknowledge the contributions of one of them, Barbara Jordan. Barbara Jordan has been to the Congressional Black Caucus what Hubert Humphrey was to the Democratic Farmer's Labor Party in Minnesota, what Susan B. Anthony was to the suffrage movement, what Jackie Robinson was to baseball, what Sojourner Truth was to early freedom fighters. She has been our guiding light, our trailblazer.

Barbara is what the E. F. Hutton commercial says—when she speaks, people listen. They listen not only in the halls of Congress and the inner sanctums of the Oval Office, but also in the towns and hamlets of America. They listen in the cities and the urban areas. They listen in the corporate board rooms and the living rooms. But even more important, they listen in the school rooms and the pool rooms. And what they hear is a beautiful black woman with pathos and passion, brilliantly articulating the omens of ill-fated clouds which hang so ominously over Western culture. They hear a voice so powerful, so awesome, so imposing that it cannot be ignored and will not be silenced. What they hear is a voice verbalizing the hopes, frustrations, aspirations of millions who have no way themselves to effectively communicate with those who dictate the social, political and economic order.

Barbara Jordan is Barbara Jordan because she has refused to let modesty prevail over truth, because she has refused to accept this nation as it is, because she has demanded it become what it ought to be.

In the words of Marvin Gaye, Barbara is devoted to an idea of "saving the children and saving a world destined to die." In the words of Gladys Knight, Barbara is the "best thing that ever happened" to the Black Caucus. In the words of the Commodores, Barbara is "once, twice, three times a lady."

Tonight, we, the members of the CBC, proudly recognize a person who carved a niche in the hearts of the American public by her probing, penetrating questions during the impeachment hearings, a person who lifted the hearts of those Americans with her sterling oratory at the Democratic National Convention. Tonight, we pay homage to the drum majorette of justice and equality, the Black Rose of Texas, Barbara Jordan.

RANGEL SUCCEEDS STOKES AS CBC CHAIRMAN

In January 1974, Charles Rangel of New York succeeded Louis Stokes as chairman of the Congressional Black Caucus. In taking over the leadership, Rangel remarked that for nearly three years, the CBC had been providing the nation with the image of psychological black unity. In concert with that posture and attitude, the organization had relied on a very heavy media focus that projected a perception of its being all things to all people. Rangel felt that posture was unrealistic. He stated that there was no clear view and understanding of the CBC's strengths and weaknesses, an understanding that was necessary if the CBC were to provide an effective leadership core, working in concert with and not simply on behalf of black Americans, poor and not poor.

In outlining the next steps in a memo he labeled "New Directions and New Definitions," Chairman Rangel said,

The CBC must gather the resources available to it, develop a system for effectively using those resources in a manner complementing CBC strengths—thereby creating the base for developing both real political power and effective leadership for many Americans seeking a betterment of existing conditions.

The CBC must now attract and utilize a broad involvement of technical resource persons—universities, businesses, institutions, and social action organizations—building also upon leadership and relationships developed through the civil rights movement.

The CBC must develop the ability to positively project the image of "there are many shades of black" and that the society contains many kinds of victims, most of whom are not black and are without effective national leadership.

The CBC must accept the responsibility for its institutionalization into the public domain and must begin adhering to some of the principles of institutional preservation, maintenance, and growth—and where these principles are in conflict with the purposes of black people, be flexible enough to create new innovations.

CBC must operate like a coalition—a clearinghouse and coordinated forum for information resources that link diverse views and priorities on common action—unity without uniformity.

CBC should become an issue-generating force that acts to project collectively certain legislative and public policy issues both locally and nationally.[29]

THE CONGRESSIONAL BLACK CAUCUS FOUNDATION

Yvonne Burke followed Rangel as chairperson of the Caucus. Under her leadership, the Congressional Black Caucus Foundation, a not-for-profit, tax-exempt organization was founded. This entity was set up to allow individuals, corporations, and labor unions to donate funds to the Caucus for charitable purposes and qualify for tax write-offs. Initially, it was used to raise funds to finance the CBC Legislative Intern Program.

In 1976, spouses of Congressional Black Caucus members, under the leadership of Rangel's wife, Alma, conceived the idea of sponsoring a training program for black students interested in government careers. She developed the idea, and the Caucus approved the program to provide educational research and public policy analysis in a structured setting to college students and recent graduates.

Gretchen Wharton of the Xerox Corporation was placed on loan for two years to facilitate the program development, and the company contributed $50,000 to cover costs of a pilot program. Sheryl Webber, an intern in the initial program, was later hired as the first staff coordinator for the Intern Program.

Wharton served the CBC for seven years. Five of those years she served without time off from her corporate job or pay from the Caucus. Her exceptional skills in organizing, fund-raising, and cutting through bureaucratic red tape enabled the spouses to develop a fashion show that has become one of the major attractions of the CBC Legislative Weekend. During her years of participation, the congressional spouses have cleared in excess of $400,000 for the Intern Program.

The primary purpose of the program is to create a mechanism for training black legislative staff and for increasing their presence on committees in the Congress. At the time of the program's inception, a survey indicated that of approximately 18,000 congressional employees, less than 800 were black. On the twenty-two standing committees of the House, blacks held fewer than twenty-five of the more than 2,000 professional positions. Therefore, the main thrust of the program was geared to prepare students for job placement on committees by adequately exposing them to the intricacies of legislative policy-making processes.

In an effort to provide greater scholarly research and public policy analysis, the Graduate Intern Program was expanded into the present Congressional Fellows Program. Upon completion of a one-year program, students are equipped to function professionally in a variety of areas. They qualify as committee staff, and as members of community and public interest organizations and other governmental legislative bodies.

In 1982, the mode of operation of the Congressional Black Caucus was forced to change because of new rules adopted by the House Administration Committee. The committee, which has jurisdiction over administrative practices of members of the House, determined that "legislative service organizations" accepting monies from outside groups were in violation of House rules. CBC, being such an organization, was thus prohibited from soliciting funds from corporations, labor unions, and others who had legislative concerns.

In 1977, rules prohibited an individual member from accepting contributions from special interest groups and using those funds to promote legislative goals. The new interpretation said in effect that a group of members of Congress could not do collectively what was prohibited by the rules for individual members. In essence, all caucuses were forbidden to raise money from outside sources.

Consequently, the CBC had to reorganize its operation. The new rules of the House required the CBC to restructure and redefine areas of responsibility. In complying with the new rules, three separate and distinct organizations were created: the CBC Foundation, the CBC Legislative Service Organization, and the CBC Political Action Committee. Each assumed a different role but pursued the original goals of the Congressional Black Caucus.

The Congressional Black Caucus continued to pursue its own legislative goals by providing members with legislative assistance in the performance of their duties. The Political Action Committee supported partisan political campaigning, and the tax-exempt CBC Foundation took over major fund-raising and research projects. It was decided the foundation would become a "black think tank," providing members with information about the impact proposed legislation would have on black Americans, and it would also conduct backup research for the members' legislative proposals.

The CBC Foundation is the recipient of the bulk of funds raised for the Caucus. Although it is completely independent of Caucus members, there is a favorable working relationship. Requests for research from members of Congress usually are given preferential treatment by board members of the foundation.

Twenty-four members constitute the board of directors of the CBC Foundation. As of mid-1992, less than a majority are black members of Congress: Representatives Wheat, Dixon, Clay, Collins, Mfume, Hayes, Stokes, Owens, Rangel. The others are highly respected members of the business and educational community.

The arrangement, though necessary, is not ideal by any means. Some members of CBC resent the fact that they do not control money raised in their names. Representative Edolphus Towns of New York, vice-chairman of the Caucus, noted that the black members of Congress do not have control over the foundation, even though some serve on the board. He said, "It's a situation that needs further discussion and resolution."

The twenty-four-member board of directors of the CBC Foundation consists of strong advocates of CBC programs and outstanding black leaders in America's corporate and academic world. They are: LeBaron Taylor, vice-president of special markets for CBS Records; Lawrence P. Doss, retired partner in the firm of Coopers and Lybrand; Nira Hardon Long, an attorney with Long, Peterson & Zimmerman; Ofield Dukes, a nationally acclaimed journalist; Bertrand Lee, businessman; Wayman Smith II, vice-president and board member of Anheuser Busch Inc.; Jesse Hill, Jr., president and chief executive officer of Atlanta Life Insurance Company; Chris Edley, Jr., professor of law at Harvard University; Albert L. Nellum, president and chief executive officer of A. L. Nellum and Associates; Percy E. Sutton, attorney, civil rights activist, businessman; Barbara Williams Skinner, vice-president of Tom Skinner and Associates; and Gwen Towns of New York, who represents the CBC spouses. Amy Robertson Goldson, an attorney engaged in private practice, serves as general counsel for the foundation.

In 1983 the CBC Foundation purchased a three-story building on Pennsylvania Avenue near the Capitol. The masonry townhouse has been designated a historic landmark by the National Historic Trust and gives evidence of the permanence and seriousness with which the foundation regards its growth and development.

NOTES

1. *Saint Louis Globe-Democrat*, February 24, 1971, editorial page.
2. Chuck Stone, *The Black Scholar*, December 1969, page 10.
3. Diggs, letters to House Speaker Carl Albert, Senate Majority Leader Mike Mansfield, Senate Majority Whip Robert Byrd, House Minority Leader Gerald Ford, and House Minority Whips John Anderson and Les Arends, all dated April 5, 1971.

4. Quoted by the Reverend Lester Kinsolving in the *San Francisco Examiner*, October 23, 1972.

5. Quoted by Paul Hathaway in "The Black Caucus," *Essence* magazine, October 1971, page 40.

6. *Newsweek*, June 7, 1971, page 31.

7. Excerpts from Congressional Black Caucus press release, July 31, 1973.

8. *Facts on File Yearbook 1970*, February 26–March 4, 1970, New York: Facts on File, 1970, page 124.

9. *Congressional Record*, February 24, 1970, 91st Congress, first session, page 4580.

10. *Ibid.*, page 4926.

11. *Ibid.*, page 4705.

12. *Ibid.*, page 4581.

13. *Ibid.*

14. Quoted in the Congressional Black Caucus press release "From the Administration Which Gave Us Benign Neglect," March 1972.

15. *Ibid.*

16. *The New York Times*, July 18, 1971, page 1.

17. *Ibid.*

18. *The Washington Post*, July 19, 1971, page A-3.

19. *The New York Times*, July 18, 1971, page 17.

20. William Raspberry, *Washington Post* editorial comment, Friday, July 23, 1971, page A23.

21. *The Congressional Record*, July 21, 1971, page 26513.

22. *Ibid.*, page 26514.

23. *Ibid.*, page 26515.

24. *Ibid.*, page 26516.

25. *Ibid.*, page 26518.

26. *Ibid.*, page 26517.

27. Quoted by Lawrence E. Taylor in the *Saint Louis Post Dispatch*, July 23, 1971, page 1.

28. *New York Times*, July 23, 1971, page 39.

29. Congressman Charles Rangel, 1974 memorandum to CBC members, "New Directions and New Definitions."

9

The Black Elected Officials'
Conference and National Black
Convention

Enthusiasm ran high for developing the political game plan of which keynote speaker Ossie Davis had spoken at the First Annual CBC Dinner. Persons from all walks of life volunteered to participate in upcoming CBC programs and projects. Eight black millionaires or their representatives met in Washington, D.C., at Billy Simpson's restaurant at the invitation of Congressman Diggs to outline plans for financially underwriting Caucus activities. Among those attending the affair were Jackie Robinson, N. B. Herndon of Atlanta Life Insurance Company, A. G. Spaulding of North Carolina Mutual, and T. M. Alexander, a Georgia businessman. This group of prominent professionals met and outlined key components of a black political agenda. Later on, a group of locally elected officials who had attended the June fundraising dinner also met in Washington, D.C., with Caucus members. One outgrowth of the meeting was a call for a conference of black elected officials (BEOs) to further develop plans for addressing the black agenda and establishing a nationwide network to lobby on its behalf.

Black elected officials from throughout the nation convened in Washington, D.C., from November 18 to 20, 1971, establishing goals to design strategies to serve the agenda and form a nationwide network to lobby on behalf of black issues. Congressman Stokes, conference chairman, said in his opening statement: "We see this conference as a means of black elected officials coming together for the purpose of effectively linking together a united program of legislative and political action for the benefit of their constituents."[1]

More than 300 panelists, speakers and delegates assembled to prepare the plan to link local and national leaders to a coordinated effort for reaching overall goals. The sessions provided opportunities for delegates to examine vital issues of local concern for incorporation into a national black agenda. Additionally, strategies were shaped for resolving local constituent problems by using the resources available to members of the Congressional Black Caucus.

Alex Haley, author of the newly published novel *Roots*, was the luncheon speaker at the conference. He captivated the audience with recitations from his book and set a motivating tone by telling of the perils of Kunta Kinte and his enslaved fellowmen.

Workshops focused on confrontational politics, voter education, registration, federal and private grant processing, social and economic concerns of health, housing, education, drugs, law enforcement, and business development. There were fourteen workshops in all:

Development of Black Political Power in the Seventies
    Chairman, Congressman William L. Clay
Congressional Redistricting and Legislative Reapportionment
    Chairman, Congressman Robert N.C. Nix
Convention Delegate Selection Process
    Chairman, Congressman Walter E. Fauntroy
Report on National Political Strategy Sessions for 1972
    Chairman, Congressman Charles C. Diggs, Jr.
Utilization of News Media for Black Political Development
    Chairman, Congressman John Conyers, Jr.
Money Resources—Federal and Foundations
    Chaired by staff
Voter Education and Registration—New Trends, New Problems,
and New Strategies
    Chairman, Congressman Louis Stokes
Employment, Income Maintenance, and Economic Opportunities
    Chairman, Congressman Augustus F. Hawkins
Vietnam Veterans—War Cost to the Black Community
    Chairman, Congressman Ronald V. Dellums
Education and Early Childhood Development
    Chairperson, Congresswoman Shirley Chisholm
Problems of Aging
    Chairman, Congressman George Collins

Health
    Chairman, Congressman Ralph H. Metcalfe
Housing and Economic Development
    Chairman, Congressman Parren J. Mitchell
Drugs, Law Enforcement, and Corrections
    Chairman, Congressman Charles B. Rangel

The workshop discussions were lively as people volleyed thoughts and strategies back and forth. They evaluated the possible roles that the Caucus could play in local politics. They worked on ways to be particularly effective in congressional districts where the black vote held the balance of power. Mayor Howard Lee of Chapel Hill, North Carolina, advocated developing black caucuses at state, district, county, and municipal levels as a prerequisite for forming coalitions with nonblack groups. The point was well taken by others, but State Senator Barbara Jordan of Texas warned that coalitions were functional for blacks only if they operated from a base of strength. Mayor Carl Stokes of Cleveland advised conference attendees to use their positions of influence to help equalize the power imbalance between aspiring black elected officials and well-established white political groups.

Percy Sutton, at the time Manhattan borough president, stressed the importance of "audacious black power," adding that power is *only* effective in organization and that the black man's first coalition must be germane to the ranks of other black groups who seek self determination.

The workshops explored education issues, the black news media, the cost of the Vietnam War to the black community, federal and private grant programs, health and housing, voter education and registration, and economic development for their constituents. A highlight of the conference was a panel entitled "Justice, Law Enforcement and Law Reform." It brought together participants from the other workshops to discuss imperfections and injustices of the criminal justice system.

CONTROVERSY ARISES

While there was real forward movement in the collective energy of the elected officials present, there also was some negative undercurrent. All was not copacetic. Serious disagreements between Caucus members had been simmering behind the scenes for several months.

Representative Stokes appealed to his colleagues for a "united force," but it was easier said than won. Fireworks began on the first day of the conference at the workshop I chaired on black political power.

In my opening statement, I reminded those assembled, "Blacks are the only people in the United States who place others' interests before their own. We must play by the rules of the game, which also say that you take whatever you can, from whomever you can and however you can."[2]

At that point, Florida State Representative Gwendolyn Cherry, a supporter of Congresswoman Shirley Chisholm's presidential aspirations, stood up and accused male members of the Congressional Black Caucus of attempting to undermine the Chisholm campaign and all hell broke loose. Cherry declared that I, as moderator of the workshop, ought to relinquish the microphone, in her words, "to our illustrious presidential candidate on the Democratic ticket, Shirley Chisholm."

I was flabbergasted by the unexpected and unjustified intrusion. I responded that I was willing to let Chisholm speak her mind. But I also emphasized that the session was not intended to enhance or promote the presidential aspirations of any particular candidate, "illustrious or otherwise."

Shirley Chisholm was given the microphone and allowed her say. For twenty minutes, she accused black males of ignoring her extraordinary talents and special contributions. She rattled off a list of criticisms against black leaders and personally attacked those of us who had not encouraged her candidacy. Some Caucus members were even described as "always plotting and planning" against her.[3]

She launched a broadside of immeasurable venom against the Stokes brothers, Louis and Carl, alleging that Representative Stokes had purposely omitted her as a panelist in the political forum. At one point, she glared at me and other members of the panel and snapped, "You'd better wake up."[4]

Conferees splintered into factions and debated the merits of Chisholm's presidential intentions. Confusion and chaos reigned, temporarily disrupting the conference and continuing for most of the remaining day. Word spread throughout the conference, and participants from other workshops scampered to the big show taking place in the session dealing with black political development. The ruckus was a devastating blow to the public image of "unity" that the Caucus had tried so meticulously to nurture. The January 1972 issue of *Race Relations Reporter* said:

The next morning, November 20, the story of Mrs. Chisholm's outburst appeared in newspapers throughout the nation, under such headlines as "Rep. Chisholm Lashes Caucus." To those with cynical minds, it seemed a masterful publicity grab. Representative Louis Stokes, who had made the assignments, said Mrs. Chisholm had known for weeks she was not on the political power panel, and had not chosen to make an issue of it. Representative Clay said he didn't see any reason why she should have been on it, either.[5]

A year later, in her book *The Good Fight*, Chisholm explained the debacle in the following way:

Representative Louis Stokes was chairman of the arrangements, and the way the meeting was organized left me convinced that he, Representative William Clay of Missouri, and other Caucus members were out to do what they could to play down my candidacy. The point of the meeting was to bring the growing number of black officials, local, state and federal, together to talk about common problems and goals; it was not to work out a strategy for the presidential election.

But, naturally, everybody was talking about PRESIDENTIAL POLITICS, and the fact was inescapable that I was the only black candidate moving at the time. The Caucus asked its members to choose what workshops they would like to take part in during the meeting and I, because of my background as an educator and my position on the House Education and Labor Committee, asked to be included in a workshop on early childhood education. When the meeting got under way, it developed that there was also a workshop on national politics.[6]

The vituperative outburst at the conference was vintage Shirley Chisholm. She was fully aware already two months prior that the session that I moderated would be held. She knew for weeks that she was not scheduled to participate on the panel and chose not to make it an issue. Representative Stokes had written a memo to all CBC members announcing in detail the nature of each workshop and asking them to state their preferences. But rather than offer her critique then, she waited until the seminar was in process, under the beaming lights of television cameras and the sharpened pencils of nationally syndicated scribes, to charge that a plot had been concocted to deny her a platform for her presidential campaign.

She wrote in her book *The Good Fight*, "It seemed to me clear that there had been a subtle but unmistakable attempt to keep me out of the limelight and that there was no possibility that I would ever gain the unified backing of the Caucus."[7]

The issue did not subside until a closed session was held later in the day to discuss congressional redistricting and plans for the 1972 national presidential campaigns. At the session, which was closed to reporters, cameramen, and curiosity seekers, arguments for and against Chisholm's candidacy continued. The focus changed, though, to a proposal by poet-playwright Amiri Baraka—supported by many black elected officials from the Newark–New York area—to create an "African People's Party." The idea was simply to run black candidates for every office in every district where there was a sizeable black population.

After much wrangling, Caucus Chairman Diggs appointed James Gibson of the Potomac Institute in Washington; Antonio Harrison of the National League of Cities/National Conference of Mayors; Howard Robinson, executive director of the CBC; and myself to study the proposals advanced. We met for several hours and produced a document that was supported by the Caucus, local elected officials, and the militants. It approved of the "black agenda" and rejected the idea of a national black political party, which satisfied the members of Congress. It also called for a national black political convention, which appeased the militant black elected officials.

Meanwhile, the squabble over Chisholm's candidacy refused to go away quietly, as some had hoped. It set in motion a series of personal attacks and counterattacks by Caucus members upon each other. Disputes that heretofore had languished in the privacy of Caucus meetings were now topics of public discussion. It was revealed that Representative Chisholm had been one of several members who initially opposed the formation of the Congressional Black Caucus, and that she was very uncooperative in support of its program. She was accused of preferring to have a single spokesperson for all black folk, similar to the leadership role once played by the incomparable Adam Clayton Powell, Jr.

Chisholm's supporters charged that black male leaders were a group of chauvinists, too timid to follow her dynamic leadership. The characterization of her as a "dynamic leader" was always a bone of contention among other Caucus members who dealt with her each day of the week. Some colleagues, including myself, described her as self-centered, opportunistic, indifferent, and aloof—actually lacking leadership qualities.

Some white politicians and political analysts attempted to portray the disagreement between Chisholm and members of the Caucus as personality clashes. That's the usual response to black leaders who disagree. It's based on whites' refusal to admit that blacks have philosophies or ideologies they can disagree over. They alleged that other Caucus members were either "male chauvinists," egotistical bastards, or envious eunuchs. Elected officials are known to have unusually large egos, but the disagreement black members of Congress and hundreds of state and local black elected officials had with Shirley Chisholm was a matter of politics, not ego. The congresswoman was difficult, if not impossible, to work with.

Mrs. Chisholm, a graduate of Brooklyn College who had earned an M.A. from Columbia University, was elected to Congress in 1968 from a newly created district, defeating Republican candidate James Farmer, former executive director of C.O.R.E. In her official biographical sketch, she is particularly credited with winning minimum-wage protection for domestic workers: "When the minimum-wage law came before the Education and Labor Committee, Mrs. Chisholm lobbied on the committee and with other women members to extend minimum-wage protection to domestic workers. And she won. So most domestics, who had been earning something like $1.60 an hour, [would] now receive $2.20 under terms of the law."[8]

Her detractors in the Caucus cited numerous occasions of Chisholm's failure to cooperate with other members in a spirit of unity. They accused her of pursuing a reckless form of self-centered politics. As politicians sometimes wrongfully do, she took credit for good deeds and successes she had little or nothing to do with. For example, the issue of a minimum wage for domestics, mentioned in Chisholm's official biography, did not come up until two years after her unsuccessful bid for the presidency. But this is the issue she cited to counter charges that she was "self-centered."

Any person intimately involved in writing the legislation to include domestic workers under protection of the Fair Labor Standards Act knows that Chisholm had nothing whatsoever to do with that inclusion. In fact, her effort to reap political mileage from passage of the legislation seriously jeopardized passage of the bill.

The language covering domestic workers was originally proposed in 1971 by me, while the bill was still in subcommittee. Phil Burton of California, the point man on the legislation, supported its inclusion. That provision was inserted in the drafting stages without objection and passed out of the full committee. The following year, on the floor of the House, a substitute provision was passed eliminating all provisions expanding coverage of the minimum wage, including that for domestics.

In 1973, another attempt was made to pass a bill that included domestics. This time the strategy was to allow a tax credit up to $480 a year to householders employing domestics. But the Ways and Means Committee claimed jurisdiction over the tax provision and the Education and Labor Committee was forced to drop the tax idea. At that time, ten Republicans did sign minority views objecting to including domestics in the bill. But no one offered an individual amendment to eliminate coverage of domestic household employees.

The House vote on the bill covering domestics in the minimum wage was scheduled for March 20, 1974. Several members of the Black Caucus got wind of Chisholm's intention to speak on the floor in behalf of domestics. Since the committee had reported the bill without debate and the minority opinion written by Congressman Earl Landgrebe, a conservative Republican from Indiana, did not oppose the inclusion, Caucus members feared a heated debate might ensue. However, they were unable to change her mind. She delivered her speech, called a press conference afterward, and issued a statement documenting how she singlehandedly had saved the domestic workers' provision. As one CBC member described it, Shirley Chisholm rescued from the perils of defeat a section of the bill that was never in danger.

Chisholm embellished on this story in later years. On numerous occasions she claimed to have telephoned Congresswoman Louise Day Hicks in Boston, an archenemy of school integration, and persuaded her to leave a hotly contested campaign for mayor against the incumbent Kevin White and return to Washington, D.C., to defeat efforts to strip coverage for domestics from the minimum wage bill. Chisholm claimed that Hicks' votes at the committee mark-up provided the margin of victory for three essential amendments.

But there were no critical votes in committee to delete domestics from the bill. There was not a single vote in committee or on the House floor to deny coverage to domestic workers. In point of fact, Mrs. Hicks' one term in Congress had expired more than a year before the legislation in question was enacted.

HISTORIAN LERONE BENNETT KEYNOTES THE BEO DINNER

The evening following Shirley Chisholm's outburst at the conference, nationally acclaimed black historian Lerone Bennett, Jr., senior editor of *Ebony* magazine, delivered a sterling keynote address at the dinner concluding the Conference of Black Elected Officials. Delivering his remarks in staccato fashion, he outlined the historical perspective of the conference for the audience of delegates and provided insight that anticipated perfectly the national strategy to emerge from the gathering. He laid out the agenda in a way that provided an unusual prelude and created an enthusiastic atmosphere for the statement calling for a national black political convention. The following are selected excerpts from his speech:

> We can no longer avoid the challenge of creating and disseminating a common black agenda. . . .
>
> It is imperative, it is a matter of life and death, for us to develop a series of comprehensive plans identifying the black interest and the black position in every field. We must plan now not only for the 1972 election but also for the 1976 election and the 1980 election.
>
> We must plan now not only for the Nixons and Agnews of today but also for the Nixons and Agnews and Rehnquists of tomorrow. . . .
>
> First of all and most importantly of all, is the question of survival. In order to plan for tomorrow, we must live today. And in order to live today, we must conceive and project emergency plans for employment, welfare, education, prison reform, and health.
>
> A second major item on the black agenda is empowerment, the solidification of existing power in the cultural, political, and economic fields, and the fulfillment of the potential power of black people on the local, state, and federal levels. . . .
>
> It goes without saying that this item includes black control of the resources and institutions of the community and of all bureaucracies which vitally affect the lives of black people. . . .
>
> A third item is black renewal. And by that I mean a renewal of the structures, energies, and values of the black community. . . .
>
> There is need, fourthly, for a massive mobilization of all the resources of the black community. Black labor, black capital, the black intellect, and the black ballot must be organized within and without existing structures within the perspective of the values and interests of the black community. . . .
>
> There is also a desperate need for machinery to tap the rage and energy of black youth and the skills and resources of the black middle class.
>
> The traditional American idea of organizing people to trade their votes for garbage collection and petty patronage jobs is not only *not power*—it is the precise opposite of power.

Political power is not garbage collection or petty patronage in a rotten political system but the ability to transform political structures so that people will not have to be aliens and adversaries for resources and services that governments should provide routinely. . . .

The fifth and final general area of importance on the black agenda of the seventies is the transformation of the institutions of American society which threaten or prevent the fulfillment of items one, two, three, and four. . . .

It is necessary for us to disengage ourselves from white people's arguments and redefine all concepts and associations in terms of the fundamental interest of black people. We are one people, and we shall survive as one people, or we shall go, one by one, Baptist, Methodist, Catholic, Protestant, Republican, Democrat, to that white doom this society is preparing for all black people. . . .

The revolution is not going to come Monday morning or the next Monday or the Monday after that. We are engaged in a long-range process . . . to incorporate this insight into a strategy of conscious and antagonistic participation. . . .

It means using the system to destroy the system . . . using the whole arsenal of parliamentary tricks to slow down, disrupt and stop proceedings which adversely affect the interest of black people. . . .

The problem is not the poor; the problem is the powerful. The problem is not the distribution of contraceptives; the problem is the distribution of income. The problem is not the ghetto; the problem is the white system which created the ghetto and which perpetuates it.[9]

THE CALL FOR A
NATIONAL BLACK POLITICAL CONVENTION

After the crowd showered a thunderous ovation upon Lerone Bennett, CBC Chairman Diggs issued a statement of political strategy calling for a national convention to be held the next spring. It sounded a clear note of unity at the end of this, the first national conference ever held for black elected officials. Immediately following Bennett's speech, Diggs rose and read the preamble of a resolution calling for the national convention:

For 300 years black people have been the victims and pawns of the American political process. The political representatives of the black community, meeting in Washington, D.C., in November 1971, have concluded that we still wear the shackles of political bondage. . . .

. . . tonight, the Congressional Black Caucus issues a call to the black people of the United States for a national political convention to be held in April or early May of 1972, for the purpose of developing a national black agenda and the crystallization of a national black strategy for the 1972 elections and beyond. . . .[10]

The Caucus went through many sessions in discussing the feasibility of participating in a national black political convention. There were many and various opinions as to the relevance and peril of such a bold move. Fauntroy and Diggs were convinced that the Caucus should exercise maximum energies to make the convention a success. Stokes, Mitchell, and I expressed the feeling that before we could talk about a convention we must deal with the question of maximizing the Caucus's unity and make sure that we were not saddled with the total expenses for such a venture.

Dellums said he thought the BEO conference had been very good substantively and the only major problem had been the strategy session. He felt the Caucus would be on thin ice if it got into the area of endorsing candidates—that would be explosive and divisive. The Caucus would do better to limit the convention agenda to those matters which were of immediate and long-range concern to blacks using the political process to advance our cause. He argued that issues of a parochial nature had no place at the conference.

THE NATIONAL BLACK CONVENTION

The National Black Political Convention (NBPC) was held in Gary, Indiana, March 10–12, 1972. All major networks, every major daily newspaper, foreign correspondents from sixty countries, and a large contingent of the black media sent representatives to document this historic event. Two cable television companies from New York City with more than 80,000 subscribers provided gavel-to-gavel live coverage of the activities.

The 5,000 delegates and several thousand guests attending the convention represented all walks of life in black America. They were Democrats, Republicans, independents, separatists, revolutionists, and reformists. One group even supported a ticket promoting Richard Nixon for president and Shirley Chisholm as his vice-presidential running mate. They contended such an illogically unbalanced ticket would attract both "anti-black and pro-black" voters. If successful, it certainly would have insulated Nixon against any assassination attempts or impeachment procedures.

The atmosphere at the gathering was bazaarlike in one sense, bizarre in another. Vendors sold balloons, t-shirts and Afro combs. Others stood on sidewalks reciting poetry about the struggle for freedom and hawking books about Marcus Garvey and Malcolm X. Caterers with food carts offered such soul food delicacies as pig-ear sandwiches, chitterlings, red beans and rice. Delegates were frocked in assorted dress: Ivy League suits, button-down collars, freedom fighter dungarees, cotton dresses, dashikis and other elaborate African garb. Colorful boubous of traditional African cloth and smartly wrapped gelees bedecked the bodies and heads of beautiful, stately black women.

Noticeably absent were those sporting do-rags on their heads or *Fortune* 500 logos in their lapels. Dixie flag wavers and cross burners were nowhere in sight. Presidential candidates of both parties, who otherwise never passed up a chance to wave the flag in a public forum, avoided Gary as if it were the Black Plague. They opted for fishing trips in Iowa or explained that they wanted to spend some quality time at home with their wives and children rather than mingle with 8,000 black voters.

Summing up the sense and purpose of the convention was the "Gary Declaration: Black Politics at the Crossroads," an angry document written by justifiably angry people who gave a perceptive analysis of black fury and its resentment toward the white political establishment. Amiri Baraka was responsible for writing a major portion of the document. It stated, in part:

> The Black Agenda . . . is our attempt to define some of the essential changes which must take place in this land as we and our children move to self-determination and true independence . . . in an hour of great crisis and tremendous promise for black Americans. . . . We stand on the edge of history and are faced with an amazing and frightening choice: We may choose in 1972 to slip back into the decadent white politics of American life, or we may press forward, moving relentlessly from Gary to the creation of our own black life.[11]

The document continued:

> The American system does not work for the masses of our people, and it cannot be made to work without radical fundamental change. . . . Both

parties have betrayed us whenever their interests conflicted with ours (which was most of the time), and whenever our forces were unorganized and dependent, quiescent and compliant. . . . For white politics seeks not to serve but to dominate and manipulate. . . .[12]

In summary, this call for a convention affirming a national black agenda concluded:

To those who say that such an agenda is "visionary," "utopian," and "impossible," we say that the keepers of conventional white politics have always viewed our situation and our real needs as beyond the realm of their wildest imaginations. . . .

. . . for a new black politics demands new vision, new hope, and new definitions of the possible. Our time has come. These things are necessary. All things are possible.[13]

Presiding over the convention's general session was Congressman Diggs. The keynote address was delivered by Yvonne Braithwaite, a state assemblywoman from California, and the plenary session was under the direction of Richard Hatcher, mayor of Gary, Indiana. Georgia State Senator Julian Bond and the Reverend Jesse Jackson of People United to Save Humanity were participants on the first day of the convention.

Although Congressmen Charles Diggs and Walter Fauntroy played leading roles in planning and executing the Gary Convention, they were not acting as official agents of the Congressional Black Caucus. After issuing the call for a national convention, several incidents developed that caused the Caucus to withdraw as a sponsor of the affair. In the early stages of planning, Diggs reported back to the Caucus that the convention would be financed through fund-raising efforts, the first of which was to be held on February 20 in Atlanta, Georgia. The second was scheduled for Indianapolis. A finance committee was established, and Dr. Frank Lloyd of Indianapolis and Al Boutte of Chicago were named cochairmen.

In the ensuing weeks, the planned events for raising money to cover the cost of the convention failed to materialize. The rules for selecting delegates to the convention were skewed to favor community-based groups, primarily those associated with the radical left. In overemphasizing the importance of grassroots involvement, the three cochairmen allotted a disproportionately small number of delegate slots to members of Congress, mayors of big cities, heads of national civil rights and social organizations, and appointed high government officials.

In trying to appease a small but vocal group, they went so far as to give Amiri Baraka's people control of the microphones and responsibility for guarding the entrance to the stage and serving as sergeants-at-arms. The process for selecting delegates was heavily weighted in favor of nonpolitical, nonelected individuals whose number of constituents was always a matter of dispute.

Some black elected officials immediately protested their lack of meaningful involvement in determining the agenda and setting priorities for the convention calendar.

Those who had taken full control of the convention, primarily the followers of a coalition developed by Baraka, were legitimate leaders of grassroots organizations, but not one of them had ever been elected to public office. They had maneuvered themselves into positions of dominance at Gary and planned the entire agenda without input from other groups. Without consulting elected officials or civil rights leaders, they had selected the site, set the dates, decided the method of determining delegates, named the convention officials, and imposed the registration fee.

The only significant role expected for members of the Congressional Black Caucus was the honor of picking up the tab—an estimated $100,000—to cover printing, equipment rentals, luncheons, travel and hotel expenses for guest speakers, telephones, telegrams, messenger services, postage, and security costs.

CBC members objected to the arrangement, refused to finance the affair, and voted not to participate officially as an organization. CBC members who attended did so as representatives of their own congressional districts and had no authority to speak for the Caucus. It was rumored that the city of Gary ended up obligated for more than $120,000 in unpaid bills incurred at the NBPC.

The arrangement we made to sponsor the Gary Convention was doomed to fail and we should have known it. By lending legitimacy and respectability to the function, we were held responsible for outcomes that we had no part in. It is doubtful that militant leaders such as Amiri Baraka and Roy Innis could by themselves have assembled such an array of prominently elected officials and established civil rights leaders as those who journeyed to Gary. Caucus sponsorship was the drawing card. Even with pervasive racial discontent, black revolutionists did not have the appeal to attract the number and the kinds of persons who showed up in Gary.

The Gary Convention Declaration stated, "Conventional white politicians have always viewed our situation as beyond the realm of their wildest imaginations." Members of the Congressional Black Caucus, in their "wildest," did not foresee the problems looming ahead. Between 7,000 and 8,000 attendees representing all philosophical and ideological shades of thinking, many of them in sync with the ideas and teachings of black separatist leaders, converged on Gary.

Blacks preaching separatism wrested control of the convention apparatus. They established local and state subcommittees with a mandate to define what they called the "collective black will." In effect, any radical community agitator able to buy a roundtrip bus ticket to Gary was now ostensibly authorized to return home and decide what black elected officials could or could not do in the name of the "collective black will."

But the most critical skirmish came when the black nationalists demanded their members make up half of the state decision-making bodies that were established to determine the position of black people on major issues of local and national import. Elected officials vigorously opposed this measure, contending that only those who had gone through the electoral process and received voter approval could effectively deal with the two political parties.

Congressman Conyers, reflecting the sentiment of many elected officials, remarked, "There are many nonpolitical people at Gary with little responsibility to a constituency."[14]

The black nationalists, however, won the procedural struggle and wrote the convention rules in such a manner that most elected officials immediately folded their tents and headed for home.

Signs of danger to the stated goal of "a new black politics demand(ing) new vision, new hope and new definitions" surfaced in the keynote address delivered by Mayor Hatcher: "We say to the two American political parties, this is their last chance. . . . These are not idle threats. Only senile fools would think them so. The choice is theirs."[15]

His undisguised warning was followed by Jesse Jackson's blunt assertion: "We must form a black political party."[16]

The Gary Convention was becoming one gigantic propaganda engagement, and the CBC was destined to be the loser in the game if the tide of convention did not turn. And even if it did, any residual political or public relations value for the Caucus as a perceived sponsor of the occasion was doomed the minute Amiri Baraka was called to address the delegates.

The scene was fit for a Hollywood epic. Twenty people clad in black military-style uniforms goose-stepped in unison down the aisle to clear a path for Baraka. They shoved people out of the way as if for the coming of the Messiah. The news media reported it widely and with prominence.

Many of the resolutions adopted by the delegates were impossible for most elected officials to support politically. The preamble to the convention drafted by Congressman Walter Fauntroy and Illinois State Senator Richard Newhouse, calling for "an independent black political movement, an independent black political agenda, and an independent black spirit" was condemned by the NAACP before the delegates assembled. Proclaiming advocacy of an independent black political party, they felt, promoted racial separatism.

John A. Morsell, assistant executive director of the NAACP, termed the preamble and the agenda of the convention "unacceptable." In a memorandum to NAACP delegates, he wrote, "It is clear that in fundamental tone and thrust, as well as in numerous specific references, it [the draft declaration] is not an acceptable document for the NAACP." He further charged, "The preamble's rhetoric is that of revolution rather than of reform, although we note that it stops short of its logical conclusion, which is revolt aimed at setting up a new nation with its own territorial base...."[17]

Roy Wilkins, executive secretary of the NAACP, wrote to Baraka and Diggs, the convention's cochairmen:

> Specific reference must be made to two propositions of the Gary Convention which we not only find repugnant to our basic principles but which we must vigorously and unqualifiedly oppose. I am speaking here of the anti-Israel and the anti-busing statements, and our objection to them is not reduced by the half-hearted and awkward revisions which they have undergone....[18]

Advocacy of an "independent black political movement" was repudiated by most black elected officials. Diggs pretty much spoke for the average officeholder when he said, "A party outside the two-party system is always a very minor thing. Blacks, if they are going to get ahead politically on a national level, have to work within the two-party system."[19]

Even Congressman John Conyers, an outspoken advocate for independent black empowerment, criticized the call for a separate black political party as unworkable: "I don't think it is feasible to go outside the two-party system. I don't know how many of us blacks could be elected without white support."[20]

Donald M. Payne, a member of the same delegation as Baraka and the Democratic committee chairman of Newark's South Ward, who sixteen years later would become a member of Congress, sided with his future colleagues, Diggs and Conyers. "I'm not knocking an independent thrust," Payne said. But, he argued, working to make one of the major parties "reflect black thinking" would be more realistic than launching an independent movement. His "whole concern" in working within the party was "to make the Democratic party more viable, more reflective of the needs of black people."[21]

The nationalists who had taken control of the convention machinery utilized their position to dominate the affair and dictate all the rules. They systematically shuffled elected officials off to the side and effectively muzzled them when important issues were debated. On several occasions, members of the CBC were greeted with scorn, sneers, and ridicule and were dispatched to address delegates in workshops as far as fifteen miles away from the center of activity.

Opposition to school busing for desegregation and antipathy to political party alliances held center stage. Roy Innis, executive director of the Congress of Racial Equality, declaimed, "We're tired of being guinea pigs for social engineers and New York liberals. Busing is obsolete and dangerous to black people—we are ready to control our own destiny."[22]

The resolutions opposing busing and condemning Israel for its "expansionist policy" led the NAACP to withdraw from the convention and issue a verbal attack on the "Black Agenda." Texas State Senator Barbara Jordan and several other public officials publicly dissociated themselves from the anti-Israel resolution.

In response to the NAACP action, Amiri Baraka, cochairman of the convention, charged that Wilkins did not represent the grassroots membership of the association and condemned him as a divisive factor during "our first kind of awkward attempt to justify, to unify an often diverse" black people. He pleaded with those in opposition not to abandon because of some minor disagreements the potential good the national convention could achieve for the black race. It was in this frame of reference that he coined the oft-quoted slogan "We can have unity without uniformity." But even his great persuasive powers were incapable of preventing a split in the ranks of black leadership.

At the conclusion of the convention, Congressman Stokes, chairman of the CBC, issued a press release reaffirming the Caucus's support of busing to achieve public school desegregation and defending the right of the State of Israel to exist. The statement relating to Israel read in part:

> As the black elected representatives to the U.S. Congress, we reaffirm our position that we fully respect the right of the Jewish people to have their own state in their historical national homeland. We vigorously oppose the efforts of any group that would seek to weaken or undermine Israel's right to existence.
>
> The American people, including black Americans, have cherished the friendship of both the peoples of Israel and the Arab states. Our government, reflecting that friendship, has sought to promote an Arab–Israeli peace and has provided both Israel and the Arab states with economic assistance to raise the living standards of their people.
>
> . . . In times of crisis—epidemics, wars, famines—Israel has sent tons of relief supplies and medical aid to her African neighbors.
>
> . . . We pledge our continued support to the concept that Israel has the right to exist in peace as a nation.[23]

Critics charged it was pressure from labor groups, liberal white organizations, and Jewish financial contributors to individual Caucus members that caused the CBC to repudiate the resolutions of the Gary Convention. But most members of the Caucus knew weeks prior to the convention that no practical, reasonable political declaration could possibly emerge from that body. The relationship between Caucus members, organized labor, and Jewish groups was one of choice and convenience, not necessity. At least one member of the Caucus (Mitchell) had defeated Jewish incumbents to get to Congress, and at least four, including myself, had defeated candidates endorsed by organized labor.

Several days after the session an agenda was issued at a press conference by the three cochairmen of the Gary Black Political Convention. The fifty-eight-page document reaffirmed the convention delegates' support of the resolutions condemning Israel for its expansionist policy and their opposition to busing for the purpose of integrating public schools. But the cochairmen themselves were in disagreement over the two issues. Mayor Hatcher and Congressman Diggs rejected the conclusions reached concerning Israel and busing. They, joined by Congressman Walter Fauntroy, issued a separate report that stated, "We feel obligated to point out that in our judgement the resolution regarding Israel and the busing element on quality education are not representative of the sentiments of the vast majority of black Americans."[24]

Hatcher attempted to soften the impact of the anti-busing resolution and called the resolution to "dismantle" Israel "very unfortunate." On the other hand, Roy Innis, executive director of C.O.R.E. hailed the two resolutions as setting a new and innovative direction for the masses of black people. The anti-busing position made it crystal clear, he said, that the black community was tired of forced integration and ready to govern their own educational institutions. Innis was elated at the convention action and claimed it was proof that a substantial number of blacks were in opposition to integration. He and others also expressed dissatisfaction with the handling of the convention by the media. It was his opinion, as it was of many other delegates, that the mass media had overemphasized the disputes and ignored the efforts to reach consensus on major issues.

However, Mayor Hatcher disagreed with Innis's interpretation of the meaning of the busing resolution, noting that the motion was passed on a voice vote in the closing hours of the session when most delegates had departed for home.

Baraka, the other cochairman, described Hatcher and Diggs as "theoretical leadership" who failed to represent grassroots members of the convention. He accused them of being "divisive forces in our first kind of awkward attempt to justify and to unify an often diverse black people."[25]

The National Black Political Convention meant different things to different people. The enthusiasm of the delegates had run high and expectations were great. Amiri Baraka said at the beginning that the delegates would seek the creation of a unified political culture and the transformation of the black potential—through structure—to political power. Diggs predicted that the convention would be similar to the 1909 Niagara founding session of the National Association for the Advancement of Colored People. The Reverend Jesse Jackson thought the gathering would mark the beginning of a movement to start an independent black political party. Mayor Dick Hatcher, in opening the convention and welcoming the delegates to his city, cheered, "This convention signals the end of hip pocket politics. We ain't in nobody's hip pocket no more."[26]

But at the conclusion of the convention, they and other prominent black leaders were reserved in their assessment.

Carl B. Stokes, former mayor of Cleveland, reacted this way:

What does it mean for black politicians? When Baraka, Roy Innis, and other nationalists can use decent politicians like Richard Hatcher and Charles Diggs to take over a national black political conference originally called by the Congressional Black Caucus. . . . Can regular, traditional politicians move far enough to the left to satisfy the new discipline that is forming? Even if they could move to the left, could they still function in government? I don't know.[27]

Congressman Charles Diggs felt that, despite legitimate criticism, the convention had served a useful purpose and that the ongoing organized efforts coming out of the convention would also serve a useful purpose. He believed there was a comprehensive representation of all the diversified elements of the black population, but he did question the Black Agenda's ability to serve as a viable political instrument to bring forth people capable of representing the diverse positions found within the total black community.

People like the founder of the United Citizens Party of South Carolina, attorney John Roy Harper, arrived in high spirits and departed the same. He was quoted in the *New York Times* as saying, "The convention was the most significant event to happen to black people since 1619, when our ancestors were first brought to the colonies as slaves."[28]

Many of the activists at Gary were highly moralistic and idealistic, but ultimately their efforts were frustrated. The National Black Political Agenda they designed called for an "independent black political movement," when hundreds of elected officials within a matter of hours would be back in the trenches of political warfare trying to elect a president in a two-party system. And the strong language in the document advocating racial separation and calling for an end to busing for the purpose of desegregating public schools forced supporters of racial integration into public dispute with other blacks. Insistence on condemning the State of Israel and calling for its dismantling was also certain to drive a wedge between black civil rights organizations and many of their long-time supporters.

The CBC has made many mistakes in its brief history, but calling for a national convention and then losing control of the administrative apparatus was probably its most regrettable blooper. The event turned into a tactically indefensible fiasco that threatened to render us politically ineffective. The adverse political fallout for the CBC was considerable. Dissociating ourselves from its negative effects would call for "pedal to the metal" action.

NOTES

1. CBC press release, November 24, 1971.

2. *The National Conference of Black Political Scientists* (NCOBPS), December 1972, Volume 1, No. 2, page 1.

3. *Race Relations Reporter*, January 1972, page 9.

4. Reported by Lawrence Taylor, *St. Louis Post Dispatch*, November 20, 1971.

5. Jack White, in *Race Relations Reporter*, January 1972, page 10.

6. Shirley Chisholm, *The Good Fight*, New York: Harper & Row, Publishers, 1973, page 50.

7. *Ibid.*

8. Michael Barone, *The Almanac of American Politics*, Boston: Gambit, 1974, page 676.

9. Lerone Bennett, "A Black Agenda for the Seventies," Sheraton-Park Hotel, Washington, D.C., November 21, 1971, *Race Relations Reporter*, January 1972, page 13.

10. Congressman Charles Diggs, Sheraton-Park Hotel, November 19, 1971, Washington, D.C., manuscript department, Moorland-Spingarn Research Center, Howard University, Washington, D.C.

11. "The Gary Declaration: Black Politics at the Crossroads," Greensboro, North Carolina, 1972, page 1.

12. *Ibid.*, pages 2, 3.

13. *Ibid.*, page 55.

14. Quoted by Dom Bonafede, *National Journal*, June 24, 1972, page 1064.

15. *New York Times*, March 12, 1972, page 1.

16. *Ibid.*

17. *New York Times*, March 10, 1972, page 20.

18. *New York Times*, May 17, 1972, page 9, column 1.

19. *National Journal*, June 24, 1972, page 1064.

20. *Ibid.*

21. Quoted by Bob Smartt. *Newark Star-Ledger*, March 12, 1972, page 18.

22. *New York Times*, March 13, 1972.

23. CBC press release, Washington, D.C., March 21, 1972.

24. *New York Times*, May 20, 1972, page 14.

25. *Ibid.*

26. *New York Times*, March 12, 1972, page 1.

27. Carl Stokes, *Promises of Power*, New York: Simon and Schuster, 1973, page 279.

28. *New York Times*, March 19, 1972, page 42.

10

The 1972 Presidential Campaign

The 1972 Democratic presidential campaign offered a challenge for the CBC to seize the opportunity to influence presidential politics. We were a cadre of black leadership determined to contravene sacrosanct rules and procedures of the past and be part of a process historically reserved for a privileged few nonblack power brokers in the privacy of smoke-filled rooms.

Our goal was an open Democratic Convention that was fairly reflective of many diverse interests. In order to accomplish this, we and other representatives of grassroots groups had to exert meaningful influence at the convention. We would have to quash the designs of quintessential Democratic power brokers and break a pattern of black spokespersons being used by the powers-that-be to achieve victories and then being denied not only rewards but simple credit for our contribution to the victory.

There were efforts to balance the ticket by coupling a southern moderate and a northern liberal, but this would not equal the meaningful participation blacks worked toward achieving for themselves at the convention. For the first time ever, the party could not get away with adopting a party platform that did not specifically address the needs of blacks, Hispanics, gays, and welfare recipients. The representatives of these groups now constituted almost a majority of the convention delegates.

Intraparty squabbling between Senators Humphrey, McGovern, McCarthy, Jackson, Kennedy, Mondale, and Muskie divided delegates mostly along lines of previous political debts. The party was not united and organized labor's preference for any candidate except pro-labor, pro-liberal, pro-peace Senator George McGovern played a significant role in this disunity. AFL-CIO President George Meany's public statements in support of anti-labor, pro-war Richard Nixon were offensive to many in the Democratic party, including a number of influential labor leaders. Those leaders, fearing Meany's capacity for vindictive response, took a neutral stance in the presidential election.

Black input in determining the presidential nominee was far greater in 1972 than at any previous Democratic or Republican convention. We were now effectively involved at every stage: from the adoption of the McGovern-O'Hara-Fraser Reform Commission rules to approving the challenges of delegates from the Mississippi Loyalist Democrats and seating them—and to successfully voting to unseat the Chicago delegation headed by Mayor Richard Daley.

Undeterred by the political disaster experienced at the Gary Convention, the Congressional Black Caucus moved with dispatch in organizing for the 1972 Democratic Convention.

A strategy to influence the Republican platform was never considered because all members of the Caucus were Democrats. That task was left to black Republicans who held high-ranking positions in the Nixon administration and boasted of having significant influence within the inner circle of their party's decision-making apparatus. They devised an agenda that advocated increased emphasis on President Nixon's call for "black capitalism." Sincerely interested in the economic plight of the black community, they believed that with enough government assistance in awarding set-aside contracts to minorities, the other problems faced by the black community would soon disappear.

Edwin T. Sexton, Jr., director of the black political division of the Republican National Committee, was one of the principal spokesmen for black Republicans. He cited the accomplishments of President Nixon as including the appointment of more blacks to high government positions than ever before; creation of the Office of Minority Business Enterprise, which gave financial aid to minority businesses; promotion of seven blacks to the rank of general in the armed services; allocation of more funds for civil rights enforcement than ever before; and increased low-income housing for the poor.

In June 1972, four months prior to the general election, the Committee of Black Republicans for the Re-election of the President gave a fund-raising dinner in Washington and raised over $200,000 for the campaign. Floyd McKissick, former national executive director of the Congress of Racial Equality, spoke at the conference that preceded the fund-raising dinner: "[Blacks] should stop sucking the sugar tit of Democratic rhetoric." McKissick, founder of the nearly all-black Soul City at Manson, North Carolina, maintained the Republican party was, for blacks, "the best vehicle of self-determination."[1]

Most CBC members believed it was the responsibility of black Republicans to handle Nixon, if that was at all possible. Our major preoccupation would remain the Democratic party. We thought that a carefully crafted plan, coordinated with local and state black leaders, could pressure the national Democratic party to abandon the centrist-to-far-right position it had been drifting toward since the 1968 elections. Many white Democrats were preaching that if the party hoped to defeat Nixon, it had to become more conservative in fiscal matters and less vocal in matters of civil rights. Black leaders warned that this change in political direction put the party at risk of losing massive black voter support not only at the national level, but also in state and municipal elections.

Black officials flexed their muscles, offering party bigwigs an "either fish or cut bait" proposition. The Congressional Black Caucus warned party leaders that serious problems existed for black Americans and that if black voters were to participate fully in the upcoming general election, certain guarantees were essential. Between 7 and 8 million blacks were expected to vote in the upcoming election. It was anticipated that a disproportionate number, perhaps more than 90 percent, would cast their votes for the Democratic candidate.

A BLACK DECLARATION OF INDEPENDENCE AND BILL OF RIGHTS

Caucus Chairman Louis Stokes announced at the Second Annual CBC Dinner in June 1972 that a "black bill of rights" would be issued. Shortly thereafter, a two-part document was released outlining major concerns. It was entitled "Black Declaration of Independence and Black Bill of Rights" and began with the following:

PREAMBLE TO THE BLACK DECLARATION OF INDEPENDENCE AND
THE BLACK BILL OF RIGHTS

Millions of black Americans look to the thirteen black members of the United States House of Representatives as their legitimate spokesmen on national issues. . . . This imposes an awesome burden on our shoulders.

Large numbers of black Americans have been subjected to intense hardships, have been denied their basic rights, and have suffered irreparable harm because the two major political parties have failed to firmly and honestly commit their powers and resources to equality and justice for all.

It has become patently obvious . . . that black Americans will no longer tolerate insensitivity and lack of concern on the part of those who benefit from black involvement in the political process.

. . . The new political mood permeating black America makes it imperative that the Democratic party address itself to the hopes, aspirations, concerns and rights of black Americans—if that party expects to continue to receive the support of black voters. . . .

THE BLACK DECLARATION OF INDEPENDENCE

We, the members of the Congressional Black Caucus, being the highest elected black officials in the United States, responding to a mandate from millions of black Americans, and in conjunction with thousands of representatives from our national constituency, do hereby demand that the following Black Bill of Rights be implemented immediately.

. . . We insist that the Democratic party, in its official pronouncements and policies, and at its national political convention, dedicate itself to the doctrine that no American shall be denied the fundamental right to be equal.

Black Americans are no longer petitioning for equal treatment, but are demanding from the Democratic party and its presidential nominee a full, honest, and unequivocal commitment to equality—in words, deeds, and most importantly, results. . . .

THE BLACK BILL OF RIGHTS

If the RIGHT TO LIVE is to be assured for blacks and other citizens, the new Democratic administration must establish a FULL EMPLOYMENT program and REPLACE the present WELFARE SYSTEM WITH A GUARANTEED ANNUAL INCOME SYSTEM.

. . . The number one priority, in our view, is the creation of jobs to alter the present IMBALANCE IN THE NATIONAL UNEMPLOYMENT RATE. . . . Confronting what is truly a national crisis, the Congressional Black Caucus calls for:

1. The establishment of a national monetary and fiscal policy designed to achieve continuous full employment and full production.
2. A direct attack on the high unemployment among minority groups and

in minority communities, through public service job programs, training programs, quality education and a computerized comprehensive national employment service.

3. A systematic approach to solving the apparent tendency of full employment to cause inflation. . . .

. . . Black Americans, like all Americans, have a RIGHT TO PEACE. If our right to peace and the right of black people on the continent of Africa to freedom from oppression are to be realized, the new Democratic administration must bring an IMMEDIATE and definite END TO THE WAR IN INDOCHINA and WITHDRAW ALL SUPPORT OF COLONIALIST or NEO-COLONIALIST FORCES ON THE CONTINENT OF AFRICA.

. . . The RIGHT to a QUALITY EDUCATION is as fundamental as any in the Bill of Rights. America can afford *every* child a quality education. To finance quality education for all, we urge the inclusion of specific tax reform recommendations in the Democratic party platform so that the cost of education will not continually be borne by the poor.

. . . The RIGHT of every American to LIVE IN HUMAN DECENCY must not be abridged by federal passiveness. Citizens of the inner city, especially blacks, are confronted with increasingly deteriorating housing conditions. To remedy the current situations, we urge that your platform include a plank calling for:

A. A new HOMESTEAD ACT, to make use of the billions of dollars worth of land now owned by federal, state, and local governments.

B. The rebuilding of the inner cities—not the removal of the poor.

. . . A major plank of any national platform must be GUARANTEED HEALTH DELIVERY SYSTEMS. The current inaccessibility of adequate health delivery to all Americans, lack of adequate or comprehensive health coverage, and seemingly uncontrollable increases in health costs combine to relegate countless Americans to a state of insufficient medical care.

. . . To correct the present inequities and to fulfill the RIGHT of black Americans to the FREE ENTERPRISE SYSTEM, we urge that your platform include:

A. A call for an increase in the number of black-owned businesses with supporting grants and loans from the federal government and major corporations.

B. The establishment of a federal policy to set aside 15 percent of all government contracts exclusively for black-owned businesses.

. . . The goal of the Democratic party must be to eliminate the illegal sale and use of drugs and to treat those who are unfortunately hooked on drugs not as criminals but as people with serious health problems. To accomplish this we urge the inclusion in your platform of a plank that:

A. Declares drug abuse and addiction a major national crisis.
B. Requires the use of all existing resources to stop the illegal entry of drugs into the United States, including suspension of economic and military assistance to any country which fails to take appropriate steps to prevent narcotic drugs produced or processed in that country from entering the United States unlawfully.

. . . The Democratic National Platform must call for black Americans receiving a proportionate amount of all appointed positions, up to and including the cabinet of the president of the United States. Furthermore, federal judgeships should reflect the percentage of minority residents in any given state or local jurisdiction.

The members of the Congressional Black Caucus were adamant in their position that unless the Democratic candidate for president publicly adopted the Black Bill of Rights as his personal campaign commitment and unless the party incorporated basically the same, we would encourage black voters to boycott the election. I really believe that our predisposition was to take that course of action.

We in the Caucus saw this as an effective way of brokering power for those we represented. However, there was no unanimity with other black leaders. Some thought the threat impossible to carry out. We knew that a majority of blacks, despite our campaign, would still vote. But we also knew the Democrats needed every vote they could muster from every quarter in the black community. Successfully keeping just 10 percent at home would render the Democratic candidate's chances for victory nil.

State Representative Julian Bond of Georgia was one who disagreed with the Caucus position. He was of the opinion that personal commitments from candidates served a much better purpose than planks in the platform. In defending his position, he said, "My feeling about platforms is that they really don't amount to much. You can say what you want in the platform and the candidate will go ahead and do what he wants anyway. You've got to get guarantees from the candidate himself."[2]

SHIRLEY CHISHOLM'S BID FOR PRESIDENT

During the latter months of 1971, it became clear that Congress-woman Shirley Chisholm was seriously considering a run for president. Problems posed for black elected officials by her decision were to become an introduction to the world of hard-ball politics for many of them. The unannounced intention of our colleague was a major concern to most Caucus members. She had not taken any of us into her confidence and never discussed her plans for seeking the highest office. Press speculation indicated she was seriously contemplating the race, but her retorts to inquiring fellow Caucus members were cautiously veiled or noncommittal. She later claimed, however, that each member of the Caucus was mailed a letter detailing her intentions and informing them of the date she would declare her candidacy three days before she officially made the announcement. In fact, none of us received such notification.

As Chisholm's candidacy advanced, the public squabbles about her intentions escalated. Several weeks following the episode at the Conference of Black Elected Officials, the Democratic national chairman announced that Patricia Harris, the first black female ambassador in the history of the United States, would chair the Credentials Committee at the convention. Immediately, she was labeled an "Uncle Tom" by some black leaders and castigated as unqualified for the position. Joining the parade of attackers were Shirley Chisholm, John Conyers, and Julian Bond. They described Harris as the hand-picked tool of anti-reform elements in the Democrat party. Their preference for the chairmanship just happened to be a white male, Harold Hughes, U.S. senator from Iowa.

That same week, Carl Stokes launched an attack on Chisholm and others who supported Senator Hughes. On the Reverend Jesse Jackson's Saturday morning "Operation Breadbasket" radio program, Stokes said,

The young men that I have always held in respect, Julian Bond and Congressman Conyers, called [Mrs. Harris] unqualified. Now I'm going to tell you it's hard for me to fight this white man about respecting my black women when these black men talk about them like that.

. . . you have heard or read about my saying that if Shirley Chisholm wants to run for president, "right on." But I'll be doggone if I didn't turn around the other day and found out that she, a black woman, said she is going to run for president of the United States in order to reflect black interests and the interests of women. I'll be doggone if she didn't turn around and was opposing this brilliant black woman as chairman of the Credentials Committee—this is, for a white man. . . . Either you're going to stand up for black women and black people, or don't stand up at all, Shirley.[3]

Shortly thereafter, Chisholm surprised many blacks by supporting Congresswoman Patsy Mink of Hawaii over Yvonne Braithwaite Burke of California for vice-chairperson of the 1972 Democratic National Convention. Again she was scorned by some black leaders for favoring an Asian-American over a highly qualified black woman who had already been selected by convention officials as an officer. Despite Chisholm's opposition, Yvonne Burke was named vice-chairperson and Patricia Harris was appointed chairperson of the Credentials Committee.

This was merely the beginning of a series of disputes black leaders would experience with the Chisholm candidacy. Late in 1971, they gathered from all sections of the country to stage a number of secret meetings in an effort to reach a consensus for the 1972 presidential election. The purpose was to forge a national strategy, if possible, to reap major benefits for the black community. Leaders in this endeavor included Jesse Jackson of Operation Breadbasket; Georgia State Senator Julian Bond; Manhattan Borough President Percy E. Sutton; Richard Hatcher, mayor of Gary, Indiana; Walter E. Fauntroy, congressional delegate for the District of Columbia; Willie Brown, California state assemblyman; Maynard Jackson, vice-mayor of Atlanta; Amiri Baraka, playwright and activist; Clarence Mitchell III, Maryland state senator; Basil Patterson, New York City ward leader; CBC members Stokes, Diggs, Conyers, Rangel, and myself; and other black politicoes.

These unannounced and unpublicized meetings were held in Detroit, Washington, D.C., Cleveland, and several other cities. Local leaders were invited to sessions in each of the cities. For three months, the meetings, the participants, and the agenda were kept from public view. How such tight secrecy was preserved and how these events eluded the attention of the daily press still mystifies many of the participants.

The media did not get wind of the sessions until the one held at Northlake, a suburban community outside Chicago's O'Hare Airport. Although Chisholm had refused to attend any of the thirteen strategy meetings, she was represented by an aide, the Reverend Thaddeus Garrett, at the meeting held at Northlake.

Some black leaders considered her absence an intentional affront. Julian Bond complained,

Mrs. Chisholm's candidacy was a unilateral candidacy. A great many black politicians resented it. She went off entirely by herself. There was a series of meetings of black politicians over the last year. She didn't attend one of them—invited to all, but didn't attend any. One meeting I had begged her to come. She sent a young kid to represent her.[4]

Although the meetings were all planned and the invitees carefully selected, the discussions and debates were not at all constrained. They covered a wide range of lively topics:

1. Should blacks endorse a presidential candidate and, if so, whom?
2. Should blacks file an independent candidate?
3. Should blacks run "favorite sons and favorite daughters" to strengthen bargaining power at the convention with committed delegates?
4. Should blacks organize into a third party and deny Democrats the black vote in the general election?
5. Should blacks advocate boycotting the presidential election if an unsuitable candidate was nominated by Democrats to oppose Richard Nixon?
6. Should blacks file a candidate in the Democratic primaries?

Meanwhile, Chisholm was planning her campaign for the presidency without consulting other black elected officials or showing concern for how they might react. Her attitude was "I don't give a damn what black men do."

As a panelist at a workshop in Chicago sponsored by Jesse Jackson and Operation Breadbasket, she displayed her contempt for black male leaders, declaring,

> . . . well, I am about ready to make my decision to run, and just want today to say a few things to my black brothers, who I know are not going to endorse me. I do not expect their support, nor will I bother them about it. I know their feelings. I have learned too much for too long in my dealings with politicians, black and white. . . . Anyone in his right mind knows that this group of men, for the most part, would only laugh at the idea. They would never endorse me.
>
> They are the prisoners of their traditional attitudes, and some of them are just plain jealous, because they have been wounded in their male egos.[5]

On November 21, 1971, on the nationally broadcast program "Face the Nation," Chisholm was asked, "Does it make any difference what the other black leaders decide they want to do? You're going to be in it, regardless?

Representative Chisholm: "Yes, I am going to run regardless because, as I said, I have—I was first projected by a number of forces five or six months ago."[6]

Some black leaders were appalled by her statement and publicly expressed their concern that, given her attitude, white women like Bella Abzug and Gloria Steinem of the women's liberation movement might be in a position to bargain with white men at the convention in the name of the black community.

In conversations with members of the Caucus, Chisholm further complicated the situation by convincing some of us she actually believed victory was within her grasp. She spoke of winning a number of the larger states. Her scenario's crowning glory was to win Florida and California. In these two states her game plan called for a coalition of women, Spanish-speaking people, liberal whites, young students, and welfare recipients to push her ahead of other candidates. It was a frightening bit of fantasy to those of us who were more earthly in our political assessments.

Months after the election, Chisholm wrote in her book *The Good Fight*:

> . . . I was not out to become only the black candidate. While I would have welcomed the support of these men, I did not seek it because, even if they had offered their backing (as I knew they never would do), I would have been locked into a false and limiting role. It was possible for me to be more than the black candidate, or the candidate of minorities generally. My potential support went far beyond the black community. It could come from the women's movement, from young voters, and even from a growing number of older white voters who had reached the end of their patience with the programs and candidates of the two major parties.[7]

These verbal gyrations clearly showed Chisholm's frame of mind during her erstwhile campaign for the presidency. As a phalanx of black leaders searched for a candidate who would make a statement about the legitimacy of black concerns and pressure the Democratic party into recognition of those concerns, Shirley Chisholm had ideas on a more grandiose scale. But no matter how unrealistic, she was entitled to her hallucinations and had every right to disagree with the opinions of black male elected officials.

For a brief moment, it looked as if the Chisholm campaign was picking up momentum and that she would be able to reconcile her differences with black male leaders. That possibility surfaced when Percy Sutton intervened on her behalf. He convinced her to establish a committee of twenty members and publicly to promise not to engage in unilateral decision-making at the convention.

The agreement was the result of several hard bargaining sessions involving the candidate, Jesse Jackson, Congressman Ron Dellums, Mayor Richard Hatcher, and others. Initially, Congressman Rangel of Harlem indicated his support of the group.

A major component of the agreement required that Chisholm not compete for delegates in any district where blacks such as Congressmen Walter Fauntroy and former Mayor Carl Stokes were running as "favorite son" candidates. The arrangement soon fell apart as Chisholm nevertheless filed in several areas where blacks were running as "favorite son" candidates. (A "favorite-son" candidate is one who is very popular in his or her local community but not necessarily well known in other areas of the country. These candidates are usually able to garner enough votes to elect all the convention delegates from a particular district. Controlling large blocs of delegate votes confers tremendous negotiating power on the spokesperson for those votes.)

In Florida, Alcee Hastings, a black lawyer who had previously conducted a serious campaign in the Democratic senatorial race, was so incensed by Chisholm's entry in the state's presidential primary that he suspended his activities as a "favorite-son" candidate. He publicly attacked Chisholm for her decision to enter a race that she probably could not win. It was generally acknowledged that Hastings would win some delegates to the Democratic Convention. It was thought, and later confirmed, that Chisholm would fail to attract enough black voters to win delegates. Hastings, announcing his withdrawal as a "favorite son" candidate, angrily stated he would rather support George Wallace than Shirley Chisholm.[8]

In Cleveland, Congressman Stokes' brother Carl ran as a "favorite-son" candidate. The election procedure in the state of Ohio for selecting delegates to the national party conventions places the name of the presidential candidate on the ballot with his or her recommended delegates listed immediately below. None of the major candidates for the presidency filed slates against the former mayor of Cleveland. The Twenty-first District elected all eight delegates to the Democratic Convention on the Stokes slate.

Chisholm believed that her campaign depended on walking into the convention with a majority of the black delegate support and did not hesitate to tell black leaders of her intention to secure them by whatever means possible. Many of her black male colleagues disagreed with Chisholm's strategy. Fauntroy and Stokes, as well as many other locally elected blacks, viewed the strategy of "favorite son" candidates as a better option for keeping white politicians from automatically corralling black delegate strength. That strategy was designed to withhold important delegate support from major white candidates and win bargaining power for black spokespersons. Chisholm's decision to enter the presidential contest in these districts forced a change in those plans.

Those attending the private sessions to devise a black strategy for the 1972 presidential election never saw a black candidate as a serious aspirant for the Democratic nomination. Perhaps our overall plan would have made more sense if we had. But certainly Shirley Anita Chisholm, for many reasons, was way down on any theoretical list of potential black candidates.

That, of course, had no bearing on her own belief that she was the only logical black choice, a candidate able to wage a viable campaign for the presidency. She charged that black male leaders were "ego tripping," but she, too, possessed a well-developed ego. This was evident in remarks she made in her book, *The Good Fight:*

> Had the meetings at Northlake and elsewhere produced a potential nominee whom I could have supported, and whom I could have seen as an effective leader in creating the national black voting bloc, I would have abandoned my campaign and worked for him as hard as I worked for myself. But no one was put forward who—to be completely candid—compared with me as a potential vote-getter. Who among the others mentioned was already under real pressure to run? Who else already had volunteers begging to be allowed to set up state and local campaign organizations? For whom else was there grassroots support among women, Spanish-speaking voters and college-age voters? The fact is that there was a vacuum into which I was propelled. This may have left, as someone told a newspaper reporter, "male egos bleeding all over the floor," but it seemed to me that there were more important issues involved than hemophilia of the masculine psyche.[9]

Carl Stokes, who played a leading role at the Gary National Black Political Convention in convincing delegates not to endorse any candidate for the presidency, alluded to Chisholm's own ego. He admitted the move was designed to stop Chisholm from playing games with the future of blacks as it related to the election of their presidential choice. Stokes wrote in his book *Promises of Power*,

> This [policy of no endorsement], admittedly, was to stop them from joining Congresswoman Shirley Chisholm on her ego trip in the presidential primaries. The view prevailed, but it was a rough fight. I looked at the situation we faced in 1972, and it was exactly what it had been in 1968. We faced the probability of four more years of Richard Nixon. Yet many people were still out there playing games.[10]

Chisholm's statement is riddled with egotistical misconceptions of self-importance. She would never have "abandoned" the race, regardless of who was unanimously endorsed by black leaders. Her face-saving dodge was the caveat "whom I could support." If she could not support talented black women such as Yvonne Burke and Patricia Harris for convention positions, what other black in her opinion would qualify for president? The assertion that "no one was put forward who—to be completely candid—compared with me as a potential vote-getter" was ludicrous.

Shirley Chisholm was never a potential or real "vote-getter." She served in the U.S. Congress not by any particular mandate of the voters but rather due to the apathy and indifference of her Brooklyn constituency. Each time she was elected to Congress, it was with fewer votes than any of the other 434 members of the House of Representatives. The first time she was elected to Congress, her opponent James Farmer received 13,777 votes. She received only 34,885 votes.

Stokes and I also were elected to Congress for the first time on the same day as Chisholm. Stokes received 86,000 votes and I received 79,295 votes. My Republican opponent, Curtis Crawford, in losing, received 9,421 votes more than Chisholm. So, her vote-getting ability pales considerably in comparison.

The fallacy of her assertion of vote-getting prowess is dispelled by a simple comparison of her 1972 general election results (in the year of her presidential campaign) with those of the other members of the New York delegation and also her colleagues in the Congressional Black Caucus. All members of Congress are elected from districts with roughly the same number of constituents. Of the thirty-nine candidates seeking to become representatives from New York State in the 1972 general elections, seventeen received more votes than Chisholm and still lost in their bid for election. The comparison with her colleagues in the Congressional Black Caucus is also revealing:

	Vote count
Ralph Metcalfe of Illinois	136,755
John Conyers of Michigan	131,353
Yvonne Burke of California	123,468
Charles Rangel of New York	104,427
Louis Stokes of Ohio	99,190
Charles Diggs of Michigan	97,562
William Clay of Missouri	95,098
Augustus Hawkins of California	95,050
Walter Fauntroy of D.C.	93,300
Barbara Jordan of Texas	85,672
Parren Mitchell of Maryland	83,749
Andrew Young of Georgia	72,289
Shirley Chisholm of New York	57,821

Most serious candidates who are defeated for Congress receive more votes in being denied a seat in the House than Chisholm ever received in winning office. In one hard-fought primary, in which both candidates spent thousands of dollars, Chisholm beat her opponent by less than 2,500 votes. He received 7,500 votes and she received not quite 10,000.

Chisholm's campaign was a failure. In Florida, she received only 4 percent of the vote; in Massachusetts, 4.8 percent; even less in Wisconsin. Surprised by Senator Humphrey's strength in black areas: 72 percent in Pennsylvania, 70 percent in Florida, and 78 percent in Ohio, she said, "My campaign for the have-nots and the disillusioned has not caught fire as hoped." In her home state of New York, forty-three of the forty-seven candidates pledged to her were rejected in the election of delegates by the voters, including two of the six proposed black delegates from her own congressional district.

BLACKS THROW THEIR SUPPORT TO GEORGE MCGOVERN

Louis Stokes, Walter Fauntroy, and I endorsed George McGovern's candidacy after we reached an understanding with him and secured his commitment to support blacks on issues of paramount concern to us. Among those was the Black Bill of Rights drafted by the Caucus. He made his support and endorsement of it public when other candidates, fearful of losing support in the white community, refused to do the same.

If it is possible to pinpoint the most critical time in the nomination of a presidential candidate, it has to be the moment 50 percent plus one of the delegates to a convention commit to that candidate. For Senator George McGovern that moment of truth came on June 26, 1972, several weeks before the convention.

At the time, McGovern had 1,347.05 delegate votes committed to him. The other candidates were far behind: Humphrey with 387.3; Wallace with 377; Muskie with 215.1; Henry Jackson with 39.75; Chisholm with 28; "favorite sons" with 58; and uncommitted numbering 484.25. Although McGovern was far ahead of the pack, unless he reached the magic number for nomination on the first ballot, he would be in serious trouble.

This count above did not include seventy-six delegates to be elected the following weekend at caucuses and conventions in New York, Delaware, Arkansas, and Washington. The count released by the news media also was in disagreement with that of Senator McGovern, who claimed to have 1,413 votes.

Many of the uncommitted were black delegates from Louisiana, Georgia, Alabama, and South Carolina.

The last week in June, following a breakfast in Washington, D.C., with uncommitted black delegates from around the country, it was announced that ninety-six formerly uncommitted delegates were now supporting McGovern. The total included the twenty-six that Stokes, Fauntroy and I personally controlled by virtue of our elected slates. Added to those already pledged to McGovern, they constituted the exact number of 1,509 delegates needed to take the senator over the top on the convention's first ballot.

The only remaining problem was for the McGovern camp to hold all committed delegates between then and the time of the first convention ballot. Pressures on delegates to retract commitments were exerted by supporters of Senator Hubert Humphrey, Senator Henry Jackson, AFL-CIO President George Meany, and old line party big-wigs. About twelve of the delegates later denied having given permission to use their names. But the rest steadfastly stayed in the McGovern column.

It was almost inevitable that McGovern would win the nomination. That was the assessment of most political professionals, but none of the traditional centers of influence in party matters was overly pleased with the prospect. Many labor leaders, led by George Meany, refused to support his campaign. Although half of the AFL-CIO unions actively supported McGovern, Meany was able to persuade the AFL-CIO executive council to take a neutral position in the campaign.

This nonendorsement meant that McGovern would not be able to mobilize a nationwide labor apparatus. Four presidents of building trade unions and two maritime unions openly endorsed and campaigned for Nixon, an avowed anti-labor politician. In the interval, Meany was so hostile to the McGovern campaign that when the Colorado AFL-CIO Labor Federation defied his orders and endorsed McGovern, he put them in trusteeship. They were forced to sue in the court to get the right to back their choice.

Even with all of the internal bickering, it was apparent that McGovern was the clear choice of representatives of grassroots organizations, including a defiant black element within the ranks of organized labor, that for once made a difference at a national convention.

Black labor leaders under the leadership of Bill Lucy, secretary-treasurer of the American Federation of State, County, Municipal Employees Union also defied Meany. They held a meeting in Chicago, where more than 1,200 in attendance announced their intention to register black voters across the country in a massive drive and to get that vote out for Senator McGovern. It was necessary, Lucy declared, for the organization to become permanent in order to deal with the peculiar problems of the black trade unionists: "It's obvious that the AFL-CIO is not doing its job for black workers. The federation may consider the problems of poor blacks, but it doesn't understand those problems."[11]

Big city party bosses like Mayor Daley of Chicago and the regular Democrats of Mississippi were not happy. Supporters of McGovern flexed their muscles at the very beginning of the convention when a minority in favor of seating the Daley delegation was defeated by 105 votes. Then the delegation led by Chicago Alderman William Singer and Jesse Jackson, which supported McGovern, was seated. The Mississippi regular Democrats, headed by arch segregationist Governor John Bell Williams, posed a challenge that was rejected by the Credentials Committee a week before the convention opened. The committee sided with a "loyalist" group of delegates headed by Aaron Henry, a civil rights activist. The Loyal Democrats of Mississippi organization was made up of liberals and blacks who had remained in the Democratic party when white elected officials deserted it over the issue of racial integration and states' rights. Included in the group were the Mississippi Freedom Democratic Party, the state Young Democrats, the Mississippi Teachers Association, the Prince Hall Masons, and the state chapter of the AFL-CIO.

THE TWO PLATFORMS

Every RADICAL in Congress VOTED for NEGRO SUFFRAGE.   Every RADICAL in the Pennsylvania Senate VOTED for NEGRO SUFFRAGE. STEVENS, FORNEY & CAMERON are for NEGRO SUFFRAGE; they are all Candidates for the UNITED STATES SENATE.   NO RADICAL NEWSPAPER OPPOSES NEGRO SUFFRAGE GEARY said in a Speech, at Harrisburg, 11th of August, 1866—"THERE CAN BE NO POSSIBLE OBJECTION TO NEGRO SUFFRAGE."

CLYMER'S
Platform is for the White Man.

GEARY'S
Platform is for the Negro.

READ THE PLATFORMS

CONGRESS says, THE NEGRO MUST BE ALLOWED TO VOTE, OR THE STATES BE PUNISHED.

[PUT THIS UP.]

An 1866 Pennsylvania gubernatorial election poster proposing Clymer and opposing Geary and his Radical Republican platform. The nation was divided on the issue of the political inclusion of blacks, and fearful of the consequences. (*Courtesy of the Library of Congress*)

This broadside seems designed to provoke fear in whites of black political participation. (*Courtesy of the Library of Congress*)

This woodcut from a sketch by Alfred R. Waud in *Harper's Weekly*, August 4, 1866, depicts blacks and whites stoning one another. (*Courtesy of the Library of Congress*)

RADICAL MEMBERS

OF THE FIRST LEGISLATURE AFTER THE WAR

SOUTH CAROLINA

Dusenberry	Mayes	Demars	Rivers	Miteford	Smith	Swails
McKinlay	Jillson	Brodie	Duncan	White	Pettengill	Percin
Dickson	Lomax	Hayes	BOOZER	Barton	Hyde	James
Wilder	Jackson	Cain	Smythe	Boston	Lee	Johnston
Hoyt	Thomas	Maxwell	Wright	Shrewsbury	Simonds	Wimbush
Randolph	Webb	Martin	MOSES	Mickey	Chesnut	Hayes
Harris	Bozeman	Cook	Sancho	Henderson	Mc Daniel	Farr
	Tomlinson	Miller	Sanders	Howell	Williams	Meade
	Wright *		Nuckles	Hayne	Gardner	Thompson
				Mobley		Rainey
				Hudson		
				Nash		
				Carmand		

* Afterwards associate Justice of the Supreme
Court of the State

This depicts the first South Carolina legislature after the Civil War.
(*Courtesy of the Library of Congress*)

Hiram R. Revels, the first black U.S. senator, chosen to fill the unexpired term of former Confederate President Jefferson Davis. Revels' term only lasted for one year. (*Courtesy of the Library of Congress*)

"Heroes of the Colored Race": Blanche K. Bruce, who served one six-year term in the U.S. Senate; abolitionist and activist Frederick Douglass; and Hiram R. Revels. (*Courtesy of the Library of Congress*)

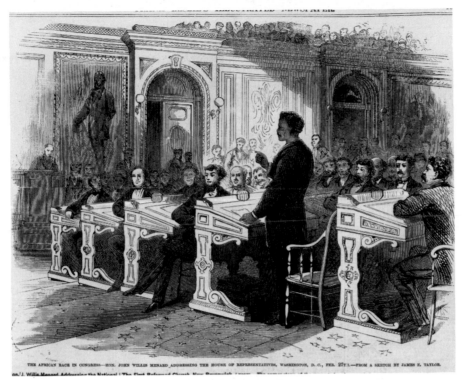

The African Race in Congress—the Honorable John Willis Bernard addressing the House of Representatives, Washington, D.C. (*Courtesy of the Library of Congress*)

Representative William L. Dawson (*left*) and Representative Adam C. Powell, Jr., in front of the Capitol on January 14, 1950. (*Courtesy of AP-World Wide Photos*)

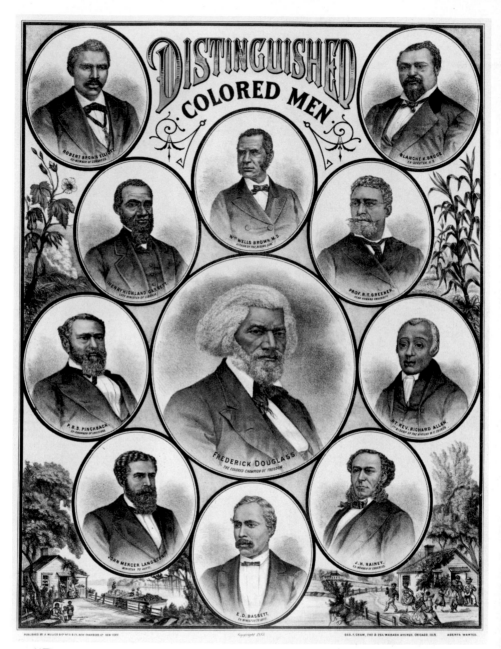

"**D**istinguished Colored Men" who belied the stereotype of black leaders and elected officials as uncouth and corrupt: (*left to right*) Robert Brown Elliot, congressman from South Carolina; Blanche K. Bruce, senator from Mississippi; Henry Highland Garnett, late minister of Liberia; William Wells Brown, M.D., author of the *The Rising Son*; Professor R. T. Greener, dean of Howard University; P. B. S. Pinchback, former lieutenant governor of Louisiana; Frederick Douglass; the Right Reverend Richard Allen, founder and first bishop of the African Methodist Episcopal Church; John Mercer Langston, minister to Haiti; E. D. Bassett, ex-minister to Haiti; and J. H. Rainey, congressman from South Carolina. (*Courtesy of the Library of Congress*)

Congressman John Conyers, Jr., of Michigan, Louis Stokes of Ohio, and myself (*in the center*). Congresswoman Shirley A. Chisholm of New York, Louis A. Stokes of Ohio, and I were sworn in on January 2, 1969, bringing the number of blacks in the House of Representatives up to nine. (*Courtesy of the Library of Congress*)

Congresswoman Chisholm talks with Congressman Charles C. Diggs, Jr., of Michigan and me. (*Courtesy of the Library of Congress*)

Young people like these at my Twenty-sixth Ward headquarters in 1968 in St. Louis helped to get me elected. (*Courtesy of the Library of Congress*)

My wife, Carol, and I on
January 15, 1969. (*Photo
by Paul Begley*)

Senator Edward Brooke in
his office in Washington,
December 1971. (*Photo by
Walter Bennett*)

Congressman Louis Stokes of Ohio and I at the Democratic National Convention in Miami, Florida, in August 1972. Black input in determining the presidential nominee was far greater than at any previous Democratic or Republican convention. (*Photo by Dev O'Neil, courtesy of William L. Clay*)

Here I am campaigning in 1972. (*Courtesy of William L. Clay*)

This same year, Ron V. Dellums of California, Louis Stokes, myself (*standing*), Charles Rangel of New York, Parren Mitchell of Maryland, and Ralph Metcalfe of Illinois received the "Top Hat" award of the year from the *Pittsburgh Courier*. (*Photo by Frank Russell Hightower, courtesy of William L. Clay*)

Ron Dellums, (unidentified woman) and the Reverend Leon Sullivan. Dellums was one of Congress's most outspoken opponents of the war in Vietnam. (*Courtesy of William L. Clay*)

Senator George McGovern, Clay, and Congressman Henry Reuss. (*Courtesy of William L. Clay, Dev O'Neil*)

Dick Gregory, a civil rights leader as well as entertainer, at the naming of a street for him in St. Louis. City Comptroller John Bass and I are holding the ladder. (*Courtesy of William L. Clay*)

Ethel Payne had a thirty-year career as an award-winning journalist and crusader against injustice and for human rights. (*Photo by David A. Brooks, courtesy of William L. Clay*)

Representative Charles Diggs of Michigan in 1975.

Black elected officials meeting with President Gerald Ford in the Oval Office: (*left to right, sitting*) Augustus F. Hawkins of California; Cardiss Collins of Illinois; Charles Rangel of New York; Yvonne Braithwaite Burke of California; myself; Parren J. Mitchell of Maryland; (*standing*) Ron Dellums of California, Robert Nix of Pennsylvania, John Conyers, Jr., of Michigan; Shirley Chisholm of New York; Andrew Young of Georgia; Stan Scott, aide to the president; Ralph M. Metcalfe of Illinois; Walter E. Fauntroy, delegate from the District of Columbia; Barbara Jordan of Texas; Louis Stokes of Ohio; and Charles C. Diggs, Jr., of Michigan. (*Official photograph, the White House*)

I shook hands and smiled with President Jimmy Carter here, but his relationship to the Congressional Black Caucus was not so friendly. (*Courtesy of William L. Clay*)

Senator Ted Kennedy addressed the 1978 Annual CBC Dinner at the Washington Hilton Hotel. I was chairperson of the dinner that year. (*K. Jewel, White House photo*)

Andrew Young and Ron Dellums. Young, elected to Congress from the Fifth District of Georgia in 1972, resigned to accept the position of ambassador to the United Nations in 1977. (*Courtesy of William L. Clay*)

Left to right: Ron Dellums, Parren Mitchell, and I at a hearing on black economic development. (*Courtesy of Dev O'Neil*)

Members of the Congressional Black Caucus in 1972 on the Capitol steps: (*second row, left to right*) Harold Ford, Charles Rangel, John Conyers, Yvonne Braithwaite Burke of California, Bill Clay, Louis Stokes, Ronald Dellums; *first row, left to right*: Walter Fauntroy, Ralph Metcalfe, Bob Nix, Augustus Hawkins, Cardiss Collins, Parren Mitchell. (Shirley Chisholm and Charlie Diggs were absent). (*House photo, K. Jewel*)

I'm gesturing to fellow members at a CBC function. *Left to right*: Congressman Esteban E. Torres, chairman of the Hispanic Caucus, Merv Dymally (*standing*), Harold Washington, Ed Town (*standing*), Mike Espy, Kweisi Mfume, Ronald Dellums, Alan Wheat, Louis Stokes (*behind me*), Gus Savage and John Conyers. (*Courtesy of William L. Clay*)

Mr. Weathers tribute in 1979. Bill Stoghill, Fred Weathers, and I. (*Courtesy of William L. Clay*)

CBC members Mervyn M. Dymally of California, Charles Rangel of New York, Esteban E. Torres of California, Charles Hayes of Illinois, Alan Wheat of Missouri, Gus Savage (*head turned*) of Illinois, myself, Kweisi Mfume of Maryland, Mike Espy of Mississippi (*head and glasses partially showing*), Ed Towns of New York, and Augustus Hawkins of California (*back to the camera*) meeting with Chicago Mayor Harold Washington (*at right*) in 1987 to discuss his campaign for re-election. (*Official photograph, the White House*)

Stokes and I accept a check for $125,000 on behalf of the CBC from Anheuser Busch employees Stephen Lambright, Wayman Smith, and Henry Brown to retire the debt on the Caucus office building. (*Photo by Beverly Swanagan*)

Elected officials have all sorts of creative ways to support their constituencies. The can of beer labeled in my name was used to raise proceeds for a senior citizens' food program. (*Courtesy of William L. Clay*)

Carl and (wife) Rhia Stokes, Louis Stokes, and Senator Ted Kennedy.
(*Courtesy of William L. Clay*)

Louis Stokes and (wife) Jay; attorney Russell Adrine at right. (*Courtesy of William L. Clay*)

Maxine Waters at a press conference after the 1992 Los Angeles riots surrounded by (*left to right*) Donald M. Payne of New Jersey, Charles Rangel of New York, Lucien Blackwell of Pennsylvania, Esteban E. Torres of California, Pat Schroeder of Colorado, myself, Ed Towns of New York (*behind Waters*), Bernard Saunders of Vermont, Harold Ford of Tennessee, Ron Dellums of California, Craig Washington of Texas, and Jose Serrano of New York. (*Courtesy of William L. Clay*)

Left to right: Walter Fauntroy, Augustus Hawkins, Ronald Dellums, myself, Charles Rangel, President Jimmy Carter, Parren Mitchell, and Ralph Metcalfe met in the Oval Office in 1977. (*Official photograph, the White House*)

I addressed this rally in St. Louis on September 13, 1987, in memory of deceased St. Louis political leader Jordan Chambers. Chambers was the premier black political leader from the thirties through the fifties in St. Louis. (*Courtesy of William L. Clay*)

Congressman Charles A. Hayes of Illinois, the late Mickey Leland of Texas, attorney Amy Goldstein, and I discussing CBC Foundation activities. (*Courtesy of William L. Clay*)

Joan Gilbert; Jay Stokes; Pier Hardy; and Carol Clay and I at a 1983 community fundraiser at the Masonic Hall in St. Louis. (*Courtesy of William L. Clay*)

Stokes on the podium at his annual picnic in Cleveland. Seated to my right is Congresswoman Mary Oakar. (*Courtesy of William L. Clay*)

I chaired a hearing of the Select Committee on the Aging focusing on protection of their rights. To my right is Congressman Matthew Rinaldo. To my left are Congressman Ed Roybal, my staff assistant Phyllis Borzi, an unidentified committee staff director, and Congressman Claude Pepper of Florida (on the end). (*Courtesy of William L. Clay*)

I'm talking with Cardiss Collins at a 1986 meeting of the CBC Brain Trust on Minorities in the Electronic Media. (*Courtesy of William L. Clay*)

General Colin Powell briefed the CBC on the war in Iraq in 1991. Julian Dixon of California is on the right. (*Courtesy of William L. Clay*)

I was proud to receive the 1989 "Good Guy Award" from the National Women's Political Caucus. Pat Schroeder presented the award. (*Photo by Jim Marks*)

Secretary of Health and Human Services Louis Sullivan at a reception in his honor sponsored by Congressman Louis Stokes. *Left to right*: Sullivan, Congressman Silvio Conte of Massachusetts, myself, and Stokes.

Charles Rangel, Mayor Sharon Pratt Kelly of Washington, D.C., and I.

Thurgood Marshall swearing in members of the CBC. Congressman Floyd Flake of New York and I stand behind Marshall. (*Courtesy of William L. Clay*)

CBC members meet with Harry Belafonte. *Left to right*: former Congressman Bill Gray, Belafonte, Congressman John Conyers, and myself. (*Courtesy of William L. Clay*)

Left to right: Gus Hawkins, Winnie Mandela, Nelson Mandela, John Conyers, Louis Stokes, Kweisi Mfume, Charles Rangel, Julian Dixon. (*Courtesy of William L. Clay*)

The new police chief of Los Angeles. Willie Williams briefs the CBC about his new assignment and his plans for improving community relations there. (*Courtesy of William L. Clay*)

Alan Wheat on the night of the 1982 Missouri primary, proclaiming his victory. (*Courtesy of William L. Clay*)

My son State Senator William L. Clay, Jr., and brother Alderman Irving C. Clay. Together we have more than eighty-two years of public service behind us. (*Photo by Ted Dargan*, St. Louis Post Disptach *staff*)

Left to right: Former Congressman Charles C. Diggs, Jr.; Congressman Edolphus ("Ed") Towns (D., New York); Amistad publisher Charles Harris; Congressman William L. Clay; and Congressman Charles B. Rangel (D., New York) at a press conference held to announce publication of *Just Permanent Interests* at the National Press Club Building in Washington, D.C., September 24, 1992.

Speaker of the House of Representatives Tom Foley (D., Washington), making introductory remarks at a reception sponsored by Time Warner Inc., held in the National Building Museum on September 24, 1992, to launch the hardcover edition of this book.

This reception for Congressman William L. Clay was the opening event for the 1992 Annual Black Congressional Caucus weekend.

Charles F. Harris welcomes Congressman Louis Stokes to the dais.

Louis Stokes (D., Ohio) making his introductory remarks.

Congressman William L. Clay spoke to approximately 2500 guests, most of whom purchased copies of the book. Congressman Clay donated his royalties from the sale of the book at this event to The William L. Clay Scholarship Research Fund. The amount was matched by a contribution from Time Warner.

Congressman Clay was joined by family members (*left to right*): Henry Rory, Michelle Clay, Michael Alexis, Bill Clay, Jr., Ivie Clay, Vicki Clay, Bill Clay, Sr., and Carol Clay.

Left to right: Henry Rory, Michelle Clay, Michael Alexis, Bill Jr., Charles Harris, Ivie Clay, Vicki Clay, Bill Clay, Sr., and Carol Clay.

Left to right: Michelle Clay, Michael Alexis, Carol Clay, Bill Clay, Sr., Bill Clay, Jr., and Vicki Clay.

Congressman William L. Clay.

McGovern, who had been meeting with the three co-chairmen of the Gary Convention, agreeing to endorse most of the convention's demands to get their support, subsequently also received endorsements from Diggs and Hatcher. Several of Chisholm's delegates, two in Virginia and one in Iowa, announced they would vote for McGovern on the first ballot.

Congressmen Dellums, Mitchell, and Conyers withdrew their support of Chisholm and joined most of the other Caucus members in endorsing McGovern. Conyers had initially limited his endorsement of Chisholm to the Michigan primary anyway.

Watching her chances of a respectable showing in delegate count diminish, Chisholm panicked. She accused black leaders, including myself, of selling out the black interest by undermining her candidacy. She even went so far as to imply that Mrs. Coretta Scott King had taken money for her endorsement of McGovern's candidacy. At that point, a lineup of black leaders, among them Julian Bond, Jesse Jackson, Conyers, Stokes, and Fauntroy, called a press conference to refute the charge. I was chosen as the spokesman for the group.

One statement I made at the press conference, which was featured on national network news, apparently rankled Chisholm. After the campaign she said in her book, *The Good Fight*, "Representative Clay told the press, 'I don't question Mrs. Chisholm's integrity, but I do question her judgement and at times her sanity.' "[12] Later she threatened to sue me for defamation of character, but apparently had second thoughts when I cautioned that if I got her on the stand and proved her insanity, they would have to commit her to an institution.

To ensure that the delegates we influenced stayed influenced, and to keep the McGovern camp on the proper course, Stokes, Fauntroy, and I moved into the convention city and set up headquarters. We lobbied and promoted the candidacy of Senator McGovern. Stokes and I occupied suites at the fashionable Fontainebleau Hotel and lavishly entertained delegates. Fauntroy set up shop two blocks away in a smaller hotel, rented typewriters and mimeograph machines, hired secretarial help, and plunged into the detailed activity of countering the usual rumors and misconceptions associated with opponent activity at national conventions.

MCGOVERN PROVES A DISAPPOINTMENT

If Shirley Chisholm's candidacy was disappointing in terms of promoting the black agenda, Senator George McGovern's was a colossal disaster. Chisholm fought an uphill battle with minimal funds for election; a campaign committee consisting of a disorganized band of inexperienced volunteers; dissatisfaction and suspicion, if not outright hostility, toward her candidacy from sectors of the black community; and more importantly, no clear identification of benefits to come to black voters withholding their support of white candidates who at least had the potential to win.

McGovern, despite the advantage of being a blue-eyed, blond-haired political aspirant, was an even greater failure when it came to winning the support of his core constituency. If the disappointing campaign of Mrs. Chisholm is to be attributed primarily to her failure to garner huge voter approval in the black precincts, then Mr. McGovern must be judged by the same standards. His attempt to appeal to traditional Democratic voting blocs in white ethnic, blue collar neighborhoods was a total wash-out. White voters went to the polls in moderate numbers for presidential elections in the sixties and seventies, and in 1972 those who went overwhelmingly cast their votes for Richard Nixon.

McGovern was ultimately guilty of the same sin as others who aspired to become president. He, too, seemed to view black voters and their elected representatives as necessary irritants in the process of nomination and election.

The main headquarters of the McGovern group was lodged on the seventeenth floor of the Doral Hotel. Blacks reserved the fifteenth floor for their area of operations. At that location, the most powerful leaders in black America assembled, believing they were gathered to devise and implement plans for the making of a president.

On June 13 McGovern called a meeting with black leaders to advise on the selection of the vice-presidential candidate. About thirty-five of us convened hurriedly and selected five among us to actually go upstairs to meet with McGovern. At about 3:00 P.M., McGovern informed the group that he had narrowed his consideration of a running mate to five individuals: Mayor Moon Landreau of New Orleans, Mayor Kevin White of Boston, Governor Pat Lucey of Wisconsin, Senator Abraham Ribicoff of Connecticut, and R. Sargent Shriver. He asked us to return to the fifteenth floor, assess the qualifications of each and call back in three hours with a recommendation.

Thirty minutes later, while several dozen black leaders were discussing the merits and demerits of those under consideration, Frank Mankiewicz, one of McGovern's top advisers, appeared on television from the lobby of the Doral Hotel announcing that Senator Thomas

Eagleton of Missouri had been selected as the vice-presidential candidate. Eagleton's name was not even on the list proffered America's top black Democratic leadership less than an hour earlier.

McGovern and his top strategists—among them Gary Hart and Rick Stearns—had no intention of involving blacks in the nuts and bolts decisions for a victorious campaign. Yancey Martin, the highest black aide on the McGovern staff, was strictly window dressing. He was excluded from every decision-making session between McGovern and the other top staffers. I'm convinced McGovern would not have included us in any meaningful way after the election if he had been successful in winning the presidency.

It seems that white politicians never miss an opportunity to "piss on black folks' parades." McGovern, like all prior presidential aspirants, with the possible exception of Harry S. Truman and Lyndon Baines Johnson, showed contempt for blacks who desired to be rewarded for their contributions. Like so many other whites before him, McGovern suffered an acute case of amnesia when the time came to give back to those who gave to him.

Some, like veteran political consultant Ofield Dukes, attribute the lack of real influence in either party to the inability of blacks to provide substantial financial contributions to candidates and campaigns. Dukes observed,

> The measure of political influence and power in Washington is not based on who runs for office—but who provides the financial resources. This is not just political theory. There is, in fact, a correlation between political influence and power and the financiers of national politics.
>
> If we accept this principle or truth, then black influence and power in the Democratic party, the dominant party for blacks, are relative—to time (at elections when we produce votes) and personalities (prominent elected officials who have some say-so in party affairs).
>
> Attend any finance council meeting of the two major parties, or of any of the presidential candidates, and you will see the real "movers and shakers" who quietly represent the "inner circle" of influence and power. You will see very few if any blacks.[13]

Apparently, Ofield's assessment held true in the case of George McGovern, Democratic candidate for president in 1972. Further confirmation of the unimportant role blacks would play in any future McGovern administration came when the names of those who were to plan the actual campaign for president were announced. Of the fifty persons selected to decide strategies at a camp based at the foot of the Black Hills in a South Dakota resort, only three were black: Congressman Fauntroy, Yancey Martin, and me.

Upon arrival at National Airport in Washington, D.C., for the scheduled trip to South Dakota, Congressman Fauntroy and I were informed by a low-level McGovern staffer that the chartered plane was overbooked and we could not board. We insisted that such a decision must be made by McGovern or his campaign manager, Gary Hart. The staffer backed down and the two of us journeyed off into the wild blue yonder, leaving a pair of secretaries awaiting a commercial flight.

Once the planning for the campaign began, it would have been just as well if we had stayed at home. We played the usual role reserved for minorities—that of advising on voter registration and getting out the vote in black precincts. Budgetary outlays for such activities and decisions about who would be in charge of policy-making and financial decisions were items left exclusively to the elite, all-white McGovern inner-circle.

Commitments to blacks for cabinet positions, top administration slots, and other business arrangements were not considered proper topics for discussion. However, all of us meeting in South Dakota knew that Senators Mondale, Ribicoff, Kennedy, and others, such as Averell Harriman, had already negotiated their deals with McGovern and had received promises of key high level positions in exchange for supporting the ticket.

In the November general election, Richard Nixon was returned to office by a landslide. McGovern lost forty-nine of the fifty states. Nixon carried the Catholic vote, a first for a Republican presidential candidate. He also received half of the young first-time voters—those between eighteen and twenty-one, for whom the Democrats had fought so hard to give the right to vote. McGovern received 85 percent of the black vote, but his inability to carry the white precincts was disastrous.

The black community had to wait six years for another chance to influence a national political agenda, only then to be hoodwinked again by another soft-spoken, slick-talking medicine man of the Democratic party, James Earl Carter.

NOTES

1. *Congressional Quarterly*, June 24, 1972, page 1522.
2. *National Journal*, June 24, 1972, page 1066.

3. As quoted in *Race Relations Reporter*, January 1972, page 11.

4. Quoted by Dom Bonafede, *National Journal*, June 24, 1972, page 1064.

5. Shirley Chisholm, *The Good Fight*, New York: Harper & Row, 1973, pages 32–33.

6. "Face the Nation," November 21, 1971.

7. Chisholm, *The Good Fight*, pages 37–38.

8. *Race Relations Reporter*, January 1972, page 11.

9. Chisholm, *The Good Fight*, page 41.

10. Carl Stokes, *Promises of Power*, New York: Simon & Schuster, 1973, pages 275–276.

11. *New York Times*, October 3, 1972, page 33.

12. Shirley Chisholm, *The Good Fight*, page 120.

13. *The Washington North Star*, September 22, 1983, page 10.

11

CBC Conferences and Hearings

Louis Stokes succeeded Charles Diggs to become the second chairperson of the Congressional Black Caucus in 1972. One of his first official acts was to initiate a program to expand black representation on various congressional committees, thereby strengthening Caucus influence in Congress. Blacks already served on eleven of the twenty-one standing committees of the House; however, none was sitting on "exclusive committees" such as Appropriations, Ways and Means, and Rules. These are the three most important committees.

Ron Dellums was making an attempt to gain a position on the Armed Services Committee, which would expand the influence of black members. Congressman Wilbur Mills, chairman of the Committee on Committees, which was responsible for determining assignments, informed the Caucus that Representative F. Edward Hébert of Louisiana, chairman of the Armed Services Committee, would accept any black member recommended by the Caucus except Dellums.

That was a bold statement, conveying a message that white folk still holding onto past tendencies would decide which blacks were qualified to speak for us. Mills and Hébert and most other whites were behind the times, unaware of the new mood of black people, especially the black people sitting in the United States Congress.

Stokes immediately convened a meeting with House Speaker Carl Albert and pointed out that, historically, southern Democrats like Mills and Hébert often voted with Republicans, while black members were more consistent and loyal supporters of the national Democratic party agenda. He described the Democratic majority as precariously feeble and threatened that the twelve voting members of the Caucus were prepared to make it even more tenuous. Stokes implied that CBC members intended to repeal the "love-in" between the party and its black supporters unless black members of the House were treated with the respect due them.

The point was well taken by Representative Hébert, who along with Wilbur Mills, made an aboutface, ardently supporting Dellums for the position. A disruptive confrontation between what could be called the "abolitionists and secessionists" was averted, and the CBC passed its first acid test of the new muscle it was flexing with the House leadership.

Stokes later was forced to meet the same kind of challenge when he sought appointment to the powerful Appropriations Committee. Congressman Charles Vanik, a senior member of the Ohio delegation, vehemently opposed Stokes' effort to gain a seat on the committee. Vanik claimed to be peeved because Stokes had supported a Republican candidate for a local office in Cleveland, Ohio. But here again, because of pressure from the Caucus and the precedent established with Dellums, Stokes was appointed to the coveted position on the Appropriations Committee.

The physical, moral, and financial support of the Caucus by people throughout the country bolstered the CBC mission to focus in on pertinent, specific issues by holding a series of public hearings and conferences. Between July 1971 and September 1972, we sponsored seven national conferences and conducted three public hearings aimed at formulating a priority agenda for black America. Except for the conferences of locally elected black officials, each session was sponsored in conjunction with other groups.

HEARINGS ON RACISM AND REPRESSION IN THE MILITARY, NOVEMBER 15–18, 1971

Representatives Shirley Chisholm and Ronald Dellums exposed racism and repression in the military at hearings in November 1971. Discriminatory actions had persisted for as long as nonwhites had served in the armed forces of the United States. After twenty-five years of "official" military desegregation, too many of the nearly 300,000 black Americans in uniform—at home and abroad—were still subjected to overt and subtle manifestations of racism.

The investigative hearings that documented racial conditions at military bases around the country and overseas were held November

15 through 18, 1971. Caucus members heard on site testimony from black officers and enlisted men stationed at Fort Bragg, North Carolina; Fort Campbell, Kentucky; Fort Hood, Texas; Fort Dix, New Jersey; Fort Meade, Maryland; Travis Air Force Base, California; Westover Air Force Base, Massachusetts; Camp Pendleton Marine Base, California; Quantico Marine Base, Virginia; and Great Lakes Naval Base, Illinois.

The congresspersons returned to Washington, D.C., to hear additional testimony from active-duty military personnel, experts in military law and administrative practices, and knowledgeable journalists. For three days, these witnesses discussed inequities in military justice, discharge policies, enlistment and promotion procedures, the failure to implement equal opportunity provisions, and other areas of concern.

At the conclusion of the hearings, the Congressional Black Caucus presented its evidence of racism in the military to Pentagon officials. Appointment by the Defense Department of a special task force to focus on discrimination resulted from the hearings.

NATIONAL CONFERENCE ON THE STATUS OF HEALTH IN BLACK AMERICA, DECEMBER 9–11, 1971

The health problems of nonwhites and the poor in the United States always have been disproportionately greater than those of other Americans. Adequate health care delivery systems always have been less accessible to minority and low-income citizens.

Statistical data motivated the National Medical Association, the National Dental Association, Meharry Medical College, and Howard University to join the Congressional Black Caucus in reviewing the status of health in black America. A conference held December 9 through 11, 1971, at Meharry Medical School in Nashville, Tennessee, attracted more than 600 participants from thirty states. The importance of the gathering was pinpointed by Congressman Metcalfe, chairman of the Health Subcommittee of the Congressional Black Caucus, in his keynote address to the registrants. He was followed by Congressman Charles Diggs, chairman of the CBC, who gave an overview of the status of health care in the black community.

Working in teams on eight major health care problems, participants in separate discussion groups repeatedly stressed that progress toward improved care would only be made when the consumer in the black community actively participated in setting priorities and policies for the system.

These are the conclusions of the various discussion groups:

GROUP 1—HEALTH CARE FINANCING

Concluded: With a legacy of serious poverty for millions, and marginal income levels for most of the rest, black Americans have not been able to afford the essential health care they need. Already far behind in receiving basic health care services taken for granted by mainstream America, the black community must now consider how to secure health care services needed for survival in the increasingly more hazardous environment of twentieth-century America.

GROUP 2—COMMUNITY HEALTH SYSTEMS

Concluded: Economic, social, and political traditions trap most black Americans in the least desirable communities throughout the United States. While all communities share a mutual concern about environmental problems which threaten life, health, and well-being, there is particular concern among blacks about negative environmental factors which historically affect their communities. The most obvious of these are health and life-threatening housing conditions; rat infestation; poor nutrition; presence of industrial and commercial enterprises which pollute air, water, and streets; and the uneven application of municipal, state, and national services responsible for control and elimination of such health hazards.

GROUP 3—HUMAN DEVELOPMENT

Concluded: Concern for human development must begin with the unborn and continue through all stages of life. Regarding the health care required to support human development, black Americans experience handicaps which at the least jeopardize optimal development and, at worst, make it unattainable. Health care should begin with quality prenatal and maternity care where existing and potential health-related development problems can be detected. Upwards of 1 million predominantly black poor women receive no prenatal care.

GROUP 4—FAMILY PLANNING V. POPULATION CONTROL

Concluded: The concepts of family planning and population control have strong negative connotations in much of the black community. Population control is seen as outright genocide aimed at an unwelcome black population—one which seems to be a problem to majority group Americans, but not to itself. This is due largely to the fact that family planning programs have been imposed upon black communities by whites rather than developed by blacks to meet our own needs as we identify them.

GROUP 5—SPECIAL MINORITY CONCERNS

Concluded: Numerous health problems of high incidence among blacks are of special concern to the black community, yet do not receive sufficient national attention. Much of this is due to a failure of the responsible authorities to consult with the black community about those health concerns which affect blacks most. The result has been that scarce funds are expended to solve problems of only limited significance to the larger black community while many other important concerns receive little or no attention.

GROUP 6—HEALTH MANPOWER DEVELOPMENT

Concluded: Much national debate continues about whether there actually is a health manpower shortage. But for those living in the black community there is a very evident shortage. In the urban ghettos and poor rural areas where blacks live and where they suffer high rates of illness and disease, that much is clear. The skills and capacities of those now serving in these areas are being overwhelmed by the sheer numbers and complexities of health problems.

GROUP 7—HEALTH CARE DELIVERY SYSTEMS

Concluded: Traditional systems of health care delivery have failed to meet the needs of poor black communities. Emergency room care and hospital clinics are notorious for their inadequacies. New systems, most notably the sixty-six neighborhood health centers in the nation, seem to hold great promise in changing the situation. Other health care delivery models are also under consideration for wider use, and still others are emerging to take their place alongside traditional, private fee-for-service models.

GROUP 8—CONSUMER HEALTH EDUCATION

Concluded: Black America traditionally has received a low level of health education. Recent efforts to improve the understanding and awareness of available health services have been underfunded, erratic, and lack sensitivity to the realities of poverty conditions in cities and rural areas. But awareness without access to real opportunities for needed health services frustrates and does not help. New methods, greater community involvement, different channels of communication, and new attitudes on the part of professionals must be explored.[1]

THE BLACK CAREERS IN COMMUNICATIONS CONFERENCES AT HOWARD UNIVERSITY, 1971 AND 1972

The School of Communications at Howard University and the Congressional Black Caucus jointly sponsored two Black Careers in Communications conferences, held in 1971 and 1972. The slogan of the gatherings was "The end of rhetoric . . . the beginning of action." Dr. James Cheek, president of Howard University, and Tony Brown, dean of the School of Communications, played leading roles in organizing and promoting phase one of the conference. Tony Brown and I co-chaired the conference, while Congressmen John Conyers, Ron Dellums, Louis Stokes, and Charles Rangel also represented the CBC in the proceedings.

In consequence of the conferences, on March 14, 1972, a seventy-six-page report edited by Lawrence A. Still, assistant dean of the Howard School of Communications, was released documenting the plight of blacks attempting penetration into the mass communications media.

In his opening remarks before several hundred students attending the 1971 conference, Dr. Cheek said, "The National Black Communication Society and the university have to correct the inequities and the imbalances that continue to exist in the communications industry, because the industry apparently is not going to do it at its own initiative."[2]

Milton Coleman, editor of *The African World* from Greensboro, North Carolina, noted that one of the more serious problems in black journalism was the rape of talented blacks by white news organizations. He said,

I think you find in every major black community, the dude who was either the best photographer at the black newspaper, who showed the most promise, or who was the best writer, turned around and two years later he either went to the white daily or he went to the TV station. And now he's . . . doing news that doesn't make any sense to anybody.

. . . So why should we try to be objective? Why should we be the only people in the world who get hung up in something that is not real? I think

Don Lee said in one poem that "niggers are the only ones who want to play fair." We're going to lose every time.[3]

Coleman, unfortunately, went on to become part of the problem he himself identified so articulately. Ten years after uttering his angry assessment of black stupidity, the same Milton Coleman who chastised "niggers" for playing "fair" could be found comfortably smothered in the financial comfort provided black employees at the citadel of perhaps the most prestigious newspaper in the country, the *Washington Post*.

For years that newspaper has been accused of journalistically raping advocates of equality for black citizens and castigating strong black leaders. Then Milton Coleman emerged on the scene as the dude "doing news that doesn't make any sense to anybody." And the dude proved his complete "objectivity" and "fair play" while white reporters at the paper were still "cheating."

In the 1984 presidential campaign, Coleman wrote an objective article based on information given to him in a confidential, off-the-record conversation with Jesse Jackson. According to his story, Jackson had referred to New York City as "Hymie town." Meanwhile, Coleman and the *Washington Post* totally ignored candidate Ronald Reagan's well-known problem of senility and barely touched on the scandalous imperfections of several Democratic candidates vying for the presidency. It was apparent that Mr. Coleman had become the "one nigger who wanted to play fair," playing up the shortcomings of a black leader while overlooking those of the white incumbent. Coleman either did not listen to the experienced voice of Lu Palmer, the speaker who followed him on the program at Howard University, or chose to ignore the sage advice given.

In his presentation at the Howard Seminar, Palmer, of the *Chicago Daily News*, had concluded:

First, I believe that some black journalists, at least, must move through the media as advocates for black people. The press has gone through a period of so-called objective journalism which was never objective at all. Then we moved into a period of so-called interpretive journalism which was not interpretive at all. Both of these phases simply allow whites in the press to continue their insidious control over the minds of our people. And I believe the time has come now for blacks somehow to engage in advocacy journalism. We must find a way to advocate for blacks as whites have and continue to advocate for whites in the press.[4]

The Congressional Black Caucus contended that the white establishment-controlled mass communications media had (1) systematically excluded or exploited black talent; (2) deliberately mishandled or distorted newsworthy events of the black community; and (3) either ignored, played down, or ridiculed significant efforts in the movement for black liberation in America.

The following recommendations were issued at the close of the Black Careers in Communications conferences:

1. Black communities should form watchdog committees to monitor all local media and investigate all possible means of utilizing the mass communications media for the maximum benefit of the black public.
2. Black leaders should demand recruitment and employment of blacks and other minorities at all levels within the media.
3. Black leaders should demand forums by which blacks could determine program content and context to eliminate gross distortion and misinterpretation of the black experience.
4. The black community should apply economic and political pressure to obtain a proportionate share of all public and private advertising budgets.
5. The black press should demand full access to information disseminated at all levels of government.
6. The black community should demand an equitable share of black ownership of television and radio stations licensed by the FCC.
7. The present vacancy at the FCC should be filled by appointment of a qualified black communications person who had demonstrated an active concern for black interests.
8. The FCC should be made to place more emphasis on how stations program in the interests of black communities when reviewing license applications.[5]

THE NATIONAL BLACK ENTERPRISE CONFERENCE, JANUARY 27–29, 1972

Representative Parren J. Mitchell invited 500 black economists and businesspersons to develop a ten-year plan for black enterprise to remedy the traditional exclusion of blacks from business. The conference was held from January 27 through 29, 1972, on the campus of Morgan State College in Baltimore, Maryland.

The civil rights thrust of the sixties gave black consumers greater access to the goods and services of society. Ownership and control of business enterprises, however, were not widely viewed as "civil rights" and remained beyond the reach of most. Decades of exclusion from the marketplace thwarted the economic growth of blacks, the development of "black capitalism," and the success of black entrepreneurial endeavors.

The CBC concluded that historical inequities should be corrected through long-range adjustments in economic planning, rather than through a series of splintered programs. Thus, the National Black Enterprise Conference met to identify objectives that would foster maximum economic growth in the black community over the next several decades.

CBC HEARINGS ON RACISM IN THE MEDIA, MARCH 6–7, 1972.

On March 6 and 7, 1972, I chaired a separate hearing to consider the issue of racism in the mass media. CBC members felt that a national forum was needed to highlight not only the incessant inequities of policies in effect within the media, but also the demoralizing effect these policies had on the black community. As I stated in my opening remarks, "It is an undeniable fact of life that what is read, seen, and heard in the white-controlled media has indelibly molded opinions and perpetrated negative images in and about the black community."

The Caucus, having itself felt the sting of media distortion, decided that this problem should be brought to national attention. The white mass media clearly had failed to interpret the black movement and issues affecting the black community properly. They were unwilling to increase minority employment on their staffs adequately, and they used insidious tactics to fire highly competent black journalists. These realities prompted us to make a thorough investigation of the industry and its practices in relation to the black community.

Twenty-three black media workers, representing a cross-section of the communications industry, told us how they, the black community, and the black movement had been "grossly excluded, distorted, mishandled, and exploited by the white-controlled news media."[6] The witnesses specifically cited the media's failure to employ blacks in decision-making capacities, discriminatory union practices, lack of meaningful minority programming, exclusion of blacks from the Federal Communications Commission (FCC), and mistreatment of members of the black press as "second-class" reporters.

We invited Samuel F. Yette, a former Washington bureau correspondent for *Newsweek*, to give testimony. He was the first and only black correspondent in the magazine's Washington bureau. An accomplished journalist and author, he had just been fired on grounds that did not seem credible to us. There seemed to be hidden reasons for his dismissal.

During the two days of hearings, more than twenty expert witnesses gave persuasive testimony and lucid analysis of *Newsweek* magazine, one of the nation's most influential media outlets.

In my opening statement I had articulated the immediate concern of all CBC members and emphasized without exaggeration, "It is our hope that from these hearings will come the recommendations for correcting the present situation and eliminating the sting of racism in the white mass media. The Congressional Black Caucus intends to pursue this issue with the relentlessness of a panther."[7]

According to the FCC, by 1971 blacks held only five of the 1,219 news executive positions in the country. The situation was equally bleak for blacks in terms of ownership. There was not one black-owned television station in the nation and, out of a total of 7,000, only nineteen black-owned radio stations.

It does not take a whole lot of brain power to see that black interests were unrepresented in the policy decisions made by the media because blacks were missing from the ranks of the communications industry, especially at managerial levels.

This is important, not only because of black employment needs, but because the exclusion of blacks from the media had left unchallenged a policy of portraying them largely as inferior, criminal, illiterate, and underachieving. One result was that black people were prompted to hate themselves just as the white society around them hated them. Carl Holman, executive director of the Urban Coalition, said it this way: "[If] I can tell you who you are or who you are not, what you can become and what you cannot, I have over you a power almost as great as the power to deny you food, clothing or housing. The media [has] the power of approval or disapproval. [It has] the power to treat black people and causes as fads . . ."[8]

Consensus was difficult to achieve among those offering analysis and sharing opinions at the sessions. While the testimony given over the two days is too lengthy to include verbatim here, I can summarize the several areas of concern and suggested remedies that emerged in our discussions. We asked,

Who controls the mass media?
What importance does it have to the black community?
How can black people counteract the present negative influence of the media?
What is the role of the black press?
What are the problems of black journalists? Of black students of communications?
What should the Congressional Black Caucus do to foster solutions to the problems?

We observed a set of circumstances that continue to hold sway even today. Since the media is controlled by whites, it is obvious that the ideas and images flowing daily via the communications media to the homes of millions of black Americans are white-oriented. Further, leaving aside the negative impact on the black psyche, the mass media's failure to provide 30 million black Americans an impartial forum to air their views makes them guilty of abridging a basic constitutional right—freedom of expression.

It was dramatically clear in the hearing that we should avoid the pitfall of thinking the media would change on its own. If changes were to come, they must be ushered in by the concerted efforts of minority citizens. First, these efforts should be aimed at getting blacks into decision-making positions; second, we should demand relevant programming on the air waves for black citizens; third, we should examine the content of children's shows to determine whether these programs were geared to meet the needs of our children; fourth, we should demand that the Federal Communications Commission assert its authority to crack down on recalcitrant local broadcasting stations that continued to discriminate racially; and finally, we should assess the burgeoning implications of cable television.

The role of the black press in the black community has been largely educational. That task has been difficult because, traditionally, the black press has been relegated to a subordinate position in the total mass media. A timely example of this inequity is President Nixon's trip to mainland China in 1972. Not a single black press person was included in the official media corps accompanying the president on this historic trip. Black newsmen were not afforded the same routine privileges as their white colleagues. For instance, during the Nixon administration, black reporters found it almost impossible to obtain White House press credentials. Neither were black reporters able to obtain congressional gallery press passes on a regular basis. Consequently, many doors to the various news sources open to white reporters were closed to black reporters.

Yet the black press has been and continues to be in the vanguard, exerting journalistic pressure on the white media to make meaningful changes. The pressure takes several forms: urging the white news media to pay proper recognition to black syndicated columnists; demanding equal footing with the white press with respect to presidential press privileges; establishing a black news service to report news from a black perspective; and creating a skills bank to train black youngsters interested in journalism.

The CBC hearings identified as an ever-present problem the both subtle and overt discrimination confronting black students at white journalism schools. A 1961 study showed that only 2 percent of the members of junior and senior college classes in journalism in the United States were minority members. In 1970, a similar survey showed that 3.2 percent of the juniors and seniors in journalism schools and programs were black. Obviously, at this rate, it would take decades before the number of black journalism students was proportionate to the percentage of black people in the total population. The CBC insisted that efforts be made to eradicate this disparity. More immediately, other efforts were to be exerted to make communications schools provide hardcore courses relating to the black perspective in their curricula.

Black institutions, which have performed a laudable function in educating generations of blacks with meager resources, were encouraged to incorporate relevant journalism courses into their curricula. It was deemed important that the education of black journalists not be left exclusively to white journalism schools, since they had clearly demonstrated their inability to relate to the interests of blacks.

One of the decisions made in our sessions was to form a coalition of black elected officials and black workers in the media to address the ills in the media. CBC members would work to amend the 1934 Communications Act to give black people more productive roles in the industry; work to enact legislation providing legal assistance for black people victimized by racist acts by the mass media; and support legislation to protect the confidentiality that all reporters need in order to do their job effectively—a protection that black reporters in particular were often denied. We also recommended monitoring white journalism schools around the country and encouraged blacks to support that part of the media where they do have some influence: the black press. A Caucus task force would assist "watchdog committees" formed by local black communities to monitor fairness in the media, challenge licenses, and file lawsuits.

CONFERENCE ON ALTERNATIVES FOR BLACKS IN EDUCATION, MARCH 29–APRIL 1, 1972

In March 1972, the Congressional Black Caucus joined with Delta Sigma Theta Sorority, the Metropolitan Applied Research Center, the NAACP Legal Defense Fund, the National Association for Equal Opportunity in Higher Education, the National Council of Negro Women, the National Urban League, the National Urban Coalition, and the United Negro College Fund to sponsor a National Policy Conference on Education for Blacks. Development of a national policy on major educational issues facing the nation and the reordering of priorities were the prime objectives of the conference.

The sessions were held March 29 through April 1, 1972, in Arlington, Virginia. Educators, lawyers, civil rights workers, parents and students, and community organizers assembled to discuss questions germane to the most urgent policy issues facing blacks in education. Congressman Hawkins, chairman of the conference, asked representatives from each group to develop ideas and to present papers. Each paper was followed by discussions among the participants. The workshops were chaired by outstanding leaders in education. Dr. Bernard Watson, professor and chairman of urban education at Temple University, served as project director.

The conference produced a wealth of raw information from black scholars in the field—information particularly valuable to the Caucus in its legislative planning.

The intellectual and psychological groundwork laid at the conference led to the creation of a permanent organization composed of educational and community leaders from all regions. It was to act as a watchdog over national educational policies and programs, to research and measure the growing and changing needs of black students, and to influence decisions at policy-making pressure points. The conference added great strength to the Caucus's attempt to improve educational policies as they affected black Americans.

The conference report concluded that any alternatives to integrated classrooms for black students must be carefully examined and questioned from the point of view of financial support, ability to produce measurable increases in achievement levels, capacity to prepare children for a pluralistic society, and the constitutionality of such approaches.

THE HARVARD FORUM, "WHAT OUR NATIONAL PRIORITIES SHOULD BE," APRIL 5–7, 1972

Next, Stokes and I organized a conference with major publishers and editors of the daily press. It was one of the more important meetings held by the Caucus and took place April 5 through 7, 1972, at Harvard University in Cambridge, Massachusetts.

This nonpartisan forum on domestic issues, entitled "What Our National Priorities Should Be," was sponsored jointly by the CBC, the *Boston Globe*, the *Chicago Sun-Times*, the *Philadelphia Bulletin*, and the Institute of Politics of Harvard University. Warren Jackson of the Gannett newspapers served as the forum coordinator. He and Dexter Eure of the *Boston Globe* played key roles in the success of the conference.

Invited as panel members and participants in the discussions were some 500 persons from a variety of backgrounds—blacks and whites who had diverse, sometimes clashing viewpoints. They were business leaders, educators, doctors, editors, economists, community leaders, activists, and scholars.

The participating newspapers felt their primary jobs were to observe, report, and interpret events, but they, too, were becoming more conscious of the responsibility imposed by their great power to mold public opinion. It was time, they felt, to take a visible, active role in organizing the conference and to subject themselves to give-and-take discussion.

In the decade of the 1960s, universities and colleges were becoming more involved in the complex problems of the real world. Recognizing the critical need to learn more about an increasing black student population, Harvard lent its full cooperation to the venture.

Stokes and I arrived a day before the scheduled conference to make sure all arrangements were in order. We were greeted by Randall Robinson, then an articulate law student, now the executive director of TransAfrica, an internationally known lobbying organization for the South African anti-apartheid movement. Robinson briefed us on the school's vast financial investments in companies doing business with South Africa and stressed that the presence of black congressmen on the campus somehow gave official, albeit indirect, sanction to the disputed policy. He demanded that we change the location of the conference. I thought him right to a point, but conference planning was too far along to allow a change of location. Hundreds of participants (publishers and editors) were already in transit. We could not decide now to cancel the engagement.

The one inconsistency in Robinson's otherwise rational argument was the fact that he, a black person, was attending classes daily on the same racially insensitive campus. But he and members of the CBC understood each other's position and came to terms. The next day the entire membership of the Congressional Black Caucus joined Robinson in a press conference and picket line criticizing Harvard's investment policies. Only after making this gesture of support for the anti-apartheid movement and the concerns of black students did we go on with the business that brought us to the Harvard campus.

Congressman Stokes chaired the session on education for this forum on national priorities. Panel members included Charles E. Taylor of the Institute for Educational Leadership; Dr. Charles G. Hurst, Jr., president of Malcolm X College; Dr. Marcus Foster, superintendent of schools in Oakland, California; Dr. Lawrence A. Johnson, president of Franklin Park Community College in Roxbury, Massachusetts; Elma Lewis, director of the National Center of Afro-American Artists; Barbara Sizemore, coordinator of proposal development for the Chicago Board of Education; Dr. Robert C. Wood, president of the University of Massachusetts; and James Hoge, editor of the *Chicago Sun-Times*.

The issues discussed were many, but a lion's share of attention fell on the Nixon administration's proposals for legislation to prohibit busing and to slow school desegregation.

Some of the recommendations we made were that:

At least $10 to $15 billion more should be appropriated for education if every child was to be assured both equality in education and an education of quality.

Blacks must assert the right of every child to early education experiences, and must, meanwhile, "mobilize their private resources" to help achieve this reality.

Blacks needed significant community involvement and control in educational decision-making at all levels.

The desperate unemployment problem of blacks was the central issue in the session on employment. Black unemployment was 9.5 percent in March 1971, when the national average was 6 percent. In April 1972, it was 10.5 percent when the national average was 5.7 percent, and the grim statistics went on and on. We had no choice but to come together as professionals and politicians to make some changes. Congressman Augustus F. Hawkins chaired the session. Panel members were John S. Atlee, of Atlee Research Associates; C. W. Cook, chairman of the board of General Foods Corporation; Dr. Maurice Dawkins, of the Opportunities Industrialization Center; Nelson Jack Edwards, vice-president of the United Auto Workers; James Hefner, of the department of economics at Princeton University; the Reverend Jesse Jackson, president of PUSH; the Honorable C. Delores Tucker, secretary of state of the Commonwealth of Pennsylvania.

Among the Caucus recommendations approved for action were:

To empower the secretary of labor to declare any area a national employment disaster area when the minority unemployment exceeded the national average and to provide special federal aid to that area.

To demand that the president desist from pitting minority against minority in an effort to "obscure the gravity of joblessness among minorities" and that all laws within his power be enforced, including Title VI of the Civil Rights Act, Executive Order 11246, and the Federal Civil Service Commission's equal employment compliance section.

To urge the promulgation of an executive order directing all agencies of government to reserve not less than 15 percent of all negotiated contracts for blacks and other minorities.

To set a full employment goal to limit unemployment to no more than 2.5 percent.

Law and justice was the subject of a panel presided over by Congressman John Conyers, Jr., with assistance from Congressman Louis Stokes. Panel members included: Judge Joseph C. Howard, of Baltimore, vice-chairman of the Judicial Council of the National Bar Association; Charles R. Jackson, Jr., chief investigator for Westchester County, New York; James F. Ahern, director of the Insurance Crime Prevention Institute; David Durk, detective sergeant with the New York Police Department; Jean Cahn, of the Urban Law Institute; James

W. Cobb, president of the National Bar Association; and Illinois State Senator Richard H. Newhouse.

Among other issues, the panel focused on the failures of the criminal justice system in all its aspects—police, courts, prisons—as it touched blacks.

On the issue of voting rights, the Caucus was particularly critical of the U.S. Department of Justice and southern elected officials, the former for ignoring the law, the latter for trying to evade provisions of Section 5 of the Voting Rights Act of 1965, designed to prevent changes in voting laws that would purposefully or effectively discriminate on the basis of race or color.

The recommendations made in these sessions included proposals requiring new state and federal legislation, such as:

Disarmament of all Americans, including policemen
Complete revamping or elimination of the bail-bondsman system
Decentralization and community control of police departments

Proposals calling for nonlegislative actions included:

Support and encouragement of black lawyers
Creation by the community of its own system of law enforcement
Full financial support of "pre-delinquent" programs and
     educational and cultural programs for young people
Recruitment of more black policemen

The Caucus viewed these merely as proposals, reserving the right to act upon them or not as prudence dictated.

I was the chairman of the session on health. The panelists included: Dr. Leonard W. Cronkite, Jr., executive vice-president of Children's Hospital Medical Center in Boston; Pierre de Vise, assistant director of the Illinois Regional Medical Program in Chicago; Dr. Lloyd Elam, president of Meharry Medical College; Dr. John Knowles, president of the Rockefeller Foundation; and Dr. Andrew Thomas, director of Project 75 in Chicago.

The issues were easy to identify: an infant mortality rate 80 percent higher among blacks than whites; a life expectancy 10 percent shorter; an incidence of serious malnutrition twice as high; a high incidence of hypertension, cancer, and heart disease, with age-adjusted death rates of 18 percent, 22 percent, and 82 percent, respectively, higher for blacks than for whites suffering from these diseases.

There was no serious disagreement over the kind of prescriptions we should call for:

An end to different standards of health care for poor and non-poor, but with the preservation of "pluralism" in the design and choice of health care delivery systems.

Everyone should be able to get "high quality" medical care.

Health care as the "vehicle" by which blacks and other medically poor people would be able to enter the mainstream of American society "spiritually, morally, and economically."

First priority in plans for delivery of comprehensive health care to be given to the medically indigent or working poor.

Congressman Walter E. Fauntroy chaired the session on housing, assisted by Congressman Parren J. Mitchell. Panelists included Paul Davidoff, director of the Suburban Action Institute; James Fuerst, president of Research & Statistics; W. Wilson Goode, executive director of the Philadelphia Housing Advisory Service Corporation; Edward J. Logue, president of the New York State Urban Development Corporation; Floyd McKissick, president of Soul City, North Carolina; Dempsey J. Travis, president of United Mortgage Bankers of America; George Packard, editor of the *Philadelphia Bulletin*.

The primary issue discussed was the continuing and largely unsuccessful struggle of a great proportion of black families to get decent housing. The CBC position paper observed that the proportion of black families in substandard housing remained unchanged from 1960 to 1970, at 22 percent. About 31 percent of all dwelling units occupied by blacks were substandard if overcrowded units were added to the total.

Recommendations adopted on the initiative of the session participants were:

Funds for new-town development should be increased, with minority developers to get at least 12 percent of funding.

In its 236 housing program, HUD should foster freedom of choice by adopting a policy of continuing to rebuild in central cities.

Authorized funding for the 235 and 236 housing programs should be doubled in the 1973 fiscal year to a total of at least $5 billion, but, until frauds were eliminated, no more money should be disbursed under these programs

Communications and the media continued to be a subject of concern, so we included a session with that issue focus at the Harvard conference as well. Congressman Charles C. Diggs presided over it. Panelists included Ben H. Bagdikian, assistant managing editor of the *Washington Post*; W. Leonard Evans, Jr., founder and publisher of Tuesday Publications, Inc.; Dr. Carlton B. Goodlett, editor and publisher of the *San Francisco Sun-Reporter*; Louis Martin, editor of the *Chicago Daily Defender*; H. Carl McCall, chairman of the editorial board of the *Amsterdam News*; Albert E. von Entress, vice-president of circulation for the *Chicago Sun-Times*; Robert Healy, executive editor of the *Boston Globe*. The myopia of the media was the central concern, as the media's failure with the black populace meant also failing the society as a whole. We recommended that:

The FCC assure by regulation "an equitable share" for blacks in ownership of television and radio stations.

Legislation require the FCC to set up and fund an office for community affairs to handle citizens' complaints and challenges.

Legislation be enacted protecting newsmen's right to refuse to testify in court or before grand juries. (Government agents were leaning heavily on black reporters to testify against black groups engaged in unpopular activity.)

More blacks be involved in electronic media decision-making, with the media to eliminate the "gross distortion and misinterpretation of the black experience."

The existing vacant seat on the FCC be given to a qualified black.

The significance of the Harvard Forum lay in the conviction of the Congressional Black Caucus that America's priorities must be changed if the country were to survive.

CONFERENCE ON BLACK POLITICS AND THE LEGISLATIVE PROCESS, SEPTEMBER 29, 1973

On September 29, 1973, the CBC convened a seminar to stress the importance of understanding how the congressional legislative process worked as it related to maximizing black political, social, and economic benefits. Emphasis was placed on how the process impacted at the state and municipal levels and how Caucus members could be helpful to local black elected officials and they to the Caucus with regard to legislation.

Interpreting Caucus policy and implementing it through legislative action are crucial to the success of the CBC. Monitoring legislation and developing a national pressure group for passage or defeat of that legislation can mean the difference between victory or defeat.

By 1973, the Caucus had already organized some forty groups, including the National Urban League, the National Council of Negro Women, Operation PUSH, the AFL-CIO, the Coalition for Human Needs and Budget Priorities, and the Southern Christian Leadership Conference, to help push through legislation on the Caucus priority list.

During the previous two years, the CBC met with more than 150 church, school, and community groups from across the country. Meetings with these groups were instructional and/or educational, to explain "how the legislative process works" and what could be done to influence legislation.

These sessions were invaluable in terms of garnering research data. In fact, it was during one of these sessions that the CBC secured legislative ammunition for saving Mississippi's Mound Bayou Hospital. When the facility was transferred from the General Services Administration to the Department of Health Education and Welfare, officials at the receiving agency claimed they did not fund hospitals, so would not be able to fund this one. The staff of the CBC learned through one of the conferences of two obscure but important programs under which HEW did in fact fund hospitals—the Public Health Service Act and the Indian Health Service Program. HEW then agreed to support Mound Bayou Hospital for another twelve-year period, which allowed it time to convert from a grant-funded operation to an operation following fiscal procedures more customary for hospitals.

Clarence Mitchell, lobbyist for the NAACP, presided over the Conference on Legislative Process. Serving as panelists were Congressman Louis Stokes; Eddie Williams, of the Joint Center for Political Studies; and Percy Sutton, Manhattan Borough president. Barbara Williams, director of the Coalition on Human Needs and Budget Priorities and former administrative assistant to Congressman Dellums, moderated the legislative process session. Bruce Meredith, a staff member of the House Appropriations Committee, gave an in-depth analysis of the appropriations process. Charles Henry, from the political science department of Howard University, wrapped up the morning session.

The afternoon session dealt with the impact of federal legislation at the state level and with the needs of black state legislators. Illinois State Senator Richard Newhouse conducted this briefing. Mayor Richard Hatcher was in charge of the session dealing with federal legislative impact at the municipal level and the needs of black mayors and councilpersons. Representing the Caucus were Shirley Chisholm, Ronald Dellums, Augustus Hawkins, and Parren Mitchell.

Moderator of the panel reacting to the discussion was Richard Austin, secretary of the state of Michigan. Panelists were Leroy Irvis, a Pennsylvania state representative; Mayor Robert Blackwell, of Highland Park, Michigan; Councilwoman Ethel Allen, of Philadelphia; New Jersey State Senator Wyona M. Lipman; and Oklahoma State Representative Hannah Atkins.

THE SOUTHERN REGIONAL FORUM

On May 25–26, 1979, the CBC held its first Southern Regional Conference in Birmingham, Alabama. This was part of a critical strategy for promoting CBC legislative programs via the establishment of an alert network to influence legislation pending before the United States Congress. This was the first of many forums held to enable black voters to demand accountability from those they elected to public office. It was sponsored jointly by the CBC and Alabama black elected officials and was a major step forward in organizing a support system to pressure members of Congress from heavily black districts.

Participants came from Arkansas, Florida, Georgia, Louisiana, North Carolina, Mississippi, South Carolina, Tennessee, Texas, and Virginia.

The conference achieved several noteworthy purposes. As the CBC developed its legislative agenda, this and subsequent forums provided a gauge of the sentiments of black Americans in the South on numerous issues of national significance. Coordinators were selected for each of the congressional districts in the eleven southern states where blacks constituted a substantial percentage of the voters.

At the conclusion of the first regional forum, the National Black Leadership Round Table and the Congressional Black Caucus agreed to an aggressive campaign to:

Restore domestic cuts in the 1980 federal budget
Support the liberation of Zimbabwe
Make all Americans aware of the plight of Haitian refugees being
    mistreated in the United States
Support the Martin Luther King Legal Holiday bill

Defeat the "Anti-Busing Civil Rights Constitutional Amendment" proposal sponsored by Congressman Ron Mottl of Ohio.

The grand finale of the two-day conference was a banquet titled "Roots: Alabama Black Homecoming Celebration." Coretta Scott King was the guest of honor.

THE SOUTHWEST REGIONAL FORUM

On February 12 through 14, 1982, Congressman Mickey Leland hosted a second CBC regional legislative forum. Eleven Caucus members journeyed to Houston, Texas, for a series of workshops on such topics as minority business, the economy, foreign affairs, criminal justice, energy policies, civil rights, women's issues, and urban development. These sessions were open to community participation and more than 1,000 persons from Louisiana, Oklahoma, Arkansas, New Mexico, and Texas attended the events. Hearings, workshops, and seminars were held at the Shamrock Hotel, the University of Houston's downtown campus, and at Texas Southern University.

Representative John Conyers chaired a hearing on criminal justice. Civil rights activists testified on the effects of police brutality in the city of Houston. Representative Ronald Dellums held hearings on urban affairs, which focused in-depth attention on President Reagan's proposed enterprise zones for inner city ghetto areas.

Congresswoman Chisholm, who had announced the day before the conference that she would not seek re-election for an eighth term, said in her opening remarks to the delegates, "New Federalism is destroying the quality of life and the poor and minorities are hurt worse, because they're always at the bottom of the pole."[9]

Congressman Walter Fauntroy, echoing the general theme of the gathering, charged, "Mr. Reagan and his economic advisers have engineered the most extraordinary transfer of funds from the very poor to the very rich in the history of the nation."[10]

On Saturday morning, a "solidarity" march through downtown Houston, from Antioch Park to City Hall, followed a prayer breakfast sponsored by the Caucus. Saturday night the Caucus sponsored a dinner and honored civic leader Mack Hannah, the first black to serve on the University of Houston Board of Regents and a former chairman of the board of directors of Texas Southern University.

It was through the various conferences and hearings that the CBC was able to determine the priority issues of black Americans, and at the same time involve black leaders at all levels and from all segments of community life in the ultimate decision as to what constituted the real "black agenda."

NOTES

1. CBC Summary of the National Conference on the Status of Health in Black America, Meharry Medical College, Nashville, Tennessee, December 5, 1971, page 5.

2. Quoted in "The End of Rhetoric . . . The Beginning of Action," report of the first and second Black Careers in Communications Conferences, Washington, D.C.: Howard University School of Communications, 1972, page 10.

3. *Ibid.*, page 27.

4. *Ibid.*, page 53.

5. *Ibid.*, page 74.

6. *Ibid.*, page 34.

7. Official transcript of hearings, "The Mass Media and the Black Community," Washington, D.C.: Congressional Black Caucus, March 6, 1972, page 2.

8. Quoted in "The End of Rhetoric . . . The Beginning of Action," page 54.

9. *Houston Post*, February 13, 1982, page 11D.

10. *Ibid.*

12

The CBC Comes of Age

Congressman Charles C. Diggs, a senior black member of Congress, was chosen as the first chairman of the Congressional Black Caucus because of his ability to keep older members like Nix and Dawson in a cordial mood to relate to younger members like Chisholm, Stokes, and me. He set about putting together a staff capable of responding to most issues, federal or other, faced by black people. His successor, Louis Stokes, refocused Caucus activity around our roles as national legislators as opposed to national case workers.

In 1974, Charles Rangel succeeded Stokes as chairman. Under his leadership, the first formal legislative agenda establishing the major priorities of Caucus members was drawn up to develop a strategy for changing old laws and enacting new ones. Attorney Barbara Williams, a former aide to Dellums, was hired as staff director and commissioned to coordinate the effort and organize support groups.

Congressman Walter Fauntroy was the driving force behind the creation of a national legislative-interest network with "centers-of-influence" in about 100 congressional districts where blacks constituted 15 percent or more of the voting age population. Putting in place this vehicle allowed the Caucus to wield considerable political clout far beyond our individual district boundaries.

In 1976, Congresswoman Yvonne B. Burke assumed the Caucus chair as the first woman to hold the position. A second legislative agenda was formulated, concentrating the priorities in ten issue-oriented areas: full employment, health care, urban revitalization, rural development, civil and political rights, education, welfare reform/social insurance, economic development/aid to minority businesses, the economy, and foreign policy.

Under each chairman, the Congressional Black Caucus's number one priority legislatively and politically was always to address the concerns that affected the lives of America's poor, minorities, and disadvantaged. In the words of Charles B. Rangel:

> Where we can provide leadership for those colleagues who represent large minority constituencies, we shall. Where there are causes that can benefit by coalition politics, we shall coalesce. And whenever we can serve impoverished and minority citizens as legislators, unquestionably we shall.[1]

CAUCUS MEMBERSHIP GROWS

In the interval between the first meeting of the Congressional Black Caucus and Yvonne Burke's assuming the chair, five other blacks (including Ms. Burke) were elected to Congress. Barbara Jordan, Andrew Young, and Cardiss Collins were elected in 1973. In 1975, Harold Ford joined the group.

The early eighties saw the number of Caucus members increase to eighteen. Nine of the original members (Chisholm, Clay, Conyers, Dellums, Fauntroy, Hawkins, Mitchell, Rangel, and Stokes) were joined by nine others (Cardiss Collins; George W. Crockett, Jr.; Julian Dixon; Mervyn Dymally; Harold E. Ford; William H. Gray, III; Mickey Leland; Gus Savage; and Harold Washington. Four of the latter group replaced original members of the Caucus. Cardiss Collins succeeded her husband, George, who was killed in an airplane crash in 1972. Crockett replaced Diggs, who resigned in 1980. Gray defeated Nix in 1978. In 1980, Washington defeated Bennett M. Stewart, who was elected after Metcalfe died in office.

Barbara Jordan

Barbara Jordan was elected to Congress from the Eighteenth District of Texas in 1972. She had been serving as a Texas state senator. The Houston-based district was 19 percent Hispanic, 42 percent black, and 39 percent white. Jordan had no trouble winning the primary or the general election. She was opposed in the primary by three black males, including a state representative who was a militant civil rights activist. But Miss Jordan proved unbeatable, receiving 80 percent of the vote, handily outpolling her three opponents. In the general election, the highly respected state senator again coasted to victory with 80 percent of the vote.

Her strong support from organized labor and other white groups caused her to be labeled an "establishment candidate" by her male opponents. But the charge did not stick, because of Miss Jordan's extensive and meaningful relationships in the black community. She was also accused by her opponents of helping to eliminate the state senate seat she formerly held in order to secure the votes to create the congressional district from which she was elected. That accusation, too, was an ineffectual issue in the campaign.

Andrew Young

Andrew Jackson Young, Jr., was elected in 1972 from the Fifth District of Georgia, which consists mainly of the city of Atlanta. This was the first time since Reconstruction that a black had been elected to Congress from the Deep South.

In the primary, Mr. Young beat Wyche Fowler and two other candidates. He tallied 35,926 to Fowler's 19,549. (Mr. Fowler is now a United States senator from Georgia.) Young was successful because he was able to turn out an unusually large number of black voters, who comprised 38 percent of the district. In the general election, Mr. Young spent considerable time in the suburbs wooing white voters and addressing their major concerns. He opposed the building of a freeway through the area and promised federal aid to clean up the Chattahoochee River. His stance on both issues paid dividends. On election day, he defeated his Republican challenger, Rodney Cook, 72,289 (with 53 percent of the vote, including 23 percent of the white vote) to 64,495. Cook was a moderate Republican who had supported civil rights when it was unpopular. Under the weight of the aggressive campaign waged by "Mr. Civil Rights" himself, Andy Young, Cook adopted an "antibusing" position in the hope of generating a large turn-out in the white community, but to no avail.

The new district lines drawn by the federal court were the key to Young's victory. Two years prior, he was easily beaten for Congress by Republican Fletcher Thompson by a vote of 78,540 to 58,394. Thompson had conduted a gutter-type campaign, alluding disparagingly to race and alleging that Young favored the destruction of Western civilization. Young had concentrated on advertising his civil rights record and stressing his personal connection with Dr. Martin Luther King,

Jr. But the new district lines drawn in 1972 left Congressman Thompson's home outside of the district and increased the percentage of blacks. This greatly influenced his decision to run eventually for the U.S. Senate.

Harold Ford

Harold E. Ford, a political activist who had served two terms in the Tennessee State Legislature, came to Congress from the Eighth District of Tennessee in 1974. Ford successfully challenged the Republican incumbent in a newly drawn district that increased the black population to 48 percent. In a six-way Democratic primary, Ford benefited from the great organization built by his family. The Fords had developed a highly organized political support network in most black neighborhoods, reaching down to the block level. One of Ford's brothers, John, was in the state senate. Another brother, James, was on the Memphis City Council.

The campaign was extremely bitter, and voters pretty much cast their ballots along racial lines. The white incumbent of eight years, Republican Dan Kuykendall, had voted consistently against positions taken by the Congressional Black Caucus and showed very little concern for the interests of his black constituents. In fact, he admitted publicly during the campaign that he had not attended any function in the black community in more than five years.

Two years earlier, in 1972, Kuykendall had defeated a black state senator, J. O. Patterson, Jr., by 19,000 votes. But in 1974, State Representative Ford pursued the seat with much greater intensity. His organization was more disciplined and better financed than the one Patterson had put together.

Two major issues dominated debate in the general election. First was the militance of the Ford family and the resulting animosity in the white community toward Harold. Ford, however, refused to accept that all whites in the district would vote against him because of his race and campaigned vigorously in the white precincts, stressing economic issues. The second issue of consequence was Kuykendall's close identification with President Richard M. Nixon. Most blacks believed that Nixon's policy initiatives were designed to reverse gains in civil rights. The Watergate scandal spilled over into the campaign and probably played a significant role in Ford's ability to garner 12 perent of the white voters and win by 574 votes (57,715 to 57,141). Two of Ford's brothers were also elected to public office on the same day— John to the state senate and Emmitt to the state house of representatives.

Julian Dixon

Julian Dixon was elected in 1979 from the Twenty-eighth District of California. He succeeded Yvonne B. Burke, who did not seek re-election that year, choosing instead to run for attorney general of California. Dixon's career in politics began when then State Senator Merv Dymally hired him as a legislative aide. But his rise in politics was not tied to Dymally's star. It was, rather, the result of a series of vacancies created by Yvonne Burke. When Burke left the state assembly, Dixon replaced her. When Burke left Congress, Dixon replaced her there.

Getting elected to Congress involved a battle royal, with eight opponents, some as well connected politically as Dixon, fighting for the vacated seat. The primary race boiled down to a dog fight between Los Angeles City Councilman David S. Cunningham, State Senator Nate Holden, and Assemblyman Dixon. Cunningham, even with the support of Mayor Thomas Bradley, was unable to raise sufficient funds to bankroll the necessary polling, direct mail solicitation, and spot television and radio announcements needed in the sprawling Los Angeles area. He was unable to compete successfully with Holden and Dixon.

Holden's chief supporter was County Supervisor Ken Hahn, a powerful dispenser of patronage and contracts. But Holden, too, was unable to overcome Dixon's tremendous edge in campaign funds. Dixon's main supporters, State Assemblyman Howard L. Berman and U.S. Representative Henry Waxman, were both adept in the art of raising money, and the well-financed Dixon campaign prevailed. In the area of issues, Dixon campaigned on his record of accomplishments in the state assembly: a juvenile justice reform bill; legislation to ban throw-away beverage containers; creation of the California Arts Council; and improvement in women's retirement benefits in the public employee retirement system. In the primary, he defeated Holden, who ran second, by 48 percent (42,988) to 34 percent (30,162). The six other candidates received 19 percent of the vote. In the general election, Dixon was unopposed.

Harold Washington

Harold Washington was elected from the First District of Illinois in 1980, after defeating incumbent Bennett Stewart in the Democratic primary. The First District covered the Loop in downtown Chicago and continued southward along Lake Michigan into the heart of the black ghetto. This was the first congressional district in the twentieth century to be represented by a black congressman, where Oscar DePriest won election in 1928. It has been represented ever since by a black. Stewart was the fourth black to succeed DePriest, following Arthur Mitchell, Bill Dawson, and Ralph Metcalfe.

Washington for many years led a progressive political reform movement in opposition to the patronage-laden organization of Chicago Mayor Richard Daley. Stewart's identification with machine politics and the manner in which he was selected to fill the seat following Metcalfe's death became the main issue in both the 1978 campaign to replace Metcalfe and in 1980, when he was challenged by Harold Washington. Before being elected to Congress, Stewart, with the blessings of the Daley machine, had held various positions, including a patronage job in the Chicago Department of Urban Renewal and the office of alderman from the Twenty-First Ward.

Metcalfe died in October of 1978, a few days before he would have been re-elected to a fifth term. In circumstances such as these, the law provides for the elected committeepeople of the district to select a substitute candidate to represent their party. In this case, they selected party loyalist Bennett Stewart to run on the Democratic ticket in the general election, which was only a few days away.

The Republicans, sensing the possibility of an upset because the majority of the voters had supported Metcalfe against the Daley machine, persuaded a nondescript candidate to resign and selected A. A. Rayner, a militant black civil rights leader and community activist, to run on their ticket.

This strategy almost succeeded. Rayner received 33,540 votes (41 percent) to Stewart's 47,581 (59 percent). That was a remarkable contest, considering that two years prior, Rayner had run against Metcalfe and received only 10,147 (7 percent) to Metcalfe's 126,632 (93 percent).

In the 1980 primary, although most machine politicians supported the incumbent, Washington capitalized on dissension among regular party leaders. Stewart was further hurt when Metcalfe's son filed and siphoned off much of the traditional machine vote. Last but not least,

Washington won overwhelmingly in the politically active white part of the district. When that vote was added to Washington's sizeable vote in the machine-controlled wards and his outright victory in five of the black wards, the election belonged to him hands down.

Shortly after Washington's victory over Stewart, he became involved in a major controversy over his own replacement in the state senate. Washington had survived and succeeded in politics despite opposition from the Democratic political machine first headed by the late Richard Daley and now by his successor, Mayor Jane Byrne. He won his seat for Congress first by pulverizing Stewart, the Byrne-backed candidate, in the primary, and then by attaining 95 percent of the vote in the general election.

When Washington heard that Mayor Byrne was attempting to have the Democratic committeemen in his state senatorial district fill the vacancy with State Representative "Bulljive" Taylor, a bitter enemy, he refused to resign his seat in the senate. He did, however, stop receiving the monthly salary of a senator. This caused a major political problem for the state Democratic party.

When the Republican governor, James Thompson, realized the situation, he immediately moved to take control of the senate, where the Democrats had only a one-vote margin, with one Democrat hospitalized in serious condition. The Republicans voted to organize the senate and by a vote of 29 to 28 elected their own members to all leadership positions and appointed all committee chairmen.

This left Washington in the driver's seat to arrange with the Democratic leaders a candidate acceptable to him and to the black community in the senatorial district. Without his cooperation, Democrats could not regain control of the state senate.

Mervyn M. Dymally

Mervyn M. Dymally was elected in 1980 from the Thirty-first Congressional District of California, located in the suburbs of Los Angeles. Born in Trinidad, educated in Missouri at Lincoln University and at California State University at Sacramento and the United States International University at San Diego, where he received a Ph.D. in human behavior, Dymally held many positions before his successful bid for Congress. He was variously a member of the California State Assembly and the state senate and served as lieutenant governor of the state.

He won a decisive victory over the nine-term incumbent, Charles

Wilson, and three other candidates. Wilson had been censured by the House of Representatives for misappropriating political campaign funds, and the adverse publicity played heavily in Dymally's favor.

Ironically, Dymally had himself been a target of various criminal and ethics investigations, prompted by two newspapers that hounded him over the sixteen-year period that he was in state government. Wilson and another candidate, former Congressman Mark Hannaford, rehashed all the allegations of Dymally wrongdoing that had been raised by the *Los Angeles Times* and the *Sacramento Bee* over the years. They dredged up unsubstantiated and disproved charges that Dymally had been bribed by leaders of a religious sect to head off a state probe; had been the recipient of illegal campaign contributions from a Las Vegas casino; and was part owner of a medical firm that had bilked the state.

But Dymally waged a positive campaign, drawing heavily on the friendships he had established while serving at the state capital. He analyzed the district carefully to determine its racial, social, and ethnic composition. The district was predominantly white, but Dymally discovered that in the previous three elections Wilson had lost the white precincts and it was black support that got him re-elected. Dymally also found out that the Hispanic population was larger than first imagined, but there were no leaders discernible in that community capable of garnering enough support to win. Because of his close friendship with Cesar Chavez, of the United Farm Workers Union, Dymally was assured the Hispanic vote.

He conducted an extensive grassroots campaign, going door to door. He utilized specially designed "mailers" to target specific voter groups. The more than 750,000 pieces of mail he sent out zeroed in primarily on two issues: economic development and reduction in residential crime.

In the five-way primary, Dymally received 29,916, slightly under 50 percent of the total 60,940 votes cast. Mark W. Hannaford ran second with 14,512—ahead of Wilson, who received only 9,320 votes. Two years prior and before being censured, Wilson had beaten a black candidate, Howard L. Bingham, by 18,000 votes. In the general election, Dymally received 69,146 votes to Republican Don Drimshaw's 38,203 votes.

Edolphus Towns

In 1982, Edolphus Towns was elected to a seat from Brooklyn, New York, which was vacated by Frederick W. Richmond, a wealthy white businessman who resigned after pleading guilty to charges of marijuana possession and income tax evasion.

The new district, drawn as a result of the 1980 census, was composed of an almost equal number of Hispanics and blacks, who together constituted the vast majority of the voters. Towns was the beneficiary of political division within the Hispanic community. Two relatively well-known Hispanics, John Jack Olivero, a former executive of the telephone company, and Louis Hernandez, an insurance broker, split the vote in their community, allowing Towns to win with less than 50 percent of the Democratic primary vote.

Towns, a social worker by training and deputy borough president of Brooklyn, was the candidate endorsed by the regular Democratic clubs headed by long-time boss Meade Esposito and also by the reform group led by Assemblyman Al Vann. His association with Esposito was the basis for attacks by his opponents, who charged him with being controlled by the political bosses. However, voters knew Towns as an agent for change who had facilitated development of new neighborhood housing projects.

Major Owens

In the same election, Major Owens was elected to replace Shirley Chisholm, the veteran legislator from the other section of Brooklyn. Owens' campaign was considerably different from that of Towns because he did not have the luxury of endorsements from the regular Democratic organizations. In fact, Owens, who had spent his entire political career fighting party regulars and advocating basic reforms in government, was opposed by both the retiring Shirley Chisholm and Brooklyn Borough President Howard Golden.

Owens' opponent was State Senator Vander Beatty, a well-heeled politician with immense power because of his position as deputy Democratic leader in the state senate. Owens' campaign against great odds was buoyed when the *Amsterdam News* and the *Village Voice* both endorsed him and he defeated Beatty 18,403 (54 percent) to 15,524 (46 percent).

The major issue developed by Owens in the campaign was the connection that Beatty had with several unsavory political characters, including some who had been convicted of felonies.

Alan D. Wheat

Alan D. Wheat, at age thirty-one, was elected to the Ninety-eighth Congress from the Fifth District of Missouri in 1982, replacing Richard

Bolling, who was retiring after thirty-four years. Wheat, who had served six years previously in the Missouri State Legislature, was among seventeen candidates (eight other Democrats and eight Republicans) who filed for the seat. Wheat had the endorsement of Freedom, Inc., the leading political organization in Kansas City's black community.

The biggest obstacle to Wheat's election was not the district's composition of less than 20 percent black residents, but black voters who initially believed that a black candidate in a southern state could not win under such circumstances. When the head of Freedom, Inc., called me about Alan, I must confess that I, too, was a bit skeptical about his chances. But I was persuaded to come to Kansas City and give assistance. Over the years, I had built a solid relationship with most of the black political leaders in Kansas City through our mutual support of the Congressional Black Caucus.

A small gathering of about eighteen or twenty financially well-heeled black citizens was arranged. All of them except two had been attending the CBC Legislative Weekend and dinner since its inception eleven years earlier. My pitch to them was based on extending the heartfelt appreciation of the Congressional Black Caucus for their support in the past. I thanked them for their generous participation and efforts, which must have cost each of them $1,000 or more a year when airfare, hotel, food, and dinner tickets were all taken into account. So my plea to them was that if they could not afford both to spend $1,000 to travel to the nation's capital and give Alan Wheat $1,000 for his campaign, they should forego the trip and invest in the project to send Wheat to Congress.

It worked. From almost every person, $1,000 checks were written on the spot.

One of the Republicans in the race was Joanne E. Collins, a black member of the city council of Kansas City, who had run unsuccessfully for the seat against Bolling four years prior. Wheat's opponents in the Democratic primary included another state representative, two lawyers, a suburban city councilman, and a physician. In this overwhelmingly white district, Wheat had two major factors going for him—seven white candidates who would possibly nullify any white bloc vote, and the delivery potential of Freedom, Inc., to turn out its usual 12,000 to 17,000 votes. In addition, he was endorsed by the Greater Kansas City Women's Political Caucus and the Statewide Missouri Women's Caucus. His campaign also received a boost when Taxpayers Unlimited, Inc., a group of retired and active fire fighters announced their support.

There were as many issues in the campaign as there were candidates. Seven of the eight Democrats voiced varying degrees of dissatisfaction with President Reagan's economic policies. Several supported anti-abortion legislation while Wheat and others opposed more government control of abortions. All proclaimed to favor a bilateral freeze on nuclear weapons production, except Mr. Wheat, who advocated a unilateral freeze by the United States, at least for a limited time.

The campaign was a vigorous one, with Alan Wheat and two others emerging early as the leading candidates in the polls. Election night was no different. There was suspense and high drama from the time the polls officially closed. Two hours later, the joy and hope and anticipation in Wheat's headquarters were shattered when Wheat's father telephoned from the election board, where he had been monitoring the voting tallies. He first commended his son for conducting a first-class campaign and for making a respectable showing in the returns. Then he informed him that he had lost—only 10,000 ballots remained to be counted and Wheat was 7,000 votes behind the leading candidate.

Some supporters cried in disappointment. Others grimaced in disgust. All quickly abandoned the headquarters, leaving Wheat and two others alone.

But by midnight the campaign headquarters was alive once again with hundreds of well-wishers. There was great joy and celebration inside and dancing in the streets outside. A political miracle had taken place. Earlier, because the official returns showed Wheat so close to the leading white candidates, it was erroneously assumed that the black precincts had been counted. Not true! Wheat had run exceptionally well in the white community. The votes remaining to be counted were in the black part of the district, and Wheat received 8,000 of the 10,000 votes there.

When the dust had settled, Alan Wheat was the winner with 21,280 votes to 20,273 for John Carnes and 16,194 for Jack L. Campbell. The five other Democrats received 10,000 votes. John Sharp, a five-term state legislator, won the Republican primary, and Wheat easily defeated him in the general election with 58 percent of the vote.

THE CBC REACHES LEGISLATIVE MATURITY

Our increased numbers strengthened the role CBC members had come to assume in Congress. We were the group that most effectively cultivated an alternative value system in the body and monitored Congress's role as a protector of people.

The Caucus had reached a kind of political sophistication and a legislative maturity matched by few other caucuses in the entire House of Representatives. Black members were now in positions that enabled us at times to place the Democratic leadership in an awkward, embarrassing posture. We had the ability to exert subtle pressures and thus to frustrate legislation effectively. The twenty-three of us, if necessary, were able to block or divert legislative proposals adverse to our cause, and in some instances were actually empowered to get our own legislative initiatives enacted. No longer were we promoting ad hoc hearings in faraway places like Cambridge, Massachusetts, or Nashville, Tennessee. Now, as chairpersons of key committees, we were sitting in ornate hearing rooms in the Rayburn, Longworth and Cannon House office buildings wielding gavels in our investigations of policies important to the national concerns of black Americans.

By 1982, the Caucus also had become extremely adept in putting together necessary coalitions within the House to preserve programs important to our constituencies that President Reagan had personally targeted for dismantling.

By the mid-eighties, our influence and power in the House of Representatives, mainly because of the seniority system, had increased to such an extent that the Democratic leadership had no alternative but to accommodate us in order to advance their own legislative agenda.

We were situated strategically to defend ourselves against the usurpers of institutional power and to protect our favorite projects from administration ax-wielders engaged in cutting funds for domestic programs. No longer was it necessary for us to go hat in hand, begging for crumbs from the table of those who held all of the key committee chairmanships. Now other members of Congress sought favors from us, and showed the proper respect for any consideration granted.

During the Reagan years, when the federal deficit reached astronomical heights, conservative Democrats and Republicans applied pressure to cut domestic programs. It was primarily through the efforts of the Congressional Black Caucus that a budget-cutting mechanism was developed that preserved programs vital to the well-being of impoverished citizens. The agreement called for a fifty-fifty reduction in appropriations for military and domestic spending, but exempted from Gramm/Rudman/Hollings fund reductions Social Security benefits; federal and military retirees benefits; veterans pensions and compensation benefits; Medicaid; Aid to Families with Dependent

Children (AFDC); Supplemental Security Income benefits (SSI); Women's, Infants', Children's program benefits (WIC); food stamps; and regular state unemployment insurance benefits.

Legislators who had traditionally shown little or no compassion for those least organized and least able to protect their interests were stymied in their efforts to reduce the deficit at the expense of the disorganized and disadvantaged. The CBC successfully exerted its influence with the House Democratic leadership in striking this arrangement.

NEW CBC SUPPORT NETWORKS

The new perception of the Congressional Black Caucus as possessing power, wielding power, and/or neutralizing the power of others was due to several key initiatives we had taken. One was Parren Mitchell's creation of a "brain trust" of experts to advise him regarding legislation in the area of black economic development. Another was Congressman Walter Fauntroy's bringing into being the National Black Leadership Roundtable (NBLR) and the convening of a national lobbying network. These two activities were perhaps the most significant programmatic strategies embraced by the CBC. They certainly were at the core of whatever caused white members of Congress to redefine their relationship with us. These two mechanisms directly enhanced our influence within the deliberative body.

Mitchell's "brain trust" idea gave us the ability to call on experts readily to provide and interpret available data from a black perspective. The Caucus put this concept to use by assembling experts in thirteen separate fields of interest, such as education, international affairs, health, and telecommunications. The development of these brain trusts, patterned after one put in place by Congressman Mitchell to assist minority businesses, and establishment of the Roundtable (NBLR), brought the Caucus to a level of parity with other political powers in the House of Representatives. (In 1973, Congressman Mitchell had welded more than 300 academicians, entrepreneurs, lawyers, and consultants into a network of influence working to increase the share of black businesses in government contracts.)

The data garnered from the various brain trusts were then used to inform and educate black constituents residing in districts represented by white congressmen about the legislative agenda and its effect on the black community. The centers of influence in each district were responsible for disseminating this information and for applying pressure on elected officials to support the CBC agenda.

Congressman Fauntroy envisioned the NBLR working hand-in-glove with the brain trusts. He advocated the brain trusts' becoming the vehicle to perform specific tasks called for by the Roundtable. As originally conceived, he made no distinction between the functions of the NBLR and that of the CBC. For example, he recommended that the national business and economic development network advocated by the Roundtable might well be achieved via the CBC Brain Trust on Minority Enterprise. He suggested that the Roundtable task force created to develop a comprehensive policy for eradicating inequalities blacks experience in employment might well serve as the CBC Brain Trust on Employment/Inflation.

The National Black Leadership Roundtable (NBLR) is composed of the heads of more than 300 national black organizations, representing 250,000 blacks in business, labor, civil rights, law enforcement, the media, government, social and fraternal organizations, science, education, international affairs, and health. The NBLR has made a concerted effort also to involve heads of black women's organizations and youth and student groups, the black elderly, entertainers, athletes, religious organizations, and black elected and appointed officials. The membership is all-inclusive.

Groups capable of exerting pressure on white members of Congress representing black populations now exist in more than 100 congressional districts.

In earlier days, the Fauntroy initiative was used with limited success. The 1973 vote in favor of the District of Columbia Home Rule Bill was definitely attributable to a campaign to target southern congressmen for special contacts by members of the NBLR. Their lobbying efforts, in some cases actually intimidating white members politically, culminated in legislation that authorized election in 1978 of the District of Columbia's own mayor and city council.

In March 1986, the NBLR became much more ambitious in setting its political goals and much more aggressive in its approach to defining black issues, especially in marginal districts. The group targeted five congressional seats for election of black candidates and identified ten Senate seats where the black vote could make the difference between electing a reactionary or a moderate-to-progressive candidate. If successful in both efforts, blacks would increase their numbers in the House to twenty-six and Democrats would recapture control of the Senate from goose-stepping, Neanderthal-type Ronald Reagan clones.

On November 6, 1986, a day after the general elections, Congressman Fauntroy exulted:

> We celebrate today the fact that blacks from across the country did send money and did travel to the target districts to work for our candidates. As a result, we are extremely proud to have helped make it possible for Congressman-elect John Lewis, of the Fifth Congressional District of Georgia; Congressman-elect Mike Espy, of the Second Congressional District of Mississippi; and Congressman-elect Floyd Flake, of the Sixth Congressional District of New York, to become members of the Congressional Black Caucus. . . . We consider the achievement of three of our five House goals a tremendous step forward in our quest as a people for political advancement. We batted .600![2]

In regard to the success of the program targeting ten seats in the Senate, Congressman Fauntroy was equally enthusiastic. Describing the returns in those ten districts, he said,

> It was in pursuit of this measurable goal that we realized why they killed Medger Evers in Jackson, Mississippi, in 1963; why they beat Chaney, Schwerner, and Goodman to death in Meridian, Mississippi, in 1964; and why they shot Viola Liuzzo, a white woman voting rights activist, to death at the close of the Selma-to-Montgomery march. The assailants knew that if blacks ever participated fully in the political process in our country, hands that picked cotton would pick not only mayors and city council persons, but also congressmen, senators, and presidents. . . .
>
> Today, we revel in the fact that blacks from across the country did send money and did travel to these states to work on behalf of moderate-to-progressive candidates. As a result, we are proud to have helped provide seven of ten senators we targeted with the winning margin of votes that black voters gave them in their successful bids. They are Senators-elect Shelby of Alabama, Cranston of California, Graham of Florida, Fowler of Georgia, Breaux of Louisiana, Mikulski of Maryland, and Sanford of North Carolina.[3]

The election of those seven Democrats to the United States Senate recaptured control of that body from ultra-conservative Republicans. It denied Republicans a majority and thus prohibited them from dictating the flow of legislation via a majority leader and the shaping of that legislation through the influence of committee chairmen from their party.

A CAREER OF DISTINCTION—
PARREN J. MITCHELL

One of the most productive legislators during the seventies and first half of the eighties was Parren J. Mitchell, the representative from the Seventh District of Maryland. Mitchell, during his sixteen years in Congress, served with distinction as a member of the House Budget Committee, vice-chairman of the Joint Committee on Defense Production, chairman of the House Small Business Committee, and chairman of the Congressional Black Caucus.

In 1976, Congressman Mitchell attached to then President Carter's $4 billion Public Works Bill an amendment that compelled state, county, and municipal governments seeking federal grants to set aside 10 percent of each grant to retain minority firms as contractors, subcontractors, or suppliers. This single amendment resulted in more than $625 million (15 percent) going to legitimate minority firms. Following numerous court challenges, "the Mitchell Amendment" was upheld as constitutional by the United States Supreme Court in July 1980.

Public Law 95-89 enacted August 4, 1977, contains three provisions written by Mitchell. The first and perhaps most important of the new statutory provisions allowed the Small Business Administration (SBA) to impose moratoriums on the repayment of loans during adverse economic periods. A second provision established SBA's associate administrator for minority small business as an Executive Level V position, which is the same held by SBA's three other associate administrators. And the third required SBA's annual report to break out the assistance provided to socially and economically disadvantaged individuals.

In January 1980, President Carter presented his annual budget recommendations, which included a 5 percent real increase in defense spending while domestic social programs were to be held at fiscal year 1980 spending levels.

As the economy worsened, President Carter retracted his original budget and caucused with the House and Senate leadership to create a balanced federal budget that would be part of the administration's three-pronged attack on inflation. It included:

A balanced federal budget
A 10 cents tax on imported oil
Consumer credit controls

The balanced budget resolution proposed by the House Budget Committee would cut hundreds of millions of dollars from domestic programs while substantially increasing defense programs. The CBC described it as an "unmitigated disaster" for the poor, the elderly, youth, and the cities. According to the Congressional Budget Office, a balanced budget would trim the inflation rate by only 0.2 percent. At the same time, it would force an additional 2 million people out of work. We denounced the budget proposal as a sham and a purely symbolic attempt to combat inflation. While the president might have been sincere in his attempts to balance the budget, to do so at the expense of poor people, in our thinking, was intolerable.

As an alternative, Parren Mitchell proposed an amendment to the first budget resolution—the "Human Needs Amendment." Backed by the Caucus, it called for restoration of monies to the domestic programs and reduction of military spending by $3 billion. The Human Needs Amendment was designed to generate $5 billion more in revenues by collecting additional taxes from excessive corporate profits and by closing tax loopholes. It included a $1.5 billion spending program targeted for energy conservation, jobs, education, and health.

In promoting the Mitchell amendment, Caucus members conducted a four-hour preliminary debate on the economic assumptions underlying the Carter budget. They rallied support in a series of statements on the House floor explaining the amendment. When all budget amendments offered by liberal legislators, including Mitchell's, were defeated, CBC called a special meeting of the National Black Leadership Roundtable. Following the meeting, the NBLR participants vigorously lobbied members of Congress to increase spending for social programs.

The first budget resolution, as recommended by the president and the congressional leadership, passed in the House and in the Senate, although not in identical form. Because of the pressure exerted by the NBLR and other liberal groups on those who opposed the measure, the conference report resolving differences between the two versions was rejected by a vote of 242 to 141 when the bill was returned to the House.

In the closing minutes of the Ninety-seventh Congress on January 6, 1983, a landmark measure authorizing record levels of funding for highway and mass transportation improvement projects was passed. The legislation covered a period of four years and projected the creation of 300,000 new jobs.

By increasing federal motor fuel taxes and adjusting other highway user fees, the nation's Highway Trust Fund authorization was allowed to grow from $8.5 billion in fiscal year 1982 to a minimum of $15 billion in 1986.

Congressman Parren Mitchell, chairman of the Committee on Small Business, secured passage of an amendment earmarking $7 billion as a set-aside for contracts with minority and small businesses. Most of the economically disadvantaged firms that were awarded 10 percent of the dollar value in this multi-billion-dollar tax/highway repair bill were black and Hispanic.

It was primarily through the personal efforts of Congressman Mitchell that minority businesses enjoyed their tremendous increase in the procurement of government contracts. In 1972, the top 100 black businesses grossed sales of only $423 million. Ten years later, in 1982, their total sales had increased to $2 billion. Much of that increase can be traced directly to the efforts of Mitchell and other members of the Congressional Black Caucus.

Parren Mitchell retired from Congress in 1986 after serving sixteen years. An educator by profession, Mitchell received many awards and honorary degrees. One citation accompanying the award of the doctor of law degree from Lincoln University in Pennsylvania echoes what the members of the Black Caucus think of Parren J. Mitchell: "Indeed this son and servant of the Seventh Congressional District of Maryland, and of the nation, has been a creative craftsman and an impassioned artisan in pursuit of goals of liberty, justice, and equality for all Americans."

Parren Mitchell's lead in the area of minority business interests was followed by several other members of the Caucus. In a major effort to direct new resources to the minority business sector, CBC member Gus Savage, on August 14, 1986, offered an amendment for a 10 percent set-aside of contracts awarded by the Department of Defense, specifically for "(1) small business concerns owned and controlled by socially and economically disadvantaged individuals . . . and (2) historically black colleges and universities; or (3) minority institutions (as defined by the secretary of education . . .)"

The amendment passed the House by almost a two-to-one margin (259–135) on a recorded vote. In conference between the House and the Senate to resolve differences in the bills the two chambers had passed, a compromise of a 5 percent set-aside was reached and became law. Through the efforts of Congressmen Savage, Conyers, and Dellums, building on initiatives taken by Congressman Mitchell, a multibillion-dollar federal program for minority businesses and historically black colleges is now in place.

DEFENDING THE RULE OF LAW—LOUIS STOKES

If Parren J. Mitchell may be regarded as one of our most productive legislators, Congressman Louis Stokes has been privileged to participate in some of Congress's most historic legislative events. Only a handful of congressmen have been as honored as our brother from the Twenty-first District of Ohio. He has been summoned to perform many very important and difficult tasks by three different House Speakers. Each time, he has carried out his responsibilities with a dedication above and beyond the call of duty.

In 1975, the Democratic Caucus of the House elected him to serve on the newly formed Budget Committee. He was re-elected to that committee twice, serving a total of six years. In September 1976, Speaker Carl Albert appointed Stokes to a select committee established to conduct a two-year investigation into the assassinations of President John F. Kennedy and Dr. Martin Luther King, Jr. Squabbling among Democratic committee members led to the resignations of the chairman, Henry Gonzales of Texas, and his chief counsel. Albert's successor, Speaker Thomas P. ("Tip") O'Neill, then named Congressman Stokes to the chairmanship.

As chairman, he performed magnificently, winning praise for himself and respect for the House of Representatives. A *Cleveland Plain Dealer* headline on January 7, 1979, declared: "Louis Stokes' Masterful Conduct of Probe Solidifies Position in House." The article following noted, ". . . as a nationwide television audience watched, [James Earl] Ray, surrounded by armed federal marshals, gave his version of what happened. Then Stokes, with his questions and evidence, drove huge holes into Ray's sworn testimony. . . ."[4]

In 1980, Stokes was appointed to the House Committee on Standards of Official Conduct, more commonly known as the Ethics Committee. He later served four years as chairman of the committee. During his tenure, Stokes presided over the ABSCAM scandal involving members of Congress accused of accepting bribes and oversaw the investigation of vice-presidential candidate Geraldine Ferraro's finances. His handling of these very sensitive issues brought additional credit to the House.

In 1983, Speaker Jim Wright appointed Stokes chairman of the House Permanent Select Committee on Intelligence. In this capacity he once again distinguished himself. During the Iran-Contra Hearings, his legislative career reached a crescendo in his now famous lecture to Lieutenant Colonel Oliver North. While eloquently rebuking the arrogant marine lieutenant colonel, Congressman Stokes gave the American public a lesson in both civics and history.

> Colonel North, at the beginning of your testimony you told us that you came to tell the truth, the good, the bad, and the ugly. I want to commend you for keeping your word. It has been good. It has been bad, and it has been ugly. I suppose what has been most disturbing about your testimony is the ugly part. In fact, it has been more than ugly. It has been chilling—in fact, frightening. I'm not talking just about your part in this but [about] the entire scenario. About government officials who plotted and conspired; who set up a straw man, fall guy; officials who lied, misrepresented, and deceived. Officials who planned to superimpose upon our government structure a layer outside of our government, shrouded in secrecy and only accountable to the conspirators. I could go on and on—but we both know the testimony—and it is ugly. In my opinion, it is a prescription for anarchy in a democratic society.
>
> In the course of your testimony I have thought often about the honor code at the U.S. Naval Academy. I have always taken great pride in these appointees, knowing that they would be imbued with the highest standard of honor, duty, and responsibility toward their government. The academy catalog speaks of the honor concept as being more than an administrative device; that it fosters the development of lasting and moral principles; it becomes part and parcel of the professionalism expected of graduates as commissioned officers. But more than that, I think of the young students all over America who are sitting in civics and government courses. You have said many times that you worry about the damage these hearings are creating for the United States around the world.
>
> I worry, Colonel, about the damage to the children of America, the future leaders of America. I worry about how we tell them that the ugly things you have told us about in our government is not the way American government is conducted. That it is not our democracy's finest hour.
>
> And then lastly, Colonel, I was touched yesterday morning by the eloquence of Senator Mitchell, who spoke so poignantly about the rule of law and what our Constitution means to immigrants.

He spoke eloquently of how all Americans are equal under our law. Senator Mitchell's words meant a great deal to another class of Americans, blacks and minorities, because, unlike immigrants, they have not always enjoyed full privileges of justice and equality under the Constitution, which we now celebrate in its two hundredth year.

If any class of Americans understands and appreciates the rule of law, the judicial process, and constitutional law, it is those who have had to use that process to come from a status of non-persons in American law to a status of equality under law. We had to abide by the slow and arduous process of abiding by law until we could change the law, through the judicial process.

In fact, Colonel, as I sit here this morning, looking at you in your uniform, I cannot help but remember that I wore the uniform of this country in World War II, in a segregated army. I wore it as proudly as you do, even though our government required black and white soldiers, in the same army, to live, sleep, eat, and travel separate and apart, while fighting and in some cases dying for our country.

Because of the rule of law, today's servicemen in America suffer no such indignity. Similar to Senator Mitchell's humble beginnings, my mother, a widow, raised two boys. She had an eighth grade education and was a domestic worker. One son became the first black mayor of a major American city—Cleveland, Ohio—the other sits here today as chairman of the Intelligence Committee of the House of Representatives.

Only in America, Colonel North. Only in America. And while I admire your love for America, I hope, too, that you will never forget that others, too, love America just as much as you—and while they disagree with you and our government on aid to the Contras, they will die for America just as quickly as you will.[5]

The influence, the respect, the congeniality shown by members of the House to Mitchell and Stokes were by no means limited to those two Caucus members. Others were also leaving their mark on vital pieces of legislation and government programs. As CBC members amassed more seniority, which brought additional chairmanships, their legislative prowess continued to expand.

THE CBC ALTERNATIVE BUDGET

On February 18, 1981, after proposing to the Congress and to the American people his plan for economic recovery, President Ronald Reagan challenged anyone who did not accept his program to come up with an alternative that offered a greater chance of balancing the budget, reducing and eliminating inflation, stimulating the creation of jobs, and reducing the tax burden.

One month later, on March 18, the Congressional Black Caucus, in a luncheon meeting with members of the media at the National Press Club in Washington, unveiled its "alternative budget." Congressman Walter Fauntroy, speaking for the Caucus, announced:

> Today, the CBC answers [the Reagan] challenge. We call it a "constructive alternative"—constructive because we, like all Americans, want to reduce inflation, increase jobs and productivity, improve our national security, and relieve the American people of a growing federal tax burden. We call it an "alternative" because, unlike the Reagan administration's cold and uneven solution to these problems, our proposal moves us toward the goal of reduced inflation and full employment with a compassion for people and a sharing of the burdens of these difficult times by the rich as well as the poor.[6]

Reagan's budget proposal called for five manned bombers, reactivation of two battleships, one heavy aircraft carrier, one SSN submarine, sixty attack aircraft, eight tankers, and the Roland missile system. Merely eliminating the new weapons systems Reagan planned would reduce spending by $21.3 billion. Delaying or denying reactivation of obsolete naval vessels would save several billions of dollars more.

Congressman Dellums' position was that these proposals should be rejected because "our military posture should be defense of America, not domination of the world."

In the final moments before House consideration of the Caucus alternative budget, the Democratic Study Group, an organization highly respected on Capitol Hill for its ability to analyze legislation, quoted supporters of the CBC budget as saying:

> The [CBC budget] takes the boldest step of any proposal being offered to the House to deal with the federal deficit. [It] also offers the largest and fairest tax cut of any of the proposals before the House. It accomplishes all this without hurting other important national programs. Spending for national defense would still be substantially higher than it was in fiscal year 1981. The [Caucus budget] makes even deeper cuts than the administration requested for other programs and achieves savings by tightening up the management of government.[7]

The Congressional Black Caucus met the challenge issued by President Reagan on February 18, 1981. We addressed the economic crisis of the nation and, indeed, offered a fairer, saner resolution of the problem. But our alternative was defeated in part because of misperceptions by the press, the public, and members of Congress who believed that federal spending for social and economic programs was the root cause of the financial ills of the country.

When the white press was not ignoring our efforts, the black press was condemning them. Some of the harshest criticism came from the same black newsmen who had championed every idiotic proposal advanced by the Nixon administration. William O. Walker, black publisher of the *Cleveland Call & Post*, attempted to defend Ronald Reagan's budgetary policies by attacking the Caucus on other matters. Castigating black legislators in his personal column, titled "Down the Big Road," Walker said,

> The Reagan regime has now forced the Caucus to face up to the challenge of change. . . . Because of these changes in politics on Capitol Hill, the Caucus now finds itself mired down in petty maneuvers and selfish personal politics. . . . The Reagan administration finds the highly paid but poorly managed Caucus staff inept, inefficient, and ill prepared to meet the important legislative issues that the Caucus members must face.
>
> . . . most of our black congressmen spend plenty of their time on the paid speaking circuit outside of their districts gathering in . . . extra money, and only appearing in their districts at those public affairs that they think enhance their own public image . . . go through their districts like strutting peacocks only to be admired. . . .[8]

The Caucus was neither disillusioned by this and similar attacks in the black media nor disturbed by the silence of the white media. Congressman Fauntroy, in his presentation to the media at the National Press Club on March 18, 1981, released the Congressional Black Caucus's Four-Point Plan for Black America. The major points were:

1. We shall defend against any assaults on the political, social, and economic gains we have made in the past. . . .
2. We shall aggressively pursue new legislation and public policies designed to improve the quality of life for black Americans and all Americans. . . .
3. We shall develop and expand our National Action Alert Commu-

nications Network in 113 congressional districts where blacks are 15 percent or more of the electorate.

4. We shall organize in coalition with white Americans, minorities [Hispanics], and other groups whose interests coincide with ours on specific items on our legislative and public policy agenda.

The plan manifested in the form of the Communications Network and coalitions with various groups enabled us to pass several significant pieces of legislation. We were successful many times. Voting for economic and political sanctions against South Africa is a case in point.

THE CBC TAKES ON THE ISSUE OF SOUTH AFRICA

When anti–South Africa sentiment in the Congress reached the boiling point, the Caucus capitalized on it. The new wave of unrest demonstrated by blacks was precipitated in 1985, when a new South African Parliament was created to include Indians and Coloreds (mixed race) but not blacks. Massive demonstrations following the government's decision were met by the declaration of a state of emergency in black townships and the suspension of even the pretense of a rule of law. Thousands of blacks conducting peaceful protests were detained and imprisoned without due process; their homes were searched and ransacked; their children and family were beaten in public; and hundreds of their supporters were slaughtered by the police.

In response to these dastardly acts, both the House and the Senate voted to impose sanctions on the government of South Africa. The two bodies conferred and an agreement was reached to: (1) ban export of computers and software to the South African police or other agencies that administered apartheid; (2) ban the sale of nuclear equipment and technology until South Africa signed the Nuclear Non-Proliferation Treaty; and (3) ban most new loans to the South African government, except loans for educational, housing, or health facilities available to all races.

A second phase of sanctions was a ban on the sale of Krugerrands in the United States. The agreement also called for imposing twelve months after enactment: (1) a ban on new investments; (2) denial of most-favored-nation trading status; and (3) prohibition against importing South African coal or uranium into the United States if South Africa did not make significant progress toward eliminating apartheid.

Regrettably, the Senate surrendered to the threat of a filibuster by Senator Jesse Helms and other reactionary Republican members and bowed to a cynical ploy by President Reagan, who issued an executive order promising stern action against South Africa. As a result, the 1985 measure never became law.

The executive order President Reagan signed on September 9, 1985, purporting to impose sanctions against South Africa, in reality imposed no sanctions at all. The government of South Africa continued its ruthless policy of apartheid without hindrance.

In 1985 and 1986, members of CBC sponsored twenty-four bills relating to United States policy toward South Africa.

Congressman William Gray introduced a 1986 Comprehensive Anti-Apartheid Act. Basically, it was the same as the conference agreement made between the House and Senate the preceding year. Congressman Ronald Dellums offered an amendment proposing sweeping restrictions and a total ban on U.S. citizens' holding South African investments. Under his bill, landing rights for the South African airline would be revoked; the export of supplies to that nation (with the exception of medical provisions) and the importation of South African products (with the exception of strategic minerals) would be forbidden; there would be a total prohibition on loans to South Africa or its constituent entities; and the sale of the Krugerrand in the United States would be declared illegal. In an extraordinary and unexpected move, the House passed the Dellums substitute on a voice vote. A companion measure was immediately introduced in the Senate, which passed with some different features.

The final version issuing from the conference committee provided for termination of the sanctions, if:

1. Nelson Mandela and other political prisoners were released
2. The state of emergency was lifted and all detainees under the emergency also were released
3. Democratic political parties were unbanned
4. The Group Areas and Population Registration Acts were repealed
5. The South African government publicly committed itself to good faith negotiations with truly representative members of the black majority without setting preconditions

President Reagan, as expected, vetoed the bill on September 26, 1986. But four days later, by a vote of 313 to 83, the House overrode his veto. Favorable action in the Senate followed.

THE CBC AT THE CREST OF THE HILL

The January 1985 election of Bill Gray to the position of Democratic Caucus chairman by his Democratic colleagues in the House was an indication that CBC members had reached the crest of "the Hill," the Caucus had come of political age. We were now bona fide, credentialed, honest-to-goodness political "insiders."

Charles Rangel was defeated by Tony Coelho of California for the position of Democratic House whip in 1988. Better judgment dictated that Democrats "tiptoe lightly through the tulips" for fear of giving the appearance that the outcome of the election was determined by the race of one of these two outstanding candidates.

After Coelho's 1989 mid-term resignation, we continued our upward mobility in the House hierarchy; Bill Gray succeeded Coelho as Democratic whip. This position is the number three leadership position in the House of Representatives and traditionally has been the apprenticeship for Speaker.

Congressman Gray's successful rise in the party ranks was due primarily to his charm and charisma, his creative approach to congressional duties, and his unique ability to build coalitions. As a freshman in the Ninety-sixth Congress, Mr. Gray was able to finesse his way to such key assignments as the Foreign Affairs Committee, the Budget Committee, and the District of Columbia Committee. In the next session, he won a seat on the powerful Appropriations Committee.

Gray's 1985 election to chair the Budget Committee placed him in the center of the fight to shape federal budget priorities and in the eye of the storm to balance the budget.

Congressman Gray's committee immediately confronted the Reagan administration's budget for fiscal year 1986, which proposed cuts in or termination of a broad range of domestic programs. The White House sought to increase Pentagon spending authority by nearly $30 billion, while slashing funding for housing for the poor, child nutrition programs, Aid to Families with Dependent Children, Urban Development Action Grants, the Small Business Administration, mass transit, support to minority educational institutions, Community Service

Block Grants, and cost of living increases for Social Security recipients.

Congressman Gray, after consulting with many and varied interest groups inside and outside the House, introduced House Concurrent Resolution 152, which revised the congressional budget for the United States government for the 1986 fiscal year. It also projected priorities for the 1986, 1987, and 1988 congressional budgets. The Gray committee ultimately restored more than $38 billion that Reagan had proposed cutting out of domestic programs, most of which had a direct impact on black Americans.

During a seven-month battle with the administration and with ultra-conservatives in Congress, Chairman Gray succeeded in his efforts to retain essential funding for programs designed to rebuild urban America and to meet the human needs of low-income Americans. Striving for a budget of compassion, fairness, and economic justice, Gray's committee provided an increase to offset inflation in thirty-two out of thirty-three low-income programs. The committee also succeeded in slowing down the growth in military spending, delivering a budget to reduce the Reagan deficit by $57 billion more than the reduction sought by the president.

Gray's climb up the leadership ladder must be viewed in the overall context of increased influence of the black members of Congress. Every challenge by every black member of Congress to every racial slur and every refusal to passively accept different treatment because of race enhanced Bill Gray's opportunities for overcoming the odds.

Congressman Bill Dawson's 1951 plea for racial tolerance on the floor of the House of Representatives surely aided Bill Gray in his quest for a leadership role. His words of wisdom, spoken thirty-four years earlier, were not lost on our generation of representatives. In a stirring address attacking segregation in the armed services, Dawson declaimed, "How long, how long . . . will you divide us Americans on account of color? . . . Give me the test that you would apply to make anyone a full-fledged American and, by the living God, if it means death itself, I will pay it—but give it to me."[9]

Congressman Adam Clayton Powell's abrasive, unyielding attack on the forces that illogically argued for racial separation and injudiciously defended subjugation of the black race likewise contributed immeasurably to Bill Gray's future accomplishments.

Congressman Augustus Hawkins' effective legislative initiatives, Charlie Diggs' quiet diplomacy in bringing about changes of attitude among his white colleagues, and John Conyers' unorthodox confrontation of racism all served to level the playing field for Bill Gray when he entered the congressional "run for the roses."

But also important to Congressman Gray's successful bid for Democratic Caucus chairman and for Democratic majority whip was the perception among many white Democrats that blacks were entitled to representation in that elite leadership group. Why they decided to reevaluate their life-long opposition to blacks' giving direction and leadership—and why they reversed their once strongly held conviction that blacks could not fairly address problems affecting white constituents—is far beyond my powers of comprehension. I don't know the answer. Like many other black leaders, I, too, am baffled in my attempt to intelligently explain this new phenomenon. But I am happy we have come this far.

A LEADER LOST TOO SOON—MICKEY LELAND

Another member who was rising in the ranks of the House of Representatives was Mickey Leland of Texas. But tragedy struck the Leland family, the Caucus, the nation, and the world in August 1989. Our brother Mickey Leland and his congressional delegation were reported missing in the mountainous terrain of Ethiopia. For eleven days, citizens of the world watched, prayed, and hoped that they would be found safe and sound. But that was not to be.

It is often said that we are our brother's keeper, and some of us do attempt to live by that homily. Feeding the hungry, clothing the naked, housing the homeless are very simple but profound actions. Our fallen brother, George ("Mickey") Leland, wasn't born knowing precisely which of these would become his life's work. Hunger was not the first or even the only cause that captured his attention and imagination. Like most of us, Mickey had to search for the set of values that would transform his life into something meaningful.

When he discovered the devastating scope of world hunger, it was a monumental challenge for him. In the role of chairman of the U.S. House of Representatives Select Committee on Hunger, Leland did his best to change the plight of those who were hungry.

On the domestic front, he introduced the Homeless Persons Survival Act—the first omnibus legislation to combat the problems of homelessness in America. Additionally, in an effort to combat the rising rate of infant mortality, he proposed a $175-million program for prenatal and pediatric care for low-income mothers and their children. Another of his great legislative goals was to ensure through proper government funding the preservation of our historically black colleges and universities.

Congressman Leland and fifteen others (seven of them Ethiopians) were killed in an airplane crash while on a mission to feed hungry people in that part of Africa. Leland was the second member of the Congressional Black Caucus to die in an airline tragedy. The first was Congressman George Collins, who was killed in December 1972 in a crash at Midway Airport in Chicago.

Congressman Kweisi Mfume in assessing the life of Mickey Leland said, "Mickey understood better than most the crisis among our youth and the risk in failing to overcome it. His life was a legacy to the children of suffering and his death is a challenge for us to do more."[10]

Leland was a person of extraordinary sensitivities. His life was dedicated to many projects and many causes that the average elected representative at any level usually disregards or at least places very low on the priority list. But Mickey Leland devoted his life to the basic needs of ordinary and forgotten people.

We in the Congressional Black Caucus loved Mickey and miss his salient counsel and pungent advice. Most of all, we have been deprived of his smiling face and soft heart. This giant of a man, with a heart as big as humanity itself, devoted his life to easing the misery of others. During his stellar career in the Congress, his philosophy of life shone through, his great passion for ending hunger and saving the children.

The best way to explain Mickey Leland is through his own words. The following are excerpts from his many speeches and writings. They tell the story.

... the tragedy of hunger affects children most gravely by denying them the future which is their basic human right. The loss of a single individual hurts all humanity ... but the loss of children is especially tragic. . . .[11]

Despite instances of injustices, poverty, and violence, we must express our common humanity and answer the cry of the hungry. . . . We have seen that economic and political systems change and vary, but individual and family needs and hopes remain much the same. Unfortunately, these hopes and physical needs are still denied to millions. That is our challenge. . . .[12]

We are an integral part of a universal struggle. Let there never exist a moment when we forget that our brothers and sisters are dying in the streets of South Africa in the name of freedom. . . .[13]

In the name of those who have fallen in battle against oppression so that we might know dignity as a people, let us commit to ourselves to stand tall for principle, to march steadfastly against injustices, and to sacrifice all that is ours to give in the quest of freedom. . . .[14]

Our actions or inactions will in a very real way determine whether our children, their children, and their children's children will have clean air to breathe, potable water, and environments free of hazardous waste. In short, our decisions will dictate whether they can expect to live in a relatively safe environment or in an unhealthy world. . . .[15]

We are all world citizens and each of us has a responsibility for dedicating some small portion of our lives "to the creation of a world where all children can live a full life" . . .[16]

I would hope that we will turn our sights on doing something to help those who are the least amongst us. . . .[17]

We're in a war, all right. It's more than a war on poverty. It's a fight to save our humanity.[18]

Congressman Ronald Dellums (speaking as chairman of the Congressional Black Caucus and certainly for all of us) said,

To [Leland's] honor and in his everlasting memory, we pledge to celebrate the joys of life, to revel in his laughter, to anchor ourselves in commitment to good, to nurture and feed our young, to champion justice everywhere and challenge injustice anywhere, to heal the sick, to house the homeless, to lead where others fear to tread, and to love unconditionally.[19]

No one individual can solve the problem of world hunger that plagues even our most affluent nations. Yet Mickey Leland showed us that we have not nearly exhausted the limits of what we can accomplish with the power we control. He has challenged all of us to keep the faith and to keep his dream alive.

NOTES

1. Congressman Charles Rangel
2. Congressman Walter Fauntroy, press release dated November 6, 1986, Washington, D.C.
3. *Ibid.*
4. *Cleveland Plain Dealer*, January 7, 1979.

5. Transcript of the Joint Hearings before the Senate Select Committee on Secret Military Assistance to Iran and the Nicaraguan Contras and the Select Committee to Investigate Covert Arms Transactions with Iran, first session, Part II, Washington, D.C.: Government Printing Office, 1988, pages 161–162.

6. Congressman Fauntroy, in remarks to National Press Club, Washington, D.C., March 18, 1981 (accession No. RXA 1890, Recorded Sound Reference Center, the Library of Congress).

7. Report by the Democratic Study Group, U.S. House of Representatives, 1981, Fact Sheet 97-2, page 11.

8. *Cleveland Call & Post*, June 31, 1981.

9. Cited in *The Washington North Star*, September 22, 1983, page S-2.

10. *Point of View*, CBCF Nineteenth Legislative Weekend, September 1989, page 5.

11. *Ibid.*, page 1.

12. *Ibid.*, page 22.

13. *Ibid.*

14. *Ibid.*

15. *Ibid.*, page 26

16. *Ibid.*

17. *Ibid.*

18. *Ibid.*, page 36.

19. *Ibid.*, page 63.

13

The CBC Almost Self-Destructs

Despite the Caucus's well-established purpose and good intentions, we, like other groups of individuals, have had our share of internal conflicts from time to time. The disputes and controversies, some personal, some ideological, some uncalled for, have occasionally threatened to take us away from our noble mission.

The squabbles concerned political philosophy, direction of the organization, contests for chairmanship of the Caucus, and legislative priorities. Some issues, such as the programmatic scope of the Annual Legislative Weekend and Chisholm's campaign for president, nearly caused the dissolution of the Congressional Black Caucus.

Marguerite Ross-Barnett (named president of the University of Houston in 1990), writing in the April 1981 edition of the NAACP's *Crisis* magazine, observed,

> By mid-1972, the view that the CBC could be a "united voice for Black America" was discredited. Never actually a monolith, the myths of unity were punctured by the events surrounding the Convention and the 1972 Democratic presidential election. It is worthwhile examining the first years of CBC with some care because for short moments during those years, the CBC came quite close to inventing a new political form with enormous potential. In a cultural, ideological, and political arena rooted in individualistic constructs and modes of thought, the CBC struggled, often subconsciously, to seek an institutional means of collective political action. However, in the absence of sufficient theoretical and/or practical exploration of this new direction, the group simply became ensnarled in debilitating conflict.[1]

The conflict was not always debilitating, but conflict there was. It took the form of disagreement and debate on matters as small as the menu for the Annual Legislative Weekend dinner and as great as the purchase of real estate for the Caucus or the question who should be endorsed for the presidency of the United States.

Two weeks following the first annual dinner, the Caucus had $125,000 on deposit in a local bank and another $20,000 on hand for operating expenses. Several months later, other large contributions had come into the till, and since a large staff had not been hired, there was very little foreseeable need for increased operating expenses.

Chairman Diggs appointed a committee headed by Executive Director Howard Robinson to locate property suitable for Caucus headquarters. Several weeks later, Robinson presented to the Caucus a proposal to purchase a four-story building in the 300 block of Pennsylvania Avenue, S.E., just a few blocks from the Capitol. The building had 4,000 square feet. Our projected need was determined to be 2,000 square feet, leaving 2,000 square feet to be rented for approximately $12,000 per year. The sale price was $165,000, with a first mortgage of $100,000 to be provided by the Industrial Bank of Washington. A cash down payment of $30,000 was required. A second mortgage of $35,000 would be taken back by the sellers. It was quite obvious that the arrangement would permit the Caucus to purchase the property and let its tenants retire the mortgage.

Some members argued that it was not ethically correct for an organization such as the CBC to own property. They contended that ownership would convey the impression of middle-class snobbishness and inevitably lead to the institutionalization of the Caucus. What in the hell that meant was Greek to those of us who were not students of Marxism. At first, we thought this argument much too deep for mere "black capitalists" like us to fathom. But remembering that even peasants, indentured servants, and share-croppers aspire to own land someday, and recalling that freed slaves looked forward eagerly to their "forty acres and a mule," we suspected some of our colleagues of pursuing a hidden agenda.

The motivation of those opposing purchase of the building, we speculated, had a lot to do with their attitude of not wanting the Caucus to succeed. Several of them earnestly believed the collective actions of the Caucus overshadowed their own intellectual brilliance and precluded them from becoming the individual kind of spokespersons for black Americans that Adam Clayton Powell, Jr., had been for many years.

Those opposed to the purchase talked at great length each time the subject was brought before the group for discussion. As a result, the issue was finally tabled and the building was sold to another buyer. Eight years later, the same building was purchased by another group for $1.4 million. That was ten times the sale price offered originally to the CBC.*

OUTSIDE PRESSURES ON CAUCUS MEMBERS

When Congressman Charles B. Rangel of New York was elected to replace Congressman Stokes as chairman of the Caucus in 1974, the Caucus had grown to seventeen members. Shortly thereafter in 1975, at the beginning of the Ninety-fourth Congress, we hired a new staff director, attorney Barbara Williams, former administrative assistant to Congressman Dellums.

By the time of Rangel's election as chairman, the Caucus was adequately equipped to discern and protect, as well as advance, the legislative interests of our constituents. We had been successful in placing our members on key committees: Charles B. Rangel (New York) on Ways and Means; Andrew Young (Georgia) on the Rules Committee; Yvonne Burke (California) on Public Works; Ralph Metcalfe (Illinois) on Interstate and Foreign Commerce.

But we did have some nagging internal problems, and one that persistently faced the Caucus at the time was the lack of political independence on the part of Chicagoan Ralph Metcalfe, a staunch, avid supporter of Chicago Mayor Richard Daley's political organization. Caucus members expressed concern because of his divided, sometimes dubious loyalty. We knew it was impossible to serve two political masters. The press was unusually blunt in identifying him as a lackey of Mayor Daley. We in the Caucus were not so inhospitable, because we were political realists. We understood the nature of Chicago politics and the significance of working with or working against that city's political machine.

---

*Fifteen years later, when House rules forced the CBC to separate into three distinct, independent entities, the Congressional Black Caucus Foundation, an offspring of the original Caucus, realizing the need for permanent facilities to house its staff, purchased a much smaller building in the same vicinity for approximately $300,000. Thanks to the generosity of August Busch, III, of Anheuser Busch Companies and his top assistants, Wayman Smith, II, and Henry Brown, the mortgage on the building was retired.

The crunch came when the Black Caucus opposed H. R. 1, a welfare bill recommended by President Nixon that would have drastically altered the manner of treatment afforded welfare recipients, a large percentage of them black. The Democratic and Republican leadership in the House, organized labor, most liberal organizations, all ultra-conservative groups, the Chamber of Commerce, and a majority in the mass media banded together in support of the president's proposal. The Congressional Black Caucus stood almost alone in defying this vile assault on the weakest and the poorest elements in our society. Only the Caucus dared to challenge such an awesome array of power.

Our opposition to the bill became a "cause celebre" for black and poor people. We denounced the racist motives of those advocating these draconian changes and accused our friends in the labor movement and liberal groups of being "summer soldiers and sunshine patriots."

The Nixon workfare/welfare proposal would have established a federal base income level of $2,400 for a family of four; the family maximum would have been $3,600 for a family of eight. The bill would have jeopardized the nutritional health of millions of poor persons because it called for the elimination of food stamp benefits without guaranteeing their replacement in cash. The CBC had documented a need for $6,500 a year for a family of four to live at a minimum level of existence.

The most obnoxious feature of the bill was the forced work provision. It was especially harsh in light of the crisis in unemployment for black adults and youths. The plan was viewed by us as punitive and unrealistic, since it would deny the lowest wage earners the protection of the federal minimum wage. Further, the provision in the bill to create only 200,000 public service jobs was ludicrously inadequate, considering the 10 percent unemployment rate in the black community. We had hoped for solidarity within our ranks in opposing the measure.

After learning that Representative Dan Rostenkowski, who served as liaison for Chicago Mayor Daley and the Illinois congressional delegation, had placed a call to Ralph Metcalfe and George Collins instructing them to vote with the president, we in the Caucus were livid. Knowing the political realities of Chicago politics, Caucus members had little hope of winning Collins' vote in this matter. He had just been elected in a district that was 58 percent white with the full support of the Daley machine. And when the federal courts ordered a new redistricting plan putting Collins and longtime white incumbent

Frank Annunzio in the same district (the Seventh), Mayor Daley personally intervened and persuaded Annunzio to run in the Eleventh District.

Metcalfe also came out of and was an integral part of Mayor Daley's political machine. He had been the handpicked choice of Daley to succeed Bill Dawson (1943–1972) in the Congress. Metcalfe was not known for taking a militant stance in behalf of his people. He normally went along with the wishes of the party bigwigs once a decision had been reached. But members of the Caucus believed that Metcalfe's national prestige and solid connections to the local black community in a district 80 percent black left no logical reason for him to kowtow to the mayor.

In a hurriedly called meeting, Metcalfe explained that he needed time to develop his own power base in order to successfully challenge Mayor Daley's influence in his district. He assured us that if we were patient, in a few months he would be so entrenched that Daley would never again be in a position to exert undue pressure on him or to intimidate him on any other political issue.

Congressman Metcalfe was correct in his time assessment. During the following year, he not only became one of the CBC's biggest supporters, but also one of Mayor Daley's most bitter and effective enemies.

In Chicago, police officers were notorious for physically abusing black suspects. Charges of police brutality were rampant in ghetto communities. The mayor always turned a deaf ear to complaints of black leaders concerning the actions of his men in blue. Metcalfe, too, was usually silent on the matter.

But all of that changed in the spring of 1972 when two black dentists, both personal friends of the congressman and prominent leaders in the black community, suffered abusive treatment at the hands of the police. One of them later died of his wounds. At this point, Metcalfe broke his silence and challenged the mayor to rid the department of sadistic officers who had no respect for the rights of black citizens.

Just prior to this incident, Metcalfe and Daley had had a disagreement, and the mayor had caved in to the congressman. The issue in that case was the mayor's endorsement of State's Attorney Edward Hanrahan for renomination. Black voters were outraged because of the role Hanrahan had played in the murders of Mark Clark and Fred Hampton, two leaders of the Black Panthers in Chicago. Metcalfe refused to follow the machine endorsement and demanded that Daley withdraw his support, which the mayor surprisingly did. But on the question of alleged police brutality, the mayor steadfastly supported the police. Metcalfe conducted a series of public hearings and dramatized the gross mistreatment inflicted upon his constituents by the police. Mayor Daley retaliated by taking all political patronage away from Metcalfe, who was also the elected Democratic committeeman of the Third Ward.

Many years after Metcalfe's death, the *Chicago Tribune* newspaper, which was not fond of him in life, wrote:

> . . . It would be an excellent idea to name a new federal office building in Chicago for the late Representative Ralph Metcalfe.
>
> Metcalfe, winner of a silver medal at the 1932 Olympics and of silver and gold medals at the 1936 Olympics, was an extraordinary figure in Chicago politics and government. But when he made a dramatic break with Mayor Richard J. Daley and the Democratic organization in 1972, he secured a place in the city's history.
>
> A silent party loyalist for years, Metcalfe proved that a black politician in Chicago could assert political independence without being squashed.
>
> Through quiet conformity to the Democratic organization he had become the city's ultimate black political insider, rising to an influential position in the Chicago City Council and later moving on to Congress. Despite his unassailable civil-rights record, he was seen by many independents as an ever-cautious toady of the Daley machine.
>
> But when he bucked Daley and launched a campaign against police brutality, he became a folk hero. By staving off a later, Daley-backed challenge to his congressional seat, he helped lay the groundwork for another generation of black leaders that included his onetime protegé, Harold Washington.[2]

When the new, independent Metcalfe ran for re-election in 1973, Mayor Daley placed him on a special "hit list" for defeat and mobilized important community resources to defeat his bid for re-election. The mayor's choice for Congress was Erwin France, a black man who also had close ties to the political machine.

The Congressional Black Caucus felt obligated to give the maximum possible assistance to Ralph Metcalfe's re-election campaign, and the decision to do so was unanimous. Congressman George Collins, the other black member of Congress from Chicago, publicly supported Metcalfe in attacking the Daley administration for laxity in controlling police brutality against blacks.

Endorsement by the Congressional Black Caucus was not an idle gesture, because the Caucus was in a position to match the mayor's organization threat for threat, dollar for dollar, man for man. Respect for us among Metcalfe's constituents and personal supporters translated into vote-getting power in his behalf on a par with Daley's machine.

When leadership of the Chicago AFL-CIO informed Congressman Metcalfe that they had to support his opponent because of obligations to Mayor Daley, the Caucus met with George Meany, international president of the AFL-CIO. Caucus Chairman Rangel gave him an ultimatum: Either endorse Ralph Metcalfe, a member with a 100-percent voting record favorable to labor, or CBC members would announce publicly the severing of all relations with organized labor. When Meany balked at the demand, Rangel immediately got up from his seat and declared there was nothing further to discuss. The entire membership of the Caucus stood with Rangel and started toward the door. Meany, unaccustomed to such blunt power plays, was visibly shaken. But he did muster enough strength to instruct an assistant to call Mayor Daley and inform him that the AFL-CIO was obligated to support Congressman Metcalfe because of his sterling record in defending the rights of American workers.

When Mayor Daley turned his city hall patronage workers loose to canvass the South Side precincts in opposition to Metcalfe, members of the Congressional Black Caucus and our staffs and friends from around the nation converged on the South Side en masse. The man-hours we contributed, supplemented by the numerous canvassers from organized labor affiliates of the AFL-CIO and parishioners of local churches, were sufficient to negate the influence of Daley's patronage workers.

When Metcalfe ran short of money, the CBC, through its numerous contacts, called in IOU chits and raised thousands of dollars to foot the necessary campaign bills.

Congressman Metcalfe, in a landslide victory, totally humiliated Mayor Daley, who was unaccustomed to losing in any election. Metcalfe's South Side constituents sent a clear message to the mayor that only black people themselves would determine who spoke for them in the halls of Congress.

Another occasion threatening our unity was the great debate as to whether the Caucus should allow Coors Brewery to participate in the annual CBC Legislative Weekend as an advertiser in the souvenir booklet or to display its products as an exhibitor. Some members rightfully argued that it was inappropriate to accept money from a company that promoted ultra-conservative causes, supported anti-black candidates for public office, and used its financial resources to underwrite the missions of reactionary think tanks such as the Heritage Foundation.

Three members of the Caucus (Conyers, Dellums, and Hayes) wrote Chairman Stokes a letter of protest at the conclusion of the weekend affair:

> . . . We write to express our extreme dismay with the Congressional Black Caucus Foundation for having allowed the Adolph Coors Company to participate in the Black Caucus' Thirteenth Annual Legislative Weekend.
>
> It was particularly shocking to receive an invitation to their exhibit reception with RSVP to the CBC Foundation, thus indicating at least tacit approval of the Coors Company and their activities.
>
> The Caucus and its Foundation can ill afford to lend legitimacy to this company. It is no secret . . . [the Coors Company] and [Mr. Coors] personally have been known as "Beacons of Ultra-Conservatism" and that he has been a long-time contributor to causes in direct philosophical opposition to those of the Caucus. . . .[3]

Joseph Coors was notorious for his opposition to liberal causes. The conservative Heritage Foundation was started with a $250,000 grant from him. He also contributed handsomely and often to such radical organizations as the John Birch Society.

The controversy arose weeks before the affair and had been debated at a CBC Foundation board meeting. Several members of the Caucus and some lay members of the Foundation board took the position that most corporations did not meet the ideal standards of community responsibility set by the Caucus, yet were not restricted in their support of the annual event. They argued that as long as the contributor was aware its money did not buy any special consideration, the firm should be allowed to buy an advertisement and purchase space for a booth to exhibit its merchandise.

We reached a compromise that allowed Coors Brewery to purchase a nominal advertisement in the souvenir booklet but not to play a prominent role in the annual weekend. The company was denied sponsorship of any expensive, prestigious receptions and the opportunity to contribute $50,000 to the Graduate Fellows Training Program, as it had proposed to do.

A CONSERVATIVE LAWSUIT AGAINST THE CBC-PAC

Another controversy emerged within the CBC when the Washington Legal Research Foundation filed suit against the CBC Political Action Committee (CBC-PAC). Panic and paranoia followed because of this direct attack against us by the ultra-conservative, anti-black reactionary organization. In all my days of involvement in the movement to liberate black people from fear of the white man's prowess, I never experienced anything like the hysteria demonstrated by black leaders in response to such frivolous accusations from these white folk. Within minutes after the white press reported that the secretive Washington Legal Research Foundation was preparing to file suit against the CBC-PAC, Caucus members fell over each other trying to be the first to deny their association with the Caucus entity—a legitimate, legally constituted body of the organization.

The charges filed with the Federal Election Commission (FEC) against me as chairman of the PAC and the Caucus were:

1. Dozens of financial irregularities on the part of the CBC-PAC
2. Illegal use of my congressional office and of government equipment and employees for campaign purposes
3. Operating a fraudulent office in a hotel suite that did not exist (having an address on the sixth floor of a five-story building)
4. Committee reports illegally signed by unauthorized persons
5. Accepting illegal contributions from corporations and unions
6. Late reports to the FEC by the CBC-PAC

The charges, if true, would have been very serious, especially the one alleging use of my congressional office, government equipment, and federal employees for political purposes. Such misbehavior would have constituted felonies punishable by prison terms. But it being that the publicity-seeking, ultra-conservative Washington Legal Research Foundation was the source of the accusations should automatically have rendered them suspect, if not incredible. My accusers acted as if I were personally attempting to repeal the Constitution. They were supposedly angered by a published headline "disclosing" that the office of CBC-PAC was located on the sixth floor of a building with only five stories. It did not faze them in the least that the manager of the hotel was quoted in the accompanying newspaper article as explaining that suite number 600 was assigned only as a "mail drop" authorized for use by the CBC-PAC.

Julian Dixon, chairman of the CBC Foundation, scheduled a meeting of the foundation and requested that I respond to inquiries concerning activities of the CBC-PAC. Before the session was even held, six members of the Caucus demanded that their names be removed forthwith from the stationery of the PAC. One was so excited about his name being involved that he wrote two letters within twenty-four hours (one on his congressional stationery and one on his personal stationery) insisting that we remove his name at once, if not sooner. Three of those who acted in such an irrational, hostile manner were distinguished members of the legal profession. They did not even ask for my side of the controversy and did not allow for any possibility that I might be innocent. Presumption of innocence until proven guilty was not a consideration in this case. I had never heard such paltry, petty excuses advanced for rationalizing a decision to quit an organization.

Why six members of the Caucus chose to believe accusations made by individuals who opposed everything we represent continues to bewilder me. The Washington Legal Research Foundation lacks total credibility in our community. It is an ultra-conservative, right-wing group that distorts facts. We often joke that their version of one Biblical incident could very easily have Jonah swallowing the whale.

The hasty response of Caucus members to the accusations implied that the CBC-PAC was guilty of illegal activities, and this before the Federal Election Commission had investigated. One member, Gus Savage, was so chagrined that he wrote a letter to the chairman of the Black Caucus, which stated:

I am not associated in any way with YOUR Political Action Committee or Foundation, illegitimate and undemocratic enterprises with which I strongly disagree. Kindly instruct YOUR Congressional Black Caucus staff and CO-LEADERS to make it clear in any decisions they make, policies they adopt, and statements they publish to indicate my disassociation— unless I have been consulted and have stated specific agreement. Furthermore, kindly be notified that I am seriously considering filing a lawsuit challenging the unauthorized use of the name Congressional Black Caucus as associated with the Foundation and the Political Action Committee.[4]

Another Caucus member, Ronald Dellums, who usually displayed a militant disregard for reactionary bombast, surprisingly wrote, "The content of the [CBC-PAC] letter . . . contradict(s) my public position on political contributions. It is my hope that my request to have my name deleted as a member of the CBC-PAC will be expeditiously considered and honored."⁵

The other four were not so incensed or so rambunctious. They merely recommended abolishing the political action committee altogether. Of course, that advice was summarily rejected as I promptly removed their names from the stationery. The PAC was a little fractured but remained intact. While admitting to three very minor technical violations—unintentionally accepting less than $300 in corporate funds; failing to include the required disclaimer on a mail solicitation; and unintentionally failing to file a timely amendment reflecting a change in treasurer—we steadfastly denied that the violations were knowing and willful.

The PAC was assessed a civil penalty of $250 by the Federal Election Commission and the matter was closed.

THREATS OF RESIGNATION

The CBC-PAC was not the only CBC entity that Caucus members threatened to dissociate themselves from. Several months before the PAC incident, George Crockett of Michigan was offended because the chairman of the CBC Legislative Weekend activities did not reserve four tables at the annual dinner for large campaign contributors from his district. Like all other members, he had been informed of a deadline for remitting money so tickets could be allocated to those persons who had mailed in more than $400,000 and were awaiting confirmation. In a fit of anger, the congressman wrote a letter unceremoniously resigning from the Caucus. Four months later, he unceremoniously rejoined.

On prior occasions, several other members had also threatened to leave the organization. Parren Mitchell, peeved by Caucus members' disagreement with his brother Clarence, wrote a letter to all CBC members announcing he wanted no further dealings with the Caucus. Shortly thereafter he reconsidered and rejoined. The most comical resignation came from newly elected Gus Savage of Illinois, immediately following his swearing-in ceremony. In a letter dated early January 1981 and hand-carried to each Caucus member, he poetically informed us on that occasion and reiterated the same one year later:

As I indicated when I first arrived in Congress, I am and shall always be a member of the Congressional Black Caucus, at least in spirit and in action when I am in agreement with its other members. However, I was elected as one among equals, not to become a subordinate in some organizational hierarchy. I believe that we should have a convener not a leader, for we are all leaders—a federation, not an organization, for we all have organizations—a multiple force, not one spokesperson, because we are all spokespersons.[6]

He was sincerely of the opinion that his constituents did not wish him to subject his individuality or his leadership mandate to group approval, so he could not join the Caucus. Later, he reconsidered and joined—I imagine, after conferring with his constituents.

DISSENSION WITHIN THE BLACK COMMUNITY

A behind-the-scenes battle between the CBC and the president of the National Newspaper Publishers Association (NNPA) also became a point of contention. Dr. Carlton B. Goodlett, publisher of the *San Francisco Sun-Reporter*, communicated his great displeasure with the Caucus to other black publishers. He expressed in vivid terms his irritation with the CBC and other civil rights organizations, and threatened that the NNPA would not fully cooperate with any of them in the future.

In a letter to Louis Stokes, chairman of the CBC, Dr. Goodlett offered a brief review of CBC–NNPA relationships:

1. In June 1971, we welcomed a delegation from the Caucus to our Atlanta convention. Our convention was in session, and we could not attend in a body the first annual CBC dinner; a number of the publishers individually and organizationally endorsed and supported the dinner.
2. . . . The Congressional Black Caucus convened its emergency meeting of "National Black Leadership" on January 31, 1972. It did not invite to participate in this forum Garth Reeves, the president of NNPA; yet, our publishers supported wholeheartedly the National Black Political Convention in March 1972.
3. When the Gary Convention was held, this lack of planning involvement on the part of NNPA, an organization with a national constituency, was quite in evidence.
4. In early 1973, the CBC called approximately 350 black leaders to Washington to make an inventory of civil rights and to develop unity in the struggle against the abrasive and destructive policies of the present

national Republican administration; again, the president of NNPA, Garth Reeves, was not invited to attend this meeting until the eleventh hour, and only then at the prodding and urging on my part of California members of the Congressional Black Caucus.

5. Reports have come from individual NNPA papers that in the 1972 campaign the black press was in the main taken for granted by black members of Congress; while thousands of dollars were spent for their re-election campaigns, little or no money was spent for advertising in their local black newspapers.[7]

Dr. Goodlett was particularly peeved with Chairman Stokes, describing the relationship with him as "despicable and insulting." He alleged that he had called Stokes' office no less than five times, telexed communications to him, and still got no reply. Goodlett later admitted that due to faulty equipment Stokes might never have received his telex message, and Stokes said he had on several occasions attempted to return the telephone calls. Failure to invite the president of NNPA to the Gary Convention, which is what really prompted the verbal assault, was not the CBC's fault. No invitations were extended by the CBC because we did not control planning for the event and were not an official sponsor of the affair.

The controversy subsided considerably when members of the Caucus showered Dr. Goodlett with special attention in a deliberate effort to massage his fragile ego. That procedure was necessary in dealing with several other prima-donna black leaders.

Confrontation with the black press was not the only battle the Caucus fought with a black group. In the 1972 election for president, the CBC found it necessary to attack black entertainers and sports figures for attempting to create "a nice fellow" image of a bad fellow, President Richard Nixon.

The Nixon campaign committee enlisted the support of black superstars in the entertainment and sports world in their bid to re-elect the president. Sammy Davis, Jr., was seen on national television embracing the president in a big bear-hug. Soul singer James Brown and former professional football star Jim Brown toured the country promoting Nixon's candidacy. They cut radio tapes supporting his re-election that were beamed to black communities.

Caucus members considered these actions to be repugnant. Unlike black people who benefited personally from administration hand-outs—recipients of federal contracts and grants, presidential appointees, and employees of federally funded programs—black superstars had no debt to repay. Entertainers who did favors for a president known for his oppression of black people, and who themselves earned most of their income from the black community, could not be excused by the Caucus.

CBC Chairman Louis Stokes declared, "Sammy Davis, Jr., Lionel Hampton, James Brown, Johnny Mathis, and Jim Brown have been duped by . . . one of their greatest oppressors."[8]

Stanley S. Scott, a black assistant to White House Communications Director Herbert C. Klein, responded to Caucus criticism in a seven-page rebuttal, charging at one point, ". . . the attack by CBC on black artists and athletes was insulting, outrageous, and posturing hot air."[9]

His counterattack, however, was not sufficient to quiet the storm of emotionalism and resentment that roiled the black community. Accusing the Caucus of partisan political motivation rang hollow. Sammy Davis, Jr., was booed by thousands in attendance at the Reverend Jesse Jackson's Black Expo in Chicago. Singer James Brown was picketed when appearing at an engagement in Baltimore, Maryland.

John Wilkes, a high-ranking black in the Nixon administration, complained, "Man, we are catching hell in the black community because black Democrats are creating the impression that the president is anti-black."[10]

It was hardly necessary to create that impression. Nixon, by his words and deeds, had done an excellent job earning such a reputation.

Jet magazine reported that the picture they printed of Sammy Davis, Jr., hugging President Nixon had prompted the greatest reader response in the history of the magazine. Robert E. Johnson, executive editor, said he had received hundreds of letters, almost 100 percent against Davis, some written in bitter and vicious language.

In June 1975, an application for membership in the Congressional Black Caucus from Congressman Fortney ("Pete") Stark of the San Francisco area of northern California caused some disagreement among Caucus members. The white congressman represented a district only 2 percent black, but his voting record on issues relating to black people was identical to that of Caucus members. His request raised a question some CBC members wanted answered: Should whites with liberal credentials be admitted to the Congressional Black Caucus?

Debate over admitting whites was vigorous but civil. It caused the Caucus to re-evaluate its original decision to exclude all but black members from membership. After thoroughly examining all sides of the question, a formal vote was taken. The decision was to deny Stark's application and that of any other nonblack member of Congress.

The Caucus, while engaging in many internal squabbles, had developed a certain sophistication and pragmatic expertise. It was flexible enough to cope with differences and yet reach amiable compromises. It had been able, as Senator Ted Kennedy said at the 1980 Democratic Convention, "to take issues seriously, but never themselves too seriously."

AT ODDS WITH PRESIDENT CARTER

Although Congresswoman Chisholm's 1972 bid for the presidency posed a more serious threat to the continued existence of the Congressional Black Caucus than any previous bone of contention, the storm she aroused was minuscule in relation to what happened during President Jimmy Carter's 1980 campaign for re-election.

Infighting among members pushing for CBC endorsement of Carter's candidacy and those opposed to it created a chasm of serious proportion. Some were fanatical in their idolatry of the president and advocated giving him "carte blanche" access to the Caucus apparatus in his bid for re-election. Others were just as adamant in their determination to deny him such preferential treatment.

Never had members of the Caucus been so close to dissolving the organization as during this period. Sides were chosen and battle lines drawn; there was no middle ground. Some accused Carter of displaying a cavalier attitude toward important Caucus issues and of sneering at individual Caucus members. His CBC supporters were accused of conveniently overlooking Carter's broken promises because of substantial government contracts awarded to constituents in their congressional districts. Those in the middle, CBC members who felt neither extreme hatred nor unrestrained love for Carter, were displeased with him for what they saw as hypocritical positions on matters of grave interest to the black community and also for his contemptuous attitude toward the CBC as an organization.

The danger to the CBC's unified group leadership was serious. President Carter had alienated many members of the Caucus by going out of his way to snub them whenever possible; by advocating anti-poor, hard-line conservative fiscal and budgetary policies; by undermining essential provisions of the Hawkins-Humphrey Full Employment Act; by opposing the Martin Luther King, Jr., Holiday Bill; and by attempting to build a black power base independent of and in opposition to the Congressional Black Caucus.

By the time of the 1978 annual CBC Legislative Weekend dinner, it was apparent that the ballroom at the Washington Hilton Hotel, the biggest in the city, could not accommodate the number of persons who wanted to attend. For several years, more than $200,000 annually had been returned to persons seeking tickets through the mail for the sold-out affair. As chairman of the 1978 dinner, I decided to use a second hotel, equip it with interchangeable, piped-in cable television, and so enable dinner guests at both ballrooms to enjoy the same program.

In an effort to make the site of the newly selected hotel more acceptable to supporters who might have felt slighted by not being in the main ballroom at the Hilton Hotel, I scheduled the presence of half of the Caucus members at each hotel. In addition, the entertainment was equally divided, with superstars at both locations. Stevie Wonder was to perform at the Hilton; Natalie Cole and internationally acclaimed gospel singer Shirley Caesar were slated for the Shoreham ballroom. We invited President Carter to speak for fifteen minutes at the Shoreham and Senator Ted Kennedy to address the crowd briefly at the Hilton. Carter refused, demanding that he be presented at the Washington Hilton Hotel or not at all. The CBC acceded to his demand, but instead of honoring our request to limit his remarks to fifteen minutes, the president commandeered the microphone and performed for one hour and fifteen minutes.

Acknowledging dozens of celebrities in the audience and inviting several of them to join him on the stage conveyed the impression that the evening was being held in his honor and that the overhead expenses were being paid by the Presidential Re-election Campaign Committee. However, the extra charges, which amounted to $31,000 for overtime pay to stage hands, television technicians, waiters, cameramen, security personnel, and musicians in two first-class hotels, were paid for by the CBC, not Jimmy Carter's political action committee.

Relations between the Caucus and Carter, which were never harmonious, got worse after his performance at the dinner. It was not surprising, therefore, that the CBC's first Southern Regional Conference in Birmingham took on the flavor and aura of presidential politics. Congressman John Conyers announced on opening night that he was organizing a "dump President Jimmy Carter campaign." He told a local news reporter, "The facts are that President Carter has not lived up to his promise. He doubled-crossed us."[11]

Congressman Diggs characterized Conyers' remarks as "premature," and Congressman Harold Ford announced, "I'm emphatically against such a move. Furthermore, I'm a supporter of the president."[12]

Lawrence O. Haygood, chairman of the Macon County Commission, predicted, "Alabama was for Jimmy Carter in 1976. Alabama will be for Jimmy Carter in 1980."[13]

Ben Brown, deputy chairman of the Carter-Mondale re-election committee, announced that he was not particularly concerned about Conyers' remark: "I didn't come here to respond to Congressman Conyers' statement. We were coming anyway. But we're not at all surprised that he would make the statements he has made."[14]

But the debate intensified as several other members supported Conyers' position. Caucus Chairperson Cardiss Collins followed Conyers in attacking the Carter administration. "We have thrown down the gauntlet against the president's cuts in the domestic employment, education, and health programs," she said. "We are opposed to cutbacks in federal programs that assist our senior citizens and our youth."[15]

The harshness of the criticism leveled at Carter by members of the Caucus revealed the low esteem in which he was held by those of us who worked with his administration on a daily basis.

UN AMBASSADOR ANDREW YOUNG'S DISMISSAL

One incident that galled CBC members intensely was President Carter's cave-in to pressure from Jewish groups in the 1979 firing of former Caucus member Andrew Young as ambassador to the United Nations. This hypocritical action came just a few days before our annual dinner. Supposedly, Mr. Young was fired for meeting secretly with representatives of the Palestine Liberation Organization (PLO) without authority of the president.

Outraged by the affront, the Caucus voted a special award to be conferred upon Ambassador Young and invited him to be the principal speaker at the dinner. Carter supporters viewed our decision to invite Young instead of President Carter as a slap in the face of the president. If so, a majority of the Congressional Black Caucus sensed it was a slap well deserved and anticipated that our former colleague, now the former ambassador, would criticize Carter for deserting black interests by capitulating to the paranoid fears of American Jews.

Not all black leaders were as incensed as some in the Caucus with the Jewish organizations that had pressured President Carter to dismiss Young. Bayard Rustin, a long-time civil rights leader and head of the A. Phillip Randolph Institute, denied that Jewish lobbyists even had anything to do with the firing. Rustin had very close ties with the leadership of the AFL-CIO and with leaders in the Jewish community.

Fourteen months after Young's dismissal, in a speech given before 1,000 Jewish people at the Washington Hebrew Congregation, Rustin blamed Jimmy Carter instead of Andy Young for the meeting with Zehdi Labib Terzi, the PLO observer at the United Nations, and absolved Jews of any blame in Young's dismissal. In his explanation, however, Rustin was extremely critical of Ambassador Young, as well as of Walter Fauntroy, delegate of the District of Columbia, and Joseph Lowery, president of the Southern Christian Leadership Conference. He linked the resurgence of the Ku Klux Klan to Young, Fauntroy, and Lowery's giving respectability to a terrorist group.

On the other hand, he said,

> I did not like what Andrew Young did nor what Fauntroy did nor what Lowery did, but the basis for what they did did not lie with themselves but with the president of the United States, Jimmy Carter. . . . The Jewish community had absolutely nothing to do with Andy Young being thrown out. . . . If Jewish leaders had spoken out more critically of that battle, it would not have taken some of us in the black community three months before we had clarified it.[16]

Ambassador Young, however, disappointed those of us who thought he would denounce the president and those responsible for his termination. In his keynote address, he skirted the controversy by remaining silent about details leading up to his dismissal. He did, however, take aim at the recalcitrant position of Israeli officials and Jewish activists:

> The essence of the message we take to Jew and Palestinian alike is that . . . they should study war no more. [It was] "unfortunate" the Israeli government [decided] not to meet with a delegation from the Southern Christian Leadership Conference or with civil rights activist the Reverend Jesse Jackson, the Reverend Walter Fauntroy and the Reverend Lowery . . . after all, [Prime Minister Menachem Begin and other Israeli government officials] did meet with [former Prime Minister of South Africa] John Vorster.[17]

He added that both the Israelis and American Jews should realize that blacks had not forgotten the Holocaust or acts of terrorism against Israeli citizens. "But neither can we ignore the constant bombing of Palestinians in Lebanon."[18]

Many of us were puzzled by Young's failure to reveal the underhanded manner in which he had been treated. We knew that he was not the only high government official to have met with the PLO. We anticipated he would assail President Carter and Secretary of State Cyrus Vance for making him the scapegoat in their discredited policy dictum. Cardiss Collins, in remarks delivered at the dinner, was not as subtle in her criticism of President Carter as Ambassador Young: "The Caucus and its allies want to make clear that no politician can take black support for granted."[19]

But President Carter's strategists would not be outmaneuvered. Clarence Mitchell, Sr., pre-eminent civil rights leader, brother of Congressman Parren Mitchell, and honorary co-chairman of the CBC Dinner, chastised members of the Caucus in an angry tone of voice for not inviting the president: "If I had been consulted, I would like to make it clear, I would have opted for the president."[20]

When booed by many in the audience, Mitchell said, "I just want to make it clear that I never run away from that kind of conduct. And those who want to boo, boo to my face and I'll meet you in the alley."[21]

John Gunther Dean, ambassador to Lebanon under President Carter, later admitted holding meetings with senior PLO leaders during the same year that Young was discharged. When he retired from government in 1989, Dean said that between 1978 and 1981 he had been authorized on thirty-five separate occasions to meet with ranking PLO officials.

Cyrus Vance, who as secretary of state fired Ambassador Young, confirmed Dean's meetings but described them as different from Andrew Young's encounters. The Dean meetings, he said, were to discuss embassy security in Beirut and the release of U.S. hostages in Iran. "They were not a violation of the pledge made to Israel by Henry Kissinger in 1975 not to negotiate with the PLO until it recognized Israel's right to exist, since there were no political discussions and it was political discussions that were banned."[22]

1980—THE CBC STRUGGLE WITH PRESIDENT CARTER COMES TO A HEAD

The struggle between the CBC and President Carter did not subside after the Ambassador Young flap. In 1980, I was asked to chair the

Annual CBC Legislative Weekend dinner for the fourth time in seven years. As a condition of acceptance, I insisted on complete control of the program. The Caucus agreed to my request in a formal meeting.

That year Carter was challenged for the presidential nomination by Senator Edward Kennedy of Massachusetts. Carter's friends in the Caucus, black personnel on the White House staff, and black supporters in civil rights groups launched a campaign to secure the president's appearance on stage at the CBC dinner. I steadfastly held to my decision not to invite him, reiterating that the president had abused his previous invitation by ignoring our request to limit remarks to fifteen minutes. I cited his scornful action in refusing to address the crowd at an alternate hotel and his insistence on seeking out the Caucus only when that was beneficial to him.

Congressman Hawkins was furious that the CBC would even consider inviting a president who had sabotaged the Hawkins-Humphrey Full Employment Act and was recommending policies that relied on massive unemployment as a vehicle for lowering inflation. Hawkins could not forget that Carter's current budget postponed the Full Employment Act's unemployment target of 4 percent for two more years and the inflation target of 3 percent for another five years.

Other members of the Caucus had their own good reasons for not wanting to allow the president to use the annual CBC dinner as a sounding board to impress an elite corps of black opinion makers.

The 1980 primary contest between President Carter and Senator Ted Kennedy, which ended before the Caucus's annual dinner, was a rancorous one for black Democrats. During the Democratic Convention, Ron Dellums was briefly a candidate for the presidency, being nominated from the floor of the convention. In public statements following a brilliant speech before the delegates in which he declined to seek the nomination, Dellums reflected the lack of respect many black elected officials had for President Carter.

... Carter thinks he can out-Reagan Reagan. But I saw Reagan in California, and I can tell him that you don't beat Reagan unless you put up a positive alternative.

... Carter thinks he can take the right wing of the Democratic party and make it win by stretching it farther over to the Republicans.

... Carter is a fool if he thinks he doesn't need us. ...

... When I asked how Andrew Young could get up in New York and praise the president's record, Mrs. Dellums chimed in: "It's that Atlanta thing. Andy's incredibly loyal."

Yes, when Andy and I were at a black convention in Austin, Texas, I spoke at lunch and said publicly to Andy that his man had failed us. When Andy spoke that night at dinner, he said the truth was bitter, but that I was probably right. Yet he can go back and work for the man after admitting that.[23]

Caucus members were not alone in their criticism of the president. Other black leaders attacked him, including many of those who supported his programs. In 1980, a three-day conference of black leaders was held in Richmond, Virginia, to revise the national black agenda. It was a follow-up to the 1972 Gary, Indiana, convention, the 1974 Little Rock, Arkansas, conference, and the 1976 Charlotte, North Carolina, confab. Representatives from 300 black organizations were in attendance when Detroit Mayor Coleman Young announced that he was supporting Jimmy Carter for re-election. Most of them booed him loudly and continuously. Young became angry and attempted to justify his position by claiming that the city of Detroit had been revitalized because "Jimmy Carter" gave him money. The booing intensified.

Hostility toward Carter's stances on domestic issues resulted in bitter attacks against his administration. In a move to solidify support in black communities, the president invited influential black ministers in the key states of New Jersey, Pennsylvania, and Ohio to meet with him in the White House just prior to each state's primary.

Congressman Stokes, of Ohio's Twenty-first District, was so riled by Carter's attempt to manipulate black church leaders that he wrote 250 members of the Cleveland Baptist Ministers Conference attacking Carter's invitation to the White House as a blatant appeal to win votes.

. . . In the event that you plan to attend this meeting, I would just like to share some concerns with you. . . . In 1976, the black ministers of this city were very instrumental in Mr. Carter's election. All of you worked . . . and as a result of it, he received 95 percent of the black vote in the Twenty-first Congressional District.

It is important for you to realize Mr. Carter has not been back to Cleveland since October 1976, when he stood next to me on a stage at Olivette Institutional Baptist Church and made a lot of unkept promises.

In 1980, with high unemployment, automotive layoffs and new plant closings being announced daily, the plight of black people in Cleveland is worsening. It is very important that Mr. Carter realize that a community which gave him 95 percent of the vote had a right to expect him to keep his promises.

. . . I hope you will give some serious thought to the fact that it is President Carter who has just sent to Congress his balanced budget for fiscal year 1981, which has over $16 billion in cuts in programs such as CETA, nutrition, food stamps, school lunch programs, LEAA, health, education, and Counter Cyclical Aid for cities. It is a budget which the Congressional Black Caucus has described as an "unmitigated" disaster for minorities, the poor, and the disadvantaged.

. . . the decontrol of oil; imposing an additional fee of 10 cents per gallon on gas; failure to use the Humphrey-Hawkins Bill to reduce unemployment and inflation; . . . he is the first president in history to deliberately induce a recession.[24]

Some Caucus members seemed comfortably tucked into the inner recesses of the administration by virtue of their personal relationships with the president and his staff. Others were impressed by the number of black judges Carter had named to the federal bench, especially in southern districts—he had appointed more black judges than any previous president, by far. These supporters insisted, indeed several demanded, that the president be invited to address the CBC dinner participants. They argued that the CBC could not afford to reject an outreach from a "sitting" president of the United States. Carter, encouraged by them, wrote a letter asking to be invited. Others countered by observing that if either Presidents Nixon or Ford had requested the same, the CBC would summarily have denied both "sitting" presidents an invitation.

Friends and supporters of the Caucus from organized labor, black fraternal organizations, and civil rights groups lobbied those of us who opposed the invitation. They premised their case on "how good Carter had been to black folk." But that was *their* perception, not ours. Their arguments were not persuasive enough to dispel unfavorable memories of past events most of us had personally experienced.

The confrontation with President Carter and his black support team in his 1980 campaign for re-election was not very different from what it had been during his entire term of office: constant battle. On Friday evening, twenty-four hours before the scheduled 1980 dinner, black staffers from the White House informed us that, invited or not, the president was going to attend the function. They insisted that under the circumstances, the Caucus was powerless to prevent him. And they almost made good on their threat, even after the Caucus in a formal vote reaffirmed the decision not to invite Carter.

President Carter hurriedly arranged a special reception at the White

House for the next morning (Saturday) in behalf of Chairperson Cardiss Collins, showering her with praise and presenting her with roses. It was an apparent move to persuade the Caucus to rescind its decision. It, too, failed to change our minds.

That Saturday afternoon, Secret Service agents appeared at the Hilton Hotel and started making security checks in anticipation of the president's arrival. They brought in dogs to sniff for explosives. Jimmy Carter and his Georgia henchmen were determined to ignore the wishes of the black elected officials who were sponsoring this private function in a private hotel.

I, as dinner chairman, informed Carter's chief supporter in the Caucus that I was prepared to pull the plug from the microphone the minute Jimmy set foot on our stage. At that point, Carter's black supporters, aware of my relish for confrontation, knew the seriousness of the situation.

Fortunately, the president decided not to attend, thus avoiding what surely would have been a confrontation nasty enough possibly to bring on the dissolution of the Congressional Black Caucus. For some members of the Caucus readily admit that they were prepared to dissociate from the group over the decision not to invite this white man from Plains, Georgia, to address 3,000 black leaders.

The issue did not end with the president's decision not to attend. That night Cardiss Collins delivered an address at the dinner calling for extreme militance in pursuit of the goals of the black agenda. "We are indisputably the group in America that's the 'razor's edge,'" she had said at one point the year before.[25] This time she went on to say that those who possessed an arrogance of power (a direct reference to Mr. Carter) must not be rewarded for deserting those who had put them in power. A cheering crowd leaped to its feet.

Although Jimmy Carter did not show up for the engagement, all of his top emissaries were in the audience: Hamilton Jordan, Anne Wexler, Sarah Wellington, James McIntyre, Frank Moore, and Evan Dobelle. These were the very advisers who had caused the rift between Carter and the Congressional Black Caucus. Jordan was quoted in one of the daily newspapers as saying, "We've always supported the Black Caucus." That is the same Mr. Jordan who refused to return calls from members of the Caucus and who orchestrated the defeat of the Martin Luther King Holiday Bill in the U.S. House of Representatives.

Regardless of disagreements among Caucus members, despite opposition of white liberals, despite efforts by power forces within the Democratic party and the media to play down and denigrate the significance of black members of Congress, the CBC has an undeniable strength playing a role in shaping national policy. The heart and soul of Ossie Davis's plan is the Congressional Black Caucus' only raison d'être.

NOTES

1. Marguerite Ross-Barnett, *NAACP Crisis* magazine, April 1981, page 119.
2. *The Chicago Tribune*, May 24, 1991, section 1, page 18.
3. Letter from Congressmen Conyers, Dellums, and Hayes to Congressman Stokes, chairman of the CBC Foundation, September 29, 1983.
4. Letter from Congressman Gus Savage to the chairman of the Congressional Black Caucus, March 24, 1982.
5. Letter from Congressman Ronald Dellums to Congressman William Clay, chairman of the CBC-PAC, May 3, 1982.
6. Letter from Congressman Gus Savage to Congressional Black Caucus members, January 1981, cited in his letter of March 24, 1982.
7. Letter from Dr. Carlton B. Goodlett to Congressman Louis Stokes, August 8, 1973.
8. Congressman Louis Stokes, press release, October 1972.
9. *The New York Times*, October 26, 1972, page 34.
10. *The New York Times*, October 17, 1972, page 29.
11. *Birmingham News*, May 26, 1979, page 1.
12. *Ibid.*
13. *Ibid.*
14. *Ibid.*
15. *Ibid.*
16. Bayard Rustin, *The Washington Post*, October 10, 1980.
17. Cited by Betty Anne Williams of the Associated Press, September 23, 1979.
18. *Ibid.*
19. *Ibid.*
20. *Ibid.*
21. *The Washington Post*, September, 24, 1979, page B12.
22. *The Washington Post*, June 4, 1989, page B1.
23. Quoted by Garry Wills, *The Washington Star*, August 22, 1980, page A7.
24. Letter from Congressman Stokes to ministers in Cleveland, Ohio, April 1980.
25. Congresswoman Collins, cited by Jacqueline Trescott and Elizabeth Bumiller, "The Raucous Caucus," *The Washington Post*, September 24, 1979, page B1.

14

A Conspiracy to Silence Dissent

Robert Maynard Hutchins, former president of the University of Chicago, describes democracy as "the only form of government that is founded on the dignity of man, not the dignity of some men, of rich men, or educated men, or of white men. Its sanction is not the sanction of force, but the sanction of human nature."[1]

Such delicate language and lofty terms explaining the phenomenon of democracy do not conform with the hard, brutal reality of life in America. No matter how much dignity poor, uneducated, nonwhite people possess, the system they live within invariably acts to defeat their efforts to improve their condition. Those who advocate radical economic, social, and political change do so at great risk, no matter how meritorious their ideas and actions. No matter how incorrect the positions and unjust the decisions of rich, educated white men, for a black person to take issue with them is to ask for trouble.

Merely advocating the constitutional right of free speech and free assembly often subjects the advocate to harassment, abuse, discredit, and jail. A government supposedly composed "of the people, by the people, and for the people" more times than not shows itself to be "of the privileged, by the few, and for the powerful." A distorted sense of self-worth justifies for the privileged an unlimited array of personal entitlements. Too many of them believe their actions cannot be limited by legal and constitutional constraints. Historically, this elitist group has assumed for itself the singular prerogative to suppress ideas by oppressing the idealists.

Evidence documents the role played by agents of federal, state, and local governments intervening on behalf of powerful people, giving the "silk stocking" element an unfair edge over rank-and-file taxpayers. When it comes to repressing the rights of workers and minorities, criminal acts of official misconduct constitute the rule rather than the exception in America's system of jurisprudence. Mayors, governors, congressmen, presidents, and prosecutors have abused the powers of office with impunity while trampling on the civil liberties and human rights of the dispossessed and unorganized.

State and federal court judges have repeatedly sanctioned the illegal behavior of economically and politically empowered individuals in their desecration of the rights of minorities and workers; legislative bodies have enacted laws favoring the rich and famous; and prosecutors have prostituted their offices to protect the aristocracy.

Industrial tycoons corrupted the instruments of government in the late nineteenth and early twentieth centuries for the purpose of maximizing their profits. They unscrupulously divided laborers into warring factions: pitting white against black, men against women, native-born against immigrants, children against parents. They established a four-tiered wage scale: one for the white native-born, which was slightly more than that paid to black workers; a third one for immigrants, which was slightly less than that paid to blacks; and a fourth one for children, which was one-half that paid to adults in all of the categories.

Our system of government aided and abetted these corporate vipers in their drive to industrialize this nation at any cost. Treatment of workers attempting to organize for the purpose of collective bargaining in the railroad, coal, and meat packing industries reveals a pattern of silencing those who protested the exploitive policies of rugged, individualistic business magnates.

Those brave enough, frustrated enough, or stupid enough to challenge the "divine right" of the Rockefellers, Carnegies, Vanderbilts, and Mellons were exposed to barbaric acts of brutal retaliation, even while exercising their legal rights. The reign of terror visited upon them was sanctioned by government officials and inflicted, for the most part, in a state of official lawlessness.

Pinkerton guards were hired to break strikes by breaking the heads of strikers. Newspapers owned by or in cahoots with major corporations reported only the illegal acts engaged in or alleged to have been engaged in by striking workers. Local police, politically subservient to corporate interests, ignored the violence inflicted upon strikers. Local prosecutors and judges, usually on the payroll of big businesses or indebted to them for their appointments to public office, only intervened when workers violently fought back. Governors and presidents called out the militia to break legitimate, legal strikes.

Today, the same tactics, somewhat moderated and much more sophisticated, are still employed to permit a privileged class to operate above the law. Injunctive power is used by the courts to break strikes effectively and destroy labor unions. When imposing this discretionary provision of law, judicial gigolos express grave concern for "the health and safety" of the community. Then these robed pimps proceed to break strikes or seriously cripple their effectiveness by issuing indecent opinions favoring management at the expense of workers.

Once an injunction is disobeyed, in many cases only allegedly disobeyed, the company becomes the exclusive beneficiary of court protection. The issue then shifts to one of respect for the dignity of the court and the majesty of the judge. Under this guise, union leaders are arrested, held in contempt, and sentenced to harsh jail terms, while their local organizations are assessed huge fines. Entire union treasuries have been confiscated by courts as "fitting" punishment for violating what, in many cases, are highly questionable court injunctions.

THE PATTERN OF OFFICIAL CONSPIRACY AGAINST BLACK ELECTED OFFICIALS

If the consortium of American economic and political powers can be said to have honed their pruning hooks on union leaders and cut their wisdom teeth in disabling the labor movement, it's clear they perfected those perverted skills in harassing black leaders and frustrating the legitimate aims of the civil rights movement. In recent years, a combination of government officials, elements of the media, and influential political personalities have joined forces for the purpose of intensifying their efforts to stymie those promoting the advancement of racial and economic justice. They have plotted and schemed to silence those who were spearheading the drive to reach these ends.

Passage of the 1965 Voting Rights Act allowed blacks to register in large numbers and enabled them to win many elected positions. Most of those who opposed extending these rights did not then and have not now accepted the Voting Rights Act as legally binding. Reactionary forces have conspired to orchestrate a reign of terror against black professionals, black elected and appointed officials, and black leaders in the business and religious communities. The campaign has taken on the aspect of nullifying the import of the Voting Rights Act.

A favorite tactic for denying black citizens equitable representation in elected government is the annexing of adjacent all-white communities into towns about to gain black majorities. Another gimmick for forestalling governance by blacks is gerrymandering legislative districts to diminish the impact of large blocs of black voters. Elections in which candidates are required to run at-large (instead of in districts) or to enter second primaries where the two top vote-getters face each other in run-offs are promoted to limit the election of blacks in districts that are more than 40 percent but less than 50 percent black.

Equally devastating to a meaningful black political presence is a grandiose strategy pursued by law enforcement personnel and the news media to indict and convict black elected officials indiscriminately. During the Nixon presidential years, we were singled out on a massive scale for a special kind of illegal attention.

The most common tactic used to ruin careers of outspoken black officeholders was to undertake a series of probes into their political and personal lives. So-called "investigative reporters" working for major news journals, using information secretly supplied by government officials, wrote outlandish articles purporting to be factual exposés of criminal activity. These highly suspicious, inflammatory allegations, in most cases outright perversions of truth, then became the basis for official government investigations by the FBI, the Drug Enforcement Administration, the Internal Revenue Service, federal criminal task forces, and postal inspectors.

After months of attacks in the daily press, quoting unnamed sources and citing leaks of grand jury testimony, with millions of libelous words printed and aired by hundreds of news organs, the frivolous charges were usually unceremoniously dropped for lack of evidence. But by then real damage was often done—a promising career halted in its tracks and/or destroyed; character, reputation, and integrity irremediably tarnished. Thus the conspirators succeeded in diluting the credibility and influence of many black leaders without producing any substantive proof of wrongdoing.

Seldom were those accused or indicted ever convicted. But even after the dismissal of charges for lack of evidence or through exoneration by juries, the press and prosecutors continued to wage a war of verbal retribution. Every news story thereafter alluded to the unproven charges.

The cases involving black officials, accused in numbers grossly disproportionate to their representation in public office and selected by overzealous prosecutors for special attention, must not be viewed as a series of incidents occurring only in isolated areas. They must be analyzed with respect to pervasive national implications and viewed exactly for what they represent—a conspiracy among reactionary elements calculated to undermine, humiliate, jail, and destroy black leaders who dared challenge a repressive and unresponsive racist society.

HARASSMENT OF BLACK STATE LEADERS

So endemic was the harassment of black leaders between 1970 and 1975 that only a few escaped the heavy hand of government scrutiny. Those who spoke out against racial injustices were hauled before grand juries on trumped-up charges, audited by the Internal Revenue Service, or slandered by scurrilous newspaper attacks. After excessive publicity alleging involvement in criminal activities, the burden of proof invariably switched from the prosecution to the accused.

George L. Brown, former lieutenant governor of Colorado, poignantly summarized the situation in a 1975 speech delivered at the annual conference of the National Association of Human Rights Workers:

> I am particularly disturbed when I examine what's happening to black and brown political leadership, black and brown professionals, black religious leaders, black business people. And I know for certain that if black leaders and brown leaders are harassed and discredited to where they fall, then poor whites—and even, then, Middle America—aren't far behind. . . . I can tell you for a certainty that the list of the fallen black leaders is growing, and that there are some folks in this nation who are rejoicing because of it.[2]

Lt. Governor Brown was eminently correct in his assessment of the situation and personally knowledgeable in this subject. He, too, had suffered character assassination and personal humiliation at the hands of government representatives. He, too, was the victim of press exaggeration and media sensationalism. In his case, the simple matter of following long-established state accounting procedures for filing personal expense vouchers and then being reimbursed resulted in two years of malicious attacks and bitter recriminations by racist elements influencing politics in Colorado.

Governor Richard Lamm, a fellow Democrat, instructed the state attorney general to impanel a grand jury to investigate the allegations, reacting solely to newspaper accusations, without first consulting Brown and asking for his side of the story. Illegal leaks from the attorney general's office appearing almost daily in the press created a lynch-type public atmosphere for the black statewide elected official.

After months of rumors and speculation, after numerous demands for impeachment, after hundreds of derogatory news articles, the grand jury, overwhelmed by the lack of substantive evidence and unimpressed by this flagrant attempt at selective prosecution, concluded that Brown had done no more than follow standard procedure for all Colorado state officials.

The grand jury further noted, when refusing to issue an indictment, that the governor, the chief justice of the Colorado Supreme Court, and even the attorney general himself were engaging in the same practice. How ludicrous that only Lt. Governor Brown, a black man, was accused, prosecuted, and persecuted for using an accounting system developed and imposed by his predecessors, white Democrats.

What the media that attacked Brown over this issue deliberately ignored was that six months after taking office and long before the press made its accusations, Brown had stopped using the established accounting procedure, which was authorized by law, and publicly recommended that other state officials also discontinue the practice.

Mervyn M. Dymally of California, the only other black lieutenant governor at the time, suffered similar treatment. The attack on him was waged over a longer period of time, was more sustained, and involved an assailant with much greater financial resources. A study of his trials and tribulations clearly demonstrates how law enforcement agents and members of the media exceeded all bounds of moral decency and legal propriety.

For approximately sixteen years, the *Los Angeles Times* crusaded against Dymally in an unprecedented and vitriolic fashion.

In 1978, Dymally's opponent for lieutenant governor accused him of illegally diverting campaign funds for personal use, of perjury, of criminal acts in regard to state health care contracts, and of conflict of interest involving a personal business transaction. *The Los Angeles Times* printed each of the allegations prominently, with large headlines to emphasize the seriousness of the charges. The news articles were usually followed by editorials disparaging the integrity of Lt. Governor Dymally and implying the allegations were factual. Not once did the newspaper mention that the same charges had surfaced years earlier and been dismissed for lack of merit by the Los Angeles district attorney's office and by the Sacramento County district attorney. Not once did the paper print Merv Dymally's statements of denial or rebuttals to any of the accusations.

While the media was hammering away at Dymally, law enforcement authorities were contributing their scurrilous bit to the campaign of smear and smut. The FBI tried unsuccessfully to place an undercover agent on Dymally's official payroll. The Internal Revenue Service audited his tax returns for three consecutive years to find only a minor discrepancy resulting in a small payment of an additional $6.00 in taxes.

Actually, Dymally was requested to pay taxes on his official per diem, which was not demanded of any other elected state official. In another audit, Dymally received a refund because he was found to have overpaid his taxes by $8,900.00. Dymally's home telephones in Los Angeles and Sacramento were tapped without court approval, and his state offices in both locations were illegally wired by government agents.

Two weeks before the 1978 general election, a California deputy attorney general leaked false information to CBS affiliate KCBS-TV that the lieutenant governor and his campaign chairman were about to be indicted by a federal grand jury. The CBS affiliate reported the leaked information in a special broadcast, even though the memo to them stated the information was a rumor.

After lengthy litigation, CBS and the attorney general apologized to Dymally's white campaign chairman, but not to Dymally. In fact, in a strange turn of events, the deputy attorney general sued Dymally for charging he'd broken a California law making it a crime to leak false information about anyone who is under investigation.

The list of black leaders accused of criminal acts, thoroughly investigated by governmental agencies, vilified in the media, and finally exonerated is as long as it is deplorable. Hundreds of black leaders have suffered this kind of humiliation. Georgia State Senator Leroy Johnson was accused of criminally evading income taxes and acquitted. C. Delores Tucker, secretary of state of Pennsylvania, was accused of misusing state travel funds and cleared of all charges. Michigan Secretary of State Richard Austin was accused of soliciting illegal campaign contributions, but no charges were filed. Leon Ralph, a California assemblyman, had his telephones tapped and his office burglarized by FBI agents and was under surveillance for six years, but no indictment was ever issued. Mississippi State Representative

Thomas Reed was indicted on a felony charge of bribery. His first two trials ended in mistrials; the third trial ended in his conviction on a misdemeanor. Georgia State Representative Hosea Williams was indicted on a felony charge as a "habitual offender" resulting from numerous traffic citations, but after thirty hours of jury deliberations, he was acquitted. William Hart, Sr., mayor of East Orange, New Jersey, was indicted for misconduct in office and bribery but was acquitted. David Cunningham, city councilman for Los Angeles, was sued for denying a person's civil rights, but the charges were dropped. Pierre Hollingsworth, city commissioner of Atlantic City, New Jersey, was accused of violating state election laws, but a grand jury refused to issue an indictment.

The names of black officials who have been attacked, smeared, investigated, and indicted flow like the mighty waters of the Mississippi River—endlessly. More than 100 black elected officials were subjected to this kind of official tyranny from 1969 to 1975, only to be found unindictable, acquitted, or exonerated. Several hundred more were so maliciously slandered they either decided against seeking re-election or were defeated.

Apologists for such abusive misuse of government power ask, since no evidence of wrongdoing was uncovered, why all the fuss? That is precisely the point. First, no grounds existed to give probable cause for investigation of wrongdoing. Second, why should Dymally and more than 100 other black citizens be forced to spend thousands and thousands of dollars to defend themselves against false allegations of crime invented by corrupt white public officials and degenerate media people?

HARASSMENT OF CBC MEMBERS

Members of the Congressional Black Caucus were by no means immune from vicious press assaults and intrusive government actions. Harassment by the press and agents of government was exposed in cases of black members of Congress when various records were made available through the courts and the Freedom of Information Act.

Congressman Ralph Metcalfe

When Representative Ralph Metcalfe of Illinois launched a campaign against the Chicago Police Department for widespread acts of brutality against black citizens and broke off relations with Mayor Richard Daley's political machine over the issue, he was singled out for intimidation and recrimination. Six years after his election to Congress, Metcalfe faced federal charges in a criminal indictment.

Amid great public fanfare, Metcalfe, in the middle of a tough 1975 political campaign for re-election against a candidate hand-picked by Daley, was indicted by the Internal Revenue Service. The government charged that ten years earlier, he had accepted bribes and kickbacks and failed to report them as taxable income while serving as the city councilman chairing the aldermanic zoning committee.

The indictment supposedly resulted from intensive investigations by the FBI, the IRS, and the U.S. attorney's office in Chicago. The citizen outcry from across the country against the preposterous charges led federal prosecutor Sam Skinner to drop all charges a few days before the election. He contended that the statute of limitations had expired. That excuse was as plausible as any, but indicative of the racist politics played against black elected officials by U.S. attorneys nationwide. Skinner knew when first seeking the indictment that the statute of limitations had already expired. If not, he should have been dismissed for incompetence or malfeasance or both.

Congressman Metcalfe's legal problems resulted primarily from two factors: First, he was black. Second, he dared to challenge the racist rule of Mayor Richard Daley. Of course, there are those who never see racism as a factor in any confrontation between whites and blacks. Falling into this category are those who later wrote news stories and editorials admitting Mayor Daley's unsavory role in securing the indictment, but also condoning his retaliatory action against Metcalfe as justifiable from a political point of view. The Chicago daily newspapers stipulated that the mayor was motivated by a legitimate desire to preserve a political system based on loyalty and fidelity. The offender's ethnic origin, according to them, was of secondary concern to the mayor. What these scribes conveniently overlooked was that just two years earlier, Democratic Alderman Edward Vrdolyak, a white political underling of Daley, had run for Cook County assessor in opposition to Daley's handpicked candidate, but there was never any attempt to punish him for disloyalty or for infidelity. Another Daley organization man of many years, Democratic Alderman and Committeeman Vito Marzullo, supported Republican Richard Milhous Nixon for re-election to the presidency in 1972, and Daley never extracted any punishment for violation of party loyalty. If two blond, blue-eyed, Democrats could violate long-established political principles and go unpunished, then Metcalfe's chastisement clearly had something to do with his large lips, kinky hair, and dark skin.

Crimes of Investigation

The indictment of Ralph Metcalfe may have puzzled some well-meaning whites. But history often repeats itself, and those of us familiar with the historical oppression of black militants were not surprised in the least. Some of us recalled the case of another black, Robert Smalls, a Republican congressman from South Carolina.

In 1877, Congressman Smalls launched a campaign to assure an "honest ballot" in the state of South Carolina and lambasted state officials for depriving blacks of their political and economic rights. Shortly thereafter, he was convicted in state court of having accepted a $5,000 bribe seven years earlier, while a member of the state senate. He was jailed for a brief period of time but was pardoned by the Democratic governor, who extracted a very unusual concession. The United States district attorney for the state of South Carolina was forced to give assurance that white Democrats accused of intimidating black voters and denying them the right to vote in Representative Smalls' previous election would not be prosecuted.

At least seven other members of the Congressional Black Caucus were illegally denied their right to privacy, maligned in character, and embarrassed by public announcements of groundless criminal charges as a result of media and government harassment. Four of them were victims of flagrant, admitted violations of rights.

Police state–type government lawlessness ran the gamut in their cases. Congressman John Conyers' Capitol Hill offices were illegally bugged by the FBI and CIA. Neither agency obtained a court order for such obtrusive activity because no "probable cause" existed for one to be issued. And when their illegal misconduct became public knowledge, both admitted their transgressions, but no official action was ever taken against those responsible for violating the law.

Congressman Ron Dellums was a logical victim for repressive governmental actions. He arrived in Congress representing the voice of protest against the immoral war in Southeast Asia, effectively exposing U.S. war crimes in Vietnam through a series of ad hoc committee hearings, and poetically imputing the racist motivations of President Nixon and Vice President Spiro Agnew.

It was only a matter of time before those in high government position retaliated against him. Telephones in his congressional offices and home were tapped without court orders. His California office was burglarized on two occasions, with only a few papers found to be missing. Electronic bugs were found in his home in Washington, D.C., and the telephone company admitted that his calls were routinely monitored.

Congressman Parren Mitchell

Prior to being elected to Congress, Parren Mitchell had been labeled an activist because he constantly and publicly challenged police brutality and other manifestations of racism. After election to Congress, he continued his activism.

Then, for a period of five years, he was followed and harassed repeatedly by state and local police. When returning nightly to Baltimore following congressional sessions, two or three police cars were always parked in front of or close to his home. They always contended that their mission was to protect the congressman.

At a public hearing on the nomination of then Baltimore Police Commissioner Donald C. Pomerleau for a second term, the question of police harassment of Mitchell was raised. The commissioner's somewhat sarcastic response was that because of the many death threats against the congressman, it was his duty to keep him under constant surveillance.

Congressman Mitchell was an effective opponent of the war in Vietnam and of the military draft. He frequently spoke at anti-war rallies and participated in anti-draft protests. In 1972, he came into possession of draft records stolen from Media, Pennsylvania. After photocopying them, he called the FBI. In surrendering the documents, he informed the agents that a copy was placed in the safe of his congressional office. Only two people knew the combination to that safe, Mitchell and his office manager. Mysteriously, the copy disappeared.

Evidence of illegal wiretapping and burglaries in his office and home subsequently came to light. Yet, these criminal acts on the part of federal, state, and local police authorities were never pursued or prosecuted.

Congressman William Clay

Not many elected officials, black or white, have suffered harassment, humiliation, or intimidation to the degree and extent that I have.

The campaign of official lawlessness directed toward me included all the tactics employed in a police state. Certain elements of the media, the business community, the judiciary, and the Justice Department engaged in a concerted effort to deny me re-election; to publicly ridicule and embarrass me; and, most of all, to send me to the penitentiary. I became the victim of:

Biased reporting, printing of false accusations, and obscene coverage by the white communications media

Harassment of family members, friends, and political associates by the Internal Revenue Service, the FBI, and the Drug Enforcement Agency, and the U.S. attorney

Release of false information by government agents and illegal surveillance by local and federal police

Illegal wiretapping, including the bugging of my home and office

Tax audits by the Internal Revenue Service for criminal violations

A suit by the Justice Department for allegedly falsified travel records

Grand jury investigations for payroll padding

FBI inquiry for unreported campaign contributions

Two attempts in ten years to gerrymander the district I represent (Both times the federal courts established boundaries that made it possible for a black to be elected.)

The purging of rolls in my congressional district of almost 20,000 black voters three days before a hotly contested election with a white candidate

In the last instance, a court injunction I solicited was granted to keep the polls open five hours past the usual closing time. Eligible voters who had arbitrarily and capriciously been stricken by the election board in an attempt to assist my white opponent were allowed to cast their ballots upon presenting utility bills or other documents showing residency.

Over a period of four years, I experienced grand jury investigations of my office payroll and for income tax evasion, FBI inquiries into my campaign contributions, Justice Department and Drug Enforcement Agency probes into my alleged drug trafficking, and examinations of my travel vouchers by the Public Integrity Section of the Justice Department. All found that *I had done absolutely nothing wrong.*

Mary R. (Warner) Sawyer, chairperson of the Committee on the Status of Minority Elected Officials, National Association of Human

Rights Workers, wrote the following summary of my harassment in a scholarly report titled "The Dilemma of Black Politics."

INGREDIENTS OF TYRANNY

"Not since Adam Clayton Powell has a black legislator been the focus of such controversy and investigation as faces William L. Clay."
—*St. Louis American*, April 8, 1976

"There are signs that those close to Clay are fed up, and that those who unthinkingly have given him blind support in the past know that they have been singularly unrepresented by the self-serving congressional charlatan. Clay enjoys the lifestyle of an emperor while vast portions of his district lie in ruins. Through his neglect of important business and his nonattendance in general, Clay has failed to represent the people of his district. Because of his early record as a black militant, Clay has considered himself untouchable. At heart he is a reverse racist who attacks and undermines the constructive forces in the community while falsely claiming that all who oppose him do so out of bigotry."
—*St. Louis Globe-Democrat*, March 13, 1975

". . . We recommend the re-election of Representative Clay, Democrat, in the First District. In his four terms, Clay has compiled a solidly progressive record; he is the only major candidate in the four congressional races unafraid to describe himself as a liberal. Mr. Clay's office, to be sure, has not been without scandal. . . . But that issue has not been decided against the representative, and on his legislative record, we recommend Mr. Clay over his Republican opponent, Robert L. Witherspoon, a decent man with an honorable civil rights record, but who would be unlikely to adequately represent the needs of the First [Congressional District]."
—*St. Louis Post-Dispatch*, October 26, 1976

The diverse opinions reflected in these comments from three different St. Louis newspapers argue strongly that attacks on black officials are waged more on the battleground of perception than on the basis of truth or fact. The expressions of the perceptions held of Bill Clay by the *St. Louis Globe-Democrat* and various governmental agencies reflect more than untruths and falsehoods, they are highly suggestive of tyranny.

It does, indeed, appear to be the case that no black official since Adam Clayton Powell has been so maligned as Congressman William Clay. Perhaps no other official has spoken out so pointedly and firmly to fight the attack being waged. No other official evidences so clearly the syndrome of "guilty until proven innocent"—and the near impossibility of clearing away the cloud of doubt once it has settled in. No other case so attests to the power of the media and the misuse of power by the federal government—and to the limited resources for fighting back.

Congressman Clay is among those who have spoken out publicly, charging a national conspiracy to undermine and eliminate outspoken black leadership. He argues that those who consider the charge of national conspiracy against black elected officials as silly must explain why 50 percent of all blacks in the U.S. House of Representatives are under investigation for criminal activity and not 50 percent of the white representatives. Certainly, they are not contending that black members as a group are more criminally inclined, less principled, more corrupt, less moral?

. . . Now in his fifth term as a U.S. Representative, Clay served previously for six years as a member of the St. Louis City Council. He was, as well, an active participant in the civil rights movement in the St. Louis community—and he traces the impetus for the assaults on him now to that involvement. "I think," he says, "the fact that I was on Nixon's enemy list had something to do with the decisions of federal agencies to attempt to destroy me. The other problem is that I was among the leaders of the civil rights movement in this town for some fifteen years, and I alienated all the important forces in the power structure. There is a great deal of hostility on their part toward me. I know that I am hated in certain circles by people who have the power and influence in the city—including the white business community."

. . . Having located the sources of attacks and the motivation for attacks, Congressman Clay recites at length the specifics of the tactics employed against him.

. . . He speaks, for example, of the "tremendous amount of intimidation and embarrassment" to which he has been subjected as a result of incidents such as one which occurred in 1974. The day before the 1974 election, a photograph of Clay with two other individuals, who had long criminal records, was printed in the *Globe-Democrat* with the caption "Hoodlum Associates of Congressman Clay," and with a lengthy endorsement of Clay's opponent. The implication was that hoodlums were involved in attempting to get Clay re-elected to office. The facts were that the photo, along with some 400 others, had been taken seven years previously at an annual 26th Ward Christmas party by a commercial photographer retained as a fund-raising device; that one of the individuals in the photo had been dead for three years, and the other had been in prison for the past two years.

This incident is typical of the effort on the part of the local media to smear Clay's reputation and defeat his re-election bids. However, as Clay points out, the "war that the *Globe-Democrat* has waged against me in an attempt to destroy my credibility and effectiveness as a leader did not start in 1974; it has been fifteen years in duration. But the war was bolstered that year when the conspiracy spread to include the Drug Enforcement Administration, the U.S. Department of Justice, the FBI, and the Internal Revenue Service."

In mid-1974, Clay began hearing rumors that his name was going to be introduced in a narcotics trial. He began writing letters of inquiry to the U.S. Attorney General, seeking to forestall such an action. But on December 10, 1974, a brief submitted in federal court by the St. Louis Task Force on Crime did, in fact, contain the name of a William Clay. In his opening statement, the chief prosecutor of the Crime Task Force, Liam Coonan, announced that he would prove, among other things, that William Clay had met with an undercover agent and arranged to sell narcotics to the agent. Within hours, the St. Louis papers carried banner headlines that Congressman Clay was allegedly involved in narcotics. The balance of the article detailed the case against the defendant, former Missouri Representative John Conley, Jr. But the headline was reserved for Congressman Clay.

"How they [the *Globe-Democrat*] assumed that the William Clay mentioned in the brief and Congressman Clay were one and the same," observes Clay, "was beyond me. . . . But there's no doubt that the Special Task Force prosecutor was referring to me, because in subsequent statements he issued, he made it clear that he was talking about Congressman Clay. Furthermore, a high-level official of the Department of Justice, in response to my letter of complaint, claimed that he had documented evidence that I was the William Clay referred to in the trial and that I had been involved in the illicit traffic of narcotics."

However, during the entire proceedings of the trial, no evidence was offered by the prosecution that Clay had done anything by way of violating the laws or control of illegal narcotics. His name was never brought forth, except on one occasion when the attorney for the defense asked one of the supposedly federal undercover agents what role William Clay had played. The agent's response was that he had met with Clay and two other individuals during the fall of 1972, and that either Clay or one of the other individuals present made some statements to the effect that, "If you don't have any money, we can't sell you any narcotics."

The government witness in question, who was initially responsible for introducing the name of Clay into the case, was, according to Clay, a $100-a-week paid informer, a convicted felon who has been involved in various narcotic crimes. Curiously, although this was the third trial of the defendant on the same charges—the first trial having ended in a hung jury, the second in a conviction and reversal—it was the first trial in which Clay's name was introduced.

. . . Characterizing the inclusion of his name in the brief as an "utterly improper and reckless act" and asserting vehemently that if he were a potential witness he (Clay) should have been contacted and questioned, he filed a motion of impeachment to have Coonan removed from his position as prosecutor of the Crime Task Force. But no punitive action was taken against Coonan.

. . . Clay also undertook to have his name cleared by the Department of Justice. After thirteen months, eleven letters to Attorneys General Saxbee and Levi, and repeated phone calls, however, he still had not received a substantive response. Rather, recounts Clay, "In flagrant and total disregard for what I consider my constitutional rights of citizenship, and my legislative responsibilities as a U.S. Congressman, various sections of the Department of Justice began conducting a witch-hunt against me. It appeared that the recent, overzealous activity of Department of Justice agents was and is designed to create or manufacture, if possible, a case involving me in the illegal trafficking of narcotics."

Eventually, Clay enlisted the aid of other members of Congress, eighty-four of whom signed a letter to Attorney General Levi demanding that he: (1) admit or deny that the William Clay referred to in the case was Representative Clay; (2) explain why, after one year of offering to answer any questions, Congressman Clay had been totally ignored; and, (3) conduct a full and thorough grand jury investigation of the allegations if there existed any credible evidence. The result of this letter was the scheduling of a meeting with Attorney General Levi, attended by Bill Clay, House Majority Leader "Tip" O'Neill, and Representatives Barbara Jordan, Louis Stokes, and Charles Rangel. At this meeting, Clay again requested a full-scale investigation, not only of the initial narcotics allegations, but of other accusations as well that had been made in the intervening time-period.

Attorney General Levi concurred that such an investigation was warranted. After the investigation was completed, Attorney General Levi sent Congressman Clay a letter completely exonerating him of any wrongdoing in the narcotics matter.

By this time, however, banner headlines and repeated stories and editorials had been played in the St. Louis newspapers for over a year that virtually convicted Clay of being a dope dealer. It seems not unreasonable to surmise that the intent of Prosecutor Coonan, knowing he had no legal case, was to try Clay in the newspapers. . . .

Not surprisingly, Clay reserves some of his choicest adjectives for the publisher of the *Globe-Democrat* and the Crime Task Force prosecutor. Of

Liam Coonan, he says, "I think it is reprehensible for a prosecutor to prostitute his oath of office, bring shame to the Department of Justice, and cast doubt on the impartiality of the system of justice—which is what Coonan did when he attempted to frame me on trumped-up charges."

. . . That Clay's anger is justified is further attested to by the fact that he was told that Coonan had talked with a man awaiting trial and had offered him leniency if he could implicate Clay in any illegal activities.

Nor is Clay alone in his appraisal of Coonan. He recounts various responses of other attorneys to the incident. The former chief counsel of the Senate Watergate Committee, Samuel Dash, issued a statement saying the Department of Justice may have violated Clay's constitutional rights. Dash, now a professor of law at Georgetown University, offered the opinion that inclusion of Clay's name in the case was improper and an abuse of prosecutorial discretion, that the act amounted to accusing Clay of a crime without providing recourse to due legal process. Said Dash, "It is a poor prosecutor who maligns an individual, when he does not have evidence of culpability to support his charges." An assistant U.S. attorney volunteered, "It was not wrong legally, but it may be wrong morally. Obviously, the guy who did it was not too sophisticated."

. . . Even before the narcotics issue was raised, Clay was being charged by the *Globe-Democrat*, the first time in July 1974, with padding his payroll, paying friends and associates who were allegedly ghost employees, and using his staff for political campaigning. In this instance, Clay himself insisted on complete investigations and voluntarily made available all of his records to substantiate his claim of innocence. As a result, his office was subjected to a seven-month grand jury investigation of eight staff members.

Clay, himself, appeared before the grand jury on four separate occasions, providing over a dozen hours of testimony. No evidence was produced to substantiate the charges. However, in the course of the investigation, evidence was found that an administrative assistant to Clay had placed one person on the payroll who for two years had received funds while doing no work. The assistant subsequently pled guilty to charges of fraud. Before the investigation was completed, at least 100 persons had been brought before the grand jury, including all of Clay's present and former employees over the preceding seven-year period. Upon the conclusion of the investigation, the grand jury issued a statement completely exonerating Clay of any wrongdoing.

This issue, however, had lingered more than two years, and the newspapers, again, missed few opportunities to keep the matter before the public mind. And, even before either the payroll issue or the narcotics issue had been resolved, the *Globe-Democrat* succeeded in sparking yet a third investigation—this time revolving around misuse of campaign funds.

In July 1975, the *Globe* ran a front-page article charging Clay with failing to report labor union contributions. The Department of Justice immediately announced a criminal investigation of the *Globe* charges. The day after this announcement, the *Globe* ran a nationally syndicated article [reporting] that [Clay] was under investigation, implying that he had stolen money or diverted political money for personal use. Clay promptly called the Department of Justice, suggesting that if there were going to be an investigation, it ought to start in his office. The Department sent two FBI agents to his office.

Asked by Clay if their investigation was based solely on the *Globe-Democrat* charges, the agents expressed denial and indicated they had obtained records of his contributions from the House Clerk. At issue, they said, were contributions from nine labor unions that he had failed to disclose. At that point, Clay took a copy of the records which the agents had brought with them and proceeded to point out that, in fact, every contribution in question was appropriately identified in the report. Clay further contended that the funds in question were not technically subject to reporting anyway, inasmuch as they were paid into his office expense account and were not for campaign purposes. This interpretation of the law was upheld by the Federal Election Commission. A presumably appropriately embarrassed Department of Justice closed the investigation. Congressman Clay received another letter of exoneration from the Attorney General shortly thereafter.

A few months later, in March 1976, an article by Jerry Landauer, staff reporter, appeared on the front page of the *Wall Street Journal* headlined, "How a Congressman Billed Government for Phony Travel." That the headline itself rendered a verdict of guilty was only the first symptom of bias in this newest attack. The article accused Congressman Clay of falsifying travel records and defrauding the government by requesting reimbursement for mileage for trips to his home district from Washington, while also claiming air fare during the same time periods for trips to other cities. The "news article" was written more in the style of an editorial, using inflammatory and derogatory phrases in describing the congressman's activities. The article was syndicated nationally and appeared in newspapers across the country the same day it appeared in the *Wall Street Journal;* the story was carried on all three national television networks that evening; and, it received prominent coverage by the *Globe-Democrat.* Clay feels strongly that this timed and coordinated coverage of the charge was a deliberate and conscious "plot."

Five weeks later, on April 30, 1976, the *Wall Street Journal* carried a second article accusing nine other members of Congress—all white—of similar abuses of travel procedures. This article, containing the same charges, written by the same reporter, appearing in the same newspaper as the one about Clay, was devoid of the editorial tone, was not syndicated, and did not receive widespread national play. It was back-page news in the St. Louis papers, although four of the nine implicated members of Congress were from the St. Louis area.

Shortly after the article on Clay appeared, a law student who read the newspaper report filed suit against Clay under an 1863 statute permitting "any citizen to sue a federal official in the name of the United States for knowingly making false claims against the government." Clay challenged the case on grounds that a 1943 amendment precluded citizens' filing suit solely on the basis of information obtained from news sources. Nevertheless, the suit was amended by the Department of Justice, with the added allegation that Clay owed the federal government $186,000 for false and fraudulent travel expense reimbursement claims. No legal action was taken, however, against the nine white members of Congress.

"To briefly elucidate on the double standard of justice," summarizes Clay, "ten members of Congress were accused of a crime—one black, nine white. The only black member found himself on trial defending himself, when the other nine had not even been interrogated by the Department of Justice or FBI."

. . . Before this issue was resolved, Clay had produced records, plane tickets, affidavits, and credit card receipts on all but seventeen of the eighty-nine trips in question and ninety-seven trips paid by personal funds to verify the validity of his claims. The Justice Department, according to Clay, conceded that, on these trips, he had substantiated beyond a doubt that his travel claims were accurate and valid. The Justice Department, "in desperation," as he describes it, approached him for an out-of-court settlement of $1,754. Considering that he had already expended $3,000 in attorney fees, and recognizing that pursuing the case would cost more in defense expenditures than the settlement, Clay agreed.

. . . Shortly after this issue was resolved, the *Globe-Democrat* wrote an editorial suggesting that the IRS ought to investigate Clay's income tax returns.

A subpoena was issued for all of Clay's congressional records. Clay's attorney challenged the subpoena in court on grounds it was illegal inasmuch as Clay was not under investigation by any grand jury. The judge then contacted the U.S. attorney, asking that the request for the subpoena be withdrawn. Subsequently, a grand jury was impaneled and a subpoena again issued—this time to Congress itself. Congress denied the subpoena on grounds that the charges against Clay were unspecific and that the subpoenaing of all his records constituted a witch-hunt. Based on the claim of the Justice Department that it was investigating through the St. Louis Grand Jury, Clay agreed to release his records. But then he learned that the records were given to the IRS, and filed suit on grounds that [that] act violated secrecy of the grand jury. In July 1977, the Department of Justice announced that the case against him had been terminated and that no indictment would be forthcoming.

In a spill-over effect, though, Clay reports that, "Approximately fifteen members of my immediate family and closest friends have been investigated by the IRS."

. . . Clay was supported in his appraisal of the attacks on him by then chairperson of the Congressional Black Caucus, Yvonne Braithwaite Burke, when she charged that the *Wall Street Journal* "apparently has joined in what is looking more and more like a conspiracy between certain federal agencies and some elements of the media to undermine the integrity, and ultimately the effectiveness, of black leaders."

Asked by a reporter at a press conference whether the three years of investigation by the Department of Justice constituted harassment of Congressman Clay, Attorney General Levi reportedly replied, "Well, I hope not." But, in a meeting four months later with Representatives Clay, Burke, Conyers, and Stokes—a meeting called by the Congressional Black Caucus to discuss the dual standard of justice applied to black members of Congress—the attorney general admitted, according to Clay, that most of the investigations of him were based on irresponsible charges made by the *St. Louis Globe-Democrat*. Attorney General Levi further admitted, says Clay, that it had cost the U.S. taxpayers hundreds of thousands of dollars to investigate the irresponsible and cheap accusations.

Recollects Clay, "I, in turn, informed him that because of these *Globe-Democrat* accusations the Department of Justice apparently felt a need and a responsibility to reward the reporter who had made the accusations. . . . He was stunned. He didn't understand what I was saying. I informed him that one of the reporters who made all of the untrue accusations against me had within past weeks been hired as an assistant U.S. attorney in the St. Louis Federal District."

Small wonder that Bill Clay is moved to speak of "a sinister, callous and calculated move to discredit me in the eyes of my constituents and the public-at-large." . . . Is that not the meaning of tyranny?[3]

Congressman Floyd Flake

The disproportionate attack upon black elected officials by the Department of Justice and the failure to convict in most instances continued through the late 1980s. Congressman Floyd Flake of New York was one of the more recent victims of this insatiable thirst to prove corruption and malfeasance among black elected officials.

In 1989, Congressman Floyd Flake of New York and his wife, Elaine, were indicted on seventeen counts of fraud and tax evasion. The charges ranged from embezzling more than $140,000 from the church that the Reverend Flake pastored to filing false congressional forms and failing to pay federal taxes on $228,000. Flake's wife was charged in nine of the seventeen counts. Both were accused of that nebulous catch-all, conspiracy.

For over two years, federal prosecutors issued damaging accounts describing in detail how the Flakes allegedly had diverted funds belonging to the 6,100-member Allen A.M.E. Church to their personal use. After extensive media coverage of the charges and the Flakes' being saddled with more than $400,000 in legal debts, the case finally went to court. But the government's evidence was so scant that in the middle of the trial the prosecution abruptly announced it was dropping all charges. The decision was prompted in part by U.S. District Court Judge Eugene Nickerson's statement in open court that he was inclined to drop all charges against Elaine Flake because no evidence had been produced to show that she was an active participant in the family's financial affairs. The next day, when the judge also ruled that the ministerial expense fund in question was, in fact, an official church account, the government's case was exposed for what it was, excessive and aggressive harassment of another black elected official. At this point, the prosecution had no choice but to withdraw all remaining charges.

Congressman Harold Ford

The case of Congressman Harold Ford of Memphis, Tennessee, is a classic example of the continued harassment of black elected officials. It followed all the precedents established to indict and to place on trial black leaders. First there were the daily newspaper reports of rumors that Congressman Ford was being investigated for criminal misconduct. Then came days of speculation by the news media, projected with a sense of high drama, that an indictment was imminent and that the charges would involve considerable sums of money being illegally transferred to Mr. Ford. Then came the government's coup d'état, an indictment handed up by a grand jury, not in the congressman's home district of Memphis, but in Knoxville, several hundred miles away. The charges were similar to those filed against many other black leaders: bank fraud, mail fraud, and, of course, conspiracy.

Mr. Ford was accused of accepting payments for political influence in the guise of bank loans from one of the Butcher brothers, who controlled twenty-seven banks in the state. The Butchers went to prison for their involvement in highly questionable lending practices that triggered the largest banking collapse in the state's history.

After more than four years of preparation, a trial lasting three months and costing Ford more than $2.8 million for legal fees, the jury of eight blacks and four whites was deadlocked. The vote for acquittal was 8 to 4. The long trial was held in the Memphis court district, which is 41 percent black, after lawyers for the congressman successfully appealed for change of venue from the Knoxville court district, which is about 85 percent white.

However, the government set a date for a new trial, and Judge Odell Horton, the black federal judge handling the case, issued a preposterous order to impanel a jury in the Jackson court district, almost 100 miles from Memphis, where blacks constituted only 17 percent of the population, and bus the jurors to trial in the predominantly black city of Memphis. This absurd arrangement was based on Judge Horton's belief that the government could not get a fair trial if the congressman was tried by black citizens. He stated publicly, ". . . there is a question of whether minority [black] jury members are willing to be open minded and fair. . . ."[4] The integrity and intelligence of eight blacks who voted for acquittal were being challenged.

The leadership of the U.S. House of Representatives and the NAACP Legal Defense Fund joined Congressman Ford in his fight against the judge's order. They filed amicus curiae (friend-of-the-court) briefs on Ford's behalf, presenting reasons the Sixth Circuit U.S. Court of Appeals should reverse the decision. The petitions cited numerous examples of the government's unlawful "jury shopping" to deny the congressman's constitutional right to a jury of his peers. The brief filed by the NAACP Legal Defense Fund declared that excluding a whole group of people because of race from a jury or jury pool was clearly illegal. "A jury selection process grounded on such racial considerations would strike at the very heart of the Fifth, Sixth and Fourteenth

Amendments.''⁵ Despite overwhelming precedents to the contrary, the appellate court upheld Judge Horton.

That is merely the newest wrinkle in this highly unusual case. First, the federal prosecutors sought an indictment in Knoxville against Congressman Ford after four grand juries in Memphis had refused to issue one. Second, Mr. Ford was forced to seek appellate court relief to change venue so he could be tried by his peers and neighbors. Third, a black judge, apparently seeking to solidify his credibility among the white establishment, issued a horrendous opinion calling for the busing of white jurors to try a black congressman some 100 miles from their home base. The asinine decision to deny a black member of Congress his constitutionally guaranteed right of trial by his peers is a tragic miscarriage of justice. It is very doubtful that the black judge in this case would have strayed so far from the established rules, procedures, and principles of law if the congressman in question had been white. Nobody in his or her right mind believes he would have pressed for a new trial busing jurors from a predominantly black community if a white congressman's case had been deadlocked in a verdict that had eight whites voting for his acquittal.

A white U.S. District Judge, Jerome Turner, replaced the ailing black judge. The new trial was held in Memphis, but the jury was selected from a panel of rural Tennessee voters. On April 9, 1993, after almost ten gruelling years and a second trial lasting five and a half weeks, the jury of eleven whites and one black found Representative Ford not guilty on all eighteen counts of conspiracy and bank and mail fraud.

IT'S TIME TO STOP THE HARASSMENT

The National Council of Churches of Christ held a conference at their headquarters in New York City on May 4, 1990. The Reverend John Fisher, a commissioner of the NCC, described the purpose of the session as being "to focus on one of the major blights on our democratic system of justice. The attack on black elected officials constitutes criminal activity on the part of the government, and subverts the democratic process."⁶

Congressman Floyd Flake, who along with Congressman Merv Dymally testified in behalf of the Congressional Black Caucus, and also as an elected official victimized by the conspiracy to destroy black leadership, remarked,

Much of the harassment is done under the color of the law and is done by those who are supposed to uphold the law . . . the harassment phenomenon is a two-phased process. On the one hand, you're seeing the elimination of young black males—one in four between the ages of twenty and twenty-nine is in jail, on parole, or on probation—and on the other hand, you're witnessing the attack on black leadership.[7]

The conference heard testimony on the subject from witnesses from many states and, at its conclusion, passed a resolution condemning the unwarranted and unjustified criminal investigations of black elected officials. The resolution stated, in part:

One-third (200) of the African-American elected officials in the state of Alabama are currently experiencing investigations or indictment, as well as African-American elected officials in North Carolina and Atlanta, Georgia.

A former FBI informer has made known the existence of an FBI program entitled "Fruhmenschen" (German for primitive man or ape). This directive called for the investigation of African-American elected officials across the country "without probable cause," on the theory that African-Americans are "intellectually and socially incapable of governing. . . ."

The widespread pattern of criminal investigations and charges against African-American elected officials suggests the possibility that people with power are misusing the criminal and civil justice system to thwart the national growth of new political forces generated by the increased power of the African-American electorate in the last two decades.

These incidents are not unrelated, and they reflect a concerted effort on the part of law enforcement agencies to discredit and remove [black officials from office].

The issue is not the possible innocence or guilt of each. . . . The issue is that this pattern of attacks by agencies of the government may constitute criminal activity on the part of the government, because it subverts and undermines the democratic process.[8]

I don't mean to suggest that all charges against black officials are frivolously contrived or racially motivated. Blacks in high offices are and have been capable of misusing their public trust. When this occurs, though, I merely advocate that the culprits be dealt with *in the same manner* and punished *to the same degree* as their white counterparts. Any course of action showing more or less stringent punishment for a black official can only be described as racist.

The indictment of Marion Barry, the mayor of Washington, D.C., for smoking cocaine and lying to a grand jury is the classic example of how differently the government and the media treat black and white officials.

Despite their protestations to the contrary, despite the lofty arguments they advance about a relatively few white elected officials having been similarly treated, and notwithstanding the ugliness of the evidence submitted, Marion Barry was subjected to treatment that white officials who break the law and public confidence are not and should not be subjected to.

The Washington Post printed millions of derogatory words over a six-year period about Barry's personal and private life that had very little to do with his public responsibilities. The television correspondents were equally dishonest in their coverage. The federal government will not acknowledge the amount spent to attain an indictment, but the estimate of $3 million they admit to is probably too low, although the $40 million Barry alleges is probably too high. What is apparent is that for that kind of money they were only able to indict him for several misdemeanors, except for the one felony charge of lying to the grand jury about the misdemeanors.

Father Timothy Healy, S.J., former president of Georgetown University and now president of the New York Public Library, speaking on the subject of Barry's arrest for possession of a small quantity of cocaine, said in his remarks to the graduating class at American University,

> Three unacceptable suppositions, however, seem to lie under the case against Marion Barry and the way it has been handled by the prosecutors, by the media, and indeed, by the rest of us. The first is that arrest equals conviction. The second that an arrest justifies the means used to make it. The third that arrest authorizes those close to it to forgo compassion. . . .
>
> It is hard for those who have never suffered that jeopardy to realize the impact of an arrest, its deep sense of violation, the terror of investigation and trial, the public ostracism and private slights that follow, and the psychological hurt to wives and children. For a public figure the experience is even worse, because it means the disgrace of contracts violated, promises broken, one's word forsworn. . . .
>
> Even this is intensified if the officeholder because of his race (as once because of his religion) represents more than a political party and has even with some hubris proclaimed that role.[9]

Black officials certainly don't have political muscle heavy enough to allow them to manipulate the judicial system. If they did, no serious investigations would have been conducted in the first place, regardless of accusations by the media and political opponents. So why have so many black officials been singled out for this selective, special kind of persecution?

Why have militant, vocal black leaders throughout the history of this country been singled out for a special kind of government harassment? Marcus Garvey, a revered black leader in the early twenties, worked to develop and influence the inclusion of blacks into the economic mainstream of American life. It was through his leadership of several organizations, including the Universal Negro Improvement Association, that our people were instilled with a deep sense of pride and self-esteem.

In the process, Marcus Garvey became the target of unreasonable attacks by a young FBI agent handling his first major case. The agent, J. Edgar Hoover, as director of investigations on Negro activities, became obsessed with destroying the influence of Garvey, who was affectionately referred to within his community as "the black Moses."

For more than four years, Mr. Garvey was the victim of illegal mail intercepts, constant surveillance, and accusations of criminal activities by paid informants of the government who had infiltrated his organization. Finally, in a patently racially hostile court proceeding, Mr. Garvey, accused of using the U.S. mails to defraud prospective investors, was convicted and sentenced to five years in the Atlanta Federal Penitentiary. In 1927, President Calvin Coolidge commuted his sentence and deported him back to Jamaica.

Unfortunately, harassment has not abated in recent years. If anything, it has intensified. Former Cleveland City Council President George L. Forbes, following investigations by a Cleveland daily newspaper, was charged along with five other council members (four blacks and one white) with theft in office related to fund-raising procedures. The practices were longstanding in the community and had never before been questioned. Forbes was acquitted and the charges against the others were dropped. Why have so many accused black elected officials been exonerated? Fair-minded, decent individuals need not ask.

NOTES

1. Robert M. Hutchins, *Democracy and Human Nature*, cited in *Bartlett's Familiar Quotations*, 14th edition, Boston: Little Brown and Company, 1968, page 1045b.

2. Cited by Mary R. Sawyer, *The Dilemma of Black Politics: A Report on Harassment of Black Elected Officials, Voter Education and Registration Action*, published by *Inc.*, July 1987, page ix.

3. Reprinted from *The Dilemma of Black Politics*, pages 41–54, with permission of the publisher. The report, by Dr. Mary R. (Warner) Sawyer, assistant professor of religious studies at Iowa State University, is a thoroughly researched, scholarly document graphically describing difficulties that black elected officials have had to face in their role as representatives of the people. It also implies, correctly, that the percentage of white elected officials subjected to this kind of abuse and scrutiny is far less than their counterparts in the black community.

Dr. Sawyer's study was funded in part through grants from the Third World Fund, the Peoples Temple Church of San Francisco, United Parcel Service, the United Methodist Church, and the Brooks-Matthews Foundation. In-kind services were provided by the A. Phillip Randolph Institute and the Joint Center for Political Studies.

4. Cited by Congressman Harold Ford, *Washington Report*, May 9, 1991, page 1.

5. *Ibid.*, page 2.

6. *New Orleans Tribune*, June 1990, page 14.

7. *Ibid.*, page 15.

8. Resolution passed by the National Council of Churches of Christ, May 4, 1990, New York City.

9. *The Washington Post*, January 31, 1990, op-ed page.

15

The CBC Revolution

Those who profess to favor freedom and yet deprecate agitation are men who want crops without plowing up the ground. They want rain without thunder and lightning. They want the ocean without the awful roar of its waters. This struggle may be a moral one, or it may be a physical one, or it may be both moral and physical, but it must be a struggle. Power concedes nothing without demand. It never did, and it never will. Find out just what people will submit to, and you have found out the exact amount of injustice and wrong which will be imposed upon them; and these will continue till they are resisted with either words or blows, or with both. The limits of tyrants are prescribed by the endurance of those whom they oppress. . . .[1]

These are the words of Frederick Douglass, an ex-slave who, in 1857, advocated revolution, a violent one if necessary, to throw off the shackles of racial oppression. In the late sixties and early seventies, a somber and impassioned black America attempted a nonviolent political revolution just as deliberate as the one envisioned by Douglass. The Congressional Black Caucus, along with scores of black mayors, state representatives, and city councilmen, was an integral part of the revolution: Gus Hawkins' telling President Nixon that "unless he faces up to the problems of black Americans, there will be chaos," articulated the angry mood of black Americans. Charles Diggs' acknowledging that blacks were increasing in numbers within the political arena and were coalescing with other deprived groups for the "purpose of enhancing strength" was truly seeing the facts of life. Louis Stokes' suggesting a boycott of the president's State of the Union address indicated the depth of dissatisfaction with current government policy.

Parren Mitchell's admonition that "the black community has [not] been blackjacked into silence or lulled into apathy," gave notice of a people determined to be involved. Charles Rangel's warning, "Where there are causes that can benefit by coalition politics, we shall coalesce," forecast the Caucus's willingness to work with other groups to achieve our goals. My call in 1971 for black communities to "develop the same degree of political sophistication as others" was therefore not farfetched. It did not appear to be the case then, but urging a new, tough approach to solving the problems of racism and discrimination was realistic.

AN EFFECTIVE VOICE FOR THE DISADVANTAGED

Tough talk and tough actions motivate the establishment to sit up and take notice and are necessary stratagems for winning respect and recognition from the movers and shakers of politics and government. Once the agitators are recognized, which lends respect to their concerns, the process for resolution of many community problems is on a solid footing.

Through legislative initiatives, Caucus members have sternly resisted efforts by the administrations of the last five presidents—Nixon, Ford, Carter, Reagan, and Bush—to reverse the social, political, and economic gains black people attained during the sixties. It was the Caucus that stood in opposition to Nixon's total assault on the Great Society programs and successfully waged battle to save most of them by refocusing goals and changing agency names. The public impression was that the president had abolished the many programs that the "silent majority" deemed expendable, but the Caucus kept them alive. It was the Caucus that challenged the conservative ideologies of the Ford, Carter, Reagan, and Bush administrations and preserved vital domestic programs that affected the economically disadvantaged when everything else was being sacrificed in the name of increased defense spending.

How would the poor have survived had it not been for programs preserved by the Caucus when President Reagan offered his slashing budget proposals and phoney "safety net"? The 23.5 million (one in ten Americans) receiving food stamps owe this modest assistance to the Congressional Black Caucus, which insisted on no further cuts in the program. More than 50 percent of food stamp recipients lived in households with gross incomes of less than $400 a month. The Reagan administration wanted to make them ineligible for food stamps. Unquestionably, the Caucus has remained the strongest advocate in government for the poor.

We admirably documented the need for preserving the programs designed to feed hungry children, house their families, and provide jobs or unemployment benefits for their parents. The Caucus did not surrender to political expedience, nor did we lose our political integrity. We understand the mandate imposed by the Constitution on those who govern—namely, to promote the general welfare.

In order for our lives to have meaning and relevance, we must continue the struggle, the crusade for racial justice and economic equality. Black members of Congress cannot afford to abandon their agenda for improving the social, economic, and political lot of 32 million black Americans. Despite the vigorous attacks on the concept of affirmative action from numerous and powerful quarters, we must continue to promote set-asides in government contracts based on race; favor scholarships for economically and educationally disadvantaged black students; support on-the-job training for minorities; and insist on goals and timetables for placing blacks on a par with the larger society in every aspect.

This effort must continue until black college graduates no longer earn, on the average, less than white high school graduates; until black males are no longer employed at only half the rate of white males; until black babies no longer die of rat bites at a rate four times that of white babies. Affirmative policies and aggressive politics will be essential as long as black workers earn 56 cents for every dollar earned by white workers; until black mothers no longer die in childbirth at a rate five times greater than white mothers.

Under present circumstances, it is too much to ask that black people proceed respectfully and passively while white America still pursues a course of stubborn resistance to racial and economic justice. Heeding the call of black conservatives and white reactionaries to judge each person on individual merit without considering the past, studying the present, or assessing the future, is too much to ask of a people who have witnessed no realistic programs to deal with their oppression and repression.

Those individuals and groups, conservative and liberal, Democrat and Republican, black and white, who accuse the Congressional Black Caucus of having "outlived its usefulness" or of "being out of touch with their black constituents" would be well advised to ponder seriously one essential question: Where would black Americans be politically, economically, and educationally if there had not been a Congressional Black Caucus?

Sufficient time has expired for most to determine if the Congressional Black Caucus has been able to reach the high standards and fulfill the original expectations of black people in the early seventies. I believe we have made a difference and that we must continue to make a difference. Today, many of the advances developed and supported by the Caucus are being eroded. Elements in society—black and white—are attempting to belittle us as unrepresentative of the black community. The age-old ploy of divide and conquer is used to dilute our strength because our enemies know that the Caucus is the only organization with the potential to mobilize the black community on a national basis for a political cause.

ATTACKS FROM WITHIN THE BLACK COMMUNITY

In the beginning, it was white liberals, white conservatives, white labor leaders, and white members of the media who led the attack on the Congressional Black Caucus. In recent years, it has been black social scientists, black educators, and black members of the media who are spearheading the criticism.

Many of the blacks who have benefited most from the aggressive, militant demands of black elected officials seem to recognize that fact the least. They now refer to themselves as "black conservatives" and spend an inordinate amount of time excoriating black leaders and denouncing programs established to give our people an equal footing in jobs, housing, and education. Most of them pretend that they arrived where they are because of unquestioned talent and recognized ability. They allege to be offended because some whites accuse them of being admitted to a prestigious school or getting a top job in corporate America because of preferential treatment accorded through affirmative action policies. The ugly truth is that, talented or not, they and other blacks did not make it to the top because of personal ability, although that may have played a part. Credit must be given to the hordes of nondescript, angry, uncompromising black men, women, and children who laid their bodies and sometimes their lives on the line to change racist policy and racist attitudes. Langston Hughes, the poet, points out the dilemma of the black bourgeois who deny their heritage.

THE CBC REVOLUTION

So I am ashamed for the black poet who says, "I want to be a poet, not a Negro poet," as though his own racial world were not as interesting as any other world. I am ashamed, too, for the colored artist who runs from the painting of Negro faces to the painting of sunsets after the manner of the academicians because he fears the strange un-whiteness of his own features. An artist must be free to choose what he does, certainly, but he must also never be afraid to do what he might choose.[2]

One group of Negroes more unappreciative of efforts of black elected officials than any other is those earning the big bucks in television, radio, and print. To prove their complete acceptance of the one world, one race, one people theory and to display their total dissociation from other blacks, they feel compelled to attack, demean, and degrade black leadership and black organizations that "constantly carp and complain" about racial injustice. Their attacks, however, have failed to negate the accomplishments of the Caucus or to persuade our followers to reject our leadership. Somehow, this new breed of reporter, ignoring the direct pressures applied by the Caucus on the communications industry to hire blacks, perceives itself as possessing awesome powers of persuasion in influencing television producers, station managers, and editors.

Typical of the ever increasing crescendo of criticism leveled against the Caucus are the following statements of black educators, reporters, and television commentators:

Traditional African-American leaders are out of line with what the common black man, woman and family are thinking today. . . . So often (these groups—CBC, NAACP, National Association of Black Lawyers) speak for black people, they don't speak to black people.[3]

—Floyd Hayes, professor at Purdue University

The Congressional Black Caucus weekend is the most glaring evidence of a two-decade-old saga of ineptness, mismanagement, lack of accountability and vision of our so-called leaders.

. . . After 20 years of CBC weekends, the most obvious evidence of black leadership having been on Capitol Hill are thousands of empty Scotch bottles, a slew of chicken bones and a host of white merchants rushing to the bank to deposit the one-half billion dollars they receive each year from CBC hotel rents and the sale of Scotch and hot Buffalo wings.[4]

—William Reed, columnist

These guys [black leaders] are sitting there watching the destruction of our race while arguing about Ronald Reagan. . . . Ronald Reagan isn't the problem. Former president Jimmy Carter was not the problem. The lack of black leadership is the problem.[5]

—Clarence Thomas, as chairman of the
Equal Employment Opportunity Commission

Civil rights leaders . . . bitch, bitch, bitch about the administration . . . they create a narcotic of dependency, not an ethic of responsibility and independence. They are at best an irrelevance, covering up some real problems and inevitably a stigma.[6]

—Clarence Thomas, as chairman EEOC

[The CBC is] demanding that blacks be politically correct. . . . They're looking at life through an elitist perspective.[7]

—Robert Woodson, executive director of
Neighborhood Housing Services

The trashy misrepresentations of the Caucus Weekend and the total distortion of the many valuable contributions imparted throughout the workshops, brain trusts, and networking of the occasion were reprinted from coast to coast by more than fifty black-owned weekly newspapers. They were then repeated by several columnists, including Courtland Milloy of the *Washington Post*. Syndicated columnist Tony Brown, who has become fanatical in his attacks on black organizations, did not miss the opportunity to attack the CBC again. He used the article by Reed almost verbatim in his column.

Either these individuals do not realize or they refuse to accept the fact that it was the CBC who orchestrated and pressured the national news media to hire blacks at all levels in their industry. It was members of the CBC who met countless times with officials of the Department of Defense in the early seventies and negotiated the deal whereby minority-owned newspapers would automatically get a percentage of the agency's huge budget for advertisement. Prior to this arrangement, they had received none of the funds for recruitment solicitation or announcements of bids for contracts and materials. Legislative set-asides for minority-owned businesses, sponsored by CBC members in the Highway Bill, Alaskan Pipe Line Construction Bill, and the Surface Transportation Act, have provided access to millions of dollars in advertisement funds for black-owned newspapers and radio stations.

In addition to black media personalities attacking us, a new breed of black spokesperson has emerged to do battle with black elected officials and heads of civil rights organizations. This cadre of "created" black leaders—people without any discernible black followers (and hence, political eunuchs)—are often referred to as the "new conservatives." It is disheartening to hear these antebellum visionaries speak of "a colorblind society," of "pulling yourself out of the quagmire of poverty and deprivation by hard work and self-reliance," of "affirmative action for black people being unfair to white males," and of "getting the government off our backs."

The Caucus has not been deterred by these attacks. We have remained steadfast in pursuit of our original goals. We have also attempted to deal logically and forcefully with the foolishness of our critics.

THE CBC FIGHT FOR A PRO-ACTIVE GOVERNMENT

Possessing an in-depth knowledge of and a keen perception of American history, it was not necessary for Caucus members to conduct extensive research to reach the conclusion that hard work and self-reliance alone have never enabled a race of people to pull itself up by its own bootstraps. Our comprehension, intelligence, and awareness inform us that it has been a combination of hard work and direct government assistance that has improved the living conditions of the average American citizen. In order to change basic, pervasive deficiencies in any society, government has always played a major role.

It has been government in partnership with enterprising citizens that enabled white Americans to make progress. After World War II, the government recognized that our cities were in shambles, that the buildings were deteriorating, that pollution from smokestack industries was taking its toll, that automation was a thing of the future. And it was government that took the lead in addressing these problems. Government decided that millions of acres of land surrounding the cities were desirable for development. It was not enterprising, hard-working, self-reliant entrepreneurs. It was government policy makers. It was the government that made resources available, including tax monies to build roads, schools, and libraries on this vacant land to make it conducive to and attractive for living. The government established a policy to guarantee loans to developers to build shopping centers and middle-income housing with front lawns and backyard swimming pools—hardworking, self-reliant, enterprising white businessmen cannot take the credit. Government policy created the Federal Home Loan Assistance Program, which subsidized the purchase of houses for middle-income Americans and guaranteed that bankers who financed those homes would not lose on their investment. The government passed laws that allowed the purchasers to deduct interest payments on home mortgages from income tax liability. So hardworking, self-reliant Americans have not done all of those wonderful things on their own—have not achieved such great heights by themselves. Government played the key role in their Horatio Alger success stories.

The big problem with this scenario is that black people were left out of the equation. We were excluded from this great American experiment launched to expand opportunity, this great program designed to lift 100 million poverty-stricken white Americans from the Hoovervilles, shanty towns, and tobacco roads and place them in the middle class with sufficient buying power. Let us be honest about it. We, black Americans, were denied an opportunity to share in this great government-financed "operation boot strap." We were not allowed to ascend the ladder in tandem with other citizens of like circumstances. We were handicapped, victimized not by accident, not by oversight, but by deliberate, conscious acts of government.

Let us not be evasive or polite in explaining what happened. It was not racial segregation or separation of the races that prevented us from taking advantage of the benefits offered by the government's policy of expansion—these are merely phrases coined to make more plausible and more acceptable the most inhumane kind of treatment one group of people can inflict on another. Simply put, it was racist policies and racist laws and racist customs enacted, employed, and enforced by racist individuals that kept us out of "operation boot strap." But more important, these insurmountable impediments were sanctioned by a racist government existing in a racist society. Any other explanation is an attempt at historical revision and denigrating to those of us who have suffered the consequences of these uncivilized, bigoted acts.

If twenty-six black members had been in Congress instead of only two, Powell and Dawson, when these post–World War II measures were enacted, benefits allocated under those programs probably would have been distributed more fairly to include black people.

The mandate of the Congressional Black Caucus, as I perceive it, is to ensure that government now becomes a partner with our people to rectify three centuries of unfair, immoral treatment. Our role must be to educate black people that there is nothing shameful about petition-ing the government for financial and economic assistance in order to right these past wrongs. We should not apologize for expecting our government to correct longstanding inequities and to abolish unequal treatment based on race. White America did not get where it is without substantial financial and economic government help. And we are not going to rebuild our inner city neighborhoods, close the wide gap in income between white and black workers, or effectively deal with intolerable joblessness in our communities by resorting to the juvenile nickel-and-dime self-help programs proposed by the so-called new black conservatives.

We need the same kind of massive dollar infusion that built subur-bia. We need government policy that guarantees insurance companies will insure our properties at reasonable and fair premiums; that forces banks to lend black property owners money for rehabilitation and remodeling under the same terms and at the same interest rates as whites. We need a government that seeks out and aggressively prose-cutes those who violate our laws against discrimination in employ-ment, just as it does those who rob banks.

Finally, the Caucus must orchestrate a campaign to reverse the psychological hangups that make the poor, and black people in partic-ular, fearful, wary, and apprehensive about accepting government assistance. The misleading slogan "Get government off our backs" is designed primarily to keep government from assisting those most in need so that those least in need, those who now get the bulk of the benefits, will not have to share. Citizens at the bottom of the economic ladder must have government on their side, and the Caucus must continue to serve as a catalyst for fostering policies that deliver services and goods to them.

Ever mindful of the history of aggressive acts against black elected officials in the nineteenth century and the continuing massive opposi-tion to their attempts to legislate fairly, we must never relax or relent in our quest for equal standing in society. Just 100 short years ago, twenty-two black members had served in the United States Congress. Surely they and their constituents, ex-slaves or poor men and women only one generation removed from slavery, thought this nation well on the way to atoning for its sins against humanity. Who among them would have guessed in 1892 that seven years later not a single black would be left sitting in Congress?

Certainly Senators Revels and Bruce from Mississippi, who cham-pioned restoring unrepentant southern rebels to citizenship with full voting rights, did not envision what eventually happened. I am sure that early freedom fighters and dedicated statesmen like the very militant Alonzo J. Ransier of South Carolina and the Civil War hero Robert Smalls, also of South Carolina, never imagined that Reconstruction would end so abruptly and that within thirty years after the first black was elected to Congress, none would serve in that august body for another twenty-seven years.

It is evident that Robert Brown Elliott had no idea what brutal repression was in store for the black race when he uttered these optimistic remarks on the floor of Congress in 1872:

> We trust the time is not far distant when all our fellow citizens—whether they be native born or whether they first drew the breath of life on the banks of the Rhine; whether they sprang from the Orient or the Occident— no longer controlled by the teachings of false political faith, shall be touched with the inspiration of a holier sentiment and shall recognize the "universal fatherhood of God and the brotherhood of man."[8]

To prevent the kind of isolation experienced by those early black members of Congress, it was important and logical that an entity such as the Congressional Black Caucus be formed. No one has so clearly defined the role that the Caucus has played in serving as the catalyst for the important advances made by blacks as Congressman Julian Dixon:

> The Caucus has been the cutting edge opposing administration policies of Nixon, Ford, Carter, and Reagan. We were the first to speak out against the nominations of G. Harold Carswell and Clement Haynesworth as Supreme Court justices, and Edwin Meese as attorney general, and to question their commitments to justice for all.
>
> On the floor of the Congress, in committee hearings, before the press and across America, we have spoken out against policies which undermine the enforcement of civil rights and civil liberties, respect for law and order, disregard for personal rights of privacy, and attempts to infringe on the rights of free speech. Whether it was a president's assault on the Civil Rights Commission, a proposal for a youth sub-minimum wage, efforts to weaken federal contract compliance, to lessen the effects of full-employment legislation, or to eliminate minority set-asides, the Caucus was there to respond. Yet, perhaps it is these very challenges which have helped energize the black community to seek change through political empowerment. In the streets

of our communities we have seen the damage of presidential economic policies.

The momentum among black voters must peak, in conjunction with that of other denied groups, so that the direction of this nation can change as we restore America's commitment to fairness and justice for all.[9]

The challenges of which Congressman Dixon speaks are the same ones that members of the CBC have consistently faced. While white leaders were joyously celebrating America's two hundredth anniversary as a nation in 1976, the Congressional Black Caucus was reminding them that the struggle for decency and justice was not over. Black leaders were addressing the sad truth of America's pitiful beginnings— a country conceived in sin, born in corruption, and continuing to live out the lies, contradictions, and hypocrisies embodied in the Declaration of Independence and the Bill of Rights.

That glorious document, the United States Constitution, which is the subject of so much fanfare and brouhaha, denied women the right to own property and to vote; defined blacks as non-persons and so sanctioned "cruel and unusual punishment" against them. But despite the imperfections in the legacy of our founding fathers, the Congressional Black Caucus—because it is in our permanent interest—has directed its efforts to perfecting the union and providing for the general welfare by working to eliminate poverty, sexism, and racism.

Lesser men and women may have been willing to accept the fate imposed by a system in which they were the constant victims, but black legislators have always fully realized, as did Frederick Douglass before, that "The hypocrisy of the Nation must be exposed; and its crimes against God and man must be denounced."[10]

Marguerite Ross-Barnett in a scholarly article poses what I consider a factual analysis and a fair critique of the Congressional Black Caucus. She establishes a reasonable yardstick for measuring the good and the bad of the Caucus:

. . . two overarching considerations must be kept in mind in drawing conclusions about the CBC. The CBC can be isolated for analytical purposes but in a political sense it is part of larger systems and subsystems. It is an intrinsic part of the black community. It can only be as powerful inside Congress as the black community is outside Congress. Its weaknesses, failures and flaws, as well as its successes, strengths and assets, should not be attributed solely to individual CBC members but should be seen in the broadest political and social context. Greater CBC accountability, philosophical coherence, political innovativeness, and so on, are changes that must reflect a transformed black political culture.

The second consideration is the difficult task faced by the CBC as it attempts to use the political system to bring about economic change. . . . Transformation of CBC potential into positive political realities will depend on a variety of factors, only some of which are in the direct control of the black members of Congress.[11]

The potential for the CBC, indeed for black elected officials generally, to transform political actions into political realities depends very much on unified support in our individual districts, but to an even greater degree depends on the will and determination of those in black communities to insist that their white elected officials support the programmatic agenda of the Caucus.

IT'S TIME TO RECOGNIZE BLACK POLITICAL MATURITY AS WELL AS BLACK RIGHTS

The process of complete political independence in black communities began in earnest in the mid-sixties when an increasing number of blacks started agitating for control of positions that affected their daily lives. The rising tide of racial consciousness enabled them to assess the problem clearly and see the enemy more lucidly. That enemy was not always white officialdom *per se;* oddly enough, more often it was indifference on the part of blacks who tolerated the lackluster leadership of white elected officials.

The politics of a militant black community took almost twenty years to reach fruition. Many suffered and agonized during the period of evolution but considered the results worth the pain. One man standing almost alone at first, Jesse Jackson, is due a great deal of credit for opening the eyes and unlocking the minds of a complacent black electorate. His campaign for the presidency of the United States in 1984 went one step farther than any program our race had ever pursued and was in line with the permanent interests of black people. He unshackled the chains of political bondage to an indifferent political system and severed the long-held psychological dependence of those who had relied exclusively on whites to give leadership at the highest level of government. His foray into the realm of the heretofore politically impossible convinced the average black person that Jackson towered head and shoulders over the other seven Democrats in the race. And most believe in their heart that if Jackson were white, the Democratic nomination would have been his for the asking.

The issues Jackson promoted and the style in which he did so, would, in a "colorblind society," have guaranteed him the privilege of being the standard-bearer of the Democratic party. However, make no mistake, we still live in a society blinded by color rather than color-blind.

Jackson's campaign provided a basis for awakening a constituency from a mental complacency. The platform objectives of the Rainbow Coalition jogged the memory of many too closely aligned to the Democratic party. Jackson did for blacks in this country what John F. Kennedy did for Catholics. Kennedy dispelled the myth that Catholics could not get elected to the highest office. Jackson shattered the ill-founded belief that a black person cannot be taken seriously when aspiring for the presidency. It is merely a matter of time before a black will be the standard-bearer or the vice-presidential candidate of one of the major political parties. What was considered comical in the beginning, lightly covered by the media and grudgingly accepted by some black leaders, blossomed into a full-fledged campaign.

Although Jackson did not win, we can also say he did not lose, because black people and the new black politics did not lose. In reality, we lost the battle and won the war. We won because we found ourselves politically, proudly acknowledging our worthiness. The country lost because it was once again revealed that its people were still steeped in racial prejudice against dark-skinned citizens regardless of their talents.

For sure, our people and our politics have come a long way since that afternoon in 1971 when the Congressional Black Caucus was first conceived. The gathering at the first annual CBC dinner on that June night in 1971 was one of the few occasions in history when members of the black race experienced an exhilarating sense of reachable freedom, a renewed self-worth, a recommitment to struggle. For one fleeting moment—more accurately, for several fleeting hours—the revolutionary spirit of Frederick Douglass, W. E. B. DuBois, Paul Robeson, Angela Davis, and Stokely Carmichael meshed into a beautiful symphony of unified determination to achieve pride of race and equality of citizenship. In a sense, Lorraine Hansberry's *Raisin in the Sun*, Richard Wright's *Native Son*, and James Baldwin's *The Fire Next Time* collided with all the other angry black artistic geniuses to produce an amalgamation of the black man's American dream. That night 2,700 participants witnessed Denmark Vesey and Nat Turner as decorated national heroes; W. C. Handy and Nikki Giovanni as space ships orbiting the world of art; Jackie Robinson and Buddy Young quietly smiling as they destroyed Americanized Aryan myths of racial superiority.

Here were 2,700 black people cheering for another 25 million at a fashionable hotel in the nation's capital—finding the soul, if not the heart of America; celebrating the memories of ancestors who advanced the hopes of a people as they marched gallantly through the ravages of the eighteenth, nineteenth, and twentieth centuries to bring us to this point in time.

They also remembered that no other group of legislators has had to endure as many hardships, suffer as many indignities, or win so little appreciation as the sixty-seven black men and women who have served in the United States Congress.

These pioneers for justice and equality, some of whose character was honed in slavery, all victims of discrimination, all schooled in the hard knocks of reality, were unwavering in their faith in mankind. They believed more deeply in the promises of democracy than did the framers of the Constitution, who viewed them as less than human. They embraced the essence of the Constitution as did no other group in America, perhaps because they had no other choice, as their very survival depended on adherence by the majority to the tenets embodied in that document.

It may be too much to expect all elements of the black community to understand and appreciate the accomplishments of the Congressional Black Caucus. However, of this I am certain: While many have contributed to efforts to lift our people from bondage, the Caucus has been the single most effective political entity we have had in articulating, representing, protecting, and advancing the interests of black people in this nation over the past twenty years. In its twenty-year history, the Congressional Black Caucus has reflected on the injustices existing in American society and has pursued a course of action designed to rid this nation of the scourge of racism.

The Congressional Black Caucus fully understands that the "man with the plan" for resolution of these problems must adhere to the dictates of several political axioms. One of the more important of these was enunciated by Ossie Davis at the first Congressional Black Caucus dinner in 1971: "[The] name of the game is power, and if you ain't playing power, you're in the wrong place."[12]

The Congressional Black Caucus, playing a leadership role in this power game, is reeling under the stress and strain of a staggering federal budget deficit that threatens programs vital to our constituents. A spineless Congress concentrates primarily on the politics of re-election and an uncaring Bush administration is attuned only to big business and the wealthy; both expect the poor and dispossessed to do with even less than they already have.

Poverty, despair, despondence, and hopelessness, the four horsemen of racial discrimination, are galloping ever faster, and the poor can no longer rely on the president to publicly defend their rights, the Congress to aggressively protect their rights, or the courts to fairly interpret their rights.

In this period of chaos, the Caucus is flexing its collective muscle and judiciously using its ofttimes balance-of-power position on many close votes, deciding key issues that affect those who have been denied. The Congressional Black Caucus has succeeded because we heeded the words of Lerone Bennett, Jr., who in 1972 advised us to disengage ourselves from white people's arguments and redefine all concepts and associations in terms of the fundamental interests of black people. We have succeeded because we understand that the destiny of each of us is inextricably bound to the destiny of 32 million other black brothers and sisters, and that their struggle and our struggle are irrevocably tied one to the other.

We have survived and will continue to succeed in protecting our interests because we have adhered to the most important political principle of all, the official motto of the Congressional Black Caucus:

BLACK PEOPLE HAVE NO PERMANENT FRIENDS,
NO PERMANENT ENEMIES,
JUST PERMANENT INTERESTS.

NOTES

1. Frederick Douglass, in a speech given August 4, 1857, cited in *Before the Mayflower: A History of Black America*, by Lerone Bennett, London: Penguin Books, 1984, pages 160–161.
2. Langston Hughes, "The Negro Artist and the Racial Mountain," *The Nation*, volume 22, number 3181, June 23, 1926, page 694.
3. Floyd Hayes
4. William Reed, in the *Capital Spotlight*, a black-owned newspaper.
5. *The Washington Post*, October 25, 1991.
6. *The Washington Post*, July 2, 1991.
7. *USA Today*, July 19, 1991.
8. *Congressional Globe*, 42nd Congress, second session, 1872, page 492.

9. Congressman Julian C. Dixon, "Annual CBCF Legislative Weekend Souvenir Program Book," September 1984, page 75.

10. Frederick Douglass, cited in *The Negro Almanac—The Afro American*, New York: The Bellwether Company, 1976, page 107.

11. *The Crisis* magazine, April 1981, page 131.

12. Ossie Davis in his keynote speech at the Sheraton-Park Hotel, Washington, D.C., June 18, 1971.

Appendix A
Brief Chronology of Blacks Who Have Served in the U.S. Congress

YEARS SERVED

U.S. SENATE

Hiram R. Revels (Mississippi) 1870–1871
Blanche K. Bruce (Mississippi) 1875–1881
Edward W. Brooke (Massachusetts) 1966–1978

U.S. HOUSE OF REPRESENTATIVES
(prior to formation of the Congressional Black Caucus)

Joseph H. Rainey (South Carolina) 1869–1879
Jefferson Long (Georgia) 1871
Benjamin S. Turner (Alabama) 1871–1873
Robert C. DeLarge (South Carolina) 1871–1873
Robert B. Elliott (South Carolina) 1871–1875
Josiah T. Walls (Florida) 1871–1875
Richard H. Cain (South Carolina) 1873–1875
                                                              1877–1879
Alonzo J. Ransier (South Carolina) 1873–1875
James T. Rapier (Alabama) 1873–1875
John R. Lynch (Mississippi) 1873–1877
                                                              1882–1883
Jeremiah Haralson (Alabama) 1875–1877
John A. Hyman (North Carolina) 1875–1877

355

Charles E. Nash (Louisiana) 1875–1877
Robert Smalls (South Carolina) 1875–1879
1881–1887
James E. O'Hara (North Carolina) 1883–1887
Henry P. Cheatham (North Carolina) 1889–1893
Thomas E. Miller (South Carolina) 1889–1891
John M. Langston (Virginia) 1889–1891
George W. Murray (South Carolina) 1893–1897
George H. White (North Carolina) 1897–1901
Oscar DePriest (Illinois) 1929–1935
Arthur W. Mitchell (Illinois) 1935–1943

PAST MEMBERS OF THE CONGRESSIONAL BLACK CAUCUS

William L. Dawson (Illinois) 1943–1970
Adam C. Powell, Jr. (New York) 1945–1971
Charles C. Diggs (Michigan) 1955–1980
Robert C. Nix (Pennsylvania) 1957–1979
Shirley Chisholm (New York) 1969–1983
George W. Collins (Illinois) 1970–1972
Ralph H. Metcalfe (Illinois) 1971–1978
Parren J. Mitchell (Maryland) 1971–1987
Yvonne B. Burke (California) 1973–1979
Barbara Jordan (Texas) 1973–1979
Andrew Young (Georgia) 1973–1977
Melvin H. Evans (Virgin Islands) 1979–1981
Bennett M. Stewart (Illinois) 1979–1981
George ("Mickey") Leland (Texas) 1979–1989
Harold Washington (Illinois) 1981–1983
Katie Hall (Indiana) 1983–1985
Alton R. Waldon, Jr. (New York) 1986–1987
George W. Crockett, Jr. (Michigan) 1980–1991
Walter E. Fauntroy (District of Columbia) 1971–1991
Augustus F. ("Gus") Hawkins (California) 1963–1991
William H. Gray, III (Pennsylvania) 1979–1991
Gus Savage (Illinois) 1981–1992
Charles A. Hayes (Illinois) 1983–1992
Mike Espy (Mississippi) 1987–1992

CONGRESSIONAL BLACK CAUCUS, 1993

Sanford D. Bishop (Georgia) 1993–
Lucien E. Blackwell (Pennsylvania) 1991–
Carol Moseley Braun (Illinois) 1993–
Corrine Brown (Florida) 1993–
William L. Clay (Missouri) 1969–
Eva M. Clayton (North Carolina) 1993–
Barbara Rose-Collins (Michigan) 1991–
Cardiss Collins (Illinois) 1973–
John Conyers, Jr. (Michigan) 1965–
James E. Clyburn (South Carolina) 1993–
Ronald V. Dellums (California) 1971–
Julian C. Dixon (California) 1979–

Appendix A

Mervyn M. Dymally (California)	1981–
Cleo Fields (Louisiana)	1993–
Floyd Flake (New York)	1987–
Harold E. Ford (Tennessee)	1975–
Gary Franks (Connecticut)	1991–
Alcee Hastings (Florida)	1993–
Earl Hilliard (Alabama)	1993–
William Jefferson (Louisiana)	1991–
Eddie Bernice Johnson (Texas)	1993–
John Lewis (Georgia)	1987–
Cynthia McKinney (Georgia)	1993–
Carrie Meek (Florida)	1993–
Kweisi Mfume (Maryland)	1987–
Eleanor Holmes Norton (District of Columbia)	1991–
Major R. Owens (New York)	1983–
Donald M. Payne (New Jersey)	1989–
Charles B. Rangel (New York)	1971–
Mel Reynolds (Illinois)	1993–
Bobby Rush (Illinois)	1993–
Bobby Scott (Virginia)	1993–
Louis Stokes (Ohio)	1969–
Bennie Thompson (Mississippi)	1993–
Ed Towns (New York)	1983–
Walter Tucker (California)	1993–
Craig Washington (Texas)	1990–
Maxine Waters (California)	1991–
Mel Watt (North Carolina)	1993–
Alan Wheat (Missouri)	1983–
Albert Wynn (Maryland)	1993–

Appendix B
Black Members of Congress:
Biographical Sketches

SANFORD D. BISHOP

Congressman from Georgia
(1993–present)

Sanford Bishop (Democrat) was elected in November 1992 from the Second District of Georgia. Born February 4, 1947, in Mobile, Alabama, he received a bachelor of arts degree from Morehouse College and a juris doctor degree from Emory Law School.

Bishop served in both houses of the Georgia State Legislature. He was in the House from 1976 to 1990 and in the Senate from 1990 to his election to Congress in 1992. As a State Representative, he served on the Ways and Means Committee and displayed a great interest in the financial affairs of the state. His priority concerns in Congress will be the boosting of federal aid to public schools and the developing of tax incentives for small-city enterprise zones.

Bishop was named to the Agriculture Committee, the Veterans Committee, and the Post Office and Civil Service Committee.

LUCIEN E. BLACKWELL

Congressman from Pennsylvania
(1991–present)

Lucien Blackwell (Democrat) was elected on November 5, 1991, to fill the Second Congressional District seat formerly held by Bill Gray, who resigned to accept the position of executive director of the United Negro College Fund. Blackwell served on the Philadelphia City Council for seventeen years, where he held important positions such as majority whip and chairman of the Finance Committee.

Prior to his election to Congress, Blackwell served as a commissioner of the Delaware River Port Authority, as board director on the Port Corporation, and also as a member of the Governor's Infrastructure Task Force.

Blackwell was born August 1, 1931, attended public schools in Philadelphia, and went to work on the waterfront docks. He worked his way up from laborer to foreman to business agent and then president of Local 1332, International Longshoremen's Association, AFL-CIO, a position he held until his election to Congress eighteen years later.

CAROL MOSELEY BRAUN

U.S. Senator from Illinois
(1993–present)

November 3, 1992, was a historic day in the annals of black America because of the election of Carol Moseley Braun (Democrat) to the United States Senate. Her victory in the general election followed her upset defeat of two-term incumbent Alan Dixon in the primary. This marked the first time in history that a black woman or a black Democrat was elected to the U.S. Senate. The three black senators who served previously were all men and all Republicans.

Born in 1947 in Chicago and the mother of one son, Carol Moseley Braun has an extensive background in the field of politics. She worked for three years as a prosecutor in the U.S. Attorney's office after graduating from the University of Chicago Law School. She was elected to the Illinois House of Representatives in 1978 and stayed for ten years, rising to the rank of assistant majority leader. In 1987 Braun was appointed the recorder of deeds, which marked the first time a woman or a black person had ever held an executive office in Cook County government.

She serves on the Senate Ethics Committee, the Judiciary Committee, the Small Business and Banking Committee, and the Housing and Urban Affairs Committee.

EDWARD W. BROOKE

U.S. Senator from Massachusetts
(1967–1979)

Edward W. Brooke (Republican) represented the state of Massachusetts in the United States Senate from 1967 to 1979. He was born in Washington, D.C., in 1919 and attended the public schools. He graduated from Howard University in 1941 just prior to entering the U.S. Army as a second lieutenant. He was awarded an LL.B. and an LL.M. from Boston University. In 1960, he ran for secretary of the Commonwealth of Massachusetts and was defeated by Kevin H. White, who later became mayor of Boston.

Two years later, Brooke was successful in his bid to become attorney general of the state, serving in that capacity until 1966, when he defeated former Governor Endicott Peabody in the general election for the United States Senate. He outpolled Peabody by a plurality of 438,712 votes to become the first black elected to the United States Senate by popular vote.

The black population of the state, only 6 percent, was not a major factor in the election. As Senator Brooke often said, he was not just the first Negro this or the highest Negro that, he could likewise be described as a Protestant in a Catholic state and a Republican in a Democratic state.

Brooke defeated Democrat John J. Droney to win a second Senate term in 1972. During that term, he introduced a resolution authorizing the attorney general to appoint a special prosecutor to investigate the Watergate crimes and later became the first senator to call publicly for President Richard M. Nixon's resignation. He was an effective spokesman for low-income housing tenants. The law requiring the government to charge no more than 30 percent of a tenant's annual earnings is called the Brooke Amendment.

In the September 1978 Republican primary, he defeated Avi Nelson, but he lost in the general election to Democrat Paul Tsongas. He later resumed the practice of law in the District of Columbia.

CORRINE BROWN

Congresswoman from Florida
(1993–present)

Corrine Brown (Democrat), with ten years of experience in the Florida House of Representatives, comes to Congress well-equipped to enhance her reputation as an advocate for the poor and the underprivileged. She was elected from the Third District of Florida in the November 1992 election. Her restless energy and sensitive concern for the plight of senior citizens resulted in her being named "Legislator of the Year" by the Florida Association of Housing for the Aging.

A native of Jacksonville, Florida, she was born November 11, 1946, and has one child. She received B.S. and master's degrees from Florida Agricultural and Mechanical University and an education specialist degree from the University of Florida. Since 1977, Brown has been a member of the faculty at Florida Community College of Jacksonville; she formerly served on the faculties of the University of Florida and Edward Waters College.

She was named to the Public Works and Transportation Committee, the Veteran's Affairs Committee, and the Committee on Government Operations.

BLANCHE KELSO BRUCE

U.S. Senator from Mississippi
(1875–1881)

Blanche K. Bruce (Republican) was a well-educated former slave. Born March 1, 1841, in Farmville, Virginia, he studied at Oberlin College in Ohio; organized Missouri's first school for blacks at Hannibal in 1864; and later moved to Mississippi, where he eventually amassed a sizeable fortune from real estate holdings. Prior to being elected to the United States Senate, Bruce held several other elected positions at the local level. In 1870, he was elected to the Mississippi State Senate; in 1871, he was appointed assessor of taxes in Bolivar County; and in 1872, he was elected sheriff of the same county.

Bruce went to the Senate in 1875 and served one six-year term. During his term of office, he was an outspoken champion of minority rights and supported legislation to defend the rights of Chinese and Indians. He was appointed chairman of the Select Committee to Investigate the Freedmen's Savings and Trust Company. The six-member committee conducted a thorough inquiry and wrote a comprehensive report documenting the crimes of bank officials in the scandal. Subsequently, more than 61,000 black depositors who had been victims of fraud or incompetence received all or part of their investments. Mr. Bruce took the same position as his predecessor, Senator Revels, when it came to the question of amnesty for unrepentant Confederate leaders. They both seriously misjudged the vengeful intentions of the recalcitrant proponents of human slavery. Bruce assiduously fought to restore all rights of citizenship, including the right to hold public office, to former Confederate officers and elected officials.

In 1880, Democrats took control of the Mississippi State Legislature and nominated a Democrat, James Z. George, to succeed Bruce. In 1881, President James A. Garfield appointed Bruce registrar of the U.S. Treasury Department. He was replaced in that office in 1885, when the Democrats regained control. Four years later President Benjamin Harrison appointed him to the position of recorder of deeds for the District of Columbia and again as registrar of the Treasury from 1887 until his death in Washington, D.C., on March 17, 1898.

YVONNE BRAITHWAITE BURKE
Congresswoman from California
(1973–1979)

Yvonne Braithwaite Burke (Democrat) was elected to the House of Representatives in 1972 from the Thirty-seventh Congressional District in Los Angeles, California.

She received a bachelor of arts degree in political science from the University of California at Los Angeles and a doctor of law degree from the University of Southern California School of Law. Before coming to Congress, she served six years in the California State Assembly. In 1972, she was the vice-chairperson of the Democratic National Convention. A scholar as well as political activist, Ms. Burke was selected in 1972 by Harvard University as a fellow in their Institute of Politics and the John F. Kennedy School of Government; she was selected by Yale University as a Chubb fellow in 1975.

She was the first woman in the history of the Congress to give birth while serving in office. She was also the first woman to chair the Congressional Black Caucus. She served as a member of the Interior Committee and the Public Works Committee for two years. In her second term, she was elected by the Democratic Caucus to the more powerful House Appropriations Committee. While a member of the Public Works Committee, she attached an amendment to the Alaska Pipeline Bill for a minority set-aside that resulted in hundreds of millions of dollars in contracts to black businesses.

Ms. Burke did not seek re-election in 1978, choosing instead to run for attorney general of the state of California. She lost her bid for that office and is now practicing law in Los Angeles.

RICHARD HARVEY CAIN
Congressman from South Carolina
(1873–1875 and 1877–1879)

Richard Harvey Cain (Republican) was a minister in the African Methodist Episcopal (AME) Church. Originally, Mr. Cain was a member of the Methodist Episcopal Church in Hannibal, Missouri, but in 1844 he left that denomination in protest of their segregationist practices, joining the AME Church. He was born of free parents and served in the army with the forces of the North during the Civil War. From 1866 to 1872, he was editor and publisher of the *South Carolina Leader* and while in that position hired as associate editor Robert B. Elliott, who later became a very influential black member of Congress.

After serving four years in the South Carolina State Senate, Cain was elected to Congress as a Republican in 1872, defeating Lewis E. Johnson, who ran as an independent. He served on the Agriculture Committee. He was an ardent supporter of Senator Charles Sumner's bill to desegregate juries, public transportation and accommodations, and schools. After the legislature eliminated his at-large seat in 1874, he declined to seek re-election. However, in 1876 he ran again and was elected over Democrat Michael P. O'Connor.

After leaving the Congress in 1878, when the Republican party nominated former Representative Edmund W. M. Mackey, Mr. Cain became a bishop in the African Methodist Episcopal Church, serving as head of the Texas-Louisiana Conference.

Cain was one of the founders of the Paul Quinn College in Waco, Texas. He was transferred to the bishopric of Washington, D.C., which covered New England, New Jersey, New York, and Philadelphia, where he died in 1887.

HENRY P. CHEATHAM

Congressman from North Carolina
(1888–1893)

Henry Plummer Cheatham (Republican) was born a slave in Henderson, North Carolina, in 1857 and earned a B.A and an honorary M.A degree from Shaw University in North Carolina. He was an educator and taught at the State Normal School in Plymouth, North Carolina. He also studied law but never entered private practice.

Cheatham ran for Congress on the Republican ticket in 1888 and was elected by a margin of less than 1,000 votes. He was re-elected in 1890 by a more comfortable margin and became the only surviving black member of the Congress. Thomas E. Miller of South Carolina and John M. Langston of Virginia, the other two blacks in Congress, were defeated in their bids for re-election. In 1892, Cheatham was defeated in his attempt for a third term. This time he faced stiff opposition in his own Republican party and also from the new Populist party. He was defeated by a Democrat, Frederick A. Woodard. In the next election, Cheatham made another effort at the seat only to be defeated by his brother-in-law, George H. White.

In 1897, President McKinley appointed him recorder of deeds for the District of Columbia, a position apparently reserved for former black members of Congress. He returned to North Carolina in 1901 and became superintendent of the Oxford Orphanage, which housed 200 students. He died in 1935 at Oxford, North Carolina.

SHIRLEY ANITA CHISHOLM

Congresswoman from New York
(1969–1983)

Shirley A. Chisholm (Democrat) was elected to Congress in 1968 from the Twelfth District of New York. The heart of the district was the Bedford-

Stuyvesant area in Brooklyn. She was the first black woman elected to Congress.

Chisholm was born in Brooklyn in 1924. She graduated from Brooklyn College in 1946 with a B.A. in sociology. In 1952, she received an M.A. from Columbia University. From 1953 until 1959, she was director of New York's Hamilton-Madison Child Care Center, then became educational consultant for New York's Division of Day Care. She also served in the New York State Assembly for four years.

Mrs. Chisholm served on the Veterans Affairs Committee for the first two years of her term in the House. In 1971, she won a seat on the House Education and Labor Committee, where her many years in the field of education were better utilized. Three years later, she was appointed to the more important Rules Committee of the House.

On January 24, 1972, Chisholm declared her candidacy for the Democratic presidential nomination. She entered primaries in a dozen states and waged an extensive campaign. Although she only won 28 delegates and received only 152 votes on the first ballot at the Democratic Convention in Miami, she won the hearts of many thousands of black, poor, and mistreated American citizens.

After fourteen years in the House, she declined to run for re-election in 1982, citing the difficulties of effectuating real and meaningful change through the political process. She returned to private life in Williamsville, New York, where she spends a quiet life preparing for occasional lectures.

WILLIAM L. CLAY
Congressman from Missouri
(1969–present)

William ("Bill") Clay (Democrat) was elected to the U.S. House of Representatives in 1968 from the First Congressional District. He serves on the Education and Labor Committee and the House Administration Committee and chairs the Post Office and Civil Service Committee.

He was born in St. Louis in 1931, received a bachelor's degree in history and political science from Saint Louis University in 1953. Shortly after his discharge from the army in 1955, he became active in civil rights and politics. He was elected to the Saint Louis Board of Aldermen in 1959, where he sponsored and secured passage of the first Fair Employment Act in the city's history. He resigned from the board in 1964 after being elected committeeman of the Twenty-sixth Ward. His political career coincided with his activity as a union official. He was a business representative for the State, County and Municipal Workers Union from 1961 to 1964 and education coordinator for Pipefitter's Local 562 from 1966 until his election to Congress.

While chairman of the Labor/Management Subcommittee on Pensions, Clay sponsored revisions in pension law that reduced the time for vesting from ten years to five. He also incorporated into the law a provision that a married person could not opt for a higher monthly retirement check that would end the pension benefits upon his or her death without consent of the spouse. He recognized that too many spouses were left without financial means because of this loophole in the law. He also sponsored legislation for family and medical leave, for mandatory notification to workers of plant closings, and for the protection of workers who exercise their right to strike.

APPENDIX B

EVA M. CLAYTON

Congresswoman from North Carolina
(1993–present)

Eva M. Clayton (Democrat) represents the First Congressional District of North Carolina. She brings to Congress more than twenty-five years of experience in both government and the private sector and ten years of experience as an elected official. She is a highly educated, community-oriented leader who has a wealth of experience in both the legislative and executive branches of government.

Congresswoman Clayton received a bachelor of science degree in biology from Johnson C. Smith University and a master's degree in science from North Carolina Central University. She attended the School of Law at the University of North Carolina at Chapel Hill, where she also attended the Government Executive Institute of the School of Business Administration.

She began her political career as an assistant secretary for community development for the North Carolina Department of Natural Resources and Community Development. She also served as executive director of the Soul City Foundation, a New Town project financed with federal funds. Before her election to Congress in 1992, Clayton served for ten years on the Warren County Commission, of which she was chairperson for seven years.

In Congress she serves on the Small Business Committee and the Agriculture Committee. Her election to Congress marks the first time a black person has represented the state of North Carolina since the defeat of George White in 1901. Clayton is the first black woman to be elected to Congress from the state and also the first black Democrat to be elected.

Born in Savannah, Georgia, she is married to Theoseus Clayton, Sr., an attorney in Warrenton, N.C., and has four adult children and two grandsons.

JAMES E. CLYBURN

Congressman from South Carolina
(1993–present)

James E. ("Jim") Clyburn (Democrat) was elected in November 1992 from the Sixth District of South Carolina. He is the first black Congressman from that state since the defeat of George Washington Murray in 1897. He is also the first black Democrat ever to serve in Congress from South Carolina.

Born in Sumter, South Carolina, in 1940, he graduated from South Carolina State College, where he led the student movement. Clyburn's wife is the former Emily England, of Moncks Corner, South Carolina. He has three daughters, Mignon, Jennifer, and Angela.

In 1968, Clyburn became executive director of the South Carolina Commission for Farm Workers, then joined the staff of Governor John C. West in 1974 as human affairs commissioner. While serving in that capacity he garnered a wealth of knowledge in the area of civil rights. During his stint with state government, Clyburn played a major role in pushing through several important civil rights bills, including the state's Bill of Rights for Handicapped Citizens in 1983 and the Fair Housing Law in 1989.

In the Democratic primary of 1992, Clyburn defeated four others by a wide margin. He received 39,802 votes, while his nearest rival, Frank Gilbert, got 10,859. The three others—Ken Mosley, John Roy Harper II and Herbert

Fledding—split approximately 20,000 votes. Democrat Robin Tallon, an incumbent of ten years with a great record on civil rights, chose not to seek re-election, because he believed it was time for a black person from South Carolina to serve in the U.S. Congress and felt that his own candidacy would be racially divisive.

In the general election, Clyburn defeated his Republican opponent John Chase by a margin of 2 to 1.

BARBARA ROSE-COLLINS

Congresswoman from Michigan
(1991–present)

Barbara Rose-Collins (Democrat) was born in Detroit, attended Wayne State University, was elected to the Michigan State Legislature in 1975, and served there until 1982, when she was elected to the Detroit City Council. She was elected to the House from the Thirteenth District in 1990 to replace Congressman George Crockett, who did not seek re-election.

CARDISS COLLINS

Congresswoman from Illinois
(1973–present)

Cardiss Collins (Democrat) was first elected in 1973 to fill the Seventh District seat of her husband, George, who was killed in an airplane crash. She later became committeewoman of Chicago's Twenty-fourth Ward Regular Democratic Organization. Mrs. Collins, a former chairperson of the Congressional Black Caucus, serves on the Government Operations Committee, the Energy and Commerce Committee, and the Select Committee on Narcotics Abuse and Control. She is chairperson of the Subcommittee on Government Activities and Transportation of the Government Operations Committee.

Collins was born in Saint Louis, Missouri, and moved to Detroit at the age of ten. After finishing high school, she journeyed to Chicago and attended Northwestern University, majoring in accounting and business. Later, she worked for the Illinois Department of Labor and for the Illinois Department of Revenue.

As chairperson of the Subcommittee on Government Activities and Transportation, she has gained national attention for her investigations of airport security and advocacy of air safety practices. In addition, her legislative efforts on the Energy and Commerce Committee include increasing access to the telecommunications industry for minority broadcasters and owners, maintaining a strong and competitive financial marketplace, improving the quality of and access to health care, and supporting various measures to protect consumers and enhance their rights as purchasers.

GEORGE W. COLLINS

Congressman from Illinois
(1970–1972)

George W. Collins (Democrat) was elected to the Congress in 1970 from Illinois's Seventh Congressional District. He was born in Chicago in 1925 and

APPENDIX B

was a 1954 graduate of Central College in Illinois. After graduation, he worked with the Chicago Municipal Court while earning a degree in business law from Northwestern University in 1957.

He was elected in 1964 to the Chicago Board of Aldermen from the Twenty-fourth Ward. He was also the Democratic committeeman of the Twenty-fourth Ward. During his brief tenure in Congress, the soft-spoken, hardworking, well-respected Mr. Collins served as a member of the Government Operations Committee and the Public Works Committee. But he devoted much time to rural and agricultural affairs and became a specialist for the Congressional Black Caucus in these areas of interest.

He succeeded Congressman Daniel J. Ronan, who won the Democratic primary but died before the general election in 1969. With the active support of the Daley machine, Collins won in the district, which was 58 percent white, covering the suburban areas of Cicero and Berwyn, as well as Chicago's West Side.

Collins supported the Nixon administration's proposals to provide a minimum federal payment to low-income families with children and to share federal tax revenues with states and localities, but sharply criticized the plan's funding levels as inadequate. He worked to increase funding for the Elementary and Secondary Education Act and advocated passage of federal highway legislation that addressed the needs of mass transit programs and of urban residents uprooted from their neighborhoods by road construction.

In December 1972, one month before he was scheduled to begin his second term in Congress, the forty-seven-year-old Collins was killed in an airplane crash at Midway Field in downtown Chicago. The United Air Lines plane crashed into a house on the city's South Side. Forty-four others died in the crash.

JOHN CONYERS, JR.

Congressman from Michigan
(1965–present)

John Conyers, Jr., (Democrat) was elected in 1964 from the city of Detroit, Michigan's First Congressional District. He is a senior member of the Judiciary Committee and the full committee chairman of the Government Operations Committee. He also serves on the Small Business Committee. He was born in Detroit in 1929, educated in the public schools of Detriot, and earned bachelor and doctor of laws degrees at Wayne State University. He worked as a legislative assistant to Congressman John Dingell from 1958 to 1961 and as a referee for the Michigan Workmen's Compensation Department from 1961 to 1963. He was active in the civil rights movement and served as general counsel for the Detroit Trade Union Leadership Council.

He was a principal sponsor of the Hawkins-Humphrey Full Employment Bill, the Martin Luther King Holiday Bill, and the Civil Rights Restoration Bill. He is an outspoken foe of the death penalty and supports legislation to curb police violence and white collar crimes and to promote grand jury reform.

His amendment to prohibit the export of any nuclear materials, technology, equipment, and information and to preclude authorization of technical personnel to work in or for South Africa became a part of the Anti-Apartheid Act, which passed the House in 1985.

GEORGE W. CROCKETT, JR.
Congressman from Michigan
(1980–1990)

George W. Crockett, Jr., (Democrat) is a graduate of Morehouse College and the University of Michigan Law School. On November 4, 1980, Mr. Crockett, after a long and distinguished career as lawyer, jurist, and activist, was elected to the House of Representatives from the Thirteenth District and sworn in on November 12, 1980, to fill the vacancy created by the resignation of Charles C. Diggs. At the same time, he was elected to serve a full term in the next Congress, which began two months later.

He was born in Jacksonville, Florida, in 1909. Before coming to Congress, he served as acting corporation counsel for the city of Detroit. In 1939, he became the first black attorney appointed to the U.S. Department of Labor. In 1943, President Roosevelt named him a hearing examiner with the Fair Employment Practices Commission. A year later he moved to Detroit and became director of a fair employment practices office with the United Auto Workers Union. He served as judge of the Recorders Court from 1966 to 1978 and in 1974 was elected presiding judge of the court. He also was a visiting judge on the Michigan Court of Appeals.

Mr. Crockett served on the Committee on Foreign Affairs, where he chaired the Western Hemisphere Affairs Subcommittee; the Committee on the Judiciary; and the Select Committee on Aging. He focused his energies on preserving the structure of social and economic justice domestically and on redirecting foreign policy and assistance globally.

In 1990, he announced that he would not seek re-election.

WILLIAM L. DAWSON
Congressman from Illinois
(1943–1970)

William L. Dawson (Democrat) graduated magna cum laude from Fisk University in Tennessee and attended Kent and Northwestern University Schools of Law. He was elected to Congress in 1942, from Illinois's First District, serving on the Government Operations Committee and the District of Columbia Committee. In 1949, he became the first black member of Congress to chair a standing committee, the Government Operations Committee.

Dawson was born in Albany, Georgia, earned a law degree from Northwestern University, and was a first lieutenant in the army during World War I. In 1935, he was elected alderman as a Republican but crossed party lines and became one of President Roosevelt's staunchest supporters. In 1940, he left the Republican party and was elected Democratic committeeman of the Second Ward. In 1944, he was appointed assistant chairman of the Democratic National Committee, and soon became the first black to be elected its vice-chairman.

Dawson served in Congress twenty-eight years and held the respect of his colleagues for the entire time. He was the indisputable political leader back home in Chicago and very influential with the most powerful political figures on the Washington scene. His quiet demeanor in later years caused blood-seeking vultures in the media to compare him unfairly to the more flamboyant Adam Clayton Powell and thus depict him as less aggressive, less militant, and less committed to the cause of justice and equality for black people. Nothing was farther from the truth. The difference was more style than substance.

Labeling Mr. Dawson an "Uncle Tom" is a distortion of fact. He was adamantly opposed to racial segregation and discrimination. He fought for better appointments for blacks in the federal civil service and the judiciary; supported efforts to increase black voter registration in the South; effectively blocked congressional efforts to discredit the integration of public schools in the District of Columbia; opposed the imposition of poll taxes; and led the fight to defeat the Winstead Amendment, which would have permitted military personnel to choose whether they wanted to serve in all-white or all-black units.

Before retiring at age eighty-six, Dawson announced support for Ralph Metcalfe as his successor. He died one year later, on November 6, 1971.

ROBERT C. DeLARGE

Congressman from South Carolina
(1871–1873)

Robert C. DeLarge (Republican) defeated another Republican, Christopher C. Bowen, for Congress in 1870 by a margin of 986 votes out of 32,000 cast. Before going to Congress, he chaired the Credentials Committee at the 1865 Colored People's Convention held in Charleston and was a member of the state house of representatives, serving as chairman of the Ways and Means Committee. Shortly before his victorious campaign for Congress in 1870, DeLarge was appointed land commissioner to supervise the sale and transfer of land to persons who promised to pay for it within an eight-year period.

DeLarge was born a slave in 1842 in Aiken, South Carolina, and was educated at Wood High School. During the period of Reconstruction, he devoted his time to farming, tailoring, and acting as agent for the Freedmen's Bureau.

He was sworn into the Forty-second Congress on March 4, 1871. His right to sit in the House was challenged by his opponent, but that did not prevent his being seated while the Congress considered the challenge. For more than seventeen months, the House Committee on Elections investigated numerous allegations of voter fraud, finally ruling that neither DeLarge nor his opponent, Christopher Bowen, was entitled to the seat.

In 1872, DeLarge did not seek re-election. Another black, Alonzo J. Ransier, replaced him in the House of Representatives.

RONALD V. DELLUMS

Congressman from California
(1971–present)

Ronald V. Dellums (Democrat) was elected in 1970 from the Eighth District of California. He defeated incumbent Jeffrey Cohelan in the primary with 57 percent of the vote. He was elected during the height of the Vietnam War as an outspoken opponent of U.S. intervention in Indochina.

He was born in Oakland, California, in 1935; earned an A.A. degree at Oakland City College, a B.A. degree from San Francisco State University, and an M.S.W. degree in psychiatric social work from the University of California,

Berkeley. He served on the Berkeley City Council from 1967 to 1971, where he emerged as a spokesman for minorities and the disadvantaged. From that position he mounted his successful campaign for Congress, focusing on the unrest and discontent in the nation because of the war in Southeast Asia and the maltreatment of minorities here in America.

He serves on the Armed Services Committee and District of Columbia Committee. In 1979, he was elected chairman of the District of Columbia Committee. He is also chairman of the Subcommittee on Military Installations and Facilities of the Armed Services Committee.

Mr. Dellums is the principal congressional leader working to slow down military spending and curb the nuclear arms race. He was the first to introduce legislation to preclude funding for the MX, Pershing II, Midgetman, and B-1 weapons programs. His 1979 advocacy of a "double-zero" option on theater nuclear weapons subsequently proved the basis for the INF Treaty approved in 1988.

He was the prime sponsor of the legislation that officially ended U.S. support for the apartheid government of South Africa. Dellums served as chairman of the Congressional Black Caucus from 1989 to 1991.

OSCAR DePRIEST

Congressman from Illinois
(1929–1935)

Oscar DePriest (Republican) in 1928 became the first black elected to Congress in the twentieth century. He was born in Florence, Alabama, in 1871. He arrived in Chicago in 1889, laboring as a plasterer, house painter, and decorator. He then ventured into the real estate business. Through his property holdings and stock market investments, he amassed a fortune.

He was elected to the Cook County Board of Commissioners in 1904 and to the Chicago Board of Aldermen in 1915. After two years (1915–1917) on the board of aldermen, he was indicted on charges of accepting bribes to provide police protection to gamblers. He resigned but was then acquitted of all charges.

After the death of incumbent Congressman Martin Madden of the South Side, DePriest was selected by local committeemen to replace him. In the November election, he defeated both a white Democrat, Harry Baker, and a black independent, William Harrison.

While in the House, he served on the Committee on Enrolled Bills, the Indian Affairs Committee, and the Invalid Pensions Committee. He introduced a bill providing for a $75 monthly pension to ex-slave citizens. He sponsored legislation to make Abraham Lincoln's birthday a legal holiday.

DePriest was defeated in his 1934 bid for a fourth term by black Democrat Arthur W. Mitchell. He returned to Chicago and was elected to the board of aldermen and served from 1943 to 1947. He died in 1951.

CHARLES C. DIGGS, JR.

Congressman from Michigan
(1955–1980)

Charles C. Diggs, Jr., (Democrat) the first black congressman from Michigan, was elected in 1954 from the Thirteenth District. He was born in Detroit in

1922, educated in the public schools, and attended the University of Michigan and Fisk University in Tennessee.

During the Second World War, he entered the army air force as a private, was later commissioned a second lieutenant, and was discharged a captain. He then enrolled in Wayne College of Mortuary Science and subsequently became a licensed mortician and board chairman of the House of Diggs, Inc., a family-owned funeral business, the largest in the state of Michigan.

Diggs was a member of the Michigan State Senate from 1951 to 1954 before being elected to Congress. During his twenty-five years in Congress, he served on the Foreign Affairs Committee and District of Columbia Committee. He was elected chairman of the District of Columbia Committee in 1973 after the defeat of its racist chairman, John L. McMillan of South Carolina. Under his leadership, residents of Washington, D.C., obtained, for the first time in 100 years, the right to elect their own mayor and city council.

Diggs was one of the organizers of the Congressional Black Caucus and served as its first chairman from 1971 to 1973. In October 1978, he was convicted of mail fraud and falsifying payroll forms. The House censured him in July 1979 and he resigned on June 3, 1980, after the Supreme Court refused to review his case.

JULIAN C. DIXON

Congressman from California
(1979–present)

Julian C. Dixon (Democrat) was elected in 1978 from the Twenty-eighth District of California. He serves on the Appropriations Committee. In 1985, he was named chairman of the House Committee on Standards of Official Conduct (Ethics Committee). He served six years in the California Assembly before election to Congress.

He was born in Washington, D.C., in 1934; earned a B.S. at California State University and a law degree from Southwestern University. He worked as legislative aide to California State Senator Merv Dymally, now Congressman Dymally, before himself being elected to Congress.

In 1983, he wrote the first economic sanctions law against South Africa, and, in 1987, he authored an urgent appropriations bill to provide humanitarian aid to southern Africa, the world's poorest region. He also was instrumental in gaining increased development assistance for Africa, disaster assistance for Jamaica, and scholarships for disadvantaged South African students. He has taken a particular interest in legislation related to mass transit, low- and moderate-income housing, and health care.

Mr. Dixon served for four years as president of the Congressional Black Caucus Foundation, a nonprofit institution engaged in public policy analysis which encourages minority participation in the legislative process. During the Ninety-eighth Congress, he also served as chairman of the Congressional Black Caucus. In 1984, he served as chairman of the Standing Committee on Rules for the Democratic National Convention.

MERVYN M. DYMALLY

Congressman from California
(1981–present)

Mervyn M. Dymally (Democrat) was elected to Congress in 1981 from the Thirty-first District of California, defeating ten-term incumbent Charles Wilson and three others in the Democratic primary. He is chairman of the District of Columbia Subcommittee on Judiciary and Education. He also serves on the Foreign Affairs Committee, where he is chairman of the Subcommittee on International Operations.

Dymally, born in Cedros, Trinidad, British West Indies, holds a B.A. in education from California State University, Los Angeles; an M.A. in government from California State University, Sacramento; and a Ph.D in human behavior from United States International University, San Diego, California. He was a member of the California State Assembly from 1963 to 1967; a member of the California State Senate from 1967 to 1975; and lieutenant governor of the state from 1975 to 1979.

From 1987 until 1989 he was chairman of the Congressional Black Caucus, and served as convener of the CBC brain trust on science and technology. He has advocated the causes of many human rights groups and devotes particular attention to United States policies toward the Caribbean.

ROBERT B. ELLIOTT
Congressman from South Carolina
(1871–1875)

Robert Brown Elliott (Republican) was born in Boston, Massachusetts, of West Indian parents in 1842, according to some sources. Other records give his birthplace as Liverpool, England. However, he attended grammar school in Jamaica and high school at the Holborn Academy in London. He graduated with high honors from Eton University in England.

Elliott moved to Charleston, South Carolina, and went to work as associate editor of the *South Carolina Leader*, a paper owned by Richard Harvey Cain, who later was also elected to the U.S. House of Representatives. He was associate editor of the *Charleston Leader* newspaper for several years.

In 1868, Elliott was elected to the state house of representatives and also admitted to the South Carolina bar. In 1870, he was nominated by the Republican party for Congress and defeated John E. Bacon.

In Congress, he served on the Education and Labor Committee and the Committee on the Militia. He was a great orator and an uncompromising defender of the civil rights of minority citizens. Elliott was in the vanguard of the movement advocating compulsory public education in this country.

In his first speech before the House, he argued against restoring political rights to ex-Confederate leaders. He was re-elected without opposition in the next election. But Elliott was forced out of office in 1877 when federal troops were withdrawn from the South and Reconstruction came to an end. Unable to continue his law practice because of malarial fever, he moved to New Orleans, where he died in poverty on August 9, 1884.

MIKE ESPY
Congressman from Mississippi
(1987–1993)

Mike Espy (Democrat) was elected to Congress from the Second District of Mississippi in 1987. He was born in Yazoo City, Mississippi, in 1953. The congressman graduated from Howard University with a degree in political science and earned a degree in law from the University of California at Santa Clara.

Espy returned to Mississippi to practice law, eventually serving as assistant secretary of state for legal services. He was appointed secretary of state of the Public Lands Division from 1980 to 1984 and served as assistant state attorney general of the Mississippi Consumer Protection Division in 1984.

Winning in a very close election in 1987, he became the first black elected from Mississippi since Reconstruction. He won a landslide victory in his 1989 bid for re-election, carrying all of the twenty-two counties in the district and receiving 66 percent of the total vote.

He served on the Agriculture Committee and the Budget Committee.

Mr. Espy was one of the few freshmen members of Congress to pass a major piece of legislation in the One Hundredth Congress, the Lower Mississippi River Valley Delta Development Act. It is the blueprint for economic development in a seven-state area. Espy resigned from the Congress in 1993 to accept a cabinet position as Secretary of Agriculture in the Clinton administration.

MELVIN H. EVANS
Delegate from the Virgin Islands
(1979–1980)

Dr. Melvin H. Evans (Republican) was elected to Congress in 1979 from the Virgin Islands. He was born in Christiansted, St. Croix, in 1917; received a B.S. in 1940 from Howard University and an M.D. from the Howard College of Medicine in 1944. From 1959 to 1967, he served as the health commissioner for the Virgin Islands. In 1969, President Nixon appointed him governor of the Virgin Islands.

In 1968, Congress enacted the Virgin Islands Elective Governor Act, which provided for the election of a governor by the territory's residents. Evans was elected to the governor's office as a Republican in 1970 and served until 1975.

In 1978, he was elected to Congress as the non-voting delegate from the islands. He served on the Interior and Insular Affairs Committee and the Armed Services Committee. He was defeated in 1980 by Ron de Lugo. The next year, President Reagan appointed him ambassador to Trinidad and Tobago, where he served until his death in 1984.

WALTER E. FAUNTROY
Delegate from the District of Columbia
(1971–1990)

The Reverend Walter E. Fauntroy (Democrat) was elected to Congress from the District of Columbia in 1971. He served on the District of Columbia Committee; the Banking, Finance and Urban Affairs Committee; and the Select Committee on Narcotics Abuse and Control. He chaired the District of Columbia Committee's Subcommittee on Fiscal Affairs and Health. During the Ninety-seventh Congress (1981–1983) he was chairman of the Congressional Black Caucus.

Before election to Congress, Fauntroy was a top aide to Dr. Martin Luther King. His first encounter with elected office was as a member of the District of Columbia City Council, where he served from 1967 until resigning in 1969 to accept a position with the Model Inner City Community Organization, a neighborhood planning agency.

Fauntroy is a native of Washington, D.C., born in 1933. He attended the city's public schools, graduated cum laude from Virginia Union University in 1955, and earned his bachelor of divinity degree from Yale University Divinity School in 1958. He began his public career in 1959 as pastor of New Bethel Baptist Church.

CLEO FIELDS

Congressman from Louisiana
(1993–present)

At the age of twenty-nine, the Honorable Cleo Fields (Democrat) of the Fourth District of Louisiana became the youngest member of the 103rd Congress. At the age of twenty-four, he was the youngest member ever to serve in the Louisiana State Senate. The youthful Cleo Fields was a serious and effective legislator. He earned a reputation as a leader in the war against illicit drugs and, while serving as chairman of the Redistricting Committee, was able to craft a 65 percent black Congressional district. He successfully ran in that district to become the first black person elected to Congress from the state since 1877.

Fields received his undergraduate degree in 1984 from Southern University and a juris doctor degree from Southern University School of Law in 1987. At Southern, he was a student leader, serving as chairman of College Students for the Statewide Registration/Education March from Shreveport to Baton Rouge. The march resulted in hundreds of students registering to vote. He was also founder and executive director of the Young Adults for Positive Action, Inc.

Fields was born on November 22, 1962, in Baton Rouge. He serves on the Small Business Committee and the Committee on Banking, Finance, and Urban Affairs.

FLOYD H. FLAKE

Congressman from New York
(1987–present)

The Reverend Floyd H. Flake (Democrat) was elected to Congress from the Sixth District of Queens, New York, to fill the vacancy created by the death of longtime incumbent Joseph Addabbo. He narrowly lost to Alton Waldon in the special election to fill the remainder of Mr. Addabbo's term, but in the next regularly scheduled primary election, Flake defeated Waldon. He was appointed to the Banking, Finance and Urban Affairs Committee; the Small Business Committee; and the Select Committee on Hunger.

Flake was born in Los Angeles in 1945 and pastors the Allen A.M.E. Church in Jamaica, New York. He graduated from Wilberforce University, Payne Theological Seminary, and Northwestern University School of Business.

When he assumed the pastorate of Allen A.M.E. Church in Queens, New York, the congregation had 1,400 members. Today, there are over 5,000 active members and the church's annual budget is $1.5 million.

Election to Congress in 1986 was Flake's first political office. His victory reflected a broad-based community effort to bring new, progressive leadership to the political front. He has taken the lead in fighting against the devastating impact of drugs on the black community and is a strong proponent for a sensible, well-financed national housing program.

HAROLD E. FORD

Congressman from Tennessee
(1975–present)

Harold E. Ford (Democrat) was elected to Congress from the Ninth District of Tennessee in 1974. He holds a bachelor of science degree in business administration from Tennessee State University, an associate of arts degree in mortuary science from John Gupton College, and a master's in business administration from Howard University.

Prior to his election to Congress, Mr. Ford served two terms in the Tennessee State Legislature. He was elected to this office at age twenty-five and represented the same geographic area of Memphis in which his grandfather had served as a squire during the post-Reconstruction era.

Ford serves on the Ways and Means Committee, which has jurisdiction over all tax and revenue-raising legislation as well as over Social Security and Medicare programs. He has served as chairman of the Subcommittee on Human Resources and is a member of the Select Committee on Aging.

Because of Mr. Ford's leadership in crafting a comprehensive welfare reform bill in the 100th Congress, he was named Child Advocate of the Year for 1987 by the Child Welfare League of America.

GARY FRANKS

Congressman from Connecticut
(1990–present)

Gary Franks (Republican) was born in Waterbury, Connecticut, one of six children. He was senior class president in high school, an honor student, and an all-state basketball player who went on to Yale University. There he was twice chosen captain of the varsity basketball team and graduated with honors. After graduation, Franks worked for three *Fortune* 500 companies, was elected alderman three times in Waterbury, and unsuccessfully campaigned for state comptroller.

Franks' bid to become the first black Republican elected as a voting member of the House of Representatives since 1935 was an uphill fight from the very beginning. Entering as a candidate at the Republican caucus for the Fifth Congressional District with the fewest delegates in a five-man race, he emerged victorious on the ninth ballot. The other four candidates, each with more delegates than Franks, eliminated each other in a five-and-a-half-hour political slugfest filled with intrigue.

In the general election, the Democrats nominated Toby Moffett, who had spent eight years in the U.S. House of Representatives before being defeated in his campaign for the U.S. Senate. (Later he was defeated in a try for governor.)

During the election, Franks was attacked for his vague position on the proposed Civil Rights Act of 1990. The Waterbury Urban Coalition expressed concern that he was not taking a strong stand on the issue. Franks said he opposed minority hiring quotas but would support legislation penalizing businesses that violate anyone's civil rights. He refused to state whether or not he would support an override of President Bush's threatened veto of the bill. In turn, Franks cited his record as an alderman in Waterbury, a member of the city's civil rights commission, chairman of an aldermanic committee investigating racial imbalance in city schools, and a member of another committee on human rights.

Moffett, on the other hand, had to fight off the label of carpetbagger pinned on him by Franks' camp. He was accused of moving from Branford in the Third Congressional District for the specific purpose of running for Congress in the Fifth District.

The district race was targeted by both the Republican and Democratic national parties, which meant the maximum allowable legal contributions would be made available for the campaign. Franks was the beneficiary of several national figures' campaigning in his behalf, including the president's wife, Barbara Bush, and the director of national drug control policy, William Bennett. The death penalty became an issue in the campaign—Moffett came out against its being imposed for any crime, while Franks stated he favored broadening the death penalty to include murders involving drug kingpins.

WILLIAM H. GRAY, III

Congressman from Pennsylvania
(1979–1991)

The Reverend William H. Gray, III, (Democrat) was elected to Congress from the Second District of Pennsylvania in 1979. He was a member of the Appropriations Committee and served as chairman of the House Budget Committee. He is pastor of Bright Hope Baptist Church in Philadelphia.

Gray was born in Baton Rouge, Louisiana, in 1941. He received a B.A. degree from Franklin and Marshall College, a master's in divinity from Drew Theological Seminary, and a master's in theology from Princeton Theological Seminary. He taught at St. Peter's College, Jersey City State College, Rutgers University, and Montclair State College.

Gray, a former chairman of the Congressional Black Caucus, was elected chairman of the Democratic Caucus and elected chairman of the House Budget Committee, and before resigning from Congress, he was the majority whip of the Democratic party, the number three leadership position in the House of Representatives. He was a leading spokesman on African policy, as reflected in his versions of the Anti-Apartheid Acts of 1985 and 1986—legislation that limited American financial support for apartheid. He also authored the legislation establishing the African Development Foundation for delivering U.S. aid to African villages.

Mr. Gray wrote the first of a series of set-aside provisions to require participation by minority and women business owners, historically black colleges, and minority private agencies in the U.S. Agency for International Development's (AID) assistance programs. As a result, minorities and females received $300 million in AID contracts in a three-year period.

Mr. Gray resigned his office in 1991 to become president of the United Negro College Fund.

APPENDIX B

KATIE BEATRICE HALL
Congresswoman from Indiana
(1983–1985)

Katie Hall (Democrat) was elected to Congress from the First District of Indiana in 1983. She served on the Public Works Committee and the Post Office and Civil Service Committee. Before coming to Congress, she served in both the Indiana State House of Representatives and the Indiana State Senate.

Mrs. Hall received a B.S. degree from Mississippi Valley State University and an M.S. degree from Indiana University. She taught in the public schools of Gary, Indiana.

As a freshman, Mrs. Hall introduced the bill to make the birthday of Dr. Martin Luther King a legal public holiday. Under her floor management, the bill passed the House in August 1983 and the Senate in October. It was signed into law by President Reagan the following month.

In the 1984 Democratic primary, Hall lost to Peter J. Visclosky in her bid for renomination.

JEREMIAH HARALSON
Congressman from Alabama
(1875–1877)

Jeremiah Haralson (Republican) was elected to Congress from the state of Alabama in 1874. Born a slave in Georgia, he went on to become one of the most influential blacks in Alabama. His career was filled with controversy because of his alleged closeness to Jefferson Davis, former president of the Confederacy. Accused of fraud in the next election, he was forced into a run-off but won it handily.

In Congress, he served on the Committee on Public Expenditures. He never spoke on the House floor during his term of office. Before going to Washington, D.C., Haralson was elected to the state house of representatives on an independent ticket in 1870. He was a powerful orator and an adroit debater. His political leanings were very conservative for a black during the period of Reconstruction.

In 1876, Haralson was defeated in the Republican primary by Jeremiah Rapier, a black member of Congress whose district had been abolished by the Democrat-controlled state legislature. After losing, he ran as an independent in the general election, splitting the black vote sufficiently to allow a white Democrat, Charles Shelley, to win the seat.

He spent his last days in Colorado, where he was believed killed in a hunting accident. His body was never recovered.

ALCEE HASTINGS
Congressman from Florida
(1993–present)

Alcee Hastings (Democrat) was elected to Congress from the Twenty-third District of Florida. A fiery speaker and well-known civil rights lawyer, Hastings practiced for thirteen years in Fort Lauderdale until he was appointed Circuit Court judge in Broward County by Governor Reubin Askew. In 1979, he was appointed to the federal bench by President Jimmy Carter, becoming the first black person in the history of the state to do so.

Born in Altamonte Springs, Florida, on September 5, 1936, Hastings, father of three children, received his bachelor of arts degree from Fisk University, attended Howard University School of Law, and eventually earned his juris doctorate from Florida A&M University School of Law.

Hastings has been appropriately described as "one of the more colorful and more interesting members" of the freshman class in the 103rd Congress. Having been indicted, tried by a jury of his peers, found innocent of charges, impeached by the Congress, and then elected to join the very institution that impeached him, his is a story of supreme triumph. It is indeed the story of the phoenix—unvengeful—rising from the ashes.

He serves on the Foreign Affairs Committee, the Merchant Marine and Fisheries Committee, and the Post Office and Civil Service Committee.

AUGUSTUS F. HAWKINS

Congressman from California
(1963–1990)

Augustus F. Hawkins (Democrat) represented the Twenty-ninth Congressional District of California. While serving twenty-eight years in the California State Assembly (1935–1963), he was author of more than 100 laws, including those mandating minimum wage coverage for all women, slum clearance and low-cost housing, workman's compensation for domestics, disability insurance, old age pensions, and child care centers. He was also author of the Fair Housing Act.

Mr. Hawkins was elected to the House in 1962. He served as chairman of the House Education and Labor Committee. After fifty-six years in elected office, he announced that he would not seek re-election in November of 1990.

During the Ninety-third Congress, Mr. Hawkins authored and saw passed into law three landmark pieces of legislation: the Juvenile Justice and Delinquency Prevention Act; the Community Service Act; and the Civil Rights Act, establishing the Equal Employment Opportunity Commission. During the second session of the Ninety-fifth Congress, his bill, the Hawkins-Humphrey Full Employment and Balanced Growth Act, was signed into law.

In the Ninety-ninth Congress, the House passed his bill to continue the School Lunch and Nutrition Program. He was also author of an amendment to the Higher Education Act to give added resources to traditional minority colleges. One of his most notable accomplishments was the restoration of honorable discharges for the 167 black soldiers dismissed from the Twenty-fifth Infantry Regiment of the U.S. Army after being falsely accused of public disturbance in Brownsville, Texas, in 1906.

CHARLES A. HAYES

Congressman from Illinois
(1983–1993)

Charles A. Hayes (Democrat) was elected to Congress from the First District of Illinois in 1983 to fill the seat left vacant by Harold Washington's election as mayor of Chicago. He defeated two prominent persons in the Democratic primary, which was tantamount to victory on the South Side of Chicago. His opponents were both outstanding and well-known personalities. Al Raby, a civil rights leader, had been one of the prime movers in organizing the effort to register several hundred thousand black voters, who became the main factor in Mayor Washington's successful campaign. The other contestant, Lu Palmer, was a radio commentator and community activist and one of Mayor Washington's early and avid supporters.

All three men were eminently qualified for the position. But when Mayor Washington announced support of Charles Hayes, the scales tilted in his favor, and he won the primary with 45 percent of the vote.

Hayes, who was born in Cairo, Illinois, in 1918, spent more than forty-five years in the trade union movement. From 1979 until his retirement in 1983, he was the international vice-president and director of Region Twelve of the United Food and Commercial Workers Union.

He served on the Education and Labor Committee; the Small Business Committee; and the Post Office and Civil Service Committee, where he was chairman of the Subcommittee on Postal Personnel and Modernization. Hayes was defeated in the 1992 Democratic primary by Bobby Rush, a former Chicago City Alderman.

EARL HILLIARD

Congressman from Alabama
(1993–present)

Earl Hilliard (Democrat) is Alabama's first black Congressman since Reconstruction. After serving three terms in the Alabama State House and four terms in the State Senate, the eighteen-year veteran was elected in November 1992 to represent the Seventh Congressional District in the Birmingham area.

Born April 9, 1942, in Birmingham, Hilliard received a bachelor of arts degree from Morehouse College, a master of business administration from Atlanta University School of Business, and a juris doctor from Howard University.

Hilliard used his power in the state legislature to advance the interests of education, particularly for black students and institutions. He successfully sponsored bills that increased state funding for Alabama State, Alabama A&M, and Tuskegee universities, and he established the Lawson State Community College scholarship program. Hilliard also serves on the boards of Tuskegee University and Miles College Law School.

He was appointed to the Committee on Small Business and the Committee on Agriculture. In addition he serves on the Congressional Rural Caucus Forestry 2000 Task Force.

Hilliard is married to the former Mary Franklin of Atlanta and is the father of two children, Alesia and Earl, Jr.

JOHN A. HYMAN

Congressman from North Carolina
(1875–1877)

John A. Hyman (Republican) was elected to Congress as the first black from the state of North Carolina in 1874. He worked for a white jeweler who, in defiance of custom and the law, taught him to read and write. Hyman was sold more than eight times from one slave owner to another because his insatiable desire to improve his education antagonized each new owner.

Prior to his election to Congress, Hyman served six years in the North Carolina State Legislature.

He ran on the Republican ticket in 1872 from a predominantly black district and was defeated by Charles R. Thomas. In 1874, he again opposed Thomas and this time easily won the nomination. He also easily defeated his general election opponent, George W. Blount, who challenged the returns. Hyman was forced to spend most of the session back home preparing his defense. The House finally rejected the claim to Hyman's seat.

The district party convention in 1876 favored former Governor Curtis Brogden for the congressional seat over Hyman. So his legislative career came to an end after one term, without his having passed any bills in Congress during his two-year term. While in Congress he served on the Committee on Manufactures.

He moved to Washington, D.C., in 1889 and died there in 1891.

WILLIAM JENNINGS JEFFERSON
Congressman from Louisiana
(1991–present)

William Jennings Jefferson (Democrat) was elected from the city of New Orleans to replace Congresswoman Lindy Boggs, who did not seek re-election. Jefferson was born in Lake Providence, Louisiana, in 1947. He finished Southern University in Baton Rouge and then earned a law degree from Harvard Law School. He clerked with U.S. District Judge Alvin B. Rubin, served as a legislative assistant for U.S. Senator J. Bennett Johnson, and was a member of the Louisiana State Senate for less than a year before being elected to Congress in 1990.

Twelve candidates ran in the primary to determine who would fill the seat vacated by the retirement of Congresswoman Lindy Boggs. Jefferson and Marc Morial, son of former Mayor Dutch Morial, faced each other in the November run-off. Voters had a difficult time deciding between these worthy candidates. In an October 16, 1990, editorial, the *New Orleans Weekly Gambit* stated its endorsement of Jefferson:

The run-off election for Lindy Boggs' Second Congressional District seat offers a choice between a bright young attorney and an experienced legislative leader. The young attorney, Marc Morial, is politically astute beyond his years. The legislative leader, Senator William Jefferson, has a strong record of accomplishments. . . . It's a tough decision, but we recommend State Senator William Jefferson. . . .

EDDIE BERNICE JOHNSON
Congresswoman from Texas
(1993–present)

Eddie Bernice Johnson (Democrat) arrived in Congress from the Thirtieth District of Texas with extraordinary experience for the job. She had distinguished careers as a successful entrepreneur, a professional nurse, a health care administrator, and a Texas lawmaker. She served in both houses of the state legislature. When elected to Congress in November 1992, she was serving her second term in the Senate after five years in the State House.

Johnson began her career in elective office in 1972 when she upset the favorite candidate for a seat in the Texas House of Representatives, winning by a landslide. In her third term, she resigned to become President Carter's regional director of the Department of Health, Education, and Welfare. After nine years away from elective office, Johnson ran successfully for the State Senate and became the first black person to represent Dallas since Reconstruction.

Born in Waco, Texas, on December 3, 1935, Johnson, a mother of one, received a bachelor's degree in nursing from Texas Christian University and a master's degree in public administration from Southern Methodist University.

She serves on two House committees, the Public Works and Transportation Committee; and the Science, Space, and Technology Committee. In addition, she was elected whip of the Congressional Black Caucus.

After her election victory for the U.S. House of Representatives in 1992, the *Dallas Morning News* wrote that Johnson "was instrumental in winning a monumental victory for Dallas blacks when she got the Legislature to finally agree to a fifty percent black district in Dallas County. . . . She is tough, shrewd, and unswervingly devoted to her principles."

BARBARA JORDAN
Congresswoman from Texas
(1973–1979)

Barbara Jordan (Democrat) was elected to Congress from the Eighteenth District of Texas in 1972. She served on the Judiciary Committee, the Government Operations Committee, and the Steering and Policy Committee. She graduated magna cum laude from Texas Southern University with a B.A. in political science and received a law degree from Boston University.

Ms. Jordan served as administrative assistant to the county judge of Harris County, Texas, until her election in 1966 to the Texas Senate. In 1972, the senate unanimously elected her president pro tempore and on June 10, 1972, in the traditional "Governor for a Day" ceremonies, she became the first black woman governor in U.S. history.

Her major legislative achievements include amendments to the Voting Rights Act that expanded its coverage and provided for the printing of bilingual ballots, repeal of federal authorization for state "fair trade" laws, which sanctioned vertical price-fixing schemes, and detailed mandatory civil rights enforcement procedures for the Law Enforcement Assistance Administration and the Office of Revenue Sharing.

During the Judiciary Committee's hearings on the possible impeachment of President Nixon, Ms. Jordan won the admiration of the nation with her eloquent interrogation of witnesses. In December 1977, she decided not to seek re-election. She became professor at the Lyndon B. Johnson School of Public Affairs at the University of Texas in Austin.

JOHN MERCER LANGSTON
Congressman from Virginia
(1889–1891)

John Mercer Langston (Republican), a lawyer, orator, author, educator, and public official, was elected to Congress from the state of Virginia in 1888. He was born in Louisa, Virginia, in 1829 and educated at Oberlin College, where he received a B.A. degree and an M.A. degree. When the two Ohio law schools of that day refused to admit him because of race, he studied under Judge Philemon Bliss, a prominent jurist in Elyria, Ohio. In 1854, he was admitted to the bar.

Before election, Langston had a long and extensive career in the public sector, serving as dean and vice-president of Howard University, minister resident to Haiti, and chargé d'affaires to Santo Domingo. He was elected clerk of Brownheim Township, becoming perhaps the first black elected to public office in the United States. He served on the board of education and the city council of Oberlin.

He was elected to the U.S. House of Representatives in 1888, in a close election that was subsequently contested. The House finally seated him.

GEORGE ("MICKEY") LELAND
Congressman from Texas
(1979–1989)

George ("Mickey") Leland (Democrat) was elected to Congress from the Eighteenth District of Texas in 1978, replacing Barbara Jordan, who did not seek re-election. He served on the Energy and Commerce Committee, the Post Office and Civil Service Committee, and the Select Committee on Hunger. He was chairman of the Committee on Hunger and the chairman of the Subcommittee on Postal Operations and Services. He also served as chairman of the Congressional Black Caucus.

Mr. Leland received a B.S. degree in pharmacy from Texas Southern University in 1970. He was instructor of clinical pharmacy at the school for several years.

He first ran for public office in 1972, when he won election to the state legislature, where he served for six years. When Barbara Jordan announced she would not seek re-election, Leland declared as a candidate and won a plurality in the Democratic primary of 1978.

Congressman Leland sponsored the Homeless Person's Survival Act. A number of its provisions were incorporated into the $1.058-billion Stewart B. McKinney Homeless Assistance Act. His active role in the legislative process varied, ranging from policy toward South Africa, Central America, and the Middle East to unemployment and the preservation of black colleges.

In 1989, he was killed in a plane crash in the hills of Ethiopia while visiting a refugee camp for the starving people of that region.

JOHN LEWIS
Congressman from Georgia
(1987–present)

John Lewis (Democrat) was elected to Congress from the Fifth District of Georgia. In the 1986 Democratic primary to fill the vacancy left by Wyche

APPENDIX B

Fowler's campaign for the U.S. Senate, Lewis defeated another civil rights activist, Julian Bond, in a very hard fought campaign.

Lewis serves on the Public Works Committee and on the Interior and Insular Affairs Committee. Before coming to Congress, he served on the Atlanta City Council for five years, was director of ACTION under President Carter, and director of community affairs for the National Consumer Co-op Bank. He was responsible for registering almost 4 million minority voters while director of the Voter Education Project.

As a former chairman of SNCC and a close associate of Dr. King, Lewis has been a leading activist since the sit-ins and freedom rides of the 1960s. He was jailed forty times and beaten on many occasions for leading peaceful demonstrations throughout the South.

Lewis was born in Troy, Alabama, in 1940. He holds bachelor of arts degrees in religion and philosophy from Fisk University in Nashville, Tennessee, and is a graduate of the American Baptist Theological Seminary.

Lewis is the chief sponsor of legislation to establish a national African American history museum in the capital.

JEFFERSON FRANKLIN LONG

Congressman from Georgia
(January 1871–February 1871)

Jefferson Franklin Long, a former slave, was born in the black belt of west central Georgia in 1836.

The state of Georgia was not readmitted to the Union until 1868 because the state legislature without cause had expelled twenty-eight black members. When Georgia was finally admitted, it was at the end of the Forty-first Congress.

Long, a Republican, was elected to Congress in 1870 by the Georgia State Republican Convention to fill the last part of the second session of the Forty-first Congress. A white person was chosen to fill the full term of office, which would begin in March 1871. Long was sworn in on January 16, 1871. He delivered the first speech by a black member on the floor of Congress on February 1, 1871, and less than a month later his term expired.

JOHN R. LYNCH

Congressman from Mississippi
(1873–1877, 1881–1883)

John R. Lynch (Republican) was first elected to Congress in 1873 from the state of Mississippi. After two terms, he was defeated but in 1881 won back the seat. He was the first black to preside over a national convention of a political party—in 1884, he was chairman of the Republican National Convention.

Lynch was born a slave in Concordia Parish, Louisiana, in 1847. After being freed, he became a photographer and eventually opened his own studio in Natchez, Mississippi. He served in the state house of representatives. In 1872, he was chosen Speaker of the state house.

He was elected to Congress at the age of twenty-six, defeating incumbent Legrand W. Perce. He was appointed to the Committee on Mines and Mining and the Committee on Expenditures in the Interior Department. In 1876, he was defeated for re-election by Democrat James R. Chalmers, a former Confederate general. In 1880, he again challenged Chambers, was declared the loser, but successfully appealed to the Congress and was seated.

Until the election of Mike Espy in 1986, for almost 100 years, Lynch was the only black congressman who had ever represented the state of Mississippi. Lynch moved to Chicago in 1911, where he died in 1939.

CYNTHIA McKINNEY
Congresswoman from Georgia
(1993–present)

Cynthia McKinney (Democrat) was elected to Congress in November 1992 to represent the Eleventh District of Georgia. Like the other sixteen black members in her freshman class, she had also distinguished herself as a public servant. At the time of her election, she was serving a second term in the State General Assembly as representative at-large from Fulton County. Her father, Billy McKinney, is also a state representative in the Georgia legislature.

During her term in the state body, she fashioned and promoted legislation to allow a portion of state gasoline revenues to be used to build a commuter rail system linking Georgia's major urban areas by high-speed trains. Articulate and convincing as a speaker, McKinney forces serious consideration of her legislative positions. During the recent debates on President Clinton's budget proposals and economic stimulus program, McKinney distinguished herself in support of the President's initiatives.

Born on March 17, 1955, McKinney, a single parent, now lives in DeKalb County. She taught political science at Clark Atlanta University, Atlanta Metropolitan College, and at Agnes Scott College. She graduated from the University of Southern California and completed postgraduate studies at Georgia State University and the University of Wisconsin. In 1984 she was a Diplomatic Fellow at Spelman College. She is now a Ph.D. candidate at the Fletcher School of Law and Diplomacy.

She serves on the Agriculture Committee and the Foreign Affairs Committee.

CARRIE MEEKS
Congresswoman from Florida
(1993–present)

Carrie Meeks (Democrat) was elected to Congress from the Seventeenth District of Florida in the Miami area, while most of her constituents were still recovering from the devastation caused by Hurricane Andrew. Meeks has an extensive background in championing educational programs and promoting minority entrepreneurship. During her twelve years in the Florida Legislature, she earned a reputation as one of the state's most successful and skillful politicians.

Meeks brings an unobtrusive demeanor and a quiet dignity to a legislative body that in recent years has been noted primarily for its rambunctious, undignified notoriety. Her legislative experience and community background earned her a spot on the coveted Appropriations Committee of the U.S. House of Representatives, an unusual assignment for a freshman member. According to House rules, a member on this major committee cannot serve on any other.

Born in 1926 in Tallahassee, the daughter of sharecroppers and the grand-daughter of slaves, Meeks earned a bachelor of arts degree from Florida A&M University and a master's degree in public health and physical education from the University of Michigan. She completed work for her doctorate in administration for higher education and continuing education at Florida Atlantic University.

RALPH M. METCALFE
Congressman from Illinois
(1971–1979)

Ralph H. Metcalfe (Democrat) was elected to Congress from the First District of Illinois in 1970. He served on the Interstate and Foreign Commerce Committee, the Merchant Marine and Fisheries Committee, and the Post Office and Civil Service Committee. Before election to Congress, he was Democratic ward committeeman and a member of the Chicago Board of Aldermen, where he was elected president pro-tempore of the council.

Metcalfe, a former college track star who won a silver medal at the 1932 Olympics and gold and silver medals at the 1936 Olympics, was a director of civil rights for the Chicago Commission on Human Relations and an Illinois state athletic commissioner. He was born in Atlanta in 1910 and received a bachelor's degree from Marquette University and an M.A. in physical education from the University of Southern California.

When Congressman Bill Dawson from Illinois's First District decided not to seek re-election after twenty-three years in the House of Representatives, he personally endorsed Metcalfe for the position. Metcalfe easily won the seat and served eight years. He died in October 1978, a month before he would have been elected to a fifth term.

KWEISI MFUME
Congressman from Maryland
(1987–present)

Kweisi Mfume (Democrat) was elected to Congress from the Seventh District of Maryland in 1987 to replace Parren J. Mitchell, who did not seek re-election. He was victorious in a crowded field of candidates. He serves on the Small Business Committee and the Banking, Finance and Urban Affairs Committee.

Having served eight years on the Baltimore City Council, Mfume brought to Washington a solid reputation as an articulate, forthright advocate for the needs of people. While on the council, he won several important legislative victories, including a bill requiring the city to divest itself of investments in companies doing business in South Africa and legislation enhancing minority business in the area of bonding and set-asides. He continues that advocacy today in the Congress on issues ranging from education to economic development.

Mfume was the author of the Minority Business Development Act, the minority outreach amendments attached to the savings and loan bailout bill, and the Beeper Abuse Prevention Act.

In his first month on Capitol Hill, he was elected treasurer of the CBC and deputy whip of the freshman Democratic class.

Congressman Mfume (born Frizell Gray), born in Baltimore in 1948, graduated magna cum laude from Morgan State University in 1976. He holds a master's degree from Johns Hopkins University. He was a member of the faculty at Morgan State University, teaching political science and communications. He has a thirteen-year background in broadcasting as a former reporter and talk show host. His African name means "conquering son of kings."

THOMAS E. MILLER

Congressman from South Carolina
(1889–1891)

Thomas E. Miller (Republican) was elected to Congress from South Carolina in 1889. A lawyer in Beaufort, South Carolina, he served in the state senate before being elected to Congress. After his one term in Congress, Mr. Miller was named president of the State Colored College at Orangeburg, South Carolina.

Miller, who served on the Library of Congress Committee, was a respected orator in the House chamber. In 1891, he addressed the House in rebuttal to a polemic made in the Senate by Senator Alfred H. Colquitt of Georgia. Mr. Colquitt attacked blacks as backward and uncouth. He alleged they were responsible for retarding the economic development of the South. Miller replied that the speech was offensive to all decent people, describing it as an "offensive mixture of theology and political economy that contained groundless slanders against black Americans." He identified white southerners as the culprits of the South's economic failures, because they "were motivated by bigotry and vengefulness in denying blacks the full rights of citizenship."

Miller was born in Ferrebeeville, South Carolina, in 1849, graduated from Lincoln University in Pennsylvania, studied law at the University of South Carolina, and was admitted to the state bar.

ARTHUR W. MITCHELL

Congressman from Illinois
(1935–1943)

Arthur W. Mitchell (Democrat) was elected to Congress from the First District of the state of Illinois. He did undergraduate work at Tuskegee Institute, completed his education at Columbia University and Harvard School of Law, and was admitted to the Washington, D.C., bar.

He was born in Lafayette, Alabama, in 1883. He entered political life as a Republican and later switched to the Democratic party. In 1934, he ran as a Democrat for Congress from the First District of Chicago but was defeated by another Democrat, Harry Baker, in the primary. Baker died before the general election and the Democratic committeemen selected Mitchell as the candidate. He defeated Oscar DePriest to become the first black Democrat ever elected to the U.S. Congress.

His most notable and most consistent legislative goals were laws to hold state and local officials accountable for lynching and to outlaw racial discrimination in the civil service.

PARREN J. MITCHELL
Congressman from Maryland
(1971–1987)

Parren J. Mitchell (Democrat) was elected to Congress from the Seventh District of Maryland in 1970. He defeated incumbent Samuel N. Friedel in a close primary contest. He served on the Small Business Committee; on the Banking, Finance and Urban Affairs Committee; and on the Budget Committee. He was chairman of the Small Business Committee. He was also chairman of the Subcommittee on Domestic Monetary Policy of the Banking Committee and served as chairman of the Congressional Black Caucus.

Mitchell was born in Baltimore in 1922 and served as a commissioned officer in the U.S. Army during World War II. He received a B.A. from Morgan State College and an M.A. from the University of Maryland. Before election to the Congress, he was a professor of political science at Morgan State College, executive secretary of the Maryland Human Relations Commission, director of the Baltimore County Action Agency, and president of Baltimore Neighborhoods, Inc.

His legislative achievements while in Congress were varied, including such successes as: the African Development Bank—initial involvement of the United States in the fund with a contribution of $25 million; an amendment increasing the Elementary and Secondary Education Act level of funding by $150 million for the 1978 budget; creation of an additional 112,000 summer youth employment jobs; an amendment to the 1978 budget increasing the business and loan investment section of the Small Business Administration Act by $271 million.

GEORGE WASHINGTON MURRAY
Congressman from South Carolina
(1893–1897)

George Washington Murray (Republican) was elected to Congress in 1892 from the state of South Carolina. He was born a slave near Sumter, South Carolina, in 1853; he graduated from the University of South Carolina and the State Normal Institute at Columbia, South Carolina. He taught school for fourteen years.

He was defeated the first time he sought the congressional seat—in 1890, he lost the Republican nomination. Two years later, he won the Republican nomination, defeating Robert Smalls and two others. He was declared the victor in the general election over E. M. Moise. In 1894, running in a gerrymandered district, Murray successfully appealed the results that at first had him declared the loser and was seated by the House.

He served on the Committee on Education and Labor and the Committee on Expenditures in the Treasury Department. After the death of Frederick Douglass in February 1895, Murray sought to have the great black abolitionist's body lie in state in the rotunda of the Capitol, but Speaker Charles F. Crisp of Georgia rejected the request.

Murray died in Chicago on April 21, 1926.

CHARLES E. NASH

Congressman from Louisiana
(1875–1877)

Charles Edmund Nash (Republican) was elected to Congress in 1874 from the state of Louisiana. He was born in Opelousas, Louisiana, on May 23, 1844; he attended the common schools and learned the bricklaying trade. During the war, he enlisted in the army and fought with the Union forces, losing a leg in combat.

During his one term, he was assigned to the Committee on Education and Labor. He had limited oratorical skills and spoke very seldom on the floor of the House. He was the victim of internal strife in the Republican party and lost in the next election to a Democrat by 4,300 votes.

ROBERT N. C. NIX

Congressman from Pennsylvania
(1957–1979)

Robert N. C. Nix (Democrat) was elected to Congress in 1956 from the state of Pennsylvania. He served on the Post Office and Civil Service Committee and the old International Relations Committee. He was for a time chairman of the Post Office and Civil Service Committee.

He was born in Orangeburg, South Carolina, in 1905, where his father was dean of South Carolina State College. He was a graduate of Lincoln University in Pennsylvania and the University of Pennsylvania Law School; a former special state deputy attorney general working in the Department of Revenue; and later a special assistant deputy attorney general for the commonwealth. Before election to Congress, he was Forty-fourth Ward Democratic committeeman, an office he was first elected to in 1932.

After Representative Earl Chudoff resigned to become a judge in Philadelphia, Nix won the special election to replace him.

In 1976, the Reverend Bill Gray came within 400 votes of upsetting the veteran congressman. Two years later, Mr. Gray was successful in ending Nix's twenty-year career. Nix remained committeeman of the Thirty-second Ward until his death in June 1987.

ELEANOR HOLMES NORTON

Delegate from the District of Columbia
(1990–present)

Eleanor Holmes Norton (Democrat) is a native-born Washingtonian. She was educated at Antioch College, received an M.A. from Yale Graduate School, and a J.D. from Yale Law School. She was appointed by President Carter in 1977 to chair the Equal Employment Opportunity Commission. She was professor of law at Georgetown University from 1982 until her election to Congress in 1990.

APPENDIX B

JAMES E. O'HARA

Congressman from North Carolina
(1883–1887)

James E. O'Hara (Republican) was elected to Congress in 1882 from the state of North Carolina. He was born in New York City in 1844, studied law at Howard University, and was admitted to the North Carolina bar in 1871. He was chairman of the Halifax County Board of Commissioners and served two terms in the North Carolina State Legislature.

The first time O'Hara ran for Congress, in 1874, he lost to another black, John A. Hyman. Four years later, he received the Republican party's endorsement for the seat, but because a second Republican candidate, James H. Harris, divided the votes, a white Democrat won.

When O'Hara was sworn into office on March 4, 1883, he was the only black member of Congress. He served on the Committee on Mines and Mining and the Committee on Expenditures on Public Buildings. One year later, Robert Smalls of South Carolina was elected and became the second black in that session of Congress.

After his terms in Congress, O'Hara practiced law in New Bern, North Carolina, where he died in 1905.

MAJOR ROBERT ODELL OWENS

Congressman from New York
(1983–present)

Major Owens (Democrat) was elected to Congress from the Twelfth District of the state of New York. He serves on the Education and Labor Committee, where he chairs the Subcommittee on Select Education. He is also a member of the Government Operations Committee. He chairs the CBC Brain Trust on Higher Education.

Mr. Owens, born in Memphis, Tennessee, in 1936, is a librarian by profession. He received a B.A. degree from Morehouse College and an M.S. degree in library science from Atlanta University.

Before coming to Congress, he served as a community coordinator for the Brooklyn Public Library. He also served for six years as commissioner of the New York City Community Development Agency, where he engineered the city's first anti-poverty program; served two years as an adjunct professor at Columbia University; and served eight years as a New York state senator.

As chairman of the Subcommittee on Select Education, Owens led the fight for the passage of the landmark civil rights bill for disabled Americans—the Americans with Disabilities Act, which was signed into law in 1990. His leadership was the primary factor in the enactment of the Domestic Volunteer Service Act, which revitalized national volunteer service programs. He also championed the Child Abuse Prevention Challenge Grants Reauthorization Act, which provided more funding to the states to alleviate the horror of child abuse.

DONALD M. PAYNE
Congressman from New Jersey
(1989–present)

Congressman Donald M. Payne (Democrat) was elected in November 1988 and is a member of the Education and Labor Committee, the Foreign Affairs Committee, and the Government Operations Committee.

Payne was born in Newark, New Jersey, in 1934. Prior to his election, Mr. Payne, a graduate of Seton Hall University with a B.A. degree in social studies, served as a member of the Newark Municipal Council for six years. In 1970, he was elected president of the YMCAs of the U.S.A., serving as that organization's first black national president. In 1972, he was elected to the Essex County Board of Chosen Freeholders and served until 1978. His colleagues selected him as the board's director in 1977, making him responsible for the administration of the operating budget of the state's then most populous county.

A long-term advocate of programs to promote literacy, Payne successfully secured passage of legislation to highlight the problems of those who lack basic reading skills through the establishment of National Literacy Day. The resolution was signed into law by the president in 1990.

ADAM CLAYTON POWELL, JR.
Congressman from New York
(1945–1970)

Adam Clayton Powell, Jr., (Democrat) was elected to Congress from New York in 1944. He served on the Labor and Education Committee, which he chaired for ten years. Powell, like his father, was pastor of the Abyssinian Baptist Church in Harlem. He earned a B.S. degree from Colgate University and received an M.A. in religion from Cornell University.

During the Great Depression, Powell organized picket lines throughout Harlem, forcing merchants to hire black clerks, accountants, and salespersons. He forced the Harlem Hospital to hire back five black doctors they had dismissed. Powell was a member of the New York City Council before being elected to Congress. He won his council seat with the largest number of votes of any prior candidate for the office.

He was elected in 1944 to represent the newly created Twenty-second District. In his first term, he served on the Indian Affairs Committee and the Invalid Pensions and Labor Committee. It was not until his second term that he was appointed to the Education and Labor Committee. He became chairman of that committee in 1961 and proceeded to compile a legislative record that is still the envy of most congressmen. As chairman, Mr. Powell took fifty progressive, controversial, some even revolutionary pieces of legislation to the House floor and saw all of them enacted. His accomplishments included expanded educational opportunities, job training, minimum wage protection, school lunches, aid to elementary and secondary education, and a slew of others.

In 1967, the House of Representatives by a vote of 307 to 116 expelled him from Congress. He sat out a full session and was re-elected overwhelmingly by his Harlem constituents. In 1968, the Supreme Court ruled that the House

APPENDIX B

lacked constitutional authority to deny Powell a seat in the House after the voters had re-elected him.

Powell was sworn into office but not restored to his chairmanship. He was defeated two years later by Charles Rangel and died in Miami on April 4, 1972.

JOSEPH H. RAINEY

Congressman from South Carolina
(1870–1879)

Joseph H. Rainey (Republican) was born a slave in Georgetown, South Carolina, in 1832. After his father purchased their freedom, the family moved to Charleston. During the Civil War, he was pressed into military service by the state of South Carolina to cook and to serve passengers on a Confederate blockade runner. Before the end of the war, he and his wife escaped and fled to Bermuda.

Before going to Congress, he served a term in the state senate. Rainey, a Republican, was elected to Congress in 1870 after the white incumbent, Benjamin F. Whittemore, was accused of selling appointments to the military academies and resigned. He was re-elected in 1872, 1874, and 1876.

He was defeated by a Democrat in 1878 as the post-Reconstruction period was taking hold. He died in 1887.

CHARLES B. RANGEL

Congressman from New York
(1971–present)

Charles B. Rangel (Democrat) was elected to Congress in 1970 from New York. Before coming to Congress, he served in the New York State Assembly. There he was chairman of the New York State Council of Black Elected Democrats.

Mr. Rangel was born in New York City in 1930. He has a degree from New York University (B.S.) and from St. John's University Law School (J.D.). He practiced law until 1961, when he was appointed assistant U.S. attorney in the Southern District of New York by Attorney General Robert F. Kennedy. He also served as general counsel to the National Advisory Commission on Selective Service, an appointment he received from President Johnson in 1966.

He served as the third chairman of the Congressional Black Caucus. He served as the senior member of the Committee on Ways and Means, chairman of the Subcommittee on Select Revenue Measurements on Ways and Means, chairman of the Select Committee on Narcotics Abuse and Control, and deputy whip for the House Democratic leadership.

Rangel is the foremost congressional authority on drug and substance abuse. He has provided continuing leadership to provide tax incentives for the development of housing for low-income families.

ALONZO J. RANSIER

Congressman from South Carolina
(1873–1875)

Alonzo J. Ransier (Republican) was born free in Charleston on January 3, 1834. In 1868, he was elected lieutenant governor of South Carolina by more than 33,000 votes. He was elected to the Congress in 1872. While in the House, he served on the Committee on Manufactures. He engaged in the lengthy debate surrounding Senator Charles Sumner's Civil Rights Bill of 1873. He spoke forcefully in favor of the bill. During the course of the legislative battle, the bill was watered down considerably and a vital clause dealing with integrated education was deleted. His disappointment with the final draft left him too indignant to cast a vote for the bill.

He lost his bid for re-election when the Republican party nominated someone other than him. He claimed that his opponent, Charles W. Buttz, spent $4,000 to buy the nomination.

His wife died in 1879 shortly after giving birth to their eleventh child. Ransier died three years later in Charleston.

JAMES T. RAPIER
Congressman from Alabama
(1873–1875)

James T. Rapier (Republican) was elected to Congress from Alabama in 1872. His victory made him the second black congressman from Alabama.

He was born in Florence, Alabama, in 1837, the fourth child of John Rapier, a barber. He studied at the experimental black community of Buxton, Ontario, and at a normal institute in Toronto, where he received a teacher's certificate. He worked as a reporter in Nashville and finally became a cotton planter on 200 acres of rented land in Maury County, Tennessee.

He moved to Alabama and became active in politics. He ran for secretary of state in 1870, the first black in the state's history to seek statewide office. However, he lost a hard-fought campaign. In 1872, he was nominated for Congress by the Republican party and was victorious in the general election. While in Congress he was assigned to the Committee on Education and Labor. He was able to push through passage of one bill of importance to the state he represented: a bill designating Montgomery a port of delivery managed by the U.S. Customs Department.

In 1876, Rapier was edged out in a close race with Jeremiah Williams, an attorney and former Confederate army major. He contested the outcome, but to no avail. In 1876, Rapier moved to Lowndes County and ran again for Congress in the only black majority district left after reapportionment. He won the Republican primary over the black incumbent, Jeremiah Haralson. Haralson then filed as an independent, siphoning off enough black votes to allow the white Democrat, Charles Shelley, to win.

HIRAM RHOADES REVELS
U.S. Senator from Mississippi
(1870–1871)

Hiram Rhoades Revels (Republican) was the first black elected to the U.S. Senate. He was born in Fayetteville, North Carolina, in 1827. He was an ordained minister in the African Methodist Episcopal Church (A.M.E.) and did missionary work in Indiana, Illinois, Kansas, Kentucky, and Tennessee. In 1860, he became pastor of a church in Baltimore. During the war, he organized two all-black regiments and fought with the North—he was chaplain of the units. He established a school for freedmen in St. Louis before moving to Natchez, Mississippi, in 1866.

In 1870, Revels was chosen by the Mississippi legislature to fill the unexpired Senate term of former Confederate president Jefferson Davis. His term in the Senate only lasted for one year. While a member, he served on the Committee on Education and Labor and the Committee on the District of Columbia.

After leaving the Senate, Revels became the first president of Alcorn A. & M. College (now University), the first land-grant college. He left the school after one year. In 1882 he taught theology at Shaw University and continued his religious work as an A.M.E. superintendent. He died in Aberdeen, Mississippi, in 1901.

MEL REYNOLDS

Congressman from Illinois
(1993–present)

Mel Reynolds (Democrat) was elected in 1992 from the Second District of Illinois on the southside of Chicago. In a bitterly contested race, he easily defeated the incumbent Congressional Black Caucus member, Gus Savage. Prior to election, Reynolds was an assistant professor at Roosevelt University, executive director of the Community Economics Development Education Foundation, and a local talk-show host.

A Rhodes Scholar, Reynolds attended Chicago City colleges and the University of Illinois at Champaign. He received his juris doctor degree while studying at Oxford University in England. He is presently completing a master's degree in public administration from the Harvard University Kennedy School of Government. He was born in Mound Bayou, Mississippi, and is married, with one child.

Reynolds serves on the Ways and Means Committee, which is an "exclusive committee," one so important that time will not permit a member to serve on any other. It is considered a great honor and quite rare for a freshman member to be selected.

BOBBY RUSH

Congessman from Illinois
(1993–present)

Bobby Rush (Democrat) was elected in 1992 from the First District of Illinois on the southside of Chicago. In a very close election, he defeated incumbent Congressional Black Caucus member Charles Hayes. Prior to election, Rush was an alderman and a ward committeeman. In Chicago, both are meaningful political positions, especially the committeeship, which controls city and state patronage.

Rush, a community leader, was an active member of the Student Nonviolent Coordinating Committee and a founder of the Illinois Black Panther Party. As a nine-year member of the City Board of Aldermen he focused on education, housing, and community development. One of his major accomplishments was the creation of more than 20,000 jobs in an Enterprise Zone.

Born November 23, 1946, in Albany, Georgia, he and his wife Carolyn have five children. Rush received a bachelor's degree in political science from

Roosevelt University, graduating with honors. He also finished the core courses and thesis for a master's degree in political science at the University of Illinois at Chicago.

He serves on the Banking, Finance, and Urban Affairs Committee and on the Committee on Government Operations.

GUS SAVAGE
Congressman from Illinois
(1981–1993)

Gus Savage (Democrat) was elected to Congress in 1980 from Illinois. He serves on the Small Business Committee and on the Public Works Committee. He holds a bachelor's degree in philosophy from Roosevelt University in Chicago, where he also did graduate work in history and political science.

He was born in Detroit in 1925. Before coming to Congress, he was publisher of a chain of community newspapers. Mr. Savage has been a militant leader for social justice and economic parity for African-Americans during his entire adult life.

His 5 percent set-aside provision in the Defense Authorization Bill of 1987 resulted in substantial contracts for minority-owned and controlled businesses.

In his campaign for re-election in 1990, Savage was targeted for defeat by the American Israel Public Affairs Committee because of his support for Palestinian national sovereignty and his criticism of U.S. foreign policy, particularly the $3 billion in foreign assistance provided annually to Israel.

Savage has not been afraid to take on the establishment or to tackle controversial subjects. He has publicly defended Minister Louis Farrakhan, voted against the impeachment of Judge Alcee Hastings, and spoken out eloquently against the U.S. invasions of Grenada, Kuwait/Iraq, and Panama.

BOBBY SCOTT
Congressman from Virginia
(1993–present)

Bobby Scott (Democrat) was elected in November 1992 from the far-flung Third District of Virginia, which includes portions of eighteen cities and counties, covering an area from Hampton Roads to Richmond, and also includes some localities on the Middle Peninsula and the Northern Neck.

Prior to election to Congress, Scott served in the Virginia General Assembly from 1978 until 1983, when he was elected to the State Senate, serving ten years. During fourteen years in office, he successfully sponsored and supported bills to expand Medicaid health care services for women and children; protect consumers; raise the state minimum wage; increase unemployment benefits; and broaden the availability of liability insurance coverage for small businesses.

Scott was known in the state legislature for his special ability to translate idealistic dreams into practical, possible legislative measures. In 1986, he almost upset the incumbent, Herbert H. Bateman, in a close race for Congress.

Born on April 30, 1947, in Washington, D.C., and raised in Newport News, Virginia, this very able state legislator became the first black member of

Congress from the Commonwealth of Virginia since 1891. He received his undergraduate degree from Harvard University and his law degree from Boston College Law School.

He serves on the Judiciary Committee; the Science, Space, and Technology Committee; and the Education and Labor Committee.

ROBERT SMALLS

Congressman from South Carolina
(1875–79, 1882–83, 1884–87)

Robert Smalls (Republican) was born a slave in 1839 in Beaufort, South Carolina. He worked as a stevedore, foreman, sailmaker, rigger, and sailor. He, like fellow South Carolinian Representative Alonzo Ransier, was conscripted into Confederate military service and put on the cotton steamer *Planter*. Smalls and his black crew dodged Confederate guns and surrendered the ship to the Union navy. He was acclaimed nationally for this heroic deed.

He was elected to the state house of representatives in 1868 and to the state senate in 1870. In 1874, he was elected to Congress for the first time. He was appointed to the Agriculture Committee. He won re-election in 1876 but was accused of taking a bribe of $5,000 while in the state senate. He was pardoned by the governor. He was defeated in 1878 by Democrat George Tillman. In 1880, he ran again and narrowly lost to Tillman but successfully contested the returns and was seated in Congress on July 19, 1882. Two months later he was defeated for the Republican nomination by Edmund W. M. Mackey. When Mackey died in 1884, Smalls was elected to fill the vacancy.

After his tenure in Congress, President Harrison appointed Smalls collector of the port of Beaufort. He died in Beaufort on February 22, 1915.

BENNETT McVEY STEWART

Congressman from Illinois
(1979–1981)

Bennett M. Stewart (Democrat) was elected to Congress from the First District of Illinois in 1978. He served on the Appropriations Committee. Before coming to Congress, he served eight years on the Chicago Board of Aldermen.

He was born in Huntsville, Alabama, in 1912. He was an associate professor of sociology at Miles College in Alabama before moving to Chicago. He was a city inspector of the Chicago Building Department and also a rehabilitation specialist with the Chicago Department of Urban Renewal.

After the death of Ralph Metcalfe, Stewart was chosen by the Democratic committeemen of the First District as the party's candidate to fill the vacancy. He defeated Republican candidate A. A. Rayner in the November election. In his 1980 effort for re-election, he was beaten in the primary by State Representative Harold Washington, who went on to win in the general election.

LOUIS STOKES

Congressman from Ohio
(1969–present)

Louis Stokes (Democrat) was elected to Congress from Ohio in 1968. He serves on the Appropriations Committee. He is chairman of the Committee on

Standards of Official Conduct (Ethics Committee), chairman of the Committee to Investigate the Assassinations of President John F. Kennedy and Dr. Martin Luther King, Jr., and served as chairman of the Intelligence Committee. He is a former chairman of the Congressional Black Caucus and former chairman of the Congressional Black Caucus Foundation.

Stokes was born in Cleveland, Ohio, in 1925. He attended Western Reserve University in Cleveland and received a doctor of law degree from the Cleveland Marshall Law School.

Stokes has used his committee assignments to ensure increased opportunities for minorities and the disadvantaged in the areas of education, health, housing, business, and research development. As a result of his efforts, Congress is taking steps to enact major legislation aimed at improving the health status of minority Americans. He is also credited with the creation of training programs for minorities in the nation's intelligence organizations and biomedical research fields, and for the inclusion of minority businesses and historically black colleges in the scientific and technological industries.

BENNIE THOMPSON

Congressman from Mississippi
(1993–present)

Bennie Thompson (Democrat) was elected from the expansive twenty-four-county-wide Second District of Mississippi to fill the Congressional seat vacated by Mike Espy, who resigned to serve in the Clinton Cabinet as Secretary of Agriculture. Espy had been elected three times since defeating Republican incumbent Webb Franklin in 1986.

Thompson defeated Republican Hayes Dent, Jr., a white candidate who was the hand-picked choice of the Republican governor of Mississippi. Thompson thus became the second black person since Reconstruction to represent that state in Congress. In the open primary election he finished second to Dent in a field of eight candidates, seven of them Democrats. It was a different story in the run-off election, when Thompson garnered approximately 55 percent of the vote. The second District has a 58 percent black voting-age population.

Born on January 28, 1948, Thompson brings to the Congress a rich background in public service that extends over twenty-three years. He has served his hometown of Bolton as both alderman (1969–73) and mayor (1973–79) and as Hinds County supervisor (1980–93). He has also held positions as Democratic Chairman of the Second Congressional District and as Democratic National Committeeman. He served, in addition, with the Teachers Corps and as an adjunct professor of political science at Jackson State University.

He holds a bachelor's degree in political science from Tougaloo College and a master's degree in educational administration and supervision from Jackson State University and is a candidate for a doctoral degree from the University of Southern Mississippi. He is married and has one daughter.

EDOLPHUS ("ED") TOWNS

Congressman from New York
(1982–present)

Edolphus ("Ed") Towns (Democrat) was elected to Congress in 1981 from the Eleventh District of New York. He served on the Public Works Committee, the Government Operations Committee, and the Select Committee on Narcotics Abuse and Control until his recent appointment to the Committee on Energy and Commerce. His new committee assignment entails handling so many important issues and consumes so much of his time that House rules required him to give up his Public Works Committee position. He is also chairman of the Congressional Black Caucus.

Towns was born in Chadbourn, North Carolina, in 1934. Before coming to Congress, he was deputy borough president of Brooklyn and Democratic state committeeman in the Fortieth Assembly District. He has an undergraduate degree from North Carolina A. & T. University and a master's degree in social work from Adelphi University.

Towns has championed legislation concerning student athletes, adolescent pregnancy, drug treatment, retention of medical records, minority farmer benefits, and bilingual education.

WALTER TUCKER

Congressman from California
(1993–present)

Walter Tucker (Democrat) served as mayor of the City of Compton immediately before being elected to Congress from the Thirty-seventh District in California in 1982. He succeeded Congressional Black Caucus member Merv Dymally, who did not seek re-election. At the age of thirty-five, Tucker captured the seat after winning a hotly contested race against Dymally's daughter, Lynn Dymally. He received 39.5 percent of the vote in the primary and in the general election won in a landslide against an independent candidate, with 86 percent of the vote.

Tucker was born in Compton, California, and spent two years at Princeton University, eventually earning a bachelor's degree in political science from the University of Southern California at Los Angeles and a juris doctor degree from Georgetown University Law Center. He served as Deputy District Attorney for the County of Los Angeles for two years and then went into the private practice of criminal law.

He serves on the Public Works and Transportation Committee and on the Small Business Committee.

BENJAMIN S. TURNER

Congressman from Alabama
(1871–1873)

Benjamin S. Turner (Republican) was born a slave in Weldon, North Carolina, in 1825. His family moved to Alabama when he was five years of age. He became a merchant and owned a livery stable. He was elected tax collector of Dallas County and served as a city councilman in Selma. In 1870, he was the Republican nominee for Congress and won the election.

Turner was another black determined to establish amnesty for former Confederate officers and leaders. He struggled mightily to remove all legal and political disabilities imposed on them by Section Three of the Fourteenth Amendment. The House never considered his proposal.

In 1872, he again won the Republican nomination, but another black candidate, Phillip Joseph, entered the race as an independent and divided the black votes sufficiently for Frederick G. Bromberg, a white Democrat, to win. Turner died in Selma in 1894.

ALTON RONALD WALDON, JR.

Congressman from New York
(1986–1987)

Alton R. Waldon, Jr., (Democrat) was elected to Congress in 1986 in a special election to fill the seat formerly held by Congressman Joseph Addabbo. He was born in Lakeland, Florida, in 1936 and received a B.S. from John Jay College and a J.D. from New York University Law School. Before being elected to Congress, he was with the New York City Housing Authority, a deputy commissioner of the New York State Division of Human Rights, assistant counsel for the Office of Mental Retardation and Developmental Disabilities, and spent four years in the New York State Assembly.

Waldon squeaked through in the special election to fill the vacancy created by the death of Representative Addabbo. He edged out the Reverend Floyd Flake only after the counting of absentee ballots. He was sworn in before Congress on July 29, 1986, and assigned to the Committee on Education and Labor and the Committee on Small Business. Two months later, he was defeated for a full term by Mr. Flake.

JOSEPH T. WALLS

Congressman from Florida
(1871–1875)

Joseph T. Walls (Republican) was born near Winchester, Virginia, in 1842. During the war, like Ransier and Smalls of South Carolina, he, too, was impressed into Confederate military service, in his case the army. He was captured by Northern troops at Yorktown, Virginia, and then enlisted in the Third Infantry Regiment, United States Colored Troops at Philadelphia. He was discharged in Florida.

In 1870, he was the Republican nominee for the state's only seat in Congress. He won by a narrow margin but was challenged. The House accepted his credentials and assigned him to the Committee on the Militia, the Committee on Mileage, and the Committee on Expenditures in the Navy Department. Two months before a new term, in January 1873, the House Committee on Elections declared his challenger, Silas L. Niblack, the winner, but he held the position only until March because Walls had defeated him in the preceding November election.

In 1874, Walls again won—this time by 371 votes—and again he was challenged. The allegation by Jesse J. Finley, his Democratic opponent, of vote tampering was upheld in a partisan vote by the full House of Representatives.

In 1876, he was defeated again for the House. That same year he was sent back to the state senate by the voters. He died in Tallahassee on May 15, 1905.

CRAIG ANTHONY WASHINGTON

Congressman from Texas
(1990–present)

Craig Washington (Democrat) replaced his friend, the late George Mickey Leland of Houston, in January 1990. He was the leading vote-getter in the primary and won the special election with ease in December 1989. He was born in Longview, Texas, in 1941 and attended Prairie View A. & M. University, where he received a B.A. in 1966. In 1969, he graduated from the Thurgood Marshall School of Law at Texas Southern University.

He was elected to the Texas House of Representatives in 1973, the same year that Mickey Leland was first elected to the state legislature. In 1983, Washington was elected to the state senate. While in the Texas State Legislature, he made a name for himself in both houses for his ability to get bills passed. Among his more important feats was a measure restricting state investment in companies doing business with South Africa.

Washington serves on the Education and Labor Committee and the Committee on the Judiciary.

HAROLD WASHINGTON

Congressman from Illinois
(1981–1983)

Harold Washington (Democrat) was elected to Congress in 1980 from Illinois. Before coming to Congress, he served twelve years in the Illinois House of Representatives and six years in the Illinois Senate.

He was born in Chicago in 1922. He received a B.S. from Roosevelt University and graduated from the Northwestern University School of Law and practiced law in Chicago. He served four years as an arbitrator for the Illinois State Industrial Commission.

In the 1980 Democratic primary, he defeated Congressman Bennett Stewart, who had filled the vacancy created by Ralph Metcalfe's death in 1978. On January 3, 1981, Washington was sworn into Congress and assigned to the Committee on Education and Labor, the Committee on Government Operations, and the Committee on the Judiciary. As a member of the latter committee, he negotiated an agreement to extend enforcement sections of the 1965 Voting Rights Act, which guaranteed that jurisdictions with a history of voting rights abuses would be unable to take advantage of the measure's "bail-out" provisions and escape coverage under the act.

Washington was elected mayor of Chicago on April 12, 1983. Three weeks later he resigned his seat in the House of Representatives. He died on November 25, 1987, shortly after being re-elected mayor for a second term.

MAXINE WATERS

Congresswoman from California
(1991–present)

Maxine Waters (Democrat) was born in Saint Louis, Missouri, earned a B.A. at California State University, and was first elected to the state assembly in 1976 and served fourteen years before being elected to Congress from the

Twenty-ninth District. She replaced Congressman Augustus Hawkins, who decided not to seek a fifteenth congressional term.

MEL WATT

Congressman from North Carolina
(1993–present)

Mel Watt (Democrat) was elected from the Twelfth District of North Carolina in 1992. He and his wife of twenty-five years, the former Eulada Paysour, have two sons, Brian and Jason. Brian served as his father's campaign manager in Watt's successful bid for the U.S. Congress.

Watt earned his bachelor of science degree in business administration from the University of North Carolina at Chapel Hill, where he graduated Phi Beta Kappa. He received a juris doctor degree from Yale University Law School, where he was selected to the *Yale Law Journal* and was the author of "Tax Exemption for Organizations Investing in Black Business."

Watt is known nationally for the role he played in managing the campaign of Harvey Gantt, which almost became the political upset of the twentieth century—the defeat in 1990 of Senator Jesse Helms for re-election to the U.S. Senate from North Carolina. Prior to his election to Congress, Watt served in the State Legislature, where he was often referred to as "the conscience of the Senate."

Watt was born on August 26, 1945, in Mecklenburg County, North Carolina, and grew up near Charlotte. His is indeed a "rags-to-riches" story. He was born in a rural section of the county, in a tin-roofed shack without electricity, running water, or indoor toilets. His parents separated when he was three, and his mother raised three boys without aid from any government assistance program. She worked as a postal employee and held other part-time jobs to keep the family intact.

Watt serves on the House Banking, Finance, and Urban Affairs Committee; the Judiciary Committee; and the Post Office and Civil Service Committee. He received a great honor for a freshman member by being placed on the Democratic Caucus Policy and Steering Committee, which selects the committees on which other members serve.

ALAN WHEAT

Congressman from Missouri
(1983–present)

Alan Wheat (Democrat) was elected to Congress from the Fifth District of Missouri in 1982. He serves on the Rules Committee—one of only three freshman members ever appointed to that committee. He is presently chairman of the Congressional Black Caucus Foundation.

Wheat, born in San Antonio, Texas, is the son of an air force officer. Educated around the globe, he received a B.A. in economics from Grinnell College in Iowa. He began his career as an economist with the Department of Housing and Urban Development in Kansas City and the Mid-America Regional Council. In 1976, he won election to the Missouri General Assembly, where he served for six years. While there, he was chairman of the Urban Affairs

Committee, chairman of the (Missouri State) Legislative Black Caucus, and treasurer of the National Black Caucus of State Legislators.

As an influential member of the powerful Rules Committee, Wheat has used his position to press for action on issues of particular interest to black Americans. He played a continuing role in the efforts to strengthen and maintain U.S. sanctions against South Africa, and as manager of the rule controlling House floor debate on the Civil Rights Act of 1990, he held the line against efforts to weaken the bill.

GEORGE HENRY WHITE

Congressman from North Carolina
(1897–1901)

George H. White (Republican) was born a slave in Rosindale, North Carolina, in 1852. He studied medicine at Howard University but changed to law when he went back to North Carolina. He taught school before being admitted to the state bar. He served in the state house of representatives and was elected to the state senate in 1884. In 1886, he was elected solicitor and prosecuting attorney for the Second District of North Carolina.

In 1894, he lost in the Republican congressional primary to his brother-in-law, Henry P. Cheatham, a former congressman. Two years later he defeated Cheatham and was victorious over the Democratic incumbent, Frederick A. Woodard, and Populist candidate D. S. Moss.

When sworn into the Fifty-fifth Congress on March 15, 1897, George H. White was the only black member of Congress. The circle of no black representatives in Congress had almost closed. He managed to win re-election in 1898, but the drive to disfranchise black citizens had been completed. When George H. White left office in 1901, it would be twenty-eight years before another black was elected to the U.S. House of Representatives and sixty-seven years before a black sat in the U.S. Senate.

ALBERT WYNN

Congressman from Maryland
1993–present

Albert Wynn (Democrat) was elected in November 1992 from the Fourth Congressional District of Maryland, which is located in the suburban area of the nation's capital, taking in parts of Prince George's and Montgomery counties. In joining Kweisi Mfume of Baltimore, Wynn becomes the state's second black member presently serving in the Congress.

Born on September 10, 1951, married and residing in Largo, Maryland, Wynn began his political career in 1982 when he was elected to the Maryland House of Delegates. After one term in the House, he was elected to the State Senate, where he rose to the rank of Deputy Majority Whip, serving eight years before being elected to Congress. While in the Senate, he served on the Ways and Means Committee and the Budget and Taxation Committee.

Wynn earned a bachelor's degree in political science from the University of Pittsburgh and a juris doctor degree from Georgetown University Law Center.

He now serves on the Banking, Finance, and Urban Affairs Committee; the Foreign Affairs Committee; and the Post Office and Civil Service Committee.

ANDREW JACKSON YOUNG, JR.
Congressman from Georgia
(1973–1977)

The Reverend Andrew Young (Democrat) was elected to Congress from the Fifth District of Georgia in 1972. After a year, he was appointed to the Rules Committee. Before coming to Congress, he was a top aide to Dr. Martin Luther King, Jr., serving as director of the Southern Christian Leadership Conference.

Young was born in New Orleans in 1932. He attended Dillard University for a while and graduated from Howard University with a B.S. degree and from the Hartford Theological Seminary with a bachelor of divinity degree. He is an ordained minister in the United Church of Christ. He was appointed ambassador to the United Nations in 1977 by President James Carter.

Young was originally assigned to the Committee on Banking and Currency during the Ninety-third Congress, but after his re-election in 1974, he became the first black to serve on the Committee on Rules.

Mr. Young was active in the successful efforts to continue and strengthen the Voting Rights Act, supported legislation to terminate South Africa's sugar quota, and supported a $125-million appropriation for an emergency school aid act to help local community school districts formulate their own desegregation plans for review by the courts.

In January 1977, Young resigned from Congress to accept the position of ambassador to the United Nations in the Carter administration. Twice, in 1981 and 1985, he was elected mayor of Atlanta.

Index

INDEX